For pastors intent on shepherding their flocks v
the most insidious forces we face today, an unse
our people and driving them to react blindly in
Today, even the foundational aspects of life for our people are being shaken,
as congregations shrink, churches close, and life becomes harder.

So this important work by James Harrichand should be seen as a must-
read guide for those seeking to address this sense of disorientation. Drawing
on the Biblical narratives and Psalms as his corpus, he rightly understands
that disorientation is as much a condition of the heart as it is the mind. Thus,
the lessons this work presents have broad application, giving Christian clergy
not just a framework but also fine-tuned strategies to care for their people.

Derek Chong, PhD
Associate Pastor of Discipleship,
Morningstar Christian Fellowship, Toronto, Canada

In this welcomed interdisciplinary study, Harrichand does a wonderful job
integrating biblical and pastoral theology with the worthy goal of fostering
compassionate pastoral care practices among those coping with grief within
Canadian immigrant communities. Harrichand's study broadens and enriches
our understanding of the prayers of disorientation in Scripture, by examining
these prayers in the narrative sections of the Old Testament, thereby filling a
lacuna in Old Testament scholarship. Harrichand's examination demonstrates
that there are many varied (verbal, physical, and emotional) responses to
grief depicted in these narratives. By engaging current research in practical theology on grief while examining the contemporary responses to grief
among Guyanese and Vietnamese immigrants to Canada, this book is also
immensely practical. Harrichand invites the reader to respond with respect,
compassion, and sensitivity to diverse cultural Christian responses to grief.
Therefore I highly recommend this study to biblical scholars, pastoral theologians, and care practitioners alike.

Rebecca G. S. Idestrom, PhD
Professor of Old Testament,
Chair, Biblical Studies Department,
Tyndale University, Canada

Although the church is blessed with plenty of scholarly and popular literature on lament prayers in the Psalter, little has been written on Old Testament prose prayers and non-verbal communication in situations of disorientation. Harrichand analyzes these texts embedded in Israel's narratives and allows them to shed light on ministry to grieving believers in our own day – particularly Christians whose culturally shaped bereavement practices resonate with (or contrast with) practices exemplified in the Hebrew Scriptures.

He mines biblical scholarship, pastoral theology, and anthropology to better understand the sufferers he interviewed and equip the church's healers with insight gleaned from this research.

I hope that this careful, wide-ranging, well-written work will not only fill some surprising gaps in theological scholarship, but that those who engage with it will become more effective "wounded healers."

Kenneth Langley, DMin
Adjunct Professor of Homiletics,
Trinity Evangelical Divinity School, Illinois, USA

As an exercise of an interdisciplinary nature – Old Testament and pastoral theology – Harrichand's monograph bridges the chasm between biblical texts and cultural sensibilities. The motif of grief he considers as the lens to reflect on the complex and dynamic relationship between them. The author aptly shows how critical engagement with the Old Testament entails the consciousness of the biblical worldview and its connection to the contemporary readers. While the author's analysis is combined with anecdotes of disorientation, the creative nature of the word of God and its power of application to our life experiences is not undermined. Readers – scholars, pastors, and lay leaders – would reap from this book practical ways of coping with laments.

Dennis Ngien, PhD
Research Professor and Former Alister E. McGrath Chair of
Christian Thought and Spirituality,
Tyndale University, Canada

James Harrichand invites us to a compassionate intercultural conversation between Hebrew Bible prayers, Western expressions of grief, and the mourning practices among Guyanese and Vietnamese Christians. This thoughtful and liberative exchange takes place through the modes of renewed form criticism, ritual theory, and post-colonial pastoral theology. Expanding Brueggemann's category of "disorientation" and emphasizing the embodied, cultural construction of grief and mourning practices, Harrichand finds a spaciousness in the tradition and calls for the church to provide space for the variety of expressions of grief and mourning practices, and for pastoral caregivers to respond with sympathy and sensitivity.

Rodney A. Werline, PhD
Dean of Howard Chapel,
Leman and Marie Barnhill Endowed Chair in Religious Studies,
Barton College, North Carolina, USA

Compassionate Intercultural Care Practices for Coping with Grief

Biblical Theology in Conversation with Pastoral Theology

James Japheth Sudarshan Harrichand

Langham

ACADEMIC

© 2024 James Japheth Sudarshan Harrichand

Published 2024 by Langham Academic
An imprint of Langham Publishing
www.langhampublishing.org

Langham Publishing and its imprints are a ministry of Langham Partnership

Langham Partnership
PO Box 296, Carlisle, Cumbria, CA3 9WZ, UK
www.langham.org

ISBNs:
978-1-83973-840-1 Print
978-1-83973-999-6 ePub
978-1-78641-000-9 PDF

British Library Cataloguing-in-Publication Data
A catalogue record for this book is available from the British Library

ISBN: 978-1-83973-840-1

Cover & Book Design: projectluz.com

Contents

Anthropological Expressions of Disorientation in Biblical Theology

Foreword

Nearly three decades ago as I approached the end of my dissertation work at Cambridge, I penned an introduction to that research which began with the following words:

> If there is a supra-language which transcends linguistic barriers it must be the language of suffering, the discourse of disorientation. Pain is part of the human journey and no one is insulated from its icy touch. When humans discover a piece of literature which succinctly unveils the reality of pain they resonate immediately with that text because they identify with the content as well as the emotion.[1]

That research was focused on the final prayer among the historical books of the Old Testament (Genesis-Esther) as arranged in most English translations today, that is, Nehemiah 9. My desire was to see the role this prayer and its theology played within the community that emerged from the exile and the foundation it provided for the Jewish and Christian communities to come.

The approach taken in my early study focused on the prayer itself within an ancient community with less attention to the literary context in which the prayer was located, something pointed out by Bob Becking in the *Review of Biblical Literature*.[2] Becking's review highlighted to me how my approach to the prayer in Nehemiah 9 was influenced by the form-critical approach developed for the study of the Psalter. Determining historical and literary settings for reading the various psalms has always been a challenge in the Psalter since each psalm appears to have its own genesis and is not clearly

---

1. Now published in Boda, *Praying the Tradition*, 1.
2. Becking, "Review of Mark J. Boda."

related to the psalms surrounding it. Form-critical theory identified various ways of categorizing the historical settings of the psalms, whether related to individual piety or social groups. Applying this traditional form-critical approach wholesale to the study of prayers in the Hebrew narrative books, however, seemed misguided since these narrative books provide clear descriptions of the social contexts in which particular prayers were used.

This realization prompted me to consider more closely the work of Sam Balentine, who brilliantly showcased the value of reading such prayers in their literary contexts.[3] As a result I reconsidered not only Nehemiah 9 but also all references to prayer within Nehemiah 1–13, highlighting the way these prayers shape the reading of a biblical book and also how the biblical book provides religious, historical and literary contexts for reading these prayers.[4] My appetite was whetted for more study along these lines as I investigated the role of prayer in the prophetic books in the years which followed.

The reason I share my own journey into research on prayer is to now introduce my former student and colleague James Harrichand who took up the challenge of examining more thoroughly prayer within the OT narrative books (Genesis-Esther) to identify the human context in which such prayers were used as well as other features of human expression including the physical and emotional manifestations that accompany verbal expressions to God.

But James was not satisfied with only analyzing the role of these expressions to God within an ancient community and Old Testament corpora. He is a practitioner within a confessional community and carried on this ministry throughout his doctoral work. With the help of my colleague Dr. Phil Zylla, Professor of Pastoral Theology, James analyzed the role of prayer in the ancient text while embedded within contemporary local communities for whom expressions to God amid suffering were a present reality. Dr. Zylla's work on suffering and expression to God provided a wise foundation for James to do his own research and James rose to the task to listen to the ways these contemporary communities engaged with God amid pain.[5] I am convinced that such listening sensitized James to the biblical texts even as his immersion in the biblical texts sensitized him to dynamics at work within

---

3. Balentine, *Prayer in the Hebrew Bible*.

4. Boda, "Prayer as Rhetoric," 279–296.

5. E.g., Zylla, *Roots of Sorrow*.

these contemporary communities of faith. James Harrichand's work even impacted his supervisors, since during his research we presented a joint paper on lament and emotion at the Society of Biblical Literature, Bible and Practical Theology Group.[6] That is one of the delights of academic hospitality which not only flows from supervisor to student, but also in reverse.

This present volume bridges scriptural and cultural horizons in a hermeneutically sensitive manner, providing pathways from Scripture to the cultural horizon as well as routes from the cultural horizon to Scripture. The hope is that this will benefit those seeking new ways of reading Scripture and culture as we move further into the twenty-first century and especially engage with the Global South.

Thus, I heartily recommend this work by James Harrichand. As part of an emerging generation of scholars of prayer he provides here a new phase of research that will advance the field and highlight its relevance to today's challenges to faith. Those who read it will discover that "supra-language" which indeed "transcends linguistic barriers," that is, "the discourse of disorientation" which expresses the pain that intersects our lives, whether showcased in vulnerable scenes in the Old Testament or within dynamic contemporary communities of faith.

Mark Boda, PhD
Professor of Old Testament,
MacMaster Divinity College, Canada

---

6. Boda and Zylla, "Catalytic Study."

Dedication

With a heart intermingled with both sorrow and joy, I gratefully dedicate this monograph to my loving immediate family – my precious mother, Jennie Rosita Harrichand, my two beloved brothers, John Jonathan Suroshan Harrichand and Joel Joshua Suvachan Harrichand, and especially my deeply missed and unforgettably cherished earthly father, the late Rev. James Jaiprakash Harrichand, who currently makes his home in heaven with our crucified-yet-resurrected Lord Jesus Christ (2 Cor 5:8). Words are insufficient to thank you amply for your steadfast love, fervent prayers, and unremitting encouragement. You truly inspire me to fix my eyes on our Lord Jesus Christ, the author and perfecter of our faith, a faith that is grounded in the historical reality that Jesus Christ is the only One who not only guarantees life after death (Phil 1:21), but even more so, life *after* life after death in his glorious presence (1 Thess 4:13–18). For as God incarnate (John 1:14; 8:58), he is the only One who not only emphatically asserted, "Destroy this temple, and in three days I will raise it up" (John 2:19), but also authenticated it by rising from the dead, without any possibility of dying again, and substantiated it by revealing himself publicly to at least five hundred people just prior to his ascension and coronation in heaven (1 Cor 15:1–57). And it is this Jesus who also avowed, "I am the resurrection and the life; he who believes in Me will live even if he dies, and everyone who lives and believes in Me will never die" (John 11:25–26). The tomb of Jesus Christ is empty; Jesus Christ is alive and alive forevermore (John 20:1–11)! And because he lives eternally, we who believe that Jesus is the Christ, the Son of God, and moreover God the Son, will also live eternally with him (John 14:19; 20:30–31). As Job declared, "As for me, I know that my Redeemer lives, and at the last He will take His stand on the earth. Even after my skin is destroyed, yet from my flesh I shall see God; whom I myself shall behold, and whom my eyes will see and not another" (Job 19:25–27). O what a joyous comfort and glorious hope we have in Jesus Christ alone!

Acknowledgments

"There comes a point in your life when you need to stop reading other people's books and write your own," is a statement credited to Albert Einstein. Thanks be to God that after reading many people's books, this book that you are now in possession of is one that I gladly call my own. Yet I would be remiss to think that it was only from reading that this book has materialized. This literary work is also a byproduct of the support of countless people too numerous to be acknowledged. Nevertheless, a handful of folks are deserving of recognition.

I begin with heartfelt gratitude to my primary doctoral supervisor, Dr. Mark J. Boda, who challenged me to think deeply about God's word, especially the Old Testament (OT), and to pay keen attention to the methodology necessary for proper hermeneutics. Thank you Dr. Boda for instilling in me a greater passion for in-depth study of the word of God, assisting me in formulating a new methodology titled "Renewed Form Criticism," and penning the beautiful and remarkable foreword on my behalf. Owing to your tutelage, I am now better equipped to bridge the Scriptural and cultural horizons in a hermeneutically sensitive manner, especially in relation to the "supra-language" of disorientation, and in so doing, not only listen to the deepest and most indispensable convictions of God's people, but even more so, to assimilate them into my life.

Second, a hearty thanks to my secondary doctoral supervisor, Dr. Philip C. Zylla, who showed me that pastoral theology is rooted in human experience, which requires, as in the case of this book, a sensitive reflection on the depth-dimension of grief. By modelling such pastoral theological acuity, you have equipped me to better connect the complex world of human experience with the gospel of our Lord Jesus Christ, even from the OT. This has thus generated the five compassionate (liberative intercultural) pastoral care expressions for coping with grief that are explicated in this book.

Third, much appreciation goes to Dr. Dennis Ngien, my mentor and friend, who treated me to several cups of hot chocolate and donuts during my doctoral studies, encouraged me to reach out to Langham Publishing for potential publication, and constantly remembers me before the throne of God. Thanks for cheering me on throughout my studies and even through the writing of your endorsement on my behalf.

Fourth, many thanks to Dr. Rebecca G. S. Idestrom for writing a reference letter for me to commence my doctoral studies, giving me the opportunity to be her graduate teaching assistant during my doctoral studies, and continued prayers and encouragement ever since I was a student of hers in the MDiv in biblical studies program at Tyndale Seminary of Tyndale University, and even happily writing an endorsement in my favor. Thanks also for recommending me to Rev. Dr. J. Kevin Livingston for the teaching position of the "Preaching the Psalms" DMin course. Thank you, Rev. Kev for the privilege of teaching this class.

Fifth, recognition goes specifically to two churches (especially the English congregations) for also playing a key role during my studies as they both allowed me the privilege of serving as a pastor while pursuing my doctoral degree: the Greater Toronto Area Vietnamese Community church, led my Senior Pastor Rev. Trung (Timothy) Nguyen, and the Richmond Hill (Chinese) Baptist Church, led collectively by the Deacon Board and several pastors: Rev. Jack Yuen (Cantonese), Pastor William Wong (Cantonese), Pastor Frank Yao (Mandarin), Pastor Heusen Lam (Youth), and Pastor Sandra Fung (Children).

Sixth, several other brothers and sisters in Christ from various other congregations also exercised their fealty toward me in supporting me through their prayers and encouragement, some of which are from Malvern Community Baptist Church (now Morningstar Christian Fellowship; my home church), New Heaven Fellowship Church (Queens, New York), and Christ Community Church – Toronto, Zion, and Guyana. Here, I also add specifically some of my dear friends who dialogued encouragingly and prayerfully with me about my doctoral studies – Dr. Anand Chetram, Pastor Alex Lee, Cymone Lee, Kenric Ng, Mari Leesment, Nathan Kwan, Regine Leung, Elizabeth Boom, Rebecca Nichol, and Xenia Chan. My appreciation also extends to Dr. Rodney A. Werline (my external examiner and one of my enthusiastic endorsers), Dr. Kelvin Mutter (for orienting me to qualitative research), Dr. Lee Beach (for support with my "Recovering the Language of Lament" article), Dr. August H. Konkel (for assistance with my theological German), Dr. Ian W. Scott (for writing a reference letter for me to commence my doctoral studies), as well as Dr. Kenneth J. Langley and Dr. Derek Chong (for joyfully endorsing this book), my ten interviewees, and still many others who are dear to my heart, though too numerous to mention, yet all of whom I appreciate so much for coming alongside me to cheer and spur me on to the finish line of my doctoral work and beyond.

Seventh, both sides of my family – the Harrichand's (also the Bhola's, Misir's, Persaud's, and Singh's) and the Chu-A-Kong's (also the Chan's) – expressed their unwavering support and relentless encouragement to me and deserve to be thanked a million times and more for their immeasurable affection and fervent prayers.

Eighth, thanks are also due to Mr. Luke Lewis, Director of Publishingat Langham Literature, for taking the time to listen with keen interest and joy to a summary of my dissertation at the 2021 Society of Biblical Literature's Annual Meeting in San Antonio, Texas. Also Dr. Mark Arnold, my reviewers, and copyeditor at Langham, kindly accept my deepest thanks for assisting me in materializing this literary work under the Langham Academic imprint.

Ultimately, no one deserves to be thanked beyond measure more than our Triune God – the Father, the Son (Jesus Christ), and the Holy Spirit – my light, my life, my salvation, my all in all, without whom this literary work really would not have seen the light of day. After all, it is only in him that I live and move and exist (Acts 17:28). Cognizant of the fact that I have been crucified with Christ, and it is no longer I who live, but Christ who lives in me, so that the life I now live in the flesh, I live by faith in the Son of God, who loved me and gave himself up for me (Gal 2:20), with ceaseless thanksgiving praise from the depths of my heart wherein the Holy Spirit (p)resides, I gratefully echo the words of Revelation 5:13, "To Him who sits on the throne, and to the Lamb [Jesus Christ, the Lion that is from the tribe of Judah, the Root of David], *be* blessing and honor and glory and dominion forever and ever" (cf. Rev 5:5; Ps 115:1; Matt 6:9; 1 Tim 1:17). *Soli Deo Gloria*! Amen.

List of Abbreviations

ACTM	Australian College of Theology Monograph
ABD	Freedman, David Noel, ed. *The Anchor Bible Dictionary*. 6 vols. New York: Doubleday, 1992.
AOTC	Apollos Old Testament Commentary
AYB	Anchor Yale Bible
BECNT	Baker Exegetical Commentary on the New Testament
BDB	Brown, Francis, et al. *Hebrew and English Lexicon of the Old Testament*. Oxford: Clarendon, 1907.
BS	Biblical Series
BZAW	Beihefte zur Zeitschrift für die alttestamentliche Wissenschaft
CBQ	*Catholic Biblical Quarterly*
CeTEAL	Center for Teaching Excellence to Advance Learning
CTJ	*Calvin Theological Journal*
OTL	Forms of the Old Testament Literature
HBT	*Horizons in Biblical Theology*
ISBE	Bromiley, Geoffrey William, ed. *International Standard Bible Encyclopedia*. 4 vols. Grand Rapids: Eerdmans, 1979–1995.
JETS	*Journal of the Evangelical Theological Society*
JSOT	*Journal for the Study of the Old Testament*
JSOTSup	*Journal for the Study of the Old Testament* Supplement Series
MJTM	*McMaster Journal of Theology and Ministry*
NAC	New American Commentary
NASB	New American Standard Bible
NCBC	New Cambridge Bible Commentary

NICOT	New International Commentary on the Old Testament
NIDB	Sakenfeld, Katherine Doob, et al., eds. *The New Interpreter's Dictionary of the Bible*. 5 vols. Nashville: Abingdon, 2006–2009.
NIVAC	New International Version Application Commentary
NSBT	New Studies in Biblical Theology
NT	New Testament
OBT	Overtures to Biblical Theology
OT	Old Testament
OTL	Old Testament Library
PNTC	Pillar New Testament Commentary
PTMS	Princeton Theological Monograph Series
SBL	Society of Biblical Literature
SBLEJL	Society of Biblical Literature Early Judaism and Its Literature
TDOT	Botterweck, G. Johannes, et al., eds. *Theological Dictionary of the Old Testament*. Translated by Geoffrey W. Bromiley et al. 16 vols. Grand Rapids: Eerdmans, 1974–2018.
TOTC	Tyndale Old Testament Commentaries
TTCS	Teach the Text Commentary Series
TWOT	Harris, R. Laird, et al., eds. *Theological Wordbook of the Old Testament*. 2 vols. Chicago: Moody, 1980.
UBCS	Understanding the Bible Commentary Series
VTSS	Vetus Testamentum Supplement Series
WBC	Word Biblical Commentary
WTJ	*Westminster Theological Journal*
ZPEB	Tenney, Merrill C., ed. *Zondervan Pictorial Encyclopedia of the Bible*. 5 vols. Grand Rapids: Zondervan, 1975

CHAPTER 1

Description of Topic and
Its Importance

The Bible, particularly Genesis 1:27,[1] records the miraculous origin of human beings when it asserts that "God created man in His own image, in the image of God He created him; male and female He created them." As creatures fashioned according to the image of the God of the Bible, whose self-revelatory personal and covenant name is Yahweh, or I AM WHO I AM, and otherwise referred to as the LORD (Exod 3:14), humans – both male and female – have thus been graciously endowed with the ability to express themselves verbally, physically, and emotionally.[2] Despite this aesthetic truth, Christopher J. H. Wright sheds light on a disturbing reality that has infiltrated the Christian community. "There is an implicit pressure to stifle our real feelings because we are urged, by pious merchants of emotional denial, that we ought to have 'faith.' So we end up giving external voice to pretended emotions we do not really feel, while hiding the real emotions we are struggling with deep inside."[3]

---

1. All Scripture references are taken from the NASB 1995, unless otherwise stated.

2. See Paul's words in Acts 17:28–29 where he sheds light on the "UNKNOWN GOD" whom the Athenian Greeks worship in declaring to them that he is none other than the One in whom we live and move and exist, and thus we are not to think of him as an image formed by human skill and thought. As a corollary, if God is the physical formation of human thought and skill, then humans should *not* be able to live and move and exist. Paul therefore assumes that it is precisely the exact opposite that is true: rather than God, it is humans who are the physical formation of God's own thought, counsel, and artistic skill, that is, God's own wisdom (see Gen 1:26–27; John 1:1–4; Jas 3:9). Reasoning from this verity, the "UNKNOWN GOD" humans worship should thus be considered as the One who, like humans, lives and moves and exists. Also, out of my deepest respect for the one, true, and living God, the name that I will employ predominantly throughout this book especially in the context of OT passages, is the name that he has graciously given to us in his word – Yahweh.

3. Wright, *God I Don't Understand*, 52.

Consequently, "rather than cry out our true feelings to God, we prefer other ways of responding to it," with the disheartening result being that of "our worship becom[ing] an exercise in pretence and concealment, neither of which can possibly be conducive for a real encounter with God."[4] Further compounding this problem is the fact that, "silencing or stifling the voice of suffering serves only to intensify it," as Betty R. Ferrell and Nessa Coyle have observed.[5] This of course understandably invites at least one obvious question: where then does a contemporary Christian find appropriate language in the crucible of disorientation,[6] encompassing the four dimensions of physical pain, psychological anguish, social degradation, and spiritual despondency,[7]

---

4. Wright, 52.

5. Ferrell and Coyle, *Nature of Suffering*, 15. Balentine (*Prayer in the Hebrew Bible*, 272–295) avows, "When the church encourages the practice of lament, it promotes an understanding of divine-human communication or partnership where radical dialogue is both normative and productive . . . The point here is that covenant relationship, like human relationships, requires communication. The better the communication, the better the relationship, that is, the healthier it is and the more possibilities it has for growth and development. In the same way, restricted communication or, worse, silence reduces the possibilities within the relationship" (288). With regards to OT prayers, Brueggemann (*Great Prayers*, xi–xxx) observes, "Israel's prayer is a refusal to accept that [imposed] silence that is most often oppressive and that works to preclude human freedom and human well-being" (xxi).

6. Boda (*Praying the Tradition*, 1–18) maintains that "If there is a supra-language which transcends linguistic barriers it must be the language of suffering, the discourse of disorientation" (1). Equating disorientation with that of lament psalms, Brueggemann (*Message of the Psalms*, 15–23) contends that, "Human life consists in anguished seasons of hurt, alienation, suffering, and death. These evoke rage, resentment, self-pity, and hatred. Matching this, we will consider 'psalms of disorientation,' poems and speech-forms that match the season in its ragged, painful disarray. This speech, the lament, has a recognizable shape that permits the extravagance, hyperbole, and abrasiveness needed for the experience" (19). Noted here, however, is that while the term *lament* is the predominant nomenclature assigned to the largest category or genre (*Gattung*) of psalms found within the OT, the lament proper only submits the problem or the disorientation of the situation in life (*Sitz im Leben*) to the LORD, whereas the supplication or the petition for liberation is perhaps the most significant element of the psalm, or the axle of the entire prayer. Stated another way, the turning point of the lament psalm does not occur at the juncture of stating the lament proper; rather, the lament psalm hinges on God's reception of the supplication. As Chiu (*Psalms: An Introduction*, 100–104) argues, "Gunkel prefers the term *lamentation* instead of *supplication*. However, *supplication* seems preferable since the lament (i.e. the evocation of the situation of distress) is not the dominant element. In fact, the psalmist recalls the past or the painful present not with resignation, but with the intent that God intervene. The supplication or petition is the dominant element" (100; emphasis original).

7. The first three categories of physical pain, psychological anguish, and social degradation are further discussed in Weil, *Awaiting God*, 44 and Soelle, *Suffering*, 13–15. In recent years, the fourth category of spiritual despondency has been proposed and explored by and in Zylla, *Roots of Sorrow*, 58–59. For Zylla (41–69), "the deeper reality of suffering is multivalent and may be better described by the unifying concept of 'affliction.' This contributes to a 'thicker' description of suffering that allows for the hidden dimensions to be brought into full view"

and which also embraces the efficacy of comforting hope coupled with legitimacy in addressing God? Generally referred to as the language of *lament*, and located in large measure within the Psalter – the prayer book and hymnal of the OT saints – such heart-wounded cry not only furnishes the contemporary Christian with reassuring hope, but also with the vernacular of unimpeachable speech directed at God, especially in prayer and song.[8] Small wonder Wright avers that, "Lament is the voice of pain, whether for oneself, for one's people, or simply for the mountain of suffering of humanity and creation itself. Lament is the voice of faith struggling with unanswered questions and unexplained suffering."[9] Stated otherwise, "lament can help us give voice to our lived experience and the reality of our pain."[10]

For decades, however, it appeared as if the Western church had given such considerable attention to *praise* that the language of *lament* was deemed incongruous for appropriation within its worship setting. This situation precipitated the clarion call for the recovery of the *lost* language of lament (particularly from the Psalter), by a plethora of scholars such as Walter Brueggemann, Sally A. Brown and Patrick D. Miller, Kathleen D. Billman and Daniel L. Migliore, Christopher J. H. Wright, and others.[11] Harkening to this inspiring

---

(56). Worth mentioning here, however, is that both affliction and disorientation are multivalent experience-rich categories. See chapter 7 for a potential working definition of disorientation.

8. For more lament language, see also especially the OT books of Job and Lamentations. Noted here are the words of Miller (*Interpreting the Psalms*, 18–28) who observes, "In the Psalter we have a large collection of words uttered to God and about God, but not by or from God. In other words, the psalms give speech to human response and human existence before God (*coram Deo*, 'in the presence of God')" (19). Wright (*God I Don't Understand*, 44–55) also notes that, "It is precisely those who have the closest relationship with God who feel most at liberty to pour out their pain and protest to God – without fear or reproach . . . God seems to want to give us as many words with which to fill in our complaint forms as to write our thank-you notes. Perhaps this is because whatever amount of lament the world causes us to express is a drop in the ocean compared to the grief in the heart of God himself at the totality of suffering that only God can comprehend" (51).

9. Wright, *God I Don't Understand*, 53.

10. Hopkins and Koppel, *Grounded in the Living Word*, 137. Adhering to such a view himself, Boda (*Praying the Tradition*, 1–18) avers that, "Pain is part of the human journey and no one is insulated from its icy touch . . . When humans discover a piece of literature which succinctly unveils the reality of pain they resonate immediately with that text because they identify with the content as well as the emotion" (1).

11. See Billman and Migliore, *Rachel's Cry*; Boda, *After God's Own Heart*; Brown and Miller, eds., *Lament: Reclaiming Practices*; Brueggemann, "Costly Loss of Lament," 57–71; Brueggemann, "Lament as Antidote," 24–25; Brueggemann, "Voice as Counter," 22–33; Campbell, "New Testament Lament," 757–772; Cohen, *Why O Lord?*; Eklund, *Practicing Lament*; Ellington, *Risking Truth*; Ellington, "Costly Loss of Testimony," 48–59; Harasta and Brock, eds., *Evoking Lament*; Harper and Barker, eds. *Finding Lost Words*; Harrichand, "Recovering the

call, the Western church is currently in the process of taking the necessary measures to respond appropriately, i.e. by employing lament in concert with praise within its worship context.[12] The upshot of this is an active engagement in fostering a healthy equilibrium between its summer and winter voices of prayer and song within the Western church.[13]

Central Theological Questions

Further reflection on the irrefragable universal theme of suffering, and more particularly the multiplex responses of Christians experiencing suffering, has nonetheless sparked two questions that loom large within this book. Question number one is: within the context of OT prosaic prayers uttered in the life setting of disorientation,[14] does the potential exist for one to discover, in association with lament and praise, other modes of expression communicated to/before God (i.e. verbal, physical, and emotional) by faithful Israelite prayers?[15] Inspired by the first question, question number two is: amidst grief, and in association with lament and praise, does the possibility exist for one to discover other modes of expression communicated to/before God (i.e. verbal, physical, and emotional) within a contemporary Western Christian

---

Language," 101–130; Lai, "The Costly Loss," 281–291; McCutchan, "Illuminating the Dark," 14–17; Ngien, *Fruit of the Soul*; Resner, "Lament: Faith's Response," 129–142; Swinton, *Raging with Compassion*; Tanner, "How Long!", 143–152; Villanueva, *It's OK*; Villanueva, "Preaching Lament," 64–84; Villanueva, '*Uncertainty of a Hearing*'; Wenham, *Psalter Reclaimed*; Witvliet, "Time to Weep," 22–26 ; Wright, *God I Don't Understand*; etc.

12. As Morganthaler (*Worship Evangelism*, 96–126) maintains, "There is widespread, almost insatiable craving for vulnerability and *authenticity* . . . It is no accident that lament and vulnerability go hand in hand. No one would want a whole service of it, but worship that is real makes room for all the colors of the emotional spectrum, not just those that are rapturous and effervescent" (110, 113; emphasis original). See also Ramshaw, "Place of Lament," 317–322; Shipp, *Timeless: Ancient Psalms*; Witvliet et al., *Psalms for All Seasons*; etc.

13. See Billman and Migliore, *Rachel's Cry*, 1.

14. In contrast to the poetic prayers, prosaic prayers are those prayers located within the prose or narrative sections of the OT and thus framed within the parameters of Genesis and Esther.

15. This question stems from the observation that the academic field appears to be flooded with research relative to OT *poetic* prayers of disorientation (especially from the Psalter) while little sustained theological attention has been apportioned to OT *prosaic* prayers of disorientation. Interestingly, when asked by a Princeton University doctoral student, "What is there left in the world for original dissertation?" Albert Einstein retorted, "Find out about prayer. Someone must find out about prayer" (in Yancey, *Prayer: Does It Make*, 11). This book will seek to fill the lacuna in scholarship regarding *OT prosaic prayers*, particularly those categorized by disorientation, rather than orientation or new orientation.

context, yet through the lens of the experiences of principally Canadian immigrants from Guyana and Vietnam?[16] The rationale for selecting a principally Guyanese and Vietnamese population is threefold:

- First, this selection stems from my affiliation with both cultural groups. Being of Guyanese heritage and serving within a Vietnamese congregation (up until the end of 2018 as the English Ministry/Youth Pastor) afforded me the opportunity of connecting easily with leaders from both cultural populations for this research.

- Second, this selection, though limited to the Guyanese and Vietnamese cultural groups, does not infer that other cultural groups (e.g., African, Chinese, First Nations, Indian, Korean, Laotian, Myanmarese, Filipino, etc.) were completely removed from any consideration. Since there was little affinity with these other groups, however, the decision was made to consider them, as well as others, for future projects. Replicating this research among the excluded cultural groups after the completion of this book is thus indispensable.

- Third, limiting my population to two cultural groups seemed sufficient for this book. Additional cultural groups would complicate the data, especially since saturation had already been achieved (i.e. the data did not yield any new results) within the current cultural populations.

---

16. The impetus for looking outside-yet-inside of the West also arises from observing that the majority-cultures in North America are more stoic, formal, and less emotional in their expression of grief, as compared to their minority-culture counterparts. For example, Scazzero (*Emotionally Healthy Spirituality*, 135–152) notes that "Americans of British ancestry tend to value a 'no muss, no fuss' rationale of experiencing loss. Funerals, for example, are practical and pragmatic. As one sister said, explaining why she had not attended the funeral of her twin sister, 'What would have been the point of spending money on the airfare to get there? She was already dead'" (138). The terms 'majority-culture' and 'minority-culture' are utilized to indicate power relationships, rather than numerical magnitude within a society. According to Irish ("Multiculturalism and the Majority," 1–10) in Canada and America, "the white majorities, have dominated, discriminated against, and even pursued genocidal practices toward their non-white minorities, the indigenous peoples, the 'First Nations,' and those who came to the New World as slaves" (2n1). This has resulted in "many minority peoples in the contemporary world to develop a heightened group consciousness by organizing themselves within and among their communities, seeking respect, equal participation in the larger national and world societies, and control over their own destinies" (2). For similar observations, see Perry, "Mourning and Funeral Customs," 51–65; Nelsen, "One Woman's Interracial Journey," 21–27. In lieu of using the terms *minority-culture* or *majority-culture*, the term *intercultural* will be employed.

Observing that both questions afford a positive response,[17] the meta-method of this book will be considered, but only after enunciating the thesis statement.

Thesis Statement

Bifocal in its objective, this book: (1) generates a domain of anthropological[18] expressions of disorientation communicated to/before God, along with their essence or meaning from both the ancient Israelite context of OT prosaic prayers of disorientation and that of a contemporary Christian intercultural context (principally among Canadian immigrants from Guyana and Vietnam) amidst grief; and (2) sensitizes contemporary pastoral caregivers to such an expressive domain with its multivalent significance, for the purpose of fostering compassionate pastoral care, couched within rituals, in the best interest of intercultural Christian communities coping with grief.[19]

---

17. For examples of other expressions, see the discussion that follows in chapters 3 and 4.

18. It should be noted here that using the word *anthropological*, I am not referring to *anthropology* in the strict sense of the scientific study of human societies and cultures and their development. Rather, I simply employ the term *anthropological* in reference to humans in general and the ways in which they express themselves verbally, physical, and emotionally to/before God, especially in the midst of disorientation (which is synonymous with affliction) of which grief is a significant component.

19. Relying on the work of Crisp ("Compassion and Beyond," 233–246), Zylla ("Inhabiting Compassion," 1–9) understands compassion as "a moral emotion that is also a pathocentric virtue. As such, compassion evokes deep feelings of pain and distress at the pain and distress of others. Compassion will result in a feeling of shared anguish, a desire to see the situation changed and actions that alleviate the root cause of the suffering observed" (2). Sharp ("Globalization, Colonialism," 422–431) maintains that pastoral theologians and caregivers who employ the liberative intercultural praxis seek to liberate, resist, empower, heal, guide, sustain, reconcile, and nurture those who find themselves in life situations of suffering (426). Swinton and Mowat (*Practical Theology*, 73–98) proffer that compassionate pastoral care responses "will enable the initial situation to be transformed into ways which are authentic and faithful" (97). Especially amidst grief, it is important to note that the bereaved seek sustainability (see Lartey, *In Living Color*, 63–64). Here, particular attention is given to the following five compassionate (liberative intercultural) pastoral care practices for coping with grief, each of which is explicated specifically in chapter 6: (i) Bearing the funeral expenses of the poor – extending offers of help; (ii) Composing and singing sad (and joyful theopoetic) songs and poems of lament – finding emotional catharsis through music; (iii) Incorporating indigenous Christian devotional songs (e.g., Bhajans) in the wake/funeral liturgy – tapping into the cultural liminal memory of a deep experience of faith; (iv) Celebrating the life of the deceased through dancing and singing upbeat gospel songs – spiritual rejoicing for having arrived home in heaven; and (v) Connecting personal grief stories to God's sacred story – experiencing hope in the crucified-yet-resurrected Christ.

CHAPTER 2

Research Framework and Methodologies

2.1. Metamethod and Methodologies

2.1.1. Revisionist Method of Mutual Critical Correlation

Achieving the foregoing thesis necessitates that one keep in mind the following central Christian theological task as espoused by David Tracy: "the dramatic confrontation, the mutual illuminations and corrections, the possible basic reconciliation between the principal values, cognitive claims, and existential faiths of both a reinterpreted post-modern consciousness and a reinterpreted Christianity."[1] Such an undertaking, Tracy believes, is best accomplished by the *revisionist method of mutual critical correlation*,[2] which he defines as, "The philosophical reflection upon the meanings present in common human experience and language, and upon the meanings present

---

1. Tracy, *Blessed Rage*, 32, 43.

2. It is "revisionist" because Tracy revises Paul Tillich's method of correlation, which correlates insights from Christian revelation in conjunction with the issues and questions raised by existential, philosophical, and psychological analysis. Whereas Tillich's method of correlation is unidirectional wherein the Christian message furnishes the answers to the questions implied in human existence, Tracy's revisionist method of critical correlation includes questions raised from within the Christian tradition with answers being furnished by human existence. This way, questions and answers flow in both directions, that is, between human existence and Christian tradition. In his own words, Tracy (*Blessed Rage*, 22–42) states that, "The reasons for the label 'revisionist' are both historical and systematic. Historically, it seems clear that classical liberalisms, classical orthodoxies, various kinds of neo-orthodoxy, and various radical alternatives are now legitimately judged inadequate models for the present theological task . . . The principal reasons for the label 'revisionist,' however, are systematic ones" (32).

in the Christian fact."[3] This revisionist method of mutual critical correlation adheres to the ensuing five theses:

1.   The two principal sources for theology are Christian texts and common human experience and language.[4]
2.   The theological task will involve a critical correlation of the results of the investigations of the two sources of theology.[5]
3.   The principal method of investigation of the source "common human experience and language" can be described as a phenomenology of the "religious dimension" present in everyday and scientific experience and language.[6]
4.   The principal method of investigation of the source "the Christian tradition" can be described as an historical and hermeneutical investigation of classical Christian texts.[7]
5.   To determine the truth-status of the results of one's investigations into the meaning of both common human experience and Christian texts, the theologian should employ an explicitly transcendental or metaphysical mode of reflection.[8]

As concerns this book, Tracy's revisionist method of mutual critical correlation will be operationalized as its metamethod. Consequently, other significant sub-methodologies will also play an important role throughout this book. These are as follows: the liberative intercultural praxis, a hermeneutical phenomenology, and renewed form criticism. Each of these sub-methodologies will be given adequate attention subsequent to an outline of the application of Tracy's revisionist method of mutual critical correlation.

Operationalizing Tracey's revisionist method of mutual critical correlation as its metamethod,[9] this book will coordinate a dialectic correlation between

---

3. Tracy, *Blessed Rage*, 43.

4. Tracy, 43–44.

5. Tracy, 45–46. Within this book, the Christian texts and the human experience of grief will both inform and form our liberative intercultural pastoral care practices.

6. Tracy, 47–48.

7. Tracy, 49–52.

8. Tracy, 52–56.

9. According to Lynch ("Tested by Practice," 164–183) one way in which Tracy's revisionist method of mutual critical correlation can be exercised is by means of following what is known as the "pastoral cycle" with its five broad steps, which is demonstrated here (178).

the liberative intercultural praxis coupled with that of hermeneutical phenomenology and of renewed form criticism. It will begin with the *concrete life situation* of the phenomenon of grief experienced among contemporary Christians from the intercultural context of the West, i.e. among Canadian immigrants from Guyana and Vietnam.

By coupling the liberative intercultural praxis with that of the hermeneutic phenomenology, a *contextual analysis* will be executed by combining the social analytical mediation of Latin American liberation theology with the religio-cultural analysis of African and Asian liberation theology. Here, the qualitative approach of hermeneutical phenomenology will aid us in a careful examination of the range of expressions communicated to/before God (i.e. verbal, physical, and emotional) amidst grief by immigrants of Guyanese and Vietnamese cultures. The intention here is to present a thick description[10] of a taxonomy of such expressions of disorientation.

What follows next is a *theological analysis*, which involves the application of renewed form criticism to the Christian tradition of the ancient context of OT prosaic prayers uttered in the life context of disorientation. The aim here is that of generating a thick description of a taxonomy of expressions of OT prosaic prayers (sub)stages, together with their accompanying physical and emotional expressions, amidst the generic life situation of disorientation.

This is followed by a *situational analysis of theology* which involves a dialectical correlation between the life situation of the grieving, contemporary Christian intercultural expressions, and the Christian tradition expressions of OT prosaic prayers accompanied by physical and emotional expressions of disorientation. Here we explore how these three poles of knowledge can influence each other so as to produce new insights into the issue under examination, namely grief. Drawn out here are the implicit and explicit theological dimensions of the situation, with an eye toward sifting through the data, and

---

10. Denzin ("Art and Politics," 500–515) states that, "A thin description simply reports facts, independent of intentions or circumstances. A thick description, in contrast, gives the context of an experience, states the intentions and meanings that organized the experience, and reveals the experience as a process" (505). Swinton and Mowat (*Practical Theology*, 99–132) add, "A thick description seeks to capture the essence of a phenomenon in a way that communicates it in all its fullness, thus making it rich, vivid, and faithful. Therefore, the implication of a thick description for the entire research process is that the process of writing, reflecting, and accurately interpreting the data is not simply epiphenomenal to data presentation and analysis, but rather a crucial part of the process" (123).

exploring the ways in which they complement and challenge each other. While the primary emphasis is placed on the expressions located in the OT (Christian tradition), some expressions located in the NT will also play a key role in the dialectic correlation. This is because the Christian intercultural expressions also embrace a close(r) affinity to those expressions found within the NT. Behind this dialectical correlation is the sensitizing of contemporary pastoral caregivers to the multivalent significance of the verbal, physical, and emotional anthropological expressions communicated to/before God within an intercultural society.

In response to this, the chapter on *pastoral care action* will propose new and challenging forms of compassionate pastoral care practices for those within a contemporary Christian intercultural locale coping with grief. At the same time, each of these practices will be couched within rituals at the heart of which is the ordering of experience, thus reorienting the disoriented. The initial situation will thus be transformed or revised into ways that are authentic and faithful to the gospel of the triune God's redemptive mission to the world. Owing to its nature as a pastoral cycle, this dynamic process never ceases, but renews by returning to the beginning and repeating the course all over again.

2.1.2. Liberative Intercultural Praxis

As noted earlier, for the objective of this book to be accomplished, it is essential for the metamethod of the revisionist method of mutual critical correlation to incorporate the sub-methodology of the *liberative intercultural praxis*, pioneered by Emmanuel Y. Lartey. This praxis will enable the researcher to take seriously the experiences of grief among Christians marginalized and oppressed within the Western culture and church, some of whom belong to a Guyanese-Canadian and a Vietnamese-Canadian heritage.

Lartey contends that, "At the heart of the 'hiddenness' of pastoral care is love . . . In Christian terms, 'we love because God first loved us.' (1 John 4:19) . . . Not only does it impel us into relationship with others, it also enables us to recognize injustice and to desire to do something about it."[11] Lartey further asserts that, "The Christian teaching of incarnation, seeks to convey an 'enfleshing' of *agape* in a historic person – Jesus Christ – who becomes

---

11. Lartey, *In Living Color*, 29.

the icon and enabler of such love for and in his followers. Such self-giving love is at the heart of the Christian gospel and is the impelling force behind Christian action."[12] What is more, "In intercultural pastoral care, love is both the motivation and the motive force. Recognizing the love of God as crucial and basic for and in the created world, intercultural pastoral caregivers seek to place themselves within this love and to become agents and conduits of it."[13] Of key importance to this intercultural pastoral care "is the realization that the love of God is for the whole world, created diverse and affirmed in its diversity by the creative energy of God. As such, all that is done must respect and uphold the diversity in which the whole of the world is created. All attempts to force uniformity upon a world created diverse are both heretical and damaging to the creation."[14]

Lartey's liberating intercultural praxis consequently "privileges situated, contextual experience and the analysis of that experience in its multi-layered and multi-factored reality."[15] Put another way, it "presupposes a multicultural group of people committed to intercultural encounter, learning, and change."[16] More than that, it seeks to "facilitate learning within a group of people from different countries and cultures, of different ages, men and women, lay and ordained, of different Christian backgrounds as well as other traditions, with varying degrees of commitment to and challenge of their various heritages. Their only commitment is to learning for the purpose of being reflective practitioners of pastoral care in one form or another."[17] When this happens, more appropriate, compassionate, holistic, liberative, intercultural pastoral care techniques, otherwise referred to as pastoral theodical practices, are cultivated that: (i) deepen one's understanding of the nature of the divine and the human, and the relationship between them, and (ii) facilitate the

---

12. Lartey, 29; emphasis original.

13. Lartey, 29–30.

14. Lartey, 30.

15. Lartey, *Pastoral Theology*, 89.

16. Lartey, *In Living Color*, 131. Lartey (*Pastoral Theology*, 121–150) also states that "Interculturality stands for an attitude that rejects both extreme relativism and exclusive absolutism. It inhabits different cultures but also seeks to transcend their narrow limits" (124–125).

17. Lartey, *In Living Color*, 131.

development of more pertinent forms of liberative intercultural healing care for persons-in-context as a result of reflections on the divine nature.[18]

Lartey's liberative intercultural praxis falls within phase two of the revisionist method of mutual critical correlation, that is, the contextual analysis. It is employed for the purpose of learning from some of the marginalized and oppressed Christians in the Western church, particularly those of Guyanese and Vietnamese cultures, as to the verbal, physical, and emotional expressions communicated to/before God amidst grief. The information collected from the use of this sub-method will then engage in a dialectic correlation, either as a complement or a challenge, to the verbal, physical, and emotional expressions communicated to/before God by leading Israelites amidst grief within the prosaic sections of the OT (Genesis to Esther). Ultimately, it is this sub-method that will lend its aid to the development of compassionate (liberative intercultural) pastoral care practices that mitigate grief, sustain the bereaved, and are thus faithful to the triune God's redemptive mission to the world. Yet this sub-method is contingent upon a hermeneutical phenomenology.

2.1.3. Hermeneutical Phenomenology

The qualitative research method, *hermeneutical phenomenology*, will be employed with the intention of addressing the assortment of verbal, physical, and emotional responses that Christian leaders of Guyanese and Vietnamese heritage communicate to/before God amidst the phenomenon of grief. While the responses are of import to constructing a taxonomy, an even more significant step is the discovery of their *essence or meaning*, which lies at the heart of the phenomenological approach to qualitative research. Employing this method of hermeneutical phenomenology thus enables one to discover fresh insights into the experience of verbal, physical, and emotional responses to/before God amidst the phenomenon of grief, insights which will raise new and challenging questions for theology and practice. When used in the service of God, nonetheless, this type of qualitative research method holds much potential in developing faithful practices and transforming understandings, Christian communities, and beyond.[19]

---

18. Lartey, *Pastoral Theology*, 91.
19. Swinton and Mowat, *Practical Theology*, 131–132.

In much the same way that, "Pastoral theology is committed to reflection on lived experience and is rooted in the concreteness of life," Zylla affirms that, "phenomenological research focuses on lived experience."[20] While Maurice Merleau-Ponty avows that, "Phenomenology is the study of essences,"[21] it is important to note that this is not "some kind of mysterious entity or discovery, nor some ultimate core or residue of meaning. Rather, the term 'essence' may be understood as a linguistic construction, a description of a phenomenon."[22] Max van Manen accordingly asserts that, "A good description that constitutes the essence of something is construed so that the structure of a lived experience is revealed to us in a fashion that we are now able to grasp the nature and significance of this experience in a hitherto unseen way."[23] The objective therefore of phenomenology "is to transform lived experience into a textual expression of its essence – in such a way that the effect of the text is at once a reflexive re-living and a reflective appropriation of something meaningful."[24] Some of the defining features of phenomenological research, according to John W. Creswell, can be summarized as follows:

- An emphasis on a phenomenon to be explored, which is phrased in terms of a single concept or idea, which, in the case of this book, is the phenomenon of grief.
- The exploration of this phenomenon of grief with a group of individuals who have all experienced the phenomenon, which should be heterogeneous, which may vary in size from three or four individuals to ten to fifteen. For this book, ten individuals were chosen, five each of Guyanese and Vietnamese heritage.
- The principle of bracketing of the researcher wherein the researcher or pastoral theologian is called upon to "bracket" all speculative and constructive views of the phenomenon in order that there might be a disciplined "seeing," that is, an inhibition of the researcher or pastoral theologian's tendency to interpret the

20. Zylla, "Shades of Lament," 764.
21. Merleau-Ponty, *Phenomenology of Perception*, vii.
22. van Manen, *Researching Lived Experience*, 39.
23. van Manen, 39.
24. van Manen, 36.

phenomenon.[25] While this aspect of bracketing does not remove the researcher entirely from the study, it does serve to identify personal experiences with the phenomenon and to partly set them aside so that the researcher or pastoral theologian can focus on the experiences of the participants.

- A data collection procedure. While such a procedure typically involves the interviewing of individuals who have experienced the phenomenon, which in this case is grief, various other sources of data, such as blogs, journals, music, sermons, taped conversations, formally written responses, accounts of vicarious experiences of drama, films, poetry, and novels, etc., can be incorporated.
- Data analysis that can follow systematic procedures that move from the narrow units of analysis (e.g., significant statements), and on to broader units (e.g., meaning), and on to detailed descriptions that summarize two elements, "what" the individuals have experienced and "how" they have experienced it.
- A phenomenology ends with a descriptive passage that discusses the *essence* of the experience for individuals incorporating "what" they have experienced and "how" they experienced it. The "essence" is the culminating aspect of a phenomenological study.[26]

Furnishing the investigator or pastoral theologian with some guidance for the grounding of lived experience in phenomenology, van Manen states that the researcher should

- Describe the experience without causal explanations.
- Describe the experience from the inside (feelings, moods, emotions).
- Focus on specific events – describe an incident.
- Focus on vivid experiences.
- Attend to the sensory: sights, sounds, smells, feelings.
- Avoid attempts to beautify your account with fancy phrases or terminology.[27]

---

25. Patton, *From Ministry to Theology*, 37.

26. Creswell, *Qualitative Inquiry*, 78–79.

27. van Manen, *Researching Lived Experience*, 64–65.

Hermeneutical phenomenology, however, is not only oriented toward the descriptive lived experience (phenomenon) in an attempt to enrich lived experience by mining its meaning, but also toward the interpretive study of the expressions and objectifications or texts of lived experience in an attempt to determine the meaning embodied in them (hermeneutics).[28] While van Manen does not approach hermeneutical phenomenology with any set of rules or methods, he offers the following dynamic interplay of research activities: The researcher turns first to a phenomenon, which is an "abiding concern" that is of serious interest to them, and in the process, they reflect on essential themes that are relative to what exactly constitutes the nature of this lived experience. Thereafter, the researcher writes a description of the phenomenon, maintaining a strong relation to the topic of inquiry, and balancing the part of the writing to the whole. Since it is a hermeneutical phenomenology, the researcher not only provides a description of the lived experience (phenomenon), but also attempts to interpret the meaning of the lived experience (hermeneutics).[29] According to van Manen, "Lived experiences gather hermeneutic significance as we (reflectively) gather them by giving memory to them. Through meditations, daydreams, inspirations and other interpretative acts we assign meaning to the phenomenon of lived life."[30]

Developing a thick description of both the *taxonomy* and the *essence* or *meaning* of the Guyanese-Canadian and Vietnamese-Canadian believers' expressions to/before God (i.e. verbal, physical, and emotional) amidst the lived experience of grief, however, necessitated the submission of an application to the McMaster Research Ethics Board (MREB). This was to ensure that ethical permission be approved prior to formal interviews with the ten interviewees.[31] The interviews were held in locations conducive to the interviewees. Several questions were asked in relation to their expressions of grief, as well as those relative to the intercultural context-sensitive responses, which offered hope and resolution to them amidst grief. These questions fell under the umbrella

---

28. van Manen, 38.

29. See also Creswell, *Qualitative Inquiry*, 80–81.

30. van Manen, *Researching Lived Experience*, 39.

31. Swinton and Mowat (*Practical Theology*, 28–72) maintain that "The interview process is a meaningful human encounter within which both parties [interviewer and interviewee] gain implicit and explicit knowledge about the other. It is a unique space for the creation and sharing of meaning" (64).

of sampling, which according to John Swinton and Harriet Mowat are of three types: (i) opportunistic, (ii) theoretical, and (iii) purposive. For this book, a single-point purposive sampling was selected for the interview process, which suggests that "All the interviewees are chosen at the time with specific criteria that are explicit and clarified in terms of the ability to answer the research questions."[32] What follows is a sample of the single-point purposive questions that were asked during the interviews.

1. What is your understanding of the word grief?
2. What concrete examples of grief have you met with?
3. What range of expressions of grief (i.e. verbal, physical, and emotional) are normal responses within your culture?
4. Do you have a mental image of your situation of grief, or how would you describe your situation of grief?
5. Where are you currently on your journey with regards to this grief?
6. What are your culture's traditional beliefs/worldviews surrounding grief?
7. What are your church's traditional beliefs surrounding grief?
8. Are there any perspectives or behaviors that help you cope with this grief?
9. What meaning do these coping mechanisms have in your life?[33]

These three responses (i.e. the verbal, physical, and emotional expressions amidst grief, along with their essence or meaning) were then recorded in a Microsoft Word document prior to being analyzed.

---

32. Swinton and Mowat, 205. Opportunistic sampling "is the least satisfactory type of sampling and as the name implies suggests that the sample is comprised of people who were available. The opportunistic sample however is a reality in time-limited and resource-tight projects" (204). In theoretical sampling the "interviewees are chosen at a number of different points in the data collection period. The data is analyzed progressively and new recruits are sought as the data yields categories that need further investigation. The interviewees are chosen progressively for what they can add to the data set. Eventually the data analysis does not produce any new categories and saturation is achieved" (204). In other words, "There comes a point when the interviews do not yield anything new in terms of insight and there is no need to interview further" (204).

33. Creswell, *Qualitative Inquiry*, 115. I am also indebted to Kelvin Mutter for his initial thoughts in formulating these questions. Here I utilize the more user-friendly word *grief* rather than the broad and multivalent experience-rich term of *disorientation*. Alternatively stated, grief is to be understood as a dimension of psychological anguish.

Imperative to the interviewing process was *bracketing* the researcher's own personal experiences in order to engage in listening authentically to the voices of the interviewees, rather than allowing the researcher's voice to intrude. As Creswell notes, "Bracketing is a process of setting aside one's own beliefs, feelings, and perceptions to be more faithful to the phenomenon."[34] It was therefore incumbent upon me as the researcher to transcend or suspend past knowledge and experience, so as to understand the phenomenon of grief at a deeper level as a means to approach the lived experience with a sense of newness to elicit rich and descriptive data.[35]

It is important to remember that the employment of a hermeneutical phenomenology is subsumed under the liberative intercultural praxis, which is part of phase two of the larger pastoral cycle of the revisionist method of mutual critical correlation, i.e. the *contextual analysis*. The contextual analysis combines these two sub-methods to generate a thick description of a taxonomy of the range of expressions (i.e. verbal, physical, and emotional) communicated to/before God amidst grief as well as their significance or meaning. Together, this information serves to engage in a dialectic correlation, which will either complement or challenge the findings of the verbal, physical, and emotional expressions to/before God amidst disorientation by leading Israelites within in the prosaic sections of the OT (Genesis to Esther). Through this dialectic correlation one will become aware of those practices of the church that are faithful to the triune God's redemptive mission to the world.

2.1.4. Renewed Form Criticism

Generating a taxonomy of expressions of disorientation (sub)stages associated with lament and praise from within the ancient context of OT prosaic prayers of disorientation, necessitates the application of *Renewed Form Criticism*. By way of a general description, and in a manner analogous to Old and New Form Criticism, *Renewed Form Criticism* adheres to four fundamental steps in its analysis of the biblical text unit. But whereas Old Form Criticism identified the genre *prior to* seeking out the comparative life setting or *Sitz im Leben*, in *Renewed Form Criticism*, a generic life setting of orientation, disorientation,

---

34. Creswell, *Qualitative Inquiry*, 331.

35. See Creswell, 331.

or new/reorientation is established *in advance of* pursuing the genre or type of the text unit. By reversing steps two and three, this hermeneutical approach will once again undergo another modification, i.e. from Old Form Criticism to New Form Criticism and now to *Renewed Form Criticism*.[36] The four essential steps of this *Renewed Form Criticism* are thus:

1. Determine the unit – Nothing more or nothing less than the entire unit is required for the correct identification of the literary genre, type, or stage.[37] With regards to this book, the determinative unit will be one wherein the prayer of disorientation is positioned.

2. Describe its setting in life (*Sitz im Leben*) – The original oral social context is assumed to be the generic life setting of either orientation, disorientation, or new orientation. The original social context assumed in this book, however, is that of the generic life situation of *disorientation*. Moreover, the answer to the question regarding the kind of thinking that gave rise to such an expression, as well as the possibility of knowing something about the people from the way they spoke and/or acted, is sought after.[38]

3. Decipher the literary genre (*Gattung*) – In this step, a robust taxonomy of the literary (sub)stages/types/categories (*Gattungen*) of OT prosaic prayers of orientation, disorientation, or new orientation will be generated. In reference to this book, however,

---

36. Cf. Sweeney and Zvi, *Changing Face*. Gratitude to Mark J. Boda for assisting me in the nomenclature of this new criticism.

37. Tucker (*Form Criticism*, 1–21) prefers "Analysis of the structure" (11), where structure refers to "the outline, the pattern or schema of a given piece of literature or a given genre" (12).

38. Tucker refers to this step as "Definition of the setting or settings" (11). It is worth mentioning here that New Form Criticism would rather emphasize an intended literary reception/readership than an intended oral original context (see e.g., Blum, "*Formgeschichte*, 45). Here, however, I take exception to this proposal by affirming that in as much as we currently have in our possession the literary texts, it seems inconceivable to think that such literary texts were devoid of an oral lifeform, especially since ancient Israel lived within both an oral and literary society simultaneously. Textual evidence lending its aid to this contention of orality appears in Ps 44:1, which states, "God, we have heard with our ears, / *Our fathers have told us*" (emphasis mine; see also Exod 12:26–27; Deut 6:20; Judg 6:13; Ps 78:3). For further support, see also Gerstenberger, *Psalms: Part 1*, 260; Toffelmire's, 265; and Tucker, *Form Criticism*, 6. This, in conjunction with my challenge to Old Form Criticism that holds to a rigid correspondence between genre and life setting, has given rise to *Renewed Form Criticism* that I am here espousing. Also, in choosing to speak of a generic life setting of disorientation rather than "hard, fixed realities," I therefore concur with Sparks ("Form," 111–113) that, "comparative taxonomies [are] created by readers" (113).

the robust taxonomy of the literary (sub)stages/types/categories will only be related to the OT prosaic prayers of disorientation.[39]

4.   Discern its purpose – This final step seeks to address the function or purpose of the prosaic or poetic prayer of orientation, disorientation, or new orientation. But in the case of this book, it refers to the OT prosaic prayer of disorientation in the original oral stage, in addition to the purpose it now serves within the larger work of which it is part (i.e. orality and literacy). Stated alternatively, it seeks to trace what changes took place in the OT saints by knowing how these two uses differ.[40]

Succinctly stated, we commence with a particular unit of the OT prosaic prayer of disorientation text, and in comparing it with other similar units, we isolate common elements and make note of significant differences. It thus becomes possible to offer legitimate grounds for comparison that are drawn from the text, while yet taking seriously the fact that the resulting (sub)stages are abstractions. But sandwiched between determining the unit of the OT prosaic prayer of disorientation text and deciphering its literary (sub)stages is the description of the life setting, which is primarily that of the generic life situation of disorientation. Subsequently, the use and function of a specific structure within a particular unit of text may be examined in light of both the abstracted (sub)stages and other instances of similar (sub)stages. In addition to this, we may also analyze the use and function of a particular text

---

39. Tucker (*Form Criticism*, 1–21) prefers "Describing the genre" (11). To prevent any further nebulosity regarding "form" and "genre" I have sought to rename this step "Decipher the literary genre (*Gattung*)." In doing so particularly with regards to this book, Boda's two-tier taxonomy (i.e. Disorientation Stage 1 Prayers and Disorientation Stage 2 Prayers) will be carried to another level. In seeking after a robust taxonomy of OT prosaic prayers of disorientation (sub) stages, however, it is not my intention to pursue an ideal genre/type, but rather a "diagnostic tool" that will enable critics to correctly divide and analyze the word of God through a careful distinction of the assortment and mixture of the OT prosaic prayers of disorientation. At the same time, by moving from the generic life situation of disorientation prior to deciphering the genre, rather than vice versa, it is hoped that Bible students will avoid further literary nomenclature squabbles over identifying the genre of the prayer as lament, complaint, protest, petitions, etc. In other words, the names given to the variety of disorientation prayers in this project will simply be as follows: *Disorientation Stage 1 through 6 Prayers* (see chapter 4 for more details).

40. Tucker (*Form Criticism*, 1–21) prefers "Statement of the intent, purpose, or function of the text" (11).

and its (sub)stages within the book or collection in which it is positioned, thus comparing the interplay between multivalent (sub)stages.[41]

Once more it is important to remember that the employment of renewed form criticism belongs to phase three of the revisionist method of mutual critical correlation, that is, the theological analysis. The aim is that of generating a thick description of a taxonomy of expressions of OT prosaic prayers (sub)stages, together with their accompanying physical and emotional expressions, amidst the generic life situation of disorientation. Particular attention is, however, given to those expressions that come to the fore amidst grief. This will allow for a dialectic correlation with the verbal, physical, and emotional expressions communicated to/before God amidst grief by leading Christians from a Guyanese or Vietnamese heritage. The result is fostering compassionate pastoral care practices that will help in sustaining Christians from intercultural communities coping with grief. Such practices work well when couched within rituals, which will be discussed in chapter 6 since it is not a methodology.[42]

2.2. Summary and Structure

By way of summary, our previous discussion has centered on the metamethod (revisionist method of mutual critical correlation), and its sub-methods (liberative intercultural praxis, hermeneutical phenomenology, and renewed form criticism) employed within this book, all of which are engaged in an effort to generate compassionate (liberative intercultural) pastoral care practices for the church. Couched within rituals, such practices are to be compassionate, and liberative interculturally, lending their aid to the mitigation of grief, and the sustainability of the bereaved, thus remaining faithful to the triune God's redemptive mission to the world.

In that light, this chapter is brought to a close with a descriptive adumbration of the book: It begins with chapter 1, which furnishes a general description of the anthropological expressions of disorientation, the central theological questions, and the thesis statement. Following this, chapter 2 outlines the metamethod of the book and also discusses its various sub-methodologies

---

41. This summary has been adapted from Toffelmire's "Form Criticism," 269–270. Toffelmire, however, uses "form" and "genre" analogously, something of which I have avoided throughout this book.

42. For the discussion on rituals in connection with grief, see pp. @@.

employed. Chapter 3 will then attend to the situational analysis by surveying the current modes of expression within pastoral theology and its relationship to the human experience of disorientation, particularly that of the phenomenon of grief, and thereafter generate a taxonomy of the anthropological expressions of disorientation from within a contemporary Christian intercultural context of Canadian immigrants from Guyana and Vietnam. Here, the essence or meaning of the various expressions will be pursued. A theological analysis will then be executed in chapter 4 wherein the current stages of OT prosaic prayers of disorientation will be explored, and thus further generate a taxonomy of (sub)stages of expressions of disorientation from within the ancient context of the OT prosaic prayers of disorientation. Encompassed within chapter 5 will be a situational analysis of theology through the exploration of a dialectic correlation between the generic life situation of grief, the contemporary Christian intercultural expressions of grief (i.e. verbal, physical, and emotional), and that of the Christian (on account of Christ the mediator and fulfillment of the OT) traditional expressions within OT prosaic prayers of disorientation (i.e. verbal, physical, and emotional). In chapter 6, compassionate (liberative intercultural) pastoral care practices, couched within rituals, will be fostered thereby sensitizing pastoral caregivers to their multivalent significance within an intercultural society for the mitigation of grief and the sustainability of the bereaved. Chapter 7 brings the book to its conclusion even as it recapitulates the foregoing research, and thereafter offer potential expansive work that can be accomplished in relation to expressions of disorientation within the twin disciplines of biblical theology and pastoral theology.

Returning to the claim of this book, I bring this chapter to a close by once again proffering the ensuing thesis statement: Bifocal in its objective, this book: (1) generates a domain of anthropological expressions of disorientation communicated to/before God, along with their essence or meaning from both the ancient Israelite context of OT prosaic prayers of disorientation and that of a contemporary Christian intercultural context (principally among Canadian immigrants from Guyana and Vietnam) amidst grief; and (2) sensitizes contemporary pastoral caregivers to such an expressive domain with its multivalent significance, the purpose of which is to foster compassionate pastoral care, couched within rituals, in the best interest of intercultural Christian communities coping with grief.

CHAPTER 3

Anthropological Expressions of Disorientation in Pastoral Theology

3.1. Recent Pastoral Theological Reflection on Anthropological Expressions of Disorientation

3.1.1. Languages and Modes of Grief Expression

Grief studies conducted by Inge B. Corless et al., have yielded several expressions of disorientation amidst the concrete life situation of bereavement.[1] Figure 1 below indicates the various languages or modes of grief expressions.[2]

Corless observes that, "Modes of Expression and the Types of Language are influenced by various contingencies that affect the manifestation of the *Languages of Grief*."[3] Their research further yielded the following modes: verbal responses (written or oral); nonverbal responses (silent or reflective); physical responses (somatic or expressions); physical activities (rituals or objects).[4] Through the mode of verbal responses, "The bereaved may express their grief using different spoken languages and in some languages there may be no direct translation of the word grief such as in Portuguese where the

---

1. Corless et al., "Languages of Grief," 135. Other life settings of disorientation might include sickness, abuse of the self and others, etc.

2. Adapted from Corless, 135.

3. Corless, 134; emphasis original. The types of language used by the bereaved to express their grief consist of four subsets – Narrative (story telling), Symbolism (representation), Metaphor (figurative), and Analysis (concretizing) (136).

4. Corless, 134.

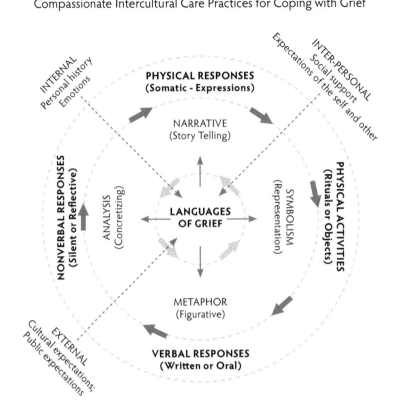

Figure 1. Languages of Grief: Manifestations and Communications

term suffering encompasses the concept of grief. Nonetheless, the concept of grief is articulated verbally in sounds that can both be heard and comprehended by others familiar with the language."[5] Nonverbal responses on the other hand are expressed through silence or reflection, that is, "ruminating on the experience of grief."[6] Physical responses, says Corless, "are composed of physical signs, bodily expressions, and sensual aspects such as seeing and hearing. The manner in which the head is held (body language) is an example of a physical response, as is weeping. Sobbing, sighing, sudden, intense emotion, or other somatic, physical responses typically occur without intention."[7]

---

5. Corless, 135–136.

6. Corless, 136.

7. Corless, 136. Of import are the words of Kleinman (*Social Origins*, 51–70) who observes that, in China and many other societies, "Somatization (the presentation of personal and interpersonal distress in an idiom of physical complaints . . .) [is] the predominant expression of difficulties in living" (51). In fact, he adds, "People experience serious personal and social

Expressions of physical activities "involve action or objects, such as attending the funerals, planning and holding memorial services, or by *sitting Shiva* [a period of seven days when the bereaved are visited by guests] in the Jewish tradition, which can have both private and public components."[8]

3.1.2. Current Scholarship on Verbal, Physical, and Emotional Expressions of Grief

In light of the above, this section surveys some of the most recent scholarship associated with the verbal, physical, and emotional expressions of grief. As will become clear, the majority of these expressions will be recognized as commonplace or universal in the West, thus presenting a lacuna in scholarship in connection with grief expressions from contemporary intercultural contexts.

Until recently, it was assumed that affliction only constituted the three categories of physical pain, psychological anguish, and social degradation.[9] At present, however, affliction encompasses a fourth category termed "spiritual desolation,"[10] submitted by Phil C. Zylla. Additionally, Zylla has developed a paradigmatic movement of affliction, consisting of three constructive movements for a pastoral theology of suffering: (i) the movement from silence to lament; (ii) the movement from indifference to compassion; and (iii) the

---

problems but interpret and articulate them, and . . . come to experience and respond to them, through the medium of the body" (51).

8. Corless, 136; another physical expression can be the sudden selling of one's house and moving far away to accommodate grief (136).

9. See Weil, *Awaiting God*, 44; Soelle, *Suffering*, 13–15. In *Roots of Sorrow*, 41–70, Zylla presents a description of physical pain, psychological anguish, and social degradation: (i) Physical pain – "It has its own night – the darkness of ache, the hurt of physical torment, and the throbbing physiological distress of injury and illness in the body" (58–59); (ii) Psychological anguish – "Suffering cuts us off from emotional freedom. It drives us to despair, disconsolation, and takes away our peace. . . . The anguish of psychological suffering is a severe experience of trauma to the human heart. The human capacity to hope is suffocated by the traumatic and blinding realities of psychological torment. Anxiety, fear, grief, and psychic numbness all take their toll on the capacity for a human being to bear under suffering" (59–62); (iii) Social degradation – Zylla identifies three types of social suffering that are interrelated and which deepen the experiences of social degradation: "abandonment (the deep disappointment of the withdrawal of support of others), rejection (the alienation from the community where companionship of life is refused), and forsakenness (the anticipation of love and acceptance is fully disappointed and, in its place, one experiences scorn or forsakenness itself)" (62–63).

10. Zylla, *Roots of Sorrow*, 54–55, 63; spiritual desolation is, "the experience of the eclipse of hope itself, which leads to experience a growing distance from God" (63). Furthermore, "At the root of the spiritual experience of desolation is the feeling that God has abandoned us and that God inflicts the suffering itself. The full dimensions of suffering are complete when the language of desolation is disclosed . . . This is the ultimate low point in the affliction" (64).

movement from loneliness to community.[11] "Each of the movements begins by entering into the perspective of persons who are suffering. The starting point of a mature theology of suffering is to engage with those who are deeply embedded in the throes of an anguishing life situation."[12] Continuing along these lines, Zylla also categorized eight lament moods from the poems written by graduate students taking his course on the theology of suffering at McMaster Divinity College (MDC). These eight lament moods/categories are as follows:

- sympathy/recognition of suffering/compassion
- bewilderment/questioning
- accusation/resistance/protest
- anguish/identification/solidarity
- pining/sorrowful/asking how long?
- regret/loss
- sadness/gloom/greyness/resignation
- darkness/despair.[13]

Thankfully, Zylla offers us a clearer view into the reality of affliction in all its dimensions. With such a thick description, we are thus able to perceive what is really going on beneath the surface of affliction. In so doing, Zylla sets the groundwork for empathy and better informed holistic compassionate pastoral care.

Assessing Job's life context of grief, R. P. Belcher observes that, "Just as there are a variety of causes to suffering, so there are a variety of responses to suffering."[14] Accordingly, Job's unjust suffering (Job 2:3) yielded the following results: "Job's initial response to suffering is *submission*. After losing his children, his wealth (1:13–19) and his health (2:7–8), he responds with *worship*. He acknowledges the sovereignty of God (1:20–21), refuses to curse God, and is willing to accept both good and calamity (2:9–10)."[15] Yet Belcher acknowledges that although "Worship and submission are the right way to respond to suffering," there are many times when "such response comes at the

---

11. Zylla, 71–130.
12. Zylla, 68–69.
13. Zylla, "Shades of Lament," 763–776.
14. Belcher, "Suffering," 777.
15. Belcher, 777; emphasis mine.

end of a process of wrestling with God, which is described in the laments."[16] In such cases, that is, "When God seems distant and unresponsive, it is natural for *questions* to arise."[17] At this juncture, "A key question in the midst of suffering, is whether the sufferer will persevere in faith. . . . Job moves from a compliant, submissive response to a challenging, questioning one."[18] But whereas Job undoubtedly gave no heed to his wife's challenge to curse God and die (2:9), he still *cursed* the day of his birth (3:1).[19]

Here, while Belcher emphasizes Job's submission to and worship of God amidst his grief, which might seem countercultural (or at least counter-spousal; see 2:9) but might very well be expressions of his faith and resilience,[20] he, nevertheless, fails to emphasize Job's other mourning expressions, such as, tearing his robe and shaving his head, the latter, of course, being a mourning rite forbidden among the people of Yahweh owing to its pagan associations (Lev 19:27; 21:5; Deut 14:1). And while cursing God seems to have incurred an imminent death penalty (Job 2:9), cursing the day of one's birth is echoed from the mouth of the prophet Jeremiah son of Hilkiah (20:14), and appears to have been considered an accustomed expression of grief. Nonetheless, both lament and *praise* are two valid expressions to/before God amidst grief.

Glen Pemberton proposes lament as the language necessary for readers "to restore a modicum of structure in times of disorientation."[21] Upon coming to the realization that lament does not always lead to thanksgiving, however, particularly when God does not respond favorably to our cries of lament, Pemberton explores the stage *after lament*. He indicates that, "Just as the Book of Psalms provided words we needed for lament, the Psalter also provides the guidance and language we need for negotiating the time after lament. . . . In other words, the laments set the agenda for what we do after lament – what

---

16. Belcher, 777.

17. Belcher, 777; emphasis mine.

18. Belcher, 778.

19. Belcher, 778; emphasis mine.

20. See for example, David's countercultural grief expressions amidst the death of his son who was conceived through his clandestine relationship with Bathsheba the wife of Uriah (2 Sam 12:15–23) and the corresponding article by Bosworth, "Faith and Resilience," 691–707, for a cogent argument in favor of David's faith and resilience, which can arguably be applied here also to Job.

21. Pemberton, *Hurting with God*, 65.

we say and how we live."[22] Pemberton subsequently offers the directions that lament points to: *trust* (Pss 11, 23, 121), *thanksgiving* (Pss 30, 92, 124), *new praise* (Pss 8, 100, 148), *rejoicing in the Lord* (Pss 65, 96, 126), *instruction* (Pss 73, 127, 133), and *broken hope* (Pss 39, 44, 88).[23] He nevertheless maintains that, "Wherever our lament may lead, it leaves us with stories of pain and scars, reminders of our wrestling with God; and it leaves us in hope – with much to work out with our God."[24] At this juncture, we are nonetheless reminded of the fact that, "our hope is not in finding a yes to every request. Our God promises grace sufficient to our need (2 Cor 12:8–10), and nothing less than life out of death, life *After Lament*."[25]

Although the title of the book of Psalms in the Hebrew Bible or Masoretic Text is סֵפֶר תְּהִלִּים, *Sepher Tehillim*, or Book of Praises, the majority genre is that of lament, at least 40 percent, as Pemberton observes.[26] And, as he also notices, the lament form (or genre) can take multiple directions (or subcategories), such as trust and praise. What are not particularly referred to as directions are *instruction* and *broken hope*. After all, the entire book of Psalms is meant to be one of *instruction* as is perceived from the introductory exhortation for all readers to "delight in the law [תּוֹרָה] of the LORD" (Ps 1:2), as well as its five-fold division/books (1–41, 42–72, 73–89, 90–106, 107–150), which serves as a reflection of the first five books of the Hebrew Bible otherwise referred to collectively as the Torah, translated instruction.[27] Furthermore, broken hope is another way of speaking of the direction or genre of lament (or pure lament). Nevertheless, in the midst of our pain and suffering, God welcomes our trust (confidence), thanksgiving, praise, and recurring laments, precisely because, as God's (emotive) image-bearers and believers in the crucified-yet-resurrected Christ, we grieve not in despair, but rather, as those who have hope (1 Thess 4:13), which is something that Pemberton undoubtedly affirms.

While it is not uncommon to verbalize one's *how long's?* or even *why's? amidst grief, according to J. Todd Billings, "The most potent questions, when

---

22. Pemberton, *After Lament*, 26.

23. Pemberton, 71–188.

24. Pemberton, 27.

25. Pemberton, 199; emphasis original.

26. Pemberton, *Hurting with God*, 32.

27. See Wenham, *Psalms as Torah*.

one pushes deeply enough, are ultimately not about our experience but about the story of God made known in Jesus Christ."[28] In conjunction with such an outlook, Billings' meditation especially on the lament psalms enables him to insist that, "In and through and by Jesus Christ, with whom Christians have been united by the Holy Spirit, we can *praise, lament, petition*, and discover that the story of our loss is not the only, or most important, story that encloses our lives. We discover that this spacious place – of living in Christ – is wide and deep enough for us to *petition, rejoice*, and also join our *laments* to Jesus Christ, who intercedes on our behalf (see Rom 8:24)."[29] Acknowledging that our lives are not our own, Billings further contends that the stories of our lives have been incorporated into what he refers to as

> the great drama of God's gracious work in the world in Jesus Christ through the Spirit. As we come to sense our role in this drama, we find that it is a path of *lament and rejoicing, protest* and *praise*, rooted in *trust* in the Triune God, the central actor; we can walk on this path even while the fog is thick. For God is bigger than cancer. God is bigger than death. The God of Jesus Christ is the God of life, whose loving promises will be shown as true in the end. Until that time, we *wait* with the psalmist for the Lord and *hope* in his Word.[30]

Embracing such a robust perspective prompts Billings to both verbally and emotionally *rejoice in lament* during his life situation of disorientation. More than this, rather than have an apathetic spirit, he also suggests that, yet another legitimate expression should be that of "giving up our life and energies for Christ, to act in *protest* and *witness* to the present and coming King."[31] For Billings, this takes the physical expression of "*compassionate action*," an example of which is that of working in a homeless shelter.[32]

Indeed, while as Christians we can lament and praise God during our grief, one of the most helpful physical expressions is that of compassionate action as a means of offering comfort and hope to those who find themselves in the

---

28. Billings, *Rejoicing in Lament*, x.
29. Billings, 15; emphasis mine.
30. Billings, 16; emphasis mine.
31. Billings, 90; emphasis mine.
32. Billings, 81; emphasis mine.

throes of grief. As a matter of fact, this book carries this physical expression forward by proposing five compassionate pastoral care responses for those coping with grief, as elucidated in chapter 6.

Reminiscent of Billings, John C. Thomas and Gary R. Habermas also advocate for the need of physically reaching out to help others in compassion. Both Thomas and Habermas are convinced that,

> The point of reaching out is not to avoid your own pain, but to take the inner turmoil you have experienced and connect it with someone else's struggle. Psychologists have found that getting clients to see themselves as helpers and givers, rather than takers and receivers, produces healing. . . . However much we may have suffered, we can find meaning in it by transforming pain into compassion. . . . Helping hurting people see how God's grace is sufficient speaks to your own unresolved questions and issues.[33]

Like Christ, wounded Christians thus become wounded healers (cf. 1 Pet 2:24; 2 Cor 1:3–4). Redeemed and transformed by God's grace, our wounds thus serve as a healing balm and a life source to the souls of those struggling with the reality of grief.

Granting there exists a place for verbal theological and philosophical theodicies that attempt to justify God in the face of evil and suffering in hopes of encouraging unwavering belief in God,[34] John Swinton prefers to engage in what he terms a *pastoral theodicy*. Extending the work of Stanley Hauerwas who calls upon Christians to build communities that absorb suffering and enable faithful living even in the midst of evil,[35] Swinton contends:

> I maintain that theodicy should not be understood as a series of disembodied arguments designed to defend God's love, goodness, and power. We require a different mode of understanding, a mode of theodicy that is embodied within the life and practices of the Christian community. Such a mode of theodicy does not seek primarily to explain evil and suffering, but rather presents

---

33. Thomas and Habermas, *Enduring Your Season*, 249.

34. The prophet Habakkuk is a good biblical example. See also Idestrom, "Habakkuk," 409–453.

35. Hauerwas, *Naming the Silences*, 49.

ways in which evil and suffering can be resisted and transformed faithfully in the midst of unanswered questions as they await God's redemption of the whole of creation. . . . Pastoral theodicy is a theodicy of action and resistance.[36]

Alternatively referred to as practical theodicy, this mode of resistance addresses issues of evil and human suffering through engagement in particular verbal, physical, and emotional expressions of Christian practices that are performed both individually and communally, with a preference for the latter. Theological and eschatological in shape and intention, pastoral theodicy seeks to mirror, embody, and participate in God's providential action in, to, and for the world. In a pastoral theodicy, God is the One who takes responsibility for the evil and suffering that has wracked and ruined God's good earth. Not necessarily implying culpability, it does however admit to God's pledge to be *with* and *for* the world in all its conflicts even as it awaits transformation and redemption. Thus, Ray S. Anderson submits that

> God does not duck and dodge the reality of evil, attributing it to human sin and blaming it on the Devil. God is the author of the drama, in which pain and pleasure, suffering and joy, good and evil are part of the plot . . . God takes full responsibility. . . . The biblical tradition has no view of evil as a problem outside the concept of God's providence. God's providence is expressed through his partnership with human persons in suffering, which is the divine power to be present as our advocate in the context of suffering and for the purpose of redeeming those who suffer. The providence of God is bound to his promise. This promise is a miracle and mystery of divine love. Suffering and injustice can produce a crisis of faith, leading us directly to God as the one who must ultimately take responsibility. In his taking responsibility through participation in the dilemma of evil, *God provides redemption from evil, not a solution to it as a problem.*[37]

From this perspective, "the 'solution' or perhaps better the response to the problem of evil lies within the forms of communal practice which actively

---

36. Swinton, *Raging with Compassion*, 4–5.

37. Anderson, *Dancing with Wolves*, 105.

engage with, resist, and seek to transform evil and suffering and struggle in solidarity to reveal love and hope to victims, survivors, and perpetrators of evil."[38] Such expressions of communal practice are thus observed in the following five verbal, physical, and emotional actions of embodied resistance, each of which make up a unified way of life in the Spirit:

> **Listening to Silence** (thoughtfulness, friendship, prayer, patience, perseverance, hope, love)
>
> **Lament** (prayer, listening to silence, friendship, hope, patience, perseverance, eschatological imagination and hope, love)
>
> **Forgiveness** (prayer, lament, faith, trust, hope, thoughtfulness, compassion, patience, perseverance, eschatological hope and imagination, love)
>
> **Thoughtfulness** (hospitality, adoption, lament, listening to silence, forgiveness, eschatological imagination and hope, friendship, love)
>
> **Hospitality** (friendship, thoughtfulness, compassion, faith, eschatological imagination and hope, perseverance, love)[39]

Swinton considers that these communal pastoral practices will "enable healing and bring comfort, hope, and transformation to both church and world. In so doing, they point towards eschatological hope and new possibilities in the present."[40] What is more, they will also "enable people to continue to love God in the face of evil and suffering and in so doing prevent tragic suffering from becoming evil."[41] Pastoral or practical theodicy is thus an alternative term to compassionate action (verbal, physical, and emotional) which is being advocated and carried forward in this book.

This section has explored some of the current research pertaining to the verbal, physical, and emotional expressions of disorientation communicated to/before God amidst affliction, inclusive of which is grief, within the discipline of pastoral theology. It should be noted here, however, that, while appreciated, the majority of these expressions are recognized as commonplace

---

38. Swinton, *Raging with Compassion*, 88.
39. Adapted from Swinton, 245.
40. Swinton, 85.
41. Swinton, 85.

in the context of grief in the West. Consequently, in the next section, we will seek to address other modes of expression, but particularly those that are found within an intercultural Canadian context.

3.2. Lacuna in Scholarship

The preceding discussion may still leave one wondering about the potential of discovering other anthropological expressions of disorientation to/before God (verbal, physical, and emotional) within a contemporary Christian *intercultural* context.[42] This inquiry is particularly significant since, as Elaine L. Graham states, "the implications of ethnic, cultural and racial diversity are *underdeveloped* in contemporary pastoral literature."[43] With a persistent rise in interculturalism in the West, especially in Canada, "A changing socioeconomic, political, cultural, and religious climate necessitates taking contexts outside of the West far more seriously than ever before."[44]

Viewed from this perspective, Lartey's definition of pastoral care becomes all the more significant. "Pastoral care," insists Lartey, "consists of helping activities, participated in by people who recognize a transcendent dimension to human life, which, by the use of *verbal or non-verbal, direct or indirect, literal or symbolic modes of communication, aim at preventing, relieving or facilitating persons coping with anxieties.*"[45] What is more, "Pastoral care seeks to foster people's growth as full human beings together with the development of ecologically and socio-politically holistic communities in which all persons may live humane lives."[46] Therefore, by definition, one of the essential elements of pastoral care from an intercultural perspective is its entailment of multivariate forms of communication.[47] At the same time, as much as verbal

---

42. Irish et al., (*Ethnic Variations*, 181–190) have suggested that "When examining death and grief in a multi-cultural context, the myths, mysteries, and mores that characterize both the dominant and nondominant groups directly affect attitudes, beliefs, practices, and cross-cultural relationships" (187). Moreover, they have observed that "lack of cultural understanding and sensitivity to cultural diversity in death and grief appear to have caused more problems than language barriers" (188).

43. Graham, *Transforming Practice*, 47; emphasis mine.

44. Lartey, *Pastoral Theology*, 29.

45. Lartey, *In Living Color*, 30; emphasis mine.

46. Lartey, 30–31.

47. Lartey, 29; other essential elements are an expression of human concern through activities, the recognition of transcendence, the motive of love, and preventing distress while

communication is an important way of conveying and receiving information, it is nonverbal communication that is currently receiving increasing recognition as a powerful mode of communication, perhaps of even greater significance than the verbal.[48] "In intercultural pastoral care, the forms of communication present in any given society are explored to ascertain their value within the society for caring interaction, especially since it is true that in many cultures, indirect forms of converse are very highly valued."[49] In fact, it has been found that such modes of communication as: "Drama, poetry, and other forms of imaginative literature may convey or mediate pastoral care of the highest order."[50]

Further, although largely overlooked, "The use of symbols, such as works of creative art and sculpture," are assigned considerable attention especially since "some of the most inspiring and liberating forms of discourse emanating from the South and Central America are in symbolic art."[51] While there is a tendency among those within and without the church to shrug their shoulders at the symbolic, as is evidenced in the all too common expression "merely symbolic,"[52] and more often than not, "seen as the poor alternatives to 'literal' or 'objective,'"[53] symbols play a very significant role in communication. As Eugene E. Lemcio asserts,

> Symbols are powerful means of communicating, especially evident when they are abused or defaced – as in the case of flag burning. Such violent treatment causes a flare-up of thoughts, emotions, and action. Head, heart, and feet are all simultaneously affected. Word symbols, as well as object symbols, can produce a similar effect. When used as a form of communication, they can be even more powerful than narrative prose. Of course, the challenge is always to avoid treating the literal symbolically and the symbolic literally.[54]

---

fostering growth (26–30).

48. Lartey, 29.

49. Lartey, 29.

50. Lartey, 29.

51. Lartey, 29.

52. As noted in Lemcio, "The Story's Conclusion," 140.

53. As noted in Lemcio, 140.

54. Lemcio, 140.

It should be pointed out, however, that, "Culture is one of the two or three most complicated words in the English language . . . mainly because it has now come to be used for important concepts in several . . . disciplines, and in several distinct and incompatible systems of thought."[55] But as Clifford Geertz maintains, "Whatever the infirmities of the concept of 'culture' there is nothing for it but to persist in spite of them."[56] Not surprisingly, Gerald A. Arbuckle contends that, "There is simply no other word to take its place."[57] In fact, Sherry Ortner avers that, "[The] issue is . . . one of reconfiguring this enormously productive concept for a changing world, a changing relationship between politics and academic life, and a changing landscape of theoretical possibilities. . . . the fate of 'culture' will depend on its uses."[58] Agreeing with Ortner, Arbuckle thus "emphasizes that cultures are not fixed entities, but processes in which people struggle for meaning in a threatening environment."[59] Arbuckle therefore proceeds to proffer a general working definition of culture as follows:

> A culture is a pattern of meanings encased in a network of symbols, myths, narratives, and rituals, created by individuals and subdivisions, as they struggle to respond to the competitive pressures of power and limited resources in a rapidly globalizing and fragmenting world, and instructing its adherents about what is considered to be the correct way to feel, think, and behave.[60]

Further, Matthew D. Kim observes that "A common image to display cultural difference is the iceberg: a few aspects of culture are above the surface, and many others (perhaps 90 percent) lie hidden below."[61] Patty Lane likewise insists that in each culture there are two types of cultural differences: objective and subjective. In keeping with the iceberg imagery, objective culture characterizes the visible portion, which might be inclusive of a culture's language, food, clothing, and greeting mannerism, and to which one might incorporate

---

55. Williams, *Keywords: A Vocabulary*, 87.

56. Geertz, *After the Fact*, 43.

57. Arbuckle, *Culture, Inculturation*, 16.

58. Ortner, *Fate of "Culture"*, 8, 11.

59. Ortner, 17.

60. Ortner, 17.

61. Kim, *Preaching with Cultural Intelligence*, 10.

anthropological expressions of disorientation. In terms of the iceberg imagery, lying for the most part below the surface of the water, is that of the subjective culture, which, according to Lane, "is the internal part of culture that drives or motivates the visible, objective culture."[62] Subjective culture is therefore less detectable, and might be inclusive of a culture's assumption, feeling, value, and motivation,[63] and in the case of this book, encompass the essence or meaning lying behind or beneath (i.e. the depth dimension) each anthropological expression of disorientation. Objective culture is therefore fueled by subjective culture, both of which rest at the core of this book.[64]

Pastoral care, with its multivariate forms of communication, consequently, opens the door for the exploration and discovery of other anthropological expressions of disorientation within a contemporary Christian intercultural context among Canadian immigrants from Guyana and Vietnam. Such an endeavor has as its purpose the development of a more comprehensive understanding of the implications and significance of ethnic, cultural, and racial diversity and similarity concerning the irrefragable universal theme of affliction, particularly the phenomenon of grief, within society even as it fosters a compassionate (liberative intercultural) pastoral care.[65]

---

62. Lane, *Beginner's Guide*, 18–19.

63. Lane, 18.

64. See also Kim, *Preaching with Cultural Intelligence*, 10–12. As a way to assist preachers in the twenty-first century towards proclaiming sermons that are culturally intelligent, Kim defines culture as "a group's way of living, way of thinking, and way of behaving in the world, for which we need understanding and empathy to guide our listeners toward Christian maturity" (5). While the outcome of this book is the sensitizing of pastoral caregivers to the multivalent anthropological expressions of disorientation, especially those related to coping with grief, coupled with their meaning, such sensitizing also fosters culturally intelligent pastoral caregivers.

65. Here we might also include potential anthropological expressions as reclusion, silence, ruminations, groans, weeping, pessimism, lamentation, trust, penitence, praise, imprecation, clothes rending, triumphalism, etc. Cole (*Good Mourning*, 9–18) has also listed several feelings associated with grief: "shock, numbness, sadness, depression, anger, frustration, impatience, anxiety, fear, loneliness, vulnerability, helplessness, fatigue, exhaustion, hopelessness, regret, guilt, shame, ambivalence, apathy, relief, and a greater sense of connection to, and value and yearning for, what we no longer have as part of our lives. The feelings that come with grief may take a physical form, too" (11).

3.3. Domain of Contemporary Christian Intercultural Anthropological Expressions of Disorientation

3.3.1. Introduction to Intercultural Anthropological Expressions of Disorientation

Gerald W. Peterman and Andrew J. Schmutzer believe that "Communities of faith that are committed to addressing a fuller spectrum of suffering must intentionally name the real ills of real people living among them, then listen to the pained testimonies of these people's suffering. Real words matter when facing real pain."[66] In light of this, attention will be given to several of the verbalized, physical, and emotional anthropological expressions of disorientation communicated to/before God amidst the phenomenon of grief by Canadian Christian immigrants from both Guyana and Vietnam. But before doing so, it is important to furnish a brief explanation of what I mean by Guyanese-Canadian and Vietnamese-Canadian.

In this book, the term Guyanese-Canadian refers to a person who was born in Guyana, but who immigrated to, and now resides in Canada as a naturalized citizen. Similarly, the term Vietnamese-Canadian refers to a person who was born in Vietnam, but who immigrated to, and currently resides in Canada as a naturalized citizen. With this is mind, we can now proceed to an examination of the verbal anthropological expressions among Guyanese-Canadian leaders.

3.3.2. The Process of Data Collection and Analysis

Following van Manen's dynamic interplay, the phenomenon of grief was chosen as an abiding concern of interest to the researcher. Writing a description of the phenomenon of grief, however, necessitated an interview process comprised of participants who have experienced grief. Ten participants were involved in this research: five Guyanese-Canadians and five Vietnamese-Canadians. Contact was made directly over phone or by email. Their contact information was furnished either by the public domain, or through a pastor (one from each cultural context). Through email, each participant was provided with a full description of the project, i.e. the Letter of Information-Consent Form, as well as the nine One-on-One Interview Questions, both

---

66. Peterman and Schmutzer, *Between Pain and Grace*, 28.

of which were approved by the McMaster Research Ethics Board. Prior to the interview, however, each participant emailed me a signed copy of their consent forms. Each participant chose a location of their convenience for the interviews.

During the interview, each participant was afforded the freedom to either respond to or refuse to answer any question that they deemed uncomfortable. Interviewed first were the five Guyanese-Canadians (five males), which was then followed by the five Vietnamese-Canadians (four males and one female). However, in connection with the latter, owing to a re-emergence of the trauma experienced while in Vietnam, two participants withdrew from the interview process. After being contacted, two other Vietnamese-Canadian leaders willingly agreed to be part of the interview.

These latter two participants from the Vietnamese-Canadian context read their responses to me during the interview. Which means that they had already taken the time to write out their answers on the One-on-One Interview Questions sheet. They also presented me with a copy of their answers to the questions. As such, I have made the decision to leave the words "groan inwardly" underlined, as indicated by VL4.

Of the five participants from the Guyanese-Canadian contexts, however, only one (GL5) did as their Vietnamese-Canadian counterparts in answering the questions prior to the interview. The others responded during the interview as the questions were asked. Nothing was specifically emphasized by GL5, such as was done by VL4.

The interviews were recorded on an Earhaus voice recorder, and thereafter transferred to a Microsoft Word document, where it was analyzed. Particular attention was given to each of the verbal, physical, and emotional expressions, along with their significance or meaning, especially those that were helpful rather than hurtful in transforming or coping with grief from each culture. In the process, the researcher tried to not only provide a description of the lived experience of the phenomenon of grief, but also an interpretation of the meaning of the lived experience. In doing so, however, care was taken to bracket out or suspend the researcher's own presuppositions and theological assumptions, yet without the tendency to inhibit the interpretation of the phenomenon.[67] As van Manen notes,

> If we simply try to forget or ignore what we already "know," we may find that the presuppositions persistently creep back into our reflections. It is better to make explicit our understandings, beliefs, biases, assumptions, presuppositions, and theories. We try to come to terms with our assumptions, not in order to forget them again, but rather to hold them deliberately at bay and even to turn this knowledge against itself, as it were, thereby exposing its shallow or concealing character.[68]

Which is to say that the researcher "hold[s] both the assumptions of their worldview at bay and open[s] themselves to the experience in front of them without judgment"[69] in an exercise of "absolute unmixed attention,"[70] which is not easy to sustain. For this reason, interviews were only conducted within a one-hour timeframe wherein the researcher "deactivate[d] his/her habitual epistemic instruments in order to situate himself/herself in a pre-categorical hearing of the other . . . which is infused by the *ethic of delicacy*."[71]

In the process of analyzing the transcription of each interviewee, van Manen's three types of reading were executed:

i. The Holistic Reading Approach: This involves attending to the text as a whole and asking, "What sententious phrase may capture the fundamental meaning or main significance of the text as a whole?"

ii. The Selective Reading Approach: This involves reading the text several times and asking, "What statement(s) or phrase(s) seem particularly essential or revealing about the phenomenon or experience being described?"

iii. The Detailed Reading Approach: This involves reviewing the text with a focus on specific sentences or sentence clusters and asking,

---

67. For this bracketing while inhibiting the tendency to interpret, see Patton, *From Ministry to Theology*, 37.

68. van Manen, *Researching Lived Experience*, 47.

69. Zylla, "Shades of Lament," 765.

70. Weil, *Gravity and Grace*, 170.

71. Mortari, "Ethic of Delicacy," 10; emphasis original.

"What does this sentence or sentence cluster reveal about the phenomenon or experience described?"[72]

In each reading, elements that were distinctive to each of the two cultures examined were given significant attention. But while it is true that "phenomenology invite[s] the use of language to express the ineffable," it is "pastoral theology that intentionally brings God-talk and theological expression into view,"[73] along with the "subtle persistence of hope."[74] And in so doing, "this articulation [is] translated into actions of compassion. Sensitive articulation reveals the path of mercy. We might say that knowing becomes being which is then transformed into doing. The cycle of pastoral imagination cannot stop short of compassion – rather, compassion is its goal and essence."[75] For this reason, this book will seek to develop compassionate (liberative intercultural) pastoral care actions that will help foster comfort and hope amidst the lived experience of grief, thus restoring the soul so that grief becomes bearable rather than unbearable as life continues for the bereaved.

At this juncture, we move toward a closer look at the verbal, physical, and emotional expressions communicated to/before God within the lived experience or phenomenon of grief. Of import here is that some expressions are culturally neutral while others are culturally specific. Mention will be made as to distinguish between the two. The first context examined is that of the Guyanese-Canadian, followed by the Vietnamese-Canadian.

3.3.3. Verbal Anthropological Expressions among Guyanese-Canadian Leaders

3.3.3.1. Lament Weeping/Wailing/Shouting/Screaming[76]

GL3's understanding of grief is that of "An outward expression of an inward feeling." This outward expression is realized in lament weeping, the significance of which can be heard in the following words from GL3: "The word grief means to me that you have a loss, and there is something to lament over that

---

72. van Manen, *Researching Lived Experience*, 93.

73. Zylla, "Shades of Lament," 767.

74. Zylla, *Roots of Sorrow*, 54–55.

75. Zylla, "Shades of Lament," 775.

76. Such expressions amidst grief are culturally neutral, meaning that they are also located within the Israelite OT context.

is beyond your control." GL3 further remarked that, "You lose a part of you, or a part of your relationship with loved ones and friends, and you cannot help them, so you grieve. . . . It's a loss that you lament over."

Sharing the example of the loss of a sister, GL3 stated that, "There is always an empty space, an empty chair there, and you lament over that." For GL3, grief in the form of lament means weeping or shedding of tears. To the accompaniment of weeping, GL1 added that, "Often accompanying wailing, which is a loud cry, some mourners scream and shout virtually at the top of their lungs. . . . It is not uncommon to hear loud wails from those stricken by grief," which, like fainting, "accentuates a deep sense of love for the deceased."

3.3.3.2. Praying Disorientation Prayers to God (Lament and Thanksgiving Praise)[77]

With the appearance of grief, GL5 articulated the interrogative or lament questions of "Why me?", "Why this?" By the same token, and acknowledging that it is only human to inquire, GL2 added: "How do we pray?" and "Why did this have to happen?" For at least these two leaders, in asking such questions of God, they recognize that when grief comes close to home, articulated prayers are hard to come by. Moreover, they both recognize that with the manifestation of death and grief, something is amiss in a world run and managed by God, the giver of life. Death, in other words, should *not* be a reality.

In lieu of trying to forget the grief, or wish it never approaches, GL4 affirmed that, "I take it to the Lord in prayer." In preference to being "bogged down" or "impacted negatively" by grief, the significance of prayer is heard when GL4 asserted that it not only demonstrates a "dependency upon the Lord," but more so, prayer fortifies GL4 with the divine potency to help "in going forward." Putting it another way, for GL4, prayer unleashes "the strength and grace of God to go through the grief or distress." Such an understanding for GL4 emanates from reading and appropriating the words of Isaiah 43:1–3 (KJV).

> But now, thus saith the LORD that created thee, O Jacob, and he that formed thee, O Israel, Fear not: for I have redeemed thee, I have called thee by thy name; thou art mine. When thou passest

---

77. Prayers of Lament and Thanksgiving amidst grief are also culturally neutral. Such prayers are also located within the Israelite OT context.

through the waters, I will be with thee; and through the rivers, they shall not overflow thee: when thou walkest through the fire, thou shalt not be burned; neither shall the flame kindle upon thee. For I am the LORD thy God, the Holy One of Israel, thy Saviour: I gave Egypt for thy ransom, Ethiopia and Seba for thee.

Along the same line of reasoning, GL3 turns to God as Father in prayer amidst grief, saying, "Dad, here is a problem, intervene." With this simple petition for divine intervention, GL3 becomes the recipient of God's "comfort and joy, a joy that money cannot pay for." Thus, GL3 can persist in going to his heavenly Father with a daily expression of thanksgiving praise saying, "Good morning, Dad. It is such a joy to have you in my life."

A former Hindu-believer-turned-Christian, GL3's significance in praying to God the Father is buttressed by the assertion that, "In my strength I am limited and weak, but with God in me, the One who called the world into existence, that God with his power and his presence in my heart, has established his kingdom and presence in the temple of my heart, and he is in full control." Embracing such a robust theological perspective, GL3 further added that, "He puts all the pieces together. He gives all the solutions, all the answers."

3.3.4. Physical Anthropological Expressions among Guyanese-Canadian Leaders

3.3.4.1. Avoiding Food and People[78]

According to GL5, the arrival of grief usually brings with it a desire to avoid food and others, to be alone in silence and solitude. "Grief consumes you and takes you so that you are not able to eat because the grief has filled you up so much. Food is not part of what you want to see because sometimes you just want to be by yourself and not be able to relate to others."

Grieving in silence and solitude while avoiding food, however, facilitates GL5's ability to "ponder mostly upon what you have lost, and whom you have lost, and all the many things that happened in the past. And it all floods back into your memory and your soul, and it goes over in your head over and over." What is more, it is during these moments of being alone and pondering these

---

78. Amidst grief, such expressions appear to be culturally neutral, especially since men generally tend to express themselves as such (see Zylla, "Aspects of Men's Sorrow," 837–854).

past memories of the lost loved one that leads GL5 to "start thinking about what you could have done, and what you should have done."

3.3.4.2. Bearing the Cost of the Funeral[79]

While not commonplace among other people groups from a Guyanese context, in times of grief, those of an East Indian heritage tend to bear the cost of funerals, especially of their parents. GL1 remarked that, "Indian people feel that it is part of their duty to take care, especially of their parents. They feel that it is part of their obligation, and in many cases, their culture will teach them that if they don't, they will have a curse on them. So, they feel that if they don't do their best for their parents, they'll be bringing a curse upon their own family. So, they gladly do it because that's part of their culture, among the Indian people especially." While it is not uncommon to have children pay for the funeral expenses of their own parents as part of their familial or parental responsibility, GL1 also observed that lending a helping hand even overflows to others external to their family. "Generally, among the Indian people more than anyone else, they will chip in to pay without being asked to pay for the funeral. They would be willing to join in and help to pay for the expenses. They would often come and ask, 'Can I help?' But you will find this almost exclusively among the Indians."

3.3.4.3. Beating Chest, Kissing the Dead, Lying Down on Grave, Fainting[80]

GL1 further remarked that, "Often accompanying wailing, which is a loud cry, some mourners scream and shout virtually at the top of their lungs all while beating their chest." On top of that, GL1 also observed that, "Some have even moved to kissing the dead, and when at the cemetery, some have even chosen to lie down on top of the grave."

Having countless opportunities to officiate at funerals of Guyanese folks both in Guyana and Canada, GL1 further commented that it is not

---

79. This expression might be distinct among East Indian Guyanese-Canadians and so will be developed in chapter 6.

80. Beating one's chest can be found within a context of mourning and/or repentance (cf. Isa 32:12; Nah 2:7; Luke 18:13; 23:48). Kissing the deceased might be analogous to Joseph's falling on his father upon Jacob's death (Gen 49:33) but bereft of fainting. Both beating one's chest and kissing the deceased therefore appear to be culturally neutral.

uncommon to see people weeping and to hear them wailing, and even faint-ing. The significance of such expressions lies in the statement that, "This is a way of telling their people that we love this person [the deceased]." As a corollary to this, if there is a lack of weeping, wailing, and fainting, the un-derlying assumption is that the expressionless griever(s) "does not love that person [the deceased]." GL5 noted that when it comes to reviving the fainting person "smelling salts or Limacol" is usually applied.[81]

3.3.4.4. Keeping Wake and Sharing Stories of the Deceased[82]

According to GL1, not only at the funeral service, but even as a way of remem-bering the departed, it is conventional to eulogize the deceased in conversa-tions that take place during the wake nights. Keeping wake usually takes place in the home of the departed. As noted by Clem Seecharan, "Death requires the public articulation of grief; the 'wake' or vigil, facilitates communal support for the bereaved, who reciprocate by providing a feast for the community."[83]

What is more, even if the person may not have been one admired within society, something good is always said about him or her, both in casual speech and writing, among family members (immediate and extended) and friends. As said by GL1, the relatives and friends of the departed "might express [their stories of the deceased] by saying things relating to the past. They might repeat words told them by the deceased, and sometimes it could be really humorous, and you probably have to put your hand to your mouth."

3.3.4.5. Sharing a Meal, and Singing and Dancing to Upbeat Gospel Music[84]

GL5 indicated that, "During the wake, close relatives and friends bring coffee, crackers, and even food." The purpose of these gestures serves "as a means of demonstrating to the immediate family members of the departed that they are there for them, and that they love and care about them."

---

81. Commonly used among Guyanese, Limacol is a perfumed product intended to rejuvenate.

82. Common among many cultures is the wake (or viewing) and sharing stories of the deceased.

83. Seecharan, "Guyana," para. 30.

84. Sharing a meal after a funeral is culturally neutral, as is singing gospel songs during the wake and funeral. What appears to be distinct here is that of dancing during the wake and funeral as part of the *Kweh-kweh* celebration of the life of the deceased.

Kweh-kweh is usually understood as an African-Guyanese pre-wedding ritualistic celebration that finds its origin among African slaves and their descendants in British Guiana, which is now named the Republic of Guyana (abridged as Guyana). According to GL1, however, in recent years, together with pre-nuptial ceremonies and parties, there has been a steady increase in the adaptation of *Kweh-kweh* to that of a pre-funeral, as well as funeral or memorial services among Guyanese and Guyanese-Canadians.

The chief purpose of *Kweh-kweh*, however, is that of serving up the engaged couple with instructions on marriage. This is comprehended from the words of Gillian Richards-Greaves, who notes that, "While less frequently referred to as karkalay and mayan, Kweh-kweh emerged among African slaves in Guyana, South America, and historically functioned as a medium for matrimonial instruction for soon-to-be-married couples."[85] What is more, Richards-Greaves comments that, "Kweh-kweh is celebrated on the eve of a wedding ceremony and has approximately six distinct segments or states, which include a procession from the groom's residence to the bride's home and the negotiation of the bride price. Each ritual segment is executed with singing, dancing and gesticulations that allow attendees to advise and instruct the bride and groom and to comment on their respective nations (relatives, friends and representatives)."[86]

A celebration of *Kweh-kweh* is virtually piecemeal, however, without partaking in the essential meal. Customized for a pre-funeral service, *Kweh-kweh* festivities include the antiphonal singing of joyful songs, dancing, and the sharing in a meal of *cook-up rice*, the contents of which are mainly black-eyed peas and rice in addition to a choice of meat (either fried chicken, beef, or pork). The significance of this modification can be heard in GL1's explanation that, "rather than mourn the death of the departed, all activities are designed to celebrate the life of the deceased."

Further to this, according to GL1, "the songs sung are upbeat Christian hymns or gospel songs, such as, 'When We All Get to Heaven' and 'Mansion Over the Hilltop.'" And as is typical of *Kweh-kweh* celebration, these upbeat songs are never sung without being accompanied by dancing, as Richard-Greaves notes above. Dancing during the *Kweh-kweh* celebration is part of

---

85. Richards-Greaves, "[Re]Constructing 'Home,'" 3.

86. Richards-Greaves, 3.

what is meant by having, as GL1 stated, "a real time expressing" themselves in celebration of the life of the deceased, and the ultimate reunion in heaven, i.e. in that mansion over the hilltop with their Lord Jesus Christ.

3.3.4.6. Writing Letters of Comfort to the Bereaved[87]

When asked if there were any perspectives or behaviors that help you cope with grief, it was GL5 who remarked that, "Some will write comforting letters to the family, which is very helpful." According to Lidia Schapira, "A written letter of condolence is also an excellent way of conveying respect and support for the family . . . A thoughtful condolence letter offers tribute to the person who died and also provides comfort to the mourners in their time of loss."[88]

3.3.4.7. Eclectic Physical Expressions

Several other eclectic physical expressions and rituals, which can be found among Guyanese during their time of grief, were enumerated by GL5. These are as follows:

- If in Guyana, the village or bell crier, also referred to as the bellman, would walk the streets of the village ringing a bell announcing the death and burial of the deceased. In Canada, this news is broadcast by family members, relatives, and friends of the deceased, in the local newspaper or on the television (Panorama TV on City TV channel 7) on Saturday mornings at 9:30 AM. Prior to the TV, telegrams were the conventional means of spreading the news of the deceased.
- Subsequent to attending a wake night or funeral service, attendees enter their homes walking backward rather than forward. The significance of this physical expression is founded upon the belief that the spirit of the dead trails the attendees home. To prevent the spirit of the dead from crossing the threshold of their homes with them, the attendees face off with the spirit of the dead symbolically communicating to the spirit that she or he is not

---

87. Perhaps with the rise of technology, hand-written letters of comfort to the bereaved are not as popular as before (e.g., Jer 29; Rev 2:8–11) as are sympathy cards.

88. Schapira, "Communication at the End," 54. From such a note, one can thus infer that this expression is culturally neutral.

allowed or welcomed here. It is the assumption of GL5 that this belief has its origin in East Indian or Hindu folklore.[89]

- As an alternative to going to the cemetery, the women usually remain with family members and friends at the home of the deceased to offer comfort to the bereaved.

- For some Guyanese, as a means of respecting the dead, no rank food, characterized as meat or fish, is consumed during the time of grief. Some Guyanese even avoid food altogether. Still, others clean their room, their clothes, and also their entire body after attending a funeral. Others even discard their clothing by burning it after returning home from a funeral. What is more, several even resolve to turn down or turn around the pictures that contain their deceased loved ones. In the year following the death of a loved one, celebrations that usually accompany special holidays like that of Christmas and Easter, are either not as extravagant, but toned down, or are deferred until the next year. All of these rituals are ways and means of expressing respect for the deceased loved one.

- If the deceased is of an East Indian descent, it is commonplace to sing bhajans at the wake and funeral. One of the most famous bhajans is "Yishu Ne Kaha: Jiwan Ki Roti," which is translated, "Jesus said: I am the Bread of Life."

3.3.5. Emotional Anthropological Expressions among Guyanese-Canadian Leaders[90]

3.3.5.1. Sadness, Depression, Listlessness, Guilt, Regret

While acknowledging that crying is the most common emotional expression, GL5 nevertheless asserted that, "Grief within your inner being makes you sad. It makes you depressed, listless, and all the things that go with it." The essence or meaning lying behind such emotions can be heard in GL5's clarification that, "On a personal level, grief is a sadness that you're overcome

---

89. Seecharan ("Guyana," para. 28) observes that, "African, Amerindian, and Indian traditional cultures have sustained folk practices that have penetrated Christianity, Hinduism, and Islam. Obeah has its roots in African folk religion but influences Indians as well, and Indian spirit possession has affected African religious sensibility."

90. Amidst grief, the following emotive expressions appear to be culturally neutral.

with, an emotion that you're going through that consumes you, and takes you, so that you're not able to eat, because the grief has filled you so much." What is more, moments of being alone and pondering past memories of the lost loved one leads GL5 to "start thinking about what you could have done, and what you should have done. All these things come back in grief, and you feel regret, and you feel guilty. These are the emotions that you pass through and you get depressed."

Relying on the work of Elizabeth Kübler-Ross, Caitlin Vieira states that, "Bargaining encompasses a lot of 'what ifs', 'if only's' and guilt. At the end of this stage is the realisation that what happened is not your fault and the beginning stages of acceptance of the situation."[91] Vieira further remarks that, "The depression stage will feel never-ending. We will feel intense sadness and withdraw from others."[92]

3.3.5.2. Anger

Once while officiating a funeral, GL5 noted that one of the immediate family members was requested to reduce his emotions. Such a demand, however, was not accepted by the bereaved family member. As a result of this, "The angry relative began pushing others around him away from him so that he could grieve freely and unhindered." Vieira remarks that, "Anger is a necessary state [in grieving] as it's an essential emotion for pain and healing. Feeling angry has never been the problem, it's how we choose to express it. There are healthy ways to express anger."[93] Vieira then goes on to quote the philosopher Aristotle who asserts that, "Anyone can become angry, that is easy. But be angry with the right person, to the right degree, at the right time, for the right purpose and in the right way – that is not easy."[94]

3.3.5.3. Sorrow, Stress, Getting Bogged Down, Mourning, Comfort, Joy, Happiness

GL4 stated that, "The basic understanding of the word grief is that of sorrow, which I experienced when my father passed away on the 1st of July 1974."

---

91. Vieira, "Grieving and Mental Health," para. 8.
92. Vieira, para. 8.
93. Vieira, para. 7.
94. Vieira, para. 7.

However, as aforesaid, GL4 maintained that "I currently do not allow the grief to stress me out or bog me down."

Earlier, it was noted by GL5 that when the mourner prays in dependency upon God, "God never lets the believer down." Here, GL5 specified that, on the contrary, "God brings comfort to the mourner through prayer. As Jesus said, 'Blessed are those who mourn, for they shall be comforted.'"[95] Such comfort, added GL5, is also found in the words of Paul who said that, "God comforts us in our affliction."[96]

GL3 avowed that, "I put my trust in God and rely on him, having the confidence that he will take my grief, and give me comfort, and cheer me up, and make me happy." As noted earlier, embracing such a positive perspective, GL3 can then go to God his heavenly Father saying, "Dad, here is a problem, intervene," which is followed by the blessed reality that, "God takes my grief and gives me comfort and joy, a joy that money cannot pay for. I [am] helped. I am happy." Such tremendous comfort, joy, and happiness have thus motivated GL3's daily expression of praise to God the Father: "Good morning, Dad. It is such a joy to have you in my life."

Perhaps the words of Lorraine Ince-Carvalhal sums up the process of grief described above, especially in relation to the exertion of one's emotional energy. "It is generally recognized that despite each individual's grief taking its own pattern, there are stages that most people go through. These are firstly accepting the reality of the loss, secondly experiencing the pain of grief before adjusting to life without the person who has passed away and finally putting less emotional energy into grieving and moving on by choosing to focus energy into something new."[97] Ince-Carvalhal, however, does admit that these three stages "can overlap and become jumbled as grievers try to find their way through and the duration of moving through the stages differs from person to person. . . . The thing to remember if you are grieving is that the feelings you are experiencing are normal."[98]

---

95. See Matt 5:4.

96. The locus of Paul's complete statement is 2 Cor 1:3–4: "Blessed *be* the God and Father of our Lord Jesus Christ, the Father of mercies and God of all comfort, who comforts us in all our affliction so that we will be able to comfort those who are in any affliction with the comfort with which we ourselves are comforted by God."

97. Ince-Carvalhal, "Unfortunate Reality of Grieving," para. 7.

98. Ince-Carvalhal, para. 8.

Having come to the end of our survey of the anthropological expressions of disorientation among Guyanese-Canadian leaders, the next move is to present the verbal, physical, and emotional expressions communicated to/before God amidst grief among Vietnamese-Canadian leaders. To reiterate, the purpose of this exercise is to identify those expressions that have proven helpful rather than hurtful, to foster compassionate (liberative intercultural) pastoral care practices that aid in the transformation of grief so that life might be lived abundantly rather than with unbearable grief.

3.3.6. Verbal Anthropological Expressions among Vietnamese-Canadian Leaders

3.3.6.1. Vocalizing Loud Cries (Weeping Lament)[99]

VL1 averred that within the Vietnamese culture it is customary for "grief to generally be expressed in sorrow and sadness and loud cries." For this reason, it is hardly surprising to hear that upon catching wind of the news of the passing of VL1's father in Vietnam, the verbal response was: "I just cried out." VL1 even went further to specify that, "I grieved one week for my dad and I couldn't even sleep." Similarly, VL5 added that "My understanding of grief is crying deeply." As such, it is not surprising to hear the remark of VL5 that "Family and relatives usually show deep grief by crying loudly."

3.3.6.2. Praying Disorientation Prayers (Lament, Cry for Comfort, and Thanksgiving)[100]

It was stated by VL1 that, "I lost two sisters, three nephews, and even a very dear female friend while crossing the seas by boat to find refuge in Canada." Subsequent to these tragedies, VL1 posed the following question to God: "Why has this happened to me and my family?"

Though familiar with the fact of life that every person will die in one way or another, without the ability to prolong one's life forever, upon the passing of VL2's father in 1997, VL2 nevertheless acknowledged, "I struggled with the idea of losing my father so soon." Trying to find an answer while simultaneously engaging in this internal struggle, VL2 posed this question to God: "Why did You create humankind in this way?" However, VL2 also

---

99. This is a culturally neutral expression amidst grief.
100. Amidst grief, such expressions are also culturally neutral.

acknowledged that "At that time, I was not good at understanding the Bible. After much struggle with thoughts about life in my mind and tears in my eyes, I finally accepted the harsh reality of birth, aging, illness, suffering and death."

Approaching grief from another angle, and with the language of lament nonetheless, rather than interrogate God, VL4 spoke of crying out to God for comfort in prayer in recognition of the fact that grief is heart-wrenching and overwhelming. "Father, you know that my heart is broken by this grief. This is too much for me to handle. Comfort me now, Father. Draw me closer to You. Shelter me from this stormy situation." VL2 likewise remarked that, "We lament in silence, we pray together, and we ask the Holy Spirit to comfort us."

At the sight of every hospital, memories of VL3's late father are regularly educed. This, however, is not cause for sadness, but rather thanksgiving. On such occasions, "I take a deep breath and thank God for taking my dad home," the significance of which is "knowing that he is now comfortable and free of pain." What is more, an added meaning lying behind such a prayer of thanksgiving from the heart of VL3 comes to the fore in the following words: "I thank God that he is there for us amidst the grief we go through."

3.3.6.3. Composing Songs and Poems; Singing Hymns; Reading through the Bible[101]

It was noted by VL1 that amidst grief, it is helpful to "Compose songs and poems, since Vietnamese music is sad music," and to "Sing hymns." For VL1, another activity to engage in is that of "Read[ing] through the Bible. Read[ing] Job, Psalms, Jesus' suffering, Isaiah 53, and Jeremiah. Read[ing] God's Word, because of the power of God's Word," which enabled VL1 to "get up from my grief and praise God."

3.3.6.4. Talking about One's Suffering, Talking to/about the Deceased[102]

It was asserted by VL4 that "People withdraw when they grieve. They would like to vent their pains or sorrows, but only to their trusted friends or relatives." VL4 further acknowledged that "Some of us are still affected by our

---

101. It is not uncommon for the bereaved to sing hymns and read their Bibles during their time of grief. What might be distinct here is composing one's personal sad songs and poems.

102. These expressions are also culturally neutral amidst grief.

cultural values. They tend not to talk much about their sufferings. But thanks to the teachings of the Scriptures concerning pain and suffering, and thanks to small group ministry, people are freer to express their grief." VL5 stated that grief is a time when Vietnamese people "Tell others of one's suffering, and tell the loved one we just lost how much we loved him or her." It was further remarked by VL5 that, "Vietnamese people spend most of their daily time at the cemetery talking to the dead."

While being Westernized and still Vietnamese, VL3 acknowledged, "My expression of grief verbally would be that I mention my dad from time to time with people." The significance of this verbal expression from the lips of VL3 is twofold and rendered thus: "I want people to know who my dad was, and it makes me happy talking about him. It brings back great memories of him." Additionally, VL3 stated that "I keep pictures of my father on my phone and talk to it as if talking to him." Dieu-Hien T. Hoang remarks that three days following the funeral of his uncle to cancer in both the abdomen and liver, "We wept and cried and talked to uncle in private."[103]

At the passing of VL2's mother, VL2 claimed, "I gathered my brothers and sisters in the hallway of the hospital and reminded them of all the good things she had done and the good life she had lived, and [we] encouraged one another to keep on with her legacy of love, dedication to the family, and faithfulness to God, which she adopted in her later years." (VL2's mother was for many years a pious Buddhist believer, but finally came to Christ towards the latter years of her life.)

Hoang also notes that following the funeral of his uncle, "for the next 49 days the family held a memorial service every seven days. Again, they shared meals with close friends and relatives and reminisced about events of uncle's passing as well as everything else in their lives."[104] According to Hoang, "Each memorial forced the family to burden others with their sorrow so that they could grieve fully."[105]

---

103. Hoang, "Death Rituals," para. 17.

104. Hoang, para. 18.

105. Hoang, para. 18.

3.3.6.5. *Worshiping God through Meaningful Songs and Prayer, Encouraging the Bereaved through Comforting Words of Scripture, and Evangelizing the Unbelievers*[106]

Following the death of a Vietnamese Christian, "We share to people who lose their loved one that whoever trusts in Jesus will be saved. Therefore they have a hope that they will see their loved one who died," stated VL5.

In terms of a funeral service, VL2 specified that, "We commemorate the life of the deceased one who was devoted to God and one's family and others, by conducting a solemn ceremony in the church or in the funeral home. During the funeral service, we worship God with meaningful songs, pray, witness to unbelievers, and strengthen our relationships." During this solemn ceremony, and among the bereaved family and friends, "We lament in silence, we pray together, and we ask the Holy Spirit to comfort us," remarked VL2. It was also noted by VL2 that even prior to the funeral service, "Ritual prayers for the comfort of the dead and also the bereaved family" are said after the death of a loved one.

3.3.7. Physical Anthropological Expressions among Vietnamese-Canadian Leaders

3.3.7.1. *Crying/Shedding Tears, Isolating Oneself, Embracing Dead Warm Body*[107]

In the opinion of VL4, "Grieving is not approvable, in our culture. Men are encouraged to show strength and courage in pain or sorrow. . . . Women tend to cry more than men." As a matter of fact, "The father never cries in front of the family, but alone. He tries to be strong," stated VL1. Further to this, VL1 specified "Grief is often bottled-up for a long time rather than expressed."

Though feeling free to question God about why he created humankind with the ability to die and without the ability to prolong life forever, VL2 declared, "After much struggle with thoughts about life in my mind and tears in my eyes, I finally accepted the harsh reality of birth, aging, illness, suffering, and death." Upon the death of a close relative, VL2 noted that it is traditional for "the bereaved, who had been closely bonded with the deceased, [to] lament the death for a long time, and [to] even relate their past experiences in tears."

---

106. Amidst grief, such expressions appear to be culturally neutral.
107. Such expressions are culturally neutral amidst grief.

Consistent with this statement, upon the passing of VL2's mother, VL2 indicated "Since my younger sister was living with our mother for a long time, she was deeply attached to her. She was the one who mourned much. She cried out in loud tears, and even embraced her still warm body, as she expressed her love for our mother."

In speaking of the death of his uncle to cancer that initiated in the liver, but which spread to the abdomen, Hoang remarks, "When uncle took his last breath, the crying began gradually as reality started to sink in. All manners of grief were shown; from stoic solemnity to weeping, crying, sobbing and screaming. The only thing not acceptable would have been laughing. All the grandchildren were present and they all cried, even the eighteen month old baby."[108]

3.3.7.2 Deep Breath

VL3 stated that when memories and sadness in relation to her father are conjured especially at the sight of every hospital, "Then I take a deep breath" or a sigh of relief. The significance of this physical expression rests in the confident "knowledge of the fact that my father is now with God, comfortable, and free from pain."

3.3.7.3. Lying Down on Casket, Hitting Oneself Hard[109]

In the midst of grief, and especially on the day of the funeral, there are times when "Someone will lie down on the casket, and hit him/herself hard, especially if s/he thought that s/he was the cause of the death of the loved one," acknowledged VL5.

3.3.7.4 Sitting Beside the Tomb, Visiting the Grave and Carrying Flowers, Keeping Memorabilia[110]

It was VL5 who remarked, "Vietnamese people grieve for our loved one who passed away for a long period. Because of this long period of thinking about the loved one, Vietnamese people spend most of their daily time at the cemetery, sitting beside the tomb and talking to the dead." Additionally,

---

108. Hoang, "Death Rituals," para. 6.
109. These also are culturally neutral expressions amidst grief.
110. Such expressions appear to be culturally neutral amidst grief.

Vietnamese people "Visit the grave and carry flowers," commented VL1. Also, VL3 stated that, "I keep pictures of my father on my phone and talk to it as if talking to him."

Here we note the words of Hoang who remarks, "Three days after the funeral . . . [t]he closest relatives and family went back to the cemetery to bring flowers and incense to the gravesite, say more prayers, and clean up the site."[111]

3.3.7.5. Wearing a White Band, and Celebrating the Life of the Deceased Annually with Lots of Food[112]

VL3 commented, "There is a traditional Vietnamese way of dealing with grief. During the funeral service, whereas in Vietnam the immediate bereaved family wear all white, the mourners in Canada wear black clothing with a white band around their head and/or their arm." Explaining the significance behind this ritual, VL3 further explained "This traditional white band is to be worn for an entire year as a sign of mourning and as a symbol of the loss of life or the ashes of the deceased."

Also implied in such a year-long ritualistic expression is the silent truth that *grief* is not terminated upon the completion of the committal (burial or cremation) of the deceased. To state it another way, wearing the traditional white band throughout the rest of the year following the death of a close family member is to suggest the unspoken statement that even when the dead is long gone and no longer physically present, grief still persists.

This finds support in the words of Hoang who notes that, "After the funeral, family members wore a small piece of black or white fabric on their clothes every day to signify that they were in mourning."[113] Hoang further remarks that this piece of fabric would usually be worn for two years. "On the second anniversary, these clothes would be burned to signify that the mourning period was over."[114] According to Hoang, "The burning of the mourning clothes signifies the incorporation of the bereaved into the normal course of

---

111. Hoang, "Death Rituals," para. 17.

112. Amidst grief, both expressions appear to be distinct among the Vietnamese-Canadians, although it might be analogous to the donning of widow's clothes (Gen 38:14).

113. Hoang, "Death Rituals," para. 21.

114. Hoang, para. 21.

life."[115] Yet Hoang also states that, "The deceased's memory is not erased and the family still observes the anniversary of the death each year."[116]

In addition to this, it was VL1 who noted that the life of the deceased is celebrated "as a memorial annually with lots of food." This expression should not be confused, however, with the offering of food to the deceased's spirit prior to sharing the meal with the gathered family members at the memorial.[117]

3.3.8. Emotional Anthropological Expressions among Vietnamese-Canadian Leaders[118]

3.3.8.1. Confusion and Depression

Due to the lengthy period of grief among Vietnamese folks, such prolonged grief can have adverse emotional consequences. Thus, VL5 noted, "Vietnamese people usually experience depression and mental problems. Some become confused, and even lose their memories."

3.3.8.2. Anger, Heartbreak, Shock

The multiple losses among immediate and extended family members and friends – two sisters, three nephews, and an especially dear female friend – resulted in VL1's elicitation of much anger on occasion. The manifestation of VL1's unholy anger rose to the surface especially in the early years of marriage, which saw both spouse and children suffering the brunt of it.

Anger was also provoked toward God by father, mother, and VL3 following the brutal and unfortunate death of VL3's brother at the tender age of fifteen. Although the bereaved family came to understand God and realized that he took VL3's brother home for a reason, thus leaving him in his hand, VL3 averred, "At first we did blame God." Unable to explain VL3's brother's unfortunate death, VL3 remarked, "We were still shocked and heartbroken and didn't understand why." To make matters even worse, their anger was further compounded by the priest's uncongenial attitude and lack of support

---

115. Hoang, para. 22.

116. Hoang, para. 22.

117. See Hoang, para. 20. But see the article by an anonymous UCA News reporter, "Vietnamese Bishops Issue Guidelines," for a Catholic perspective on ancestor worship, including the use of ancestor altars with candle, incense, flowers, fruits and the deceased's pictures, which are allowed under the altars of God in their houses (para. 7).

118. Such emotive responses appear to be culturally neutral amidst grief.

toward the bereaved family. When asked to go to the cemetery "to give a final saying for my brother," stated VL3, "the priest told my dad it was rainy so he would not go." What is more, to add further insult to injury, "the priest told my dad that his job was done, and he was not interested in doing anything extra." Thus, VL3 commented, "My parents were shocked and angry." Perhaps this is a case of insensitivity upon the part of the priest.

3.3.8.3. Pain, Sadness, and Sorrow

VL4 asserted, "People withdraw when they grieve. They would like to vent their pains or sorrows, but only to their trusted friends or relatives." VL1 averred that within the Vietnamese culture it is customary for "grief to generally be expressed in sorrow and sadness and loud cries." For VL3, the sight of any hospital evokes memories of VL3's dad, and with it, "sadness hits me."

3.3.8.4. Hope

VL5 noted, "As Vietnamese Christians, we value our tradition as our heritage, especially in time of grief. But we rather trust the Bible than our tradition about the afterlife. We sorrow with hope."

Interestingly, according to Lam, prior to their death, some Vietnamese believers experience a pre-resurrection, that is, a foretaste of heaven in their *dreams*,[119] which provides ample proof of their belief in the afterlife. As Lam puts it: "One thing confirms that God's miracles are still effective, and that is the resurrection of followers of Christ *before* their death."[120] In this way, Vietnamese believers can sorrow with hope.

---

119. Lam, *God's Miracles*, 200.
120. Lam, 199; emphasis mine.

3.4. Domain of Anthropological Expressions of Disorientation in Pastoral Theology

Verbal Anthropological Expressions	Loud Cries/Lament Wailing/ Screaming/Shouting; Praying Disorientation Prayers (Lament, Cry for Comfort, and Thanksgiving Praise); Sharing Stories of and/or Talking to/about the Deceased; Talking of One's Grief; Worshiping God through Meaningful Songs and/or Singing Psalms, Hymns, and Spiritual songs to the Lord [such as Upbeat Gospel Songs and Bhajans]
Physical Anthropological Expressions	Avoiding Food and People; Bearing the Cost of the Funeral; Beating One's Chest/Hitting Oneself Hard; Celebrating the Life of the Deceased Annually with Lots of Food; Composing Sad Songs and Poems; Deep Breath; Embracing the Deceased's Body; Encouraging the Bereaved through Comforting Words from the Scripture; Fainting; Keeping Memorabilia; Keeping Wake; Kissing the Dead; Lying Down on a Casket and or Grave; Proclaiming an Evangelistic Message of Hope in the Lord Jesus Christ alone/Evangelizing the Unbelievers; Reading through the Bible; Sharing a Meal; Sitting beside the Tomb; Thinking about the Lost Loved One; Visiting the Grave and Carrying Flowers; Wearing a White Band on Head and/or Arm; and Writing Letters to Comfort the Bereaved
Emotional Anthropological Expressions	Anger/Heartbreak/Shock; Confusion/ Depression; Pain/ Sadness/Sorrow/Listlessness/Guilt/Regret; Stress/Getting Bogged Down/Mourning; Hope/Comfort/Joy/Happiness

These verbal, physical, and emotional anthropological expressions communicated to/before God will subsequently engage in a dialectic correlation with the verbal, physical and emotional anthropological expressions communicated to/before God within the context of prosaic prayers in the life setting of disorientation in the OT (Genesis to Esther). Through this dialectic correlation, it is hoped that compassionate (liberative intercultural) pastoral care practices will be fostered in an attempt to transform grief making it manageable, rather than destructive, for the bereaved. For this reason, the next chapter will generate the verbal, physical, and emotional anthropological expressions collected within the parameters of Genesis and Esther, that is, within the OT prosaic context of prayers of disorientation.

CHAPTER 4

Anthropological Expressions of Disorientation in Biblical Theology

4.1. Recent Scholarship on Anthropological Expressions of Disorientation in Old Testament Prosaic Prayers

In this chapter, our focus turns to the multivalent expressions (verbal, physical, and emotional) and their attentiveness to the ancient human experience of disorientation within the prosaic sections of the OT (Genesis to Esther). Such expressions, interestingly enough, are detected in non-death-related contexts (i.e. individual and communal prayers of disorientation) and also death-related contexts.[1] As Saul M. Olyan perceives, "The texts narrating the mourning rites of penitents, humiliated individuals, and persons seeking a divine revelation, among others, do not use a different vocabulary to describe their behaviour; rather, they utilize the vocabulary of mourning the dead."[2] The fact that such expressions are recorded in both non-death-related and death-related contexts allows the researcher to better explore a dialectic correlation with the expressions examined amidst grief within the intercultural contexts of Guyanese-Canadians and Vietnamese-Canadians. It therefore seems worth proffering a brief overview of prayer, especially

---

1. Rather than prayers of disorientation, Olyan (*Biblical Mourning*, 1–27) prefers petitionary mourning, that is, "mourning rites employed by individual and communal supplicants in time of need" (5).

2. Olyan, 19.

prayers of disorientation, alongside which other expressions (i.e. physical and emotional) communicated to/before God are recorded in the prosaic sections of the OT prior to any explication and generation of a taxonomy of these multivalent expressions.

4.2. Description and Definition of Prayer

In this section I endeavor to establish a description or a working definition of prayer as understood within the OT. But as will become clear, such an endeavor is very complex, as there seems to be an enigmatic side to prayer. Mysterious as it may be, however, it seems important to attempt a definition or description of prayer. Such an effort is twofold: (i) it will aid in the process of identifying prayers within the prosaic sections of the OT, and (ii) it will serve the greater purpose of helping in the categorization of such prayers, especially those uttered within a context of disorientation.

It is not unusual to hear prayer defined or understood as dialogical, or conversational in its very nature. Terence E. Fretheim, for example, asserts that, "Prayer is communication between believers and their God within a relationship of consequence."[3] Even more explicit is Walter C. Kaiser who avers that prayer is "conversation with God."[4] This definition, however, begs the following question: Does Adam and Eve's conversation with God in the Garden of Eden (Gen 3:9–13) meet the requirement for prayer? Should one assume that Cain's conversation with God (4:9–15) also qualifies as prayer? J. Gary Millar claims that "prayer is taken to refer to the deliberative activity when human beings call on God *when he is not immediately present.*"[5] In other words, prayer *"asks God to deliver on his covenantal promises."*[6] But what about

---

3. Fretheim, *Creation Untamed*, 124. Grenz (*Prayer*, 8–30) states that, "Prayer is direct communication with God. . . . At its heart, prayer entails communion with God. . . . prayer is the activity of communicating with the God in whose presence we exist. This activity presupposes a standing-over-against Another, a relationship of the pray-er to the one addressed in prayer. Understood as communication with God, prayer moves in two directions. It includes both the human person speaking to God and God speaking to the human person" (27). Similarly, Bloesch (*Struggle of Prayer*, 50–66) defines prayer as "a two-way communication between the Creator and the creature" (50).

4. Kaiser, *I Will Lift Up*, 4.

5. Millar, *Calling on the Name*, 19n1; emphasis original.

6. Millar, 18; emphasis original.

prayers of thanksgiving and praise? Do they ask God, or do they thank and praise God for being faithful to his covenant promises, hence his deliverance?

Samuel E. Balentine understands prayer as "address to God in the second person, which is initiated by humans, intentional in design, and introduced by prayer terminology (e.g., *hitpallēl*, 'to pray'; *qārā' bešem*, 'to call on the name')."[7] P. W. Ferris observes,

> The more common terms used in the OT for "prayer" are *tepilla* (77x; 17x in the Prophetic Books [e.g., Is 5:15]) and the cognate verb *pll* Hithpael (e.g., Jer 29:12), "to advocate, intercede." . . . Other terms include: *'atar*, :to plead, entreat" (e.g., Is 19:22); *hanan*, "to implore compassion" (e.g., Hos 12:4 [12:5]; cf. Is 33:2); *qara'*, "to call" upon God (e.g., 2 Sam 22:7); *za'aq*, "to cry out" (e.g., Ezek 11:13); *šw'* Piel,"to call for help" (e.g., Is 58:9); *daraš*, "to seek" God (e.g., Amos 5:4); and *ša'al*, "to inquire, beg" (Jon 4:7).[8]

Yet, as we will see from our discussion on the prayers uttered within a context of disorientation within the prosaic scope of the OT, prayer is also present when none of these terms are made explicit within the text.

Judith H. Newman affirms that prayer is "address to God that is initiated by humans; it is not conversational in nature; and it includes address to God in the second person, although it can include third person description of God."[9] Furthermore, Newman avers that "Prayer can be understood broadly to comprehend human communication to God, which may include words and related ritual acts."[10] This will be shown to be true as we attend to the auxiliary ritual expressions (e.g., donning sackcloth and pouring dirt) that accompany OT prosaic prayers of disorientation.

Miller, nonetheless, offers a more panoramic view on prayer as found within the Bible. Miller suggests that prayer may (i) involve a vocabulary that suggests its character as a *conversation or dialogue with God*, (ii) be associated with formal places and situations of worship, (iii) be identified by a specific set of terms that all have to do with "crying out" or "calling out"

---

7. Balentine, *Prayer in the Hebrew*, 31.

8. Ferris, "Prayer," 583–587.

9. Newman, *Praying by the Book*, 6–7.

10. Newman, "Prayer," 579.

for help, and (iv) involve vocabulary that has to do with seeking direction or instruction from God.[11]

Mindful of such an extensive and yet what appears to be an inconclusive understanding of prayer, one can give more careful attention to Mark J. Boda's observation that, "There are occasions when third-person speech is employed and when prayer vocabulary is absent, and yet the composition appears to be prayer."[12] All things being equal, Boda therefore affirms that "This is a needed reminder that identifying prayer is often more of an *art* than a *science*."[13] In other words, prayer can either be *bidirectional* or *unidirectional*, and encompass both second and third-persons, as well as the presence and absence of prayer vocabulary. Whether or not God responds is only a matter of secondary importance, though it is assumed that the pray-er would earnestly desire that God would reply, and do so favorably.[14] Otherwise, prayer would seem purposeless.

In sum, in this section I have attempted to give a brief overview and definition of prayer for the purpose of identifying prayers, especially prayers of disorientation, within the contexts of the prosaic sections of the OT.

4.3. Synopsis of Scholarship on OT Prosaic Prayers

This brings us to a synopsis of scholarship with respect to prayers recorded in the prosaic sections of the OT, which will subsequently aid the researcher in identifying prayers of disorientation along with their auxiliary expressions as recorded in such a context. For the purposes of this book, attention is given primarily to prosaic rather than poetic prayers of the OT. Here I take the term *prosaic* prayers to refer to prayers referenced within the prose or narrative sections of the OT, that is, within the parameters of Genesis and Esther.[15] It is worth acknowledging here, however, that there are other prose

---

11. Miller, *They Cried*, 46–48; emphasis original.

12. Boda, "Prayer," 806.

13. Boda, 806; emphasis mine.

14. Even in prayers of thanksgiving and praise, which one might think does not necessarily warrant it, one of God's favorable responses can be that of inhabiting the praises of his people. God is the one enthroned upon both the descriptive and the declarative praises of Israel (Ps 22:4 [3]).

15. While Esther is part of the prosaic section of the OT, it is worth mentioning that no prayer category is yielded therein.

sections in the OT, especially the prophetic books, and also that prayers can be identified in those sections as well (e.g., Isa 38). Additionally, though many prosaic prayers are largely poetic, the key in my decision-making process is that of the context as prosaic, rather than independent or poetic.

The impetus for this endeavor is threefold: (i) a plethora of work in recent years has been completed within the poetic prayers of the OT, to the virtual neglect of the prosaic prayers, (ii) in comparison to the poetic prayers, the prosaic prayers of the OT yield a greater variety of prayer categories, especially those uttered within a context of disorientation, and (iii) with the actual context of disorientation furnished by the text itself, *conjecturing* the *Sitz im Leben* or life situation of the prayer category no longer becomes a necessity, as is usually the case with the employment of Form Criticism to prayers in the Hebrew Bible (especially the Psalms).

Contained within the parameters of Genesis and Esther, prosaic prayers are generally believed to move from a place of orientation to disorientation and then to new orientation. But while it is claimed by the likes of Boda, Brueggemann, etc., that prayers located within the context of disorientation are of the categories of lament, confidence, and penitence,[16] this section will highlight the *inadequacy* of such a proposal. As will become clearer, categories such as imprecation, vow, and thanksgiving praise are *also* uttered within a prosaic context of disorientation. The remainder of this book will therefore illustrate the development of other categories or stages of prayers uttered amidst a prosaic context of disorientation, thus filling a great lacuna within scholarship executed on the prosaic prayers of the OT (Genesis to Esther).

4.3.1. Development of Prayers

Westermann avows that within the OT, prayer appears to have had an historical development in relation to its form.[17] Prayer therefore seems to have

---

16. Boda, "Form Criticism in Transition," 187–190; Boda, "Prayer," 806–811; Boda, "Varied and Resplendid Riches," 61–82. Although as a psalm genre the lament form can include other subcategories (e.g., imprecation, thanksgiving praise, etc.), it is noted that within the prosaic sections of the OT, these other subcategories are yet to be acknowledged and explicated.

17. Although "form" and "genre" have been used analogously, Tucker (*Form Criticism*, 1–21) maintains, "If the term *form* is used in reference to genre or *Gattung*, it should be made clear that the word has taken on a secondary connotation" (12). In this book, however, "form" will be used distinctly from "genre." Sweeney ("Form Criticism," 227–241) asserts, "'Form' (German, *Form*) refers to the unique formulation of an individual text or communication,

evolved from its early simple prosaic forms, to the more complex poetic forms (as found within the Psalter), and then to the extremely complex forms (as witnessed in such passages as 1 Kgs 8; Ezra 9; Neh 1, 9; Dan 9).[18] The impression here is that during the pre-exilic period, a strong emphasis was placed on protest and complaint while confession of sin was virtually nonexistent. During the postexilic period, however, the complaint essentially vanished and, in its place, there is found a preponderance of confession of sin accompanied by petitions for forgiveness. As such, "This move from protest to penitence is in keeping with the historical trauma of exile, in the aftermath of which any protest of innocence would seem to have lost its foundation."[19]

4.3.2. Levels of Prosaic Prayers

Objecting to such an historical development, however, Moshe Greenberg contends that within the OT, one can discover three levels of prosaic prayers running concurrently. These are: patterned prose prayer speech, ritual prayers (psalms), and totally unconventional and artless or extemporaneous speech.[20] Greenberg adds, "These three levels of praying were *coeval*, and one and the same biblical character is attested as praying on more than one of them (e.g., Hannah [1 Sam 1:12 and 1 Sam 2:10]; Samson [Judg 15:18 and 16:28])."[21] In other words, "All three levels were available throughout the period of biblical literature, and narrators might choose to place their character on any level according to circumstances."[22]

---

whereas 'genre' (German, *Gattung*) refers to the typical conventions of expression or language that appear within a text. Genre does not constitute form; it functions within form" (227). Campbell ("Form Criticism's Future," 15–31) differentiates "genre" from "form" as follows: literary genre or type is equivalent to the typical, a matrix for the text [German: *Gattung*], while literary form or structure is equivalent to the text itself and all its individuality [German: *Form*] (24–25). Perhaps it would be helpful for form critics to compare "form" to the proverbial "forest" (the entire unit) and "type" to the proverbial "trees" (the distinctive varieties within the entire unit), to avoid the repeated discombobulation of the forest for the trees and likewise the trees for the forest.

18. Westermann, *Praise and Lament*, 165–213; see also Westermann, *Living Psalms*; see also Boda, "Prayer," 806.

19. Balentine, *Prayer in the Hebrew Bible*, 28. Boda ("Prayer," 806–811) adds, "this development occurred not only on the stylistic level, but also on the theological level, as can be discerned in the shift from lament to penitence for communal supplication forms" (806).

20. Greenberg, *Biblical Prose Prayer*, 45.

21. Greenberg, 46.

22. Greenberg, 46.

4.3.3. Prayers of Orientation, Disorientation, and New Orientation

Miller categorizes prayers into prayers for help, doxology and trust, confession and penitence, others, and blessing and curse.[23] Yet it is Brueggemann's work on prayer types, i.e. orientation, disorientation, and new orientation, which, according to Boda, has been most beneficial. "The basic categories advanced by Walter Brueggemann are helpful because they root the forms of prayer more firmly in human experience."[24] Citing 1 Chron 16:4–6 as warrant for each of these three types of prayers articulated by Brueggemann, Boda further notes that "the Chronicler presents David's commission to the Asaphites to 'minister before the ark of the Lord, to make petition [prayers of disorientation], to give thanks [prayers of reorientation], and to praise [prayers of orientation] the LORD, the God of Israel.'"[25] Alternatively stated, a panoramic viewpoint captures OT prosaic prayers as moving from seasons of orientation (a life situation deprived of affliction), to disorientation (a life situation encompassing affliction), and then to new orientation (a life situation after affliction).[26] Approaching them from this standpoint, the prosaic prayers of the OT can thus be associated with *human experience*, which is a better alternative to locating its specific liturgical contexts.

4.3.4. Stages of Disorientation Prayers

Although such a diversity exists with regards to prayer types located throughout the OT,[27] particular attention is given here to the prosaic prayers of dis-

---

23. Miller, *They Cried*, 55–133, 244–299.

24. Boda, "Prayer," 806.

25. Boda, 807. Of import here is that the NASB1995 renders the Hebrew *lehazkir* "to celebrate." While a precise translation remains ambiguous, McComiskey ("זָכַר," in *TWOT* 1:241–43) submits that it might be better to translate it as, "to invoke the name of the LORD in relation to Pss 38 and 70" (242), which might lend credence to Boda's translation "to make petition."

26. Brueggemann, *Message of the Psalms*, 19–23; cf. Brueggemann, *Psalms and the Life*, 8–15. Brueggemann adapts the three Ricoeurian categories of orientation, disorientation, and reorientation. Pemberton (*Hurting with God*, 61–75) comments, "In a liminal state, we are caught by circumstances in an in-between time or space of ambiguity, and as a result we feel displaced, confused, frustrated, or even angry. . . . Our challenge is not only how to live faithfully in a season of disorientation but also how to negotiate the liminal space as we move into a season of disorientation. The concept of liminal space and seasons of disorientation are both helpful ways to describe and so talk about the difficult times we encounter" (63–64).

27. Examples of prayers of orientation are 1 Chron 29:20; 2 Chron 5:13; Ezra 3:10–11. Examples of prayers of new orientation are 1 Sam 2:1–10; 1 Kgs 3:6–9; Neh 12:27.

orientation. Such prayers, says Boda, "arise from an experience of difficulty in which the supplicant or community is in need of God's rescue, and they often include physical rites such as fasting, sackcloth, ashes, loud wailing and crying, and various postures (lying, sitting, standing)."[28] Despite his appreciation, Boda nevertheless takes exception to Brueggemann's characterization of prayers of disorientation, especially since he only affords accommodation to the subcategory of *lament* therein.[29] By taking into consideration what he calls *Ausblick aufs Lebens*, that is, "the outlook/perspective on life,"[30] Boda has recently developed the following two-tier taxonomy of disorientation prose prayers based on the level of protest in the OT:

1. Disorientation Stage 1 Prayers (i.e. those prayers that are prayed within a period of distress, expressing despair and longing for salvation; the tone of this type of prayer is noted by the stinging lament questions to God of "why?" and "how long?").[31]

2. Disorientation Stage 2 Prayers (i.e. those prayers that arise within a context of distress, but with a different tone: on the one hand, they express confidence in God's salvific work,[32] or on the other hand, they express contrition before God's discipline and do not question God's action or inaction, that is, they possess

---

28. Boda, "Prayer," 807. Ferris ("Prayer," 583–87) has proffered the following auxiliary expressions of prayer: (i) Body language, such as, kneeling before the God (Dan 6:10), or falling on their faces (Ezek 9:8; 11:13), and imploringly raise their hands (Jer 4:31; Lam 1:17). (ii) Fasting, which is accompanied by sackcloth and ashes (Dan 9:2–4; Joel 1:1–4; Jon 3:4–6) (586). Miller (*They Cried*, 32–54) adds Ezra's tearing of clothes, pulling of hair from his beard, sitting down, along with fasting and falling on his knees before the Lord with his hands to the LORD his God (Ezra 9:3–5), and Elijah stretching himself out upon a sick child as he prayed for healing (1 Kgs 17:21) (50–54).

29. See Brueggemann, *Psalms and the Life*, 11–12; Brueggemann, *Praying the Psalms*, 10–11; Brueggemann, *Message of the Psalms*, 19. Note also the words of Pemberton (*Hurting with God*, 61–75) who contends, "What we really need and what the psalms of *lament* provide is a way to live through times of disorientation with God as an intimate traveling companion" (65; emphasis mine).

30. Boda, "Form Criticism in Transition," 181–192; Boda, "Varied and Resplendent Riches," 61–82.

31. E.g., Josh 7:6–9; Judg 21:2–4; 1 Kgs 17:20–21; described in Judg 2:4; 3:9, 15; 4:3; 6:6; 1 Sam 1:10–18, 27; 8:18; 9:16; Esth 4:1–3.

32. E.g., Josh 10:12; Judg 13:8; 2 Sam 15:30–31; 1 Kgs 3:6–9/2 Chron 1:8–10; 1 Kgs 8:22–53/2 Chron 6:14–22; 1 Kgs 8:55–61; 18:36–38; 2 Kgs 6:17–20; 19:14–19; 20:2–3; 1 Chron 4:10; 29:10–19; 2 Chron 14:9–11; 20:4–19; Ezra 8:21–23; Neh 5:19; 6:9, 14; 13:14, 22, 29, 30; described in 1 Sam 6:8; 2 Kgs 19:4; 1 Chron 5:20; 2 Chron 15:4; Ezra 6:10; Neh 2:4; 4:9.

a sense of penitence that God will forgive).[33] Corresponding to Disorientation Stage 2 Prayers is the "vow" form, which according to Boda, "requests something from God and provides a motivation in a human response following the divine intervention (Judg 11:30; 1 Sam 1:11)."[34]

Interestingly, Boda's sub-division of disorientation prayers finds a close affinity with that of Gunkel's sub-genres of communal lament prayers, especially within the Psalter:

1. Confession of Innocence (i.e. lament prayers wherein the supplicants protest their innocence and try to persuade God to recognize it as well).[35]
2. Penitential Prayers (i.e. lament prayers wherein the supplicants confess their sins to God and request his forgiveness).[36]

4.3.5. Prayers of Disorientation

This recent research prompts further analysis. *First*, Boda's two-tier taxonomy of disorientation prose prayers encourage the potential of discovering other (sub)stages/types/categories of prayers uttered within the situation of disorientation and within the context of the prosaic prayers of the OT (Genesis to Esther).[37] *Second*, and in conjunction with the first observation, although Ferris, Miller, and Boda have offered a few auxiliary expressions that accompany OT prose prayers, further exploration will enable one to discover other anthropological expressions of disorientation that *complement* the OT prosaic prayers of disorientation (sub)stages/types/categories, thus augmenting Boda's two-tier taxonomy. While all three levels of prayer (patterned prose, ritual, and extemporaneous) were coeval, as Greenberg has duly noted, and

---

33. E.g., Judg 10:10, 15; 1 Sam 6:6; 12:10, 19; 2 Sam 24:10/1 Chron 21:8; 2 Sam 24:17/1 Chron 21:16–17; 2 Chron 30:19; Ezra 9:1 – 10:1; Neh 1:4–11; 9:5–37; described in Neh 9:1–5; Ezra 10:6; 2 Chron 33:12–13.

34. Boda, "Form Criticism in Transition," 187–190; Boda, "Prayer," 806–811; Boda, "Varied and Resplendent Riches," 61–82.

35. Gunkel, *Psalms: Form-Critical*, 14.

36. Gunkel, 35–36. See also Fretheim (*Creation Untamed*, 123–147) for this distinction within the individual lament psalms wherein he proffers Ps 51 as a psalm of a penitent heart, and Ps 13 as a psalm of an innocent sufferer (139).

37. This effort is an attempt to expand the work of Boda in "Form Criticism in Transition," 181–192; Boda, "Prayer," 806–811; Boda, "Varied and Resplendent Riches," 61–82.

since scholars tend to disagree on classifying such disorientation prayers as complaint, lament, protest, etc., it seems better in light of what will follow, to retain Boda's nomenclature.

In as much as research executed on the prosaic prayers of disorientation within the OT and its attention to ancient human experience has generated some result, an existing lacuna in scholarship persists. This is particularly regarding the (sub)stages/types/categories of disorientation OT prosaic prayers that are often accompanied by other multivalent modes of expression of disorientation (physical and emotional).

4.4. Anthropological Expressions of Disorientation Prayers and Their Auxiliaries in the OT

4.4.1. Expressions of Suffering within the OT

Peterman and Schmutzer avow that, "within a distinctly theological worldview, the Old Testament affirms that any description of suffering and evil must factor God into the equation. Without a *theocentric* worldview, neither suffering nor evil necessarily calls the *meaning* of suffering into question."[38] The two further observe that, "Expressions of suffering in the Old Testament range from dire human experiences to a cacophony of sounds expressing the suffering of men and women. The OT registry is pervasive, indicating the ongoing dilemma of humankind."[39] With God therefore at the center of their theological worldview, one finds an intriguing number of verbal as well as physical and emotional anthropological expressions that the Israelite saints of the OT communicated to or before God during their prosaic prayers of disorientation.

---

38. Peterman and Schmutzer, *Between Pain and Grace*, 28. See also Balentine, "Suffering and Evil," 390.

39. Peterman and Schmutzer, 24.

4.5. Prayers of Disorientation

4.5.1. Categorization of Disorientation Prayers: Verbal Typology

One of the aims of this book is to expand and carry forward the subcategories or stages of disorientation prayers or prayers uttered in the prosaic context of disorientation commenced by Boda, which are: Disorientation Stage 1 Prayers (lament) and Disorientation Stage 2 Prayers (confidence and penitence), thus adding other (sub)stages to the classification, as will be presented below. The rationale for further classification stems from the fact that there appears to be other important elements within prosaic prayers of disorientation that have gone unnoticed under the radar of genre categorization. As we make our way through our genre recategorization, we will continue by looking more closely at the verbal expressions that leaders from within the ancient Israelite community of faith of the OT communicated to/before God amidst a life situation of disorientation. Here it should be noted, however, that, although Boda's subcategories of confidence and penitence are both accommodated within his Disorientation Stage 2 Prayers, within the prosaic sections of the OT, they are all located independently of each other, and should thus be viewed as such; that is, as two distinct subcategories. Altogether then, our robust taxonomy of prosaic prayers of disorientation in the OT would include what I would like to refer to by nomenclature as:

- Disorientation Stage 1 Verbal Expressions: DS1 Lament Prayers
- Disorientation Stage 2 Verbal Expressions: DS2 Imprecatory Prayers
- Disorientation Stage 3 Verbal Expressions: DS3 Vow Prayers
- Disorientation Stage 4 Verbal Expressions: DS4 Penitential Prayers
- Disorientation Stage 5 Verbal Expressions: DS5 Confidence Prayers
- Disorientation Stage 6 Verbal Expressions: DS6 Thanksgiving Praise Prayers

Each of these six subcategories or stages of prayers uttered within a prosaic context of disorientation in the OT will be fleshed out below.[40]

---

40. For a comprehensive analysis of the different subcategories of Disorientation Prayers Prayers, see my appendix to this volume at https://langhamliterature.org/9781839738401-appendix-1.

4.5.1.1. Disorientation Stage 1 Verbal Expressions:
DS1 Lament Prayers

The first and the majority subcategory accommodated within the prose prayers of disorientation in the OT is *DS1 Lament Prayers*. Oddly, the first lament is heard *metaphorically* from one who was slain by his own brother: "The voice of Abel's blood cries out to the LORD from the ground" (Gen 4:10). The final lament, however, comes from Nehemiah as he petitions God, "But now, O God, strengthen my hands" (Neh 6:9), as Sanballat and Geshem conspire to harm him. Sandwiched between these two laments are those of the patriarchs and matriarchs: Abraham who prays for an heir amidst Sarah's barrenness (Gen 15:2); Hagar who intercedes for the life of her son Ishmael (Gen 21:16b); Ishmael who cries out to God amidst malnutrition (Gen 21:17); Isaac who intercedes on behalf of his barren wife Rebekah (Gen 25:21); Rebekah who inquires of the LORD concerning the squabble between her twin sons within her belly (Gen 25:22); Leah who prays to God for another child (Gen 30:17); and Jacob who asks God for deliverance from his brother Esau (32:9–12).

Further to this, the children of Israel groan under the weight of their oppression (Exod 2:23; 3:7, 9); Moses laments his inability to lead the children of Israel out of Egyptian bondage under Pharaoh (5:22–23). Joshua, Moses's successor, also questions God concerning the serious blow he experiences owing to Achan's covetousness (Josh 7:7–10). During the days of the judges, the children of Israel repeatedly cry out to God for deliverance (Judg 10:10, 15). Even the judges bring their laments to God: Gideon asks the angel of the LORD whether or not the LORD is really with his people (Judg 6:13); Samson asks the LORD if he would allow him to die of thirst and fall into the hands of the uncircumcised (13:18).

Also conveying their lament to the LORD are the prophets: Samuel cries out to the LORD for Israel after they ask for a king like that of the surrounding nations (1 Sam 7:9); Elijah intercedes on behalf of the son of the widow at Zarephath (1 Kgs 17:21); Elisha also intercedes for the life of the son of the Shunammite woman to be restored to him (2 Kgs 4:33); Isaiah intercedes on behalf of Hezekiah (2 Kgs 20:11); Ezra seeks God for protection for himself and all those who return to Jerusalem (Ezra 8:21, 23); and Nehemiah prays to God after hearing of the condition of Jerusalem (Neh 2:4).

The kings also approach the throne of God with their laments: Saul inquires of the LORD concerning his battle against the Philistines (1 Sam 28:6); David inquires of the LORD concerning the life of the child to be born through his adulterous affair with Bathsheba, the wife of Uriah (2 Sam 12:16); Hezekiah asks the LORD for healing from his illness (2 Kgs 20:3); through the prophetess Huldah, Josiah inquires of the LORD for himself, the people, and all Judah concerning the words of the book of the law (2 Kgs 22:13–14); and Manasseh entreats the LORD while in captivity (2 Chron 33:12). This is just a sample of the plethora of laments, both individual and communal, located within the parameters of Genesis to Esther.

Westermann observes, "The texts in the O.T. show that throughout its history (that is, both in the Psalms and its earlier and later development) lamentation is a phenomenon characterized by three dominant elements: the one who laments, God, and the others, i.e. that circle of people among whom or against whom the one who laments stands with a complaint."[41] To whom is the lament directly addressed? The One who alone can bring deliverance, namely God. God, in other words, is the savior, the deliverer, the problem-solver. As Longman remarks, "when in great distress he has nowhere to turn but to God."[42] Hence, DS1 lament prayers, according to Allen P. Ross, "are cries to God in times of need, whether sickness, affliction, slander, war, or some other crisis. In ancient Israel, the worshiper could cry out to God anytime, anywhere; but if possible, he would normally go to the sanctuary to offer the petition, and in many cases the officiating priest might offer the prayer on his behalf. Laments form the starting point of the prayer and praise cycle."[43] Which is to say that prayers begin with lament and end with praise, though not always *after* or outside a crisis; praise can erupt even *amidst* distress.

Although not the norm, there are times when the brunt of the anguish found within the lament is directed toward God. Which is to say that the one responsible for the problem at hand is not a human (non)covenant partner, but rather *Yahweh*. As June F. Dickie remarks, "The essence of lament is the relationship with God, the lamenter's refusal to give up the relationship, even as he/she grapples with God about *God's part* in the difficulty being

---

41. Westermann, *Praise and Lament*, 169.

42. Longman, *Psalms: An Introduction*, 26.

43. Ross, *Commentary on the Psalms*, 111.

experienced."[44] So, for example, when Pharaoh refused the let the children of Israel worship Yahweh in the wilderness, Moses runs to God and interrogates him, saying, "O Lord, why have You brought harm to this people? Why did You ever send me? Ever since I came to Pharaoh to speak in Your name, he has done harm to this people, and You have not delivered Your people at all" (Exod 5:22–23). Nevertheless, there is no one the lamenter can turn to but God himself, for deliverance is found in none other.[45] Even in times of disorientation through no fault of Yahweh, but rather a member either within or outside of his covenant community (e.g., Pharaoh, the Philistines, etc.), the appeal is still made to Yahweh for his mighty deliverance.[46] That is, "When Yahweh is not to be blamed, he is nonetheless regarded as the only one who can intervene in a decisive and helpful way."[47]

DS1 lament prayers can therefore be described as those prayers that arise out of a situation of disorientation,[48] the anguished plea or passionate cry for help of the supplicant indicative of the fact that the supplicant is helpless, in grief and despair, and thus in desperate need of Yahweh's salvific intervention.[49] Even on occasion when Yahweh appears to be the enemy,[50] Yahweh is nonetheless the only deliverer that the supplicant mightily clings to. While it is not atypical for DS1 lament prayers to ask the stinging question "Why?"[51] when words are difficult to come by, *groans*,[52] which are deep, inarticulate, and mournful sounds, as well as bitter weeping,[53] are evoked from the heart of the supplicant, consequently activating Yahweh's compassionate response in effecting his salvific rescue mission in favor of the helpless supplicant. At the

---

44. Dickie, "Practising Healthy Theology."

45. Longman, *Psalms*, 27.

46. Brueggemann, *Message of the Psalms*, 88.

47. Brueggemann, 89.

48. Balentine (*Prayer in the Hebrew*, 146–189) states, "Lament has its origin in the existential experience of suffering" (168).

49. See also Harrichand, "Recovering the Language of Lament for the Western Evangelical Church," 102–103, 120.

50. For more on God as enemy, see Blumenthal, *Facing the Abusing God*; Fløysvik, *When God Becomes*.

51. It is worth mentioning here that while the stinging lament question of "Why?" is extant within DS1 lament prayers, "How long?" is nonexistent.

52. See also Judg 10:8–9; 1 Sam 5:12; 15:11; 2 Sam 22:7; cf. Pss 18:7 [6]; 34:16 [15]; 39:13 [12]; 40:2 [1]; 102:2 [1]; 145:20 [19]; Jer 8:19; Lam 3:56; Acts 7:34; Rom 8:26.

53. Cf. 1 Sam 1:10–11.

same time, it should be noted that even beyond Yahweh's salvific intervention on behalf of the supplicant, or even the "recovery of communion with God,"[54] is that of the ultimate goal of the DS1 lament prayers: joyful thanksgiving praise to Yahweh, the God who saves.[55] In this connection, it does seem reasonable to say that thanksgiving praise prayers ring hollow where DS1 lament prayers to Yahweh God are not first vocalized.

4.5.1.2. Disorientation Stage 2 Verbal Expressions: DS2 Imprecatory Prayers

The second subcategory accommodated within the prose prayers of disorientation in the OT is *DS2 Imprecatory Prayers*. The first two imprecations or curses within the prosaic parameters of Genesis and Esther are articulated by Moses. As the children of Israel proceed from the mountain of Yahweh to a resting place of Yahweh's choosing, Moses adjures Yahweh to "Rise up, O LORD! And let Your enemies be scattered, and let those who hate You flee before You" (Num 10:35). Then, in the context of a wrangle between him and Dathan and Abiram (the sons of Eliab), an exasperated Moses implores Yahweh, "Do not regard their offering!" (Num 16:15a).

Samson voices the next imprecation after his capture at the hands of the Philistines. In Judges 16:28, he beseeches Yahweh, saying, "O Lord GOD please remember me and please strengthen me just this time, O God, that I may at once be avenged of the Philistines for my two eyes."

Three imprecations are uttered by David, two of which are related to the death of Abner. In 2 Samuel 3:28–29, David asserts that "I and my kingdom are innocent before the LORD forever of the blood of Abner the son of Ner. May it fall on the head of Joab and on all his father's house; and may there not fail from the house of Joab one who has a discharge, or who is a leper, or who takes hold of a distaff, or who falls by the sword, or who lacks bread." A few verses later, David adds, "May the LORD repay the evildoer according to his evil" (3:39). Then, having learned that Ahithophel is among the conspirators with Absalom to usurp his throne in Jerusalem (15:12, 31a), David

---

54. See Soll, "Israelite Lament," 77–88. This of course assumes that there is a breakdown in the divine-human dialogue of which Ellington (*Risking Truth*, 1–32) observes, "Biblical lament at its core is about the threat of the breakdown of relationship between the one praying and his or her covenant partner" (10).

55. See also Broyles, "Lament, Psalms of," 396.

adjures Yahweh, saying, "O LORD, I pray, make the counsel of Ahithophel foolishness" (15:31).

As the Aramean army plots to capture him, the prophet Elisha requests of Yahweh to "Strike this people [the Arameans] with blindness" (2 Kgs 6:18). When the sons of Ammon, Moab, and Mount Seir attempt an incursion on the southern kingdom of Judah, King Jehoshaphat enters the house of Yahweh, and as he stands in the assembly of Judah and Jerusalem, he prays:

> "O LORD, the God of our fathers, are You not God in the heavens? And are You not ruler over all the kingdoms of the nations? Power and might are in Your hand so that no one can stand against You. Did You not, O our God, drive out the inhabitants of this land before Your people Israel and give it to their descendants of Abraham Your friend forever? They have lived in it, and have built You a sanctuary there for Your name, saying, 'Should evil come upon us, the sword, *or* judgment, or pestilence, or famine, we will stand before this house and before You (for Your name is in this house) and cry to You in our distress, and You will hear and deliver us.' Now behold, the sons of Ammon and Moab and Mount Seir, whom You did not let Israel invade when they came out of the land of Egypt (they turned aside from them and did not destroy them), see *how* they are rewarding us by coming to drive us out from Your possession which You have given us as an inheritance. *O our God, will You not judge them?* For we are powerless before this great multitude who are coming against us; nor do we know what to do, but our eyes are on You." (2 Chron 20:5–12; emphasis mine)

Though an explicit cry for divine judgment, Jehoshaphat, however, does not specify the manner in which he desires his enemies to be destroyed. Rather, he leaves that up to Yahweh, tacitly understood as the righteous Judge in heaven and on earth. From the remainder of the passage the reader discovers that it is divine judgment in the form of *supernatural annihilation*. "When they began singing and praising, the LORD set ambushes against the sons of Ammon, Moab and Mount Seir, who had come against Judah; so they were routed. For the sons of Ammon and Moab rose up against the inhabitants of

Mount Seir destroying *them* completely; and when they had finished with the inhabitants of Seir, they helped to destroy one another" (20:22–23).

The prophet Nehemiah furnishes the reader with the final three occurrences of an imprecatory prayer of disorientation primarily against Sanballat and Tobiah. In the first incident, as Sanballat and Tobiah stir up trouble and mock the Jews engaged in rebuilding the wall of Jerusalem, Nehemiah entreats Yahweh, saying, "Hear, O our God, how we are despised. Return their reproach on their own heads and give them up for plunder in a land of captivity. Do not forgive their iniquity and let not their sin be blotted out before You, for they have demoralized the builders" (Neh 4:4–5).[56] Two chapters later, Nehemiah returns to Yahweh with a cry that hints at vengeance against Sanballat, Tobiah, and Noadiah, all of whom make an earnest attempt to frighten him. "Remember, O my God, Tobiah and Sanballat according to these works of theirs, and also Noadiah the prophetess and the rest of the prophets who were trying to frighten me" (6:14).[57] The final reference sees Nehemiah imploring Yahweh against some of the Jews who were guilty of engaging in intermarriage, thus defiling themselves, rather than being holy as Yahweh their God is holy (cf. Lev 11:44–45). "Remember them, O my God, because they have defiled the priesthood and the covenant of the priesthood and the Levites" (Neh 13:29). While Nehemiah's cries for divine remembrance in the latter two prayers do not explicitly state a curse against his opponents, the tone or mood appears to be aimed at divine judgment, the content of which seems to be that of the nature of exile and divine unforgiveness. The fact that he also drives one of his own Jewish counterparts away from him (13:28) gives

---

56. Note the contrast in Neh 13:14 where the prophet asks the LORD not to blot out his loyal deeds performed for the house of God and its services.

57. Whenever Nehemiah asks God to remember him, it is always for his good, that is, that God would act favorably on his behalf for his name's sake (13:14; 22). Contrast this with Nehemiah's cry to God to remember his opponents such as Sanballat, Tobiah, and Noadiah, and even those who defiled the priesthood (6:14; 13:29). In this case, God is petitioned to act negatively or unfavorably toward, and thus to the disadvantage of Nehemiah's opponents, especially in light of their fierce opposition to the very work that God himself has commissioned Nehemiah to do for the sake of God's holy name (2:18). In both cases of God's remembrance, however, it is worth emphasizing that God always acts in consonance with his holy character, which encompasses his lovingkindness, justice, and righteousness, and which are his glorious delight (Gen 18:25; Exod 34:6–7; Deut 1:17; 32:4; Job 8:3; Ps 58:12 [11]; 94:3 [2]; Jer 9:24; Rom 3:56).

the impression of something unpleasant in Nehemiah's supplication for God to remember those who have defiled the priesthood.[58]

From the examples furnished above, it is observed that the supplicant's imprecation can be directed against one internally (Num 16:15; Neh 13:29) or externally related to the covenant community of Yahweh (2 Kgs 6:18; Neh 4:4–5; 6:14). By submitting their imprecation to Yahweh, the supplicants – Moses, Samson, David, Elisha, Jehoshaphat, and Nehemiah – thus avert the fatal error of vengeance (Lev 19:18), the sole prerogative of Yahweh the just Judge of all the earth (Deut 32:35; Ps 94:1; Isa 35:4; Nah 1:2; cf. Rom 12:19; Heb 10:30). Imprecatory prayers, however, are not simply complaints about the experiences of injustice at the hands of the unrighteous, but rather complaints submitted to Yahweh for the express purpose of *"moving God to be just. These are prayers offered in the certain conviction that God must stay in the world as a God of justice,"*[59] as Balentine avers.

Miller asserts that, "The corollary of blessing is curse . . . While such curse prayers, or imprecation, as they are sometimes called, do not seem to be as numerous as the blessings, they are present, most noticeably within the Psalms."[60] He moreover affirms that, "In form they are similar to the blessings. That is, the curses are a prayer-wish, usually jussive in form, 'May the Lord do . . .' The content, however, is a prayer for disaster of some sort to fall upon another individual or group. . . . As with the blessings, the Lord is not

---

58. Nehemiah's cry for divine remembrance with an implicit cry for divine imprecation in 6:14, appears to bear a modicum of semblance to that of Ps 137, wherein the psalmist's cried out to God: "Remember, O LORD, against the sons of Edom" (v. 7; cf. 83:6), even while sitting by the rivers of Babylon, weeping, and remembering Zion (v. 1). See McCann, "Prayer and Activity," 118–119 for his comments on Ps 137 and the importance of remembrance/memory by the psalmist's in relation to Zion/Jerusalem. He notes that while it is not explicit, "this submission of anger to God obviates the need for actual revenge on the enemy" (119).

59. Balentine, *Prayers in the Hebrew*, 286. Alternatively stated, should Yahweh forget it, evil will have free rein to perpetuate its unimaginable and ineffable horrors. When Yahweh remembers it, however, evil is brought to justice by God the righteous Judge, thus allowing for the perpetuity of justice rather than evil on God's good earth.

60. Miller, *They Cried*, 299–300. While the majority of imprecatory invocations are positioned within the Psalter (e.g., Pss 5, 6, 11, 12, 35, 40, 52, 54, 56, 58, 69, 79, 83, 89, 109, 137, 139, and 143), with a minimal number scattered throughout the prophetic corpus (e.g., Hos 10:14–15; Mic 7:16–17; Jer 8:21–22), shorter examples can also be detected within the prosaic sections of the OT (e.g., Num 10:35; 11:11–15; 16:15, 35; Judg 16:28, 30; 2 Sam 3:29; 15:31; 2 Kgs 6:18; 2 Chron 20:6–12; Neh 4:4–5; 6:14; 13:29).

always mentioned in the curse, but the divine agency is to be assumed and frequently made explicit."[61]

Contended here is that such prayers of imprecation calling for the administration of Yahweh's justice are indeed prayed within a prosaic context of disorientation.[62] By inference, the subcategory of DS2 imprecatory prayers acknowledge before Yahweh that the predicament at hand from which the supplicant seeks divine deliverance, has been instigated by the supplicant's enemy who is deserving of divine punishment. Such imprecatory prayers do not simply state one's complaint before Yahweh and also confidently petition him for liberation or divine favor. From the data gathered, it is observed that DS2 imprecatory prayers even periodically venture to take the bold step of faith to explicate the manner in which Yahweh should unleash his judgment or curse upon the opponent(s) of the supplicant.[63] This is not to say that Yahweh necessarily responded to such a degree as that of the supplicant's every entreaty for divine imprecation upon their opponent(s). But it nevertheless allows for Yahweh's human covenant and righteous prayer partners to beseech him with such detailed intensity without ever being censured by him. In that way, Yahweh seemingly sanctioned their supplications for divine imprecation to be inflicted upon their enemy, be it that of a person of Gentilic or Israelite stock. Said otherwise, in DS2 imprecatory prayers, with a verdict of guilty having been reached by the righteous supplicant, justice must be meted out in vengeance against the one who has acted in an unrighteous manner toward Yahweh's righteous servant, and that by the righteous Judge of all the earth. Which is to say that "The appeal is not to the enemy that the

---

61. Miller, *They Cried*, 300.

62. The subcategory of imprecatory prayers was never afforded accommodation within the prosaic prayers of disorientation. It is also worth mentioning here that, in light of Christ's call to pray and bless, rather than curse those who curse us (Matt 5:44; Luke 6:28; cf. Rom 12:14; 1 Cor 4:12), scholars are divided on this issue with some arguing *against* and others arguing *for* the employment of imprecation. Examples of those *opposed to* its employment are: Lewis, *Reflections on the Psalms*; Miller, "Heaven's Prisoners"; Westermann, *Praise and Lament*; and Wright, "Preaching and Teaching." Examples of those who argue *in favor of* its employment are: Beal, "Biblically Sanctioned Speech?"; Byassee, *Praise Seeking Understanding*; Bonhoeffer, *Psalms: The Prayer Book*; Brueggemann, *Praying the Psalms*; John Goldingay, *Psalms, Vol. 1*; deClaissé-Walford, "Theology of the Imprecatory"; Merrill, *Psalms for Praying*; Nehrbass, *Praying Curses*; Sherbino, *Re:Connect: Spiritual Exercises*; Swinton, *Raging with Compassion*; Volf, *Exclusion and Embrace*; Zenger, *God of Vengeance?*

63. Cf. 2 Sam 3:29; 15:31; 2 Kgs 6:18; Neh 4:4–5.

enemy should desist, for that is a hopeless plea. The appeal is that Yahweh should intervene to right the situation and punish the destabiliser."[64]

DS2 imprecatory prayers can therefore be described as those prayers that arise out of a situation of disorientation, the contents of which are either an implicit or explicit cry for divine judgment or curse to be administered to one's opponent(s). In DS2 imprecatory prayers, the source of the emergency at hand is the opponent(s) whose identity can be either one internal or one external to the covenant community of Yahweh. DS2 imprecatory prayers call on Yahweh to right the wrong that has been done, and in his perfect justice, execute his righteous judgment upon the unscrupulous offender(s) with the objective of reversing instability, and resuming peaceful (*shalom*) relations within a human-human dynamic.

4.5.1.3. Disorientation Stage 3 Verbal Expressions: DS3 Vow Prayers

The third subcategory accommodated within the prose prayers of disorientation in the OT is *DS3 Vow Prayers*. Four occurrences of a vow appear within the parameters of Genesis to Esther. First, in Numbers 21:2, as the Canaanites take up arms against them, Israel entreats Yahweh, saying, "If You will deliver this people into my hand, then I will utterly destroy their cities." Second, in Judges 11:30–31, as the sons of Ammon wage war against the children of Israel, Jephthah adjures Yahweh, saying, "If You will indeed give the sons of Ammon into my hand, then it shall be that whatever comes out of the doors of my house to meet me when I return in peace from the sons of Ammon, it shall be the LORD's, and I will offer it up as a burnt offering." Sadly, the text says, "At the end of two months she returned to her father, who did to her according to the vow which he made" (11:39a). Third, in her struggle with infertility, Hannah implores Yahweh, saying, "O LORD of hosts, if You will indeed look on the affliction of Your maidservant and remember me, and not forget Your maidservant, but will give You maidservant a son, then I will give him to the LORD all the days of his life, and a razor shall never come on his head" (1 Sam 1:10–11). The final vow can be heard coming from Absalom

---

64. Brueggemann, *Message of the Psalms*, 88.

who *apparently* prays to Yahweh, saying, "If the LORD shall indeed bring me back to Jerusalem, then I will serve the LORD" (2 Sam 15:7–8).[65]

It is observed from these four examples, that the vow subcategory stands *alone*. Having its own merit, the vow prayer neither accompanies prayers of penitence, nor prayers of confidence, as Boda suggests.[66] As a matter of fact, the presence of the word "if" within DS3 vow prayers appear to indicate an *absence*, rather than a presence of confidence. Which is to say that there is *no* assurance on the part of the supplicant that Yahweh will answer favorably. Nevertheless, the supplicant brings their vow before Yahweh in hopes that their response will be in their favor.

What is also worth mentioning here is that while Westermann refers to the vow prayer as "a vow of praise,"[67] as evidenced in our four examples, there is no inherent promise on the part of the supplicant to offer any praise to Yahweh. Even in Hannah's case, praise erupts only sometime *after* Yahweh responds favorably (i.e. Hannah's praise comes at least nine months after her vow prayer, and thus, within a context of new orientation). Moreover, should one understand the sacrifice of Jephthah's daughter as a sacrifice of praise to Yahweh? That does seem unreasonable, to say the least. However, it is possible for one to interpret Absalom's vow prayer as an intention to praise Yahweh. But from reading 2 Samuel 15:9–11, one learns that Absalom deceived his father. He gained his chance to go to Hebron, but not for the purpose of serving or praising Yahweh. Rather, Absalom was resolute about usurping the throne of his father David. So, although it is conceivable, there is no evidence in favor of praise as the outcome of the vow prayer. Praise prayer is therefore not intrinsically connected to the vow prayer.

DS3 vow prayers can thus be described as those prayers that arise out of a situation of disorientation wherein the supplicant presents a conditional petition to Yahweh ("If . . .), which is accompanied by a promise to do something in favor of Yahweh which the supplicant deems approving to Yahweh

---

65. The word *apparently* is employed here because it is not certain whether Absalom actually spoke this vow to the LORD. In light of the succeeding verses, it would appear that he told his father David about this vow so that he could go to Hebron and conspire with his followers against his father so as to usurp David's throne. Nevertheless, the vow is included here as it is a vow found within a context of disorientation.

66. Boda, "Form Criticism in Transition," 187–190; Boda, "Prayer," 806–811; Boda, "Varied and Resplendid Riches," 61–82.

67. Westermann, *Praise and Lament*, 77.

should Yahweh deliver the supplicant ("Then . . ."). It is this *promise* that thus appears to function as the motivating factor for the divine favorable answer. In response to obtaining Yahweh's deliverance, the supplicant then proceeds to honor their part of the vow to Yahweh. Accentuated here is the fact that the supplicant's vow prayers are made amidst a life context of disorientation, yet without any connection to penitence or confidence or even praise.

4.5.1.4. Disorientation Stage 4 Verbal Expressions: DS4 Penitential Prayers

The fourth subcategory accommodated within the prose prayers of disorientation is *DS4 Penitential Prayers*. The first penitential prayer is recorded in Exodus 32:31–32, wherein Moses petitions Yahweh, saying, "Alas, this people has committed a great sin, and they have made a god of gold for themselves. But now, if You will forgive their sin – and if not, please blot me out from Your book which You have written." The locus of the last recorded penitential prayer is Nehemiah 9:5–38, wherein the following penitent words shine through: "Now therefore, our God, the great, the mighty, and the awesome God, who keeps covenant and lovingkindness, do not let the hardship seem insignificant before You, which come upon us, our kings, our princes, our priests, our prophets, our fathers and on Your people, from the day of the kings of Assyria to this day. However, You are just in all that has come upon us; for You have dealt faithfully, but we have acted wickedly" (9:32–33). Sandwiched between these two penitential prayers, one finds the prophet Moses constantly mediating on behalf of the children of Israel who make it a habit of offending Yahweh, and thus kindling his anger. So, for example, when the children of Israel grumble against Moses and Aaron, even desiring to return to Egypt, igniting Yahweh's anger, Moses steps in and importunes Yahweh for their forgiveness (Num 14:13–19). When Yahweh sends fiery serpents to inject venom into their bodies causing the death of some of them, Moses acknowledges their sin and implores Yahweh to pardon them (21:7). And Balaam finally comes to his senses and confesses his sin to Yahweh after his donkey speaks with him (22:34).

In Judges 10:10, the sons of Israel cry out to Yahweh, saying, "We have sinned against You, for indeed, we have forsaken our God and served the Baals." Upon realizing their sin in soliciting the prophet Samuel for a king like that of the nations around them, Samuel and all Israel pray to Yahweh, saying, "We have sinned against the LORD" (1 Sam 4:6). Approaching Samuel after failing to utterly destroy everything belonging to the Amalekites, Saul confesses, "I have sinned; I have indeed transgressed the command of the LORD and your words, because I feared the people and listened to their voice. Now please pardon my sin and return with me, that I may worship the LORD" (15:24–25; cf. 15:30). Having been reprimanded for his adultery with Bathsheba, and the murder of her husband Uriah, David confesses to the prophet Nathan that "I have sinned against the LORD" (2 Sam 12:13). And upon taking the census for Israel and Judah, David also admits, "I have sinned greatly in what I have done. But now, O LORD, please take away the iniquity of Your servant, for I have acted foolishly" (24:20; cf. 24:14, 17). Recognizing the danger of partaking in the Passover meal without being purified, Hezekiah prays for the unholy multitude of people, saying, "May the good LORD pardon everyone who prepares his heart to seek God, the LORD God of his fathers, though not according to the purification rules of the sanctuary" (2 Chron 30:18–19). And finally, in Ezra 9:1–10:1, Ezra the priest and scribe articulates the penultimate penitential prayer as he confesses to Yahweh that his people, Israel, have engaged in unlawful intermarriage with the peoples of the land – the Canaanites, Hittites, Perizzites, Jebusites, Ammonites, Moabites, Egyptians, and Amorites. Particularly, Ezra 9:15 reads, "O LORD God of Israel, You are righteous, for we have been left an escaped remnant, as *it is* this day; behold, we are before You in our guilt, for no one can stand before You because of this."

From the few examples presented here, DS4 penitential prayers can be understood as those prayers containing a confession of sin and a plea for forgiveness, either directly from Yahweh, or through the mediation of one of Yahweh's prophets. Whereas in most disorientation prayers "blame for a lamentable condition is attached to enemies or to sickness" (e.g., DS1, DS2, DS3), Craig C. Broyles maintains that penitential prayers tend to be "introspective before God."[68] Further, the awareness of sin appears to be prompted either "by circumstances or the inner conscience instructed by God."[69] Within DS4 penitential prayers, the penitent pray-er realizes that their disoriented life is a result of their own sin or that of the covenant community of which they

---

68. Broyles, *Psalms*, 226.
69. Broyles, 226.

are part. Thus, resting on the foundation of God's grace, compassion, slow anger, and forgiving nature (cf. Exod 34:6–7),[70] the penitent pray-er appeals to Yahweh to forgive them, and with that, restore the ruptured relationship. The forgiveness of sin and the restoration of the divine-human relationship then is not primarily predicated upon the repentance of the penitent pray-er,[71] but rather on account of Yahweh's forgiving character. By virtue of his inherent character to forgive the authentically penitent pray-er, Yahweh does not despise a heart that comes broken and contrite before him (cf. Pss 34:18 [17]; 51:17 [16]; Isa 66:2).

DS4 penitential prayers can thus be described as those prayers that arise out of a situation of disorientation, wherein the pray-er, through introspection, comes to the realization that they have sinned (in)directly against Yahweh, which has resulted in a rupture within the divine-human relationship. Accordingly, for restoration to occur, the penitent pray-er sincerely repents of their sin(s) or that of the covenant community, and receives Yahweh's merciful forgiveness, which is entirely predicated upon Yahweh, whose inherent nature it is to forgive all who are humble and contrite of spirit, and who tremble at his word.

4.5.1.5. Disorientation Stage 5 Verbal Expressions: DS5 Confidence Prayers

The fifth subcategory accommodated within the prose prayers of disorientation in the OT is *DS5 Confidence Prayers*. Three prayers of confidence come to the fore within the borders of Genesis and Esther. First, in Genesis 20:17, Abraham intercedes for Yahweh's healing of Abimelech, and especially his wife and maids whose wombs Yahweh has closed because Abimelech has taken Sarah as his wife, even while she still remains Abraham's wife, as well as his half-sister. Second, in Exodus 8:12, Moses cries to Yahweh concerning the removal of the frogs. Third, in Exodus 9:33, Moses supplicates Yahweh concerning the removal of the thunder and hail. Confidence is the subcategory assigned to these three prayers because in each case, the supplicant is certain that Yahweh stands ready to answer favorably.

---

70. One might even contend that Exod 34:6–7 is the heartbeat of the entire Bible, that is, both the Old and New Testaments (see also Boda's *Heartbeat of the Old*).

71. Longman, *Psalms*, 219.

Confidence or trust prayers (DS5) lie somewhere between the prayers of lament (DS1) and the prayers of thanksgiving praise (DS6). Such prayers, according to Mark D. Futato, "lack the anguish and the structural elements that characterize the laments."[72] They express a sense of confidence in "God's power to save,"[73] even while God's salvation is yet to be realized. Which is to say that while the supplicant has moved from a place of deep anguish expressed in their lament to or before God, they still anticipate the day when a prayer of thanksgiving for God's salvation can erupt in the assembly of God's people.[74] This confidence is possible, however, not only because the supplicant firmly believes that Yahweh is ever-present to hear and to help (cf. Ps 23:4), but also because Yahweh's ability to help the supplicant has already been (in) directly hinted at or disclosed *prior to* the supplicant's petition.

Accordingly, in the case of Abimelech acquiring Sarah the wife of Abraham as his wife or concubine, Yahweh appears to Abimelech in a dream and says to him, "Now therefore, restore the man's wife, for he is a prophet, and *he will pray for you and you will live.* But if you do not restore *her*, know that you shall surely die, you and all who are yours" (Gen 20:7; emphasis mine). Then in v. 17 we read, "Abraham prayed to God, and God healed Abimelech and his wife and his maids, so that they bore *children.*"

Then in connection with Moses' first example, we observe Pharaoh imploring Moses to plead with Yahweh to remove the frogs (Exod 8:8). At that point, Moses replies, "The honor is yours to tell me: when shall I entreat for you and your servants and your people, that the frogs be destroyed from you and your houses, *that* they may be left only in the Nile?" (Exod 8:9) After Pharaoh replies "Tomorrow," Moses then assures him, "*May it be* according to your word, that you may know that there is no one like the LORD our God. *The frogs will depart* from you and your houses and your servants and your people; they will be left only in the Nile" (v. 10; emphasis mine). At this, Moses petitions Yahweh concerning the frogs, and Yahweh does exactly according to the word of Moses: the frogs die outside of the houses, the courtyards, and the fields (vv. 12–13).

---

72. Futato, *Interpreting the Psalms*, 160. One might also include the anguish of the imprecations and the sorrow of penitence alongside laments. Such prayers also go beyond the vow, which begins with "If," and which expresses an uncertainty in its tone.

73. Futato, 161.

74. Cf. Bullock, *Encountering the Book*, 170.

But in Moses' second example, Pharaoh pleads with Moses and Aaron to make supplication to Yahweh to stop the thunder and hail (Exod 9:28–29), at which point Moses says to him, "As soon as I go out of the city, I will spread out my hands to the LORD; *the thunder will cease and there will be hail no longer*, that you may know that the earth is the LORD's" (9:29; emphasis mine). We then read in v. 33, "So Moses went out of the city from Pharaoh, and spread out his hands to the LORD; the thunder and hail ceased, and rain no longer poured on the earth." It is worth mentioning here that in light of the fact that Moses supplicates Yahweh verbally in the cases for the removal of the frogs (8:12), the swarms of flies (8:30), and the locusts (10:18), and also in light of the fact that he has a speech impediment (4:10), Moses' act of spreading out his hands to Yahweh should arguably by understood as a substitute for his verbal supplication, otherwise referred to as Moses' sign language to Yahweh.[75]

DS5 confidence prayers can therefore be described as those prayers that arise out of a situation of disorientation, the pray-er confident of Yahweh's ever-abiding and comforting presence as well as his forthcoming favorable answer. This favorable answer, however, comes as a revelation to the suppli-cant, disclosed (in)directly by Yahweh even prior to the supplicant's petition. Owing to this prior knowledge, DS5 confidence prayers therefore lack the discomfort and uncertainty of lament, imprecation, penitence, and even a vow, yet they occur in the life context of disorientation. However, the con-fidence of a favorable answer is awakened for the very reason that there is a guaranteed assurance that Yahweh's mighty deliverance will prevail.

4.5.1.6. Disorientation Stage 6 Verbal Expressions: DS6 Thanksgiving Praise Prayers

The final subcategory accommodated within the prose prayers of disorienta-tion in the OT is *DS6 Thanksgiving Praise Prayers*. Within the parameters of Genesis and Esther, only one occurrence of thanksgiving praise is observed, the locus of which is that of the disorientation context of a strife (enemy war-fare). In 2 Chronicles 20, the sons of Moab, the sons of Ammon, and some of the Meunites band together to make war against King Jehoshaphat of Judah.

---

75. Exod 17:8–16 furnishes yet another example of this expression. For more on this expression, see the discussion below under "Outstretching Hands."

Following his DS2 imprecatory prayer to Yahweh (vv. 6–12), and Jahaziel's priestly word of victory (vv. 14–17), we read in vv. 18–19, "Jehoshaphat bowed his head with his face to the ground, and all Judah and the inhabitants of Jerusalem fell down before the LORD, worshiping the LORD. The Levites, from the sons of the Kohathites and of the sons of the Korahites, stood up to praise the LORD God of Israel, with a loud voice." Then on the day of the battle, before victory is even realized, we read: "When he [Jehoshaphat] had consulted with the people, he appointed those who sang to the LORD and those who *praised Him* in holy attire, as they went out before the army and said, 'Give thanks to the LORD, for His lovingkindness is everlasting.' When they began singing and praising, the LORD set ambushes against the sons of Ammon, Moab and Mount Seir, who had come up against Judah; so they were routed" (vv. 21–22).[76] Accordingly, on both days, even within a life context of disorientation (since the battle is yet to be fought, and the victory yet to be won) there is a joyful outburst of thanksgiving praise prayers to Yahweh.

Jacob Myers suggests that "Apparently the writer viewed the whole expedition as a holy war, since the cultic personnel accompanied the army and played a major role in the campaign."[77] But whereas, "In most battles a battle cry is heard," John A. Thompson avers that, "Here it is replaced by singing and praise."[78] In contradistinction to Thompson, however, Louis C. Jonker posits, "The Chronicler conducts this battle with the liturgy of a holy war: the vanguard is to sing to the LORD and to praise him for the splendor of his holiness. *Their battle cry is*, Give thanks to the LORD, for his love endures forever (20:21)."[79] Not surprisingly, Raymond B. Dillard remarks that, "One must not forget the role of music in warfare . . . Particularly within Israel's tradition of holy war, music has been assigned an important function (2 Chron

---

76. Here it is also worth mentioning in relation to the phrase "holy attire," the words of Holladay (*Psalms through Three Thousand*, 17–25) who observes that, "the same word that has been translated 'beauty' or 'array' (Hebrew *hadrat*) turns up in a Ugaritic text in parallelism with the word meaning 'dream' or 'vision'. . . . That is to say, the word in Ugaritic does not mean 'beauty' or 'ornament' but '(splendor of) divine visitation' or 'revelation'. It refers to a theophany, an appearance of the god. . . . The word does not refer to the vestments of the worshipers but to the glory of God" (20). On this note, it thus seems more plausible to say that the Levitical musicians and singers in 2 Chronicles 20:21 did not necessarily (or only) worship Yahweh in their holy attire, but rather (or also) in Yahweh's holy visitation.

77. Myers, *II Chronicles: Introduction*, 116.

78. Thompson, *1, 2 Chronicles*, 295.

79. Jonker, *1 & 2 Chronicles*, 231; emphasis mine.

13:11–12; Josh 6:4–20; Judg 7:18–20; Job 39:24–25); music accompanies the appearance of the divine warrior to execute judgment."[80] Which is exactly what we view in 2 Chronicles 20:21–23.

It is worth mentioning here, however, that from his reading of the OT, Westermann arrives at the following conclusion:

> In the Old Testament . . . there is as yet no verb that means only "to thank." *Hōdāh*, which is usually translated as "to thank," is not used in the Old Testament a single time for an expression of thanks between men. Thus it is clear from the start that this *hōdāh* cannot be equated with our "to thank," which can directed equally to God and to man. In those places in the O.T. where our "thank" as something taking place between men is most clearly found, the verb used is *bērēk*, which does not have the primary meaning of "praise" but means "bless." In view of these facts, it is clear that the O.T. does not have our independent concept of thanks. The expression of thanks to God is included in praise, *it is a way of praising*.[81]

Opposing any endeavor to constrain one Hebrew word into one German word, Frank Crüsemann challenges Westermann's assertion by demonstrating that "הודה does not refer to a public confession in the third person (about Yahweh), because it is often used in the language of direct address of praise to God in the second person."[82] Crüsemann thus proffers two possibilities for הודה: *loben/preisen* and *danken*. "Danken (to thank) is the traditional translation, but Westermann had argued that there is no such concept in Hebrew thought, suggesting that *loben/preisen* as more suitable."[83] In contra-distinction to Westermann, Crüsemann contends that "when הודה is used it looks to a recent deliverance by God. *Loben/preisen* is used to translate הלל and ברך (both Pi'el), which are used differently from הודה. He contradicted Westermann by affirming the traditional translation of 'danken.'"[84] From these considerations, *thanksgiving*, or more precisely *thanksgiving praise*, will

---

80. Dillard, *2 Chronicles*, 158.

81. Westermann, *Praise and Lament*, 27; emphasis original.

82. As noted by Boda, "Words and Meanings," 282.

83. Boda, 282.

84. Boda, 282.

thus be regarded as a distinct subcategory (DS6 thanksgiving praise prayers) within the spectrum of disorientation prayers.

Further to this, though Westermann avers that, "While the so-called song of thanks praise God for a specific deed, which the one who has been delivered recounts or reports in his song (declarative praise; it could also be called confessional praise),"[85] it is of import to note here that in the aforementioned Scripture passage, no such deliverance has yet occurred. Thanksgiving praise erupts to Yahweh in advance of any deliverance, and even in the midst of a situation of disorientation, *not* new orientation or reorientation.

It is significant to note here, however, that prayers of thanksgiving, according to Brueggemann, surface only within a context of new orientation. For Brueggemann, the most obvious prayer of new orientation is the subcategory of thanksgiving. It is in thanksgiving that the speaker is believed to be on the other side of a lament or complaint, that is, on the other side of disorientation. The occasion for such thanksgiving prayer is that "The speaker has complained to God and God has acted in response to the lament. The result of God's intervention is that the old issue has been overcome. The speech concerns a rescue, intervention, or inversion of a quite concrete situation of distress which is still fresh in the mind of the speaker."[86] Likewise, Futato avers that such prayers of thanksgiving "functioned as one key component of grateful worship that celebrated the goodness of God in delivering people from trouble in this life."[87] Consequently, such prayers of thanksgiving, he argues, "are sequels to the laments."[88] Even Longman claims that prayers of thanksgiving are "a response to answered lament," a "praise to God for answered prayer," and which is "most easily identified by a *restatement of the lament* which is now answered."[89] On a similar note, Boda also contends that, "The condition of disorientation does not endure forever, and when it is resolved and the supplicant experiences salvation, a new form of prayer is employed: the prayer of reorientation – that is, the prayer thanking God for salvation from distress."[90]

---

85. Westermann, *Praise and Lament*, 31.
86. Brueggemann, *Message of the Psalms*, 126.
87. Futato, *Interpreting the Psalms*, 158.
88. Futato, 158.
89. Longman, *Psalms*, 30–31; emphasis original.
90. Boda, "Prayer," 807.

Far from being the case, however, it is observed that the context of the situation at hand in 2 Chronicles 20:21–22a is *not* new orientation or reorientation but rather *disorientation*, for God is *yet* to act favorably on behalf of the supplicant(s) effecting divine victory. Nonetheless, the supplicant(s), amidst disorientation, explodes in doxological thanksgiving praise to Yahweh. Which is to say that the situation is still one of distress wherein Yahweh's salvific intervention is yet forthcoming. Contrary to Brueggemann then, it is not on the other side of, but rather *inside* of disorientation that such jubilant thanksgiving praise surges from the heart and through the lips of Yahweh's disoriented people. Even if there is an oracle of salvation from, for example, a priestly voice such as Jahaziel (vv. 14–17)[91] that foreshadows imminent divine deliverance, Yahweh has not yet fully and favorably answered the supplicant(s) in DS6 thanksgiving praise prayers; the prayer is yet to be answered completely on the battlefield when Yahweh effects victory on behalf of his covenant supplicant(s) for the sake of his great Name. Through a priestly voice, Yahweh evidently commits himself to acting favorably on behalf of the supplicant(s) who eagerly anticipates Yahweh making good on his promise of victory on their behalf. Yahweh thus becomes the object of the optimistic supplicant's jubilant thanksgiving praise even amidst disorientation because the supplicant is fully assured that Yahweh will be faithful to his promise (see also Josh 21:45; 23:14; Jer 1:12). In other words, "Praise is the sublime practice of trust. God's people sing praise with joy, not because all has gone their way, but because they are practicing imaginative hope and trust"[92] in the God who alone always honors his promise, and thus honors his holy covenant name, Yahweh.

---

91. See also 1 Sam 1:17 where Eli offers a priestly word of salvation to Hannah, which in effect assures Hannah that God has heard her vow and has already begun the process of answering her favorably, that is, he will make good on his promise to bless her with the child of her vowing (v. 11). However, the reason that Eli's priestly word of salvation from infertility to Hannah is excluded in this section of DS6 Thanksgiving Praise is because Hannah's thanksgiving praise to Yahweh God only erupts *after* the boy Samuel has been weaned and presented to God in the house of Yahweh at Shiloh (in 1 Sam 2:1–10). Which is to say that since Hannah's thanksgiving praise to God did not arise in the very context of her still *not* being with child while eagerly anticipating Yahweh's faithfulness to his promise to her on account of Eli's priestly word of salvation from infecundity, it cannot be considered as DS6 Thanksgiving Praise Prayer. Hannah's praise thus occurs in a situation of new orientation. Nevertheless, 1 Sam 1:17 does offer an example of a priestly word of salvation through the mouth of God's servant, Eli.

92. Pemberton, *After Lament*, 88.

DS6 thanksgiving praise prayers can thus be described as those prayers that arise out of a situation of disorientation, the content of which is joyful thanksgiving praise, even in full assurance of the actualization of Yahweh's deliverance in favor of his disoriented covenant people. Located not within a context of orientation nor new orientation or reorientation, as is typically the case, but rather amidst a context of disorientation, a DS6 thanksgiving praise prayer might be followed by a priestly word of divine deliverance, yet it nevertheless awaits a visibly manifested favorable answer from Yahweh. Owing therefore to a promise of imminent salvation through Yahweh's priestly messenger (which might then contribute to a positive outlook or perspective on life as Boda suggests), DS6 thanksgiving praise prayers go a step further than DS5 vow prayers, and thus lift an extolling voice of jubilant thanksgiving praise to Yahweh, even in the intermission of an oracle of salvation and its subsequent fulfillment, which is still nonetheless, a context of disorientation.

4.5.2. Summary

By way of recapitulation, in this section, a lacuna in prayers of disorientation within the prosaic sections of the OT (Genesis to Esther) is addressed and filled. Whereas in previous scholarship on prayers of disorientation only *two* stages (as proposed by Boda) were said to be extant, this section has demonstrated the possibility of *six* stages or subcategories bearing the following nomenclatures:

- Disorientation Stage 1 Verbal Expressions: DS1 Lament Prayers
- Disorientation Stage 2 Verbal Expressions: DS2 Imprecatory Prayers
- Disorientation Stage 3 Verbal Expressions: DS3 Vow Prayers
- Disorientation Stage 4 Verbal Expressions: DS4 Penitential Prayers
- Disorientation Stage 5 Verbal Expressions: DS5 Confidence Prayers
- Disorientation Stage 6 Verbal Expressions: DS6 Thanksgiving Praise Prayers

These six subcategories of disorientation prayers range from *lament* (consisting of either words, or at times, groans, and wailing or weeping) to *thanksgiving praise*. Whereas *thanksgiving praise* was said to be located only within a context of new orientation, that is, after God's intervention and deliverance, here it is observed *also* within a context of disorientation. Interestingly, *imprecation* was never considered as a subcategory of prayer uttered within a context of disorientation. At the same time, whereas the *vow* was associated with both *confidence* and *penitence*, here it appears to have no such relationship.

DS1 Negative / Sorrowful	DS2	DS3	DS4	DS5	DS6 Positive / Joyful

Considered along a continuum, disorientation prayers move from a language of negativity (sorrowful) to a language of positivity (joyful). This movement appears to depend on the outlook or perspective of the disoriented supplicant, a key player being that of a priestly or prophetic word of salvation from Yahweh when it comes to disorientation language located to the right of the continuum. At the two ends of the continuum, one finds the first language of disorientation, DS1 lament prayers, positioned at the negative end, and the final language of disorientation, DS6 thanksgiving praise prayers, positioned at the positive end of the continuum. Following closely behind DS1 lament prayers is the second language of disorientation, DS2 imprecatory prayers, which encompass both explicit and implicit vocabulary for divine judgment. The third language of disorientation, DS3 vow prayers, comprise a vow to God aimed at motivating his favorable answer. In DS1 lament prayers, DS2 imprecatory prayers, and DS3 vow prayers, the disorientation lies outside of the disoriented supplicant. However, with the introduction of the fourth language of disorientation, DS4 penitential prayers, positioned in the middle of the continuum, a shift appears to take place in that the disoriented supplicant recognizes that the disorientation falls *within* them, and Yahweh is thus petitioned for deliverance in the form of forgiveness. The sequence then continues with the fifth language of disorientation, DS5 confidence prayers, which is then followed by the sixth and final language of disorientation, DS6 thanksgiving praise prayers. But whereas the fifth language of disorientation, DS5 confidence prayers, only anticipates Yahweh's forthcoming deliverance, the sixth and final language of disorientation, DS6 thanksgiving praise prayers, anticipate *and* celebrate Yahweh's character and deliverance even *prior to* the realization of Yahweh's favorable answer, owing to a joyful outlook mediated through a prophet or a priest, who delivers Yahweh's word, which will not return void.

It is worth mentioning here, however, that this continuum is not constructed to prove that the order of the languages of disorientation *always* move from DS1 lament prayers to DS6 thanksgiving praise prayers. At the same time, the order of the languages of disorientation from DS1 lament prayers to DS6 thanksgiving praise prayers in no way accentuate any on the continuum as being less or more important. Rather, this continuum simply serves to demonstrate that there are, at the very least, *six* languages of disorientation, in lieu of two, as was previously proposed. Further, room is left for the likelihood of any of these six languages of disorientation to occur coevally. Any attempt to fit these six languages of disorientation into a *rigid* movement from DS1 lament prayers to DS6 thanksgiving praise prayers, without leaving room for other movements, should thus be avoided. Below is a table showcasing the six subcategories of disorientation prayers and their description.

Categories	Description
Disorientation Stage 1 Verbal Expressions: DS1 Lament Prayers	Prayers uttered within a context of disorientation at the heart of which is a cry for help; it is occasionally accompanied by the stinging lament question of "Why?" or even simply groans, and sometimes wailing or weeping.
Disorientation Stage 2 Verbal Expressions: DS2 Imprecatory Prayers	Prayers uttered within a context of disorientation that call for a divine judgment or curse upon one's enemies.
Disorientation Stage 3 Verbal Expressions: DS3 Vow Prayers	Prayers uttered within a context of disorientation wherein a promise is made to God that is predicated on a favorable answer from him, that is, "If . . . then."
Disorientation Stage 4 Verbal Expressions: DS4 Penitential Prayers	Prayers uttered within a context of disorientation the content of which is penitence over one's (in)direct sins.

Categories	Description
Disorientation Stage 5 Verbal Expressions: DS5 Confidence Prayers	Prayers uttered within a context of disorientation in confident anticipation of God's readiness to answer favorably, something of which has been (in)directly disclosed to the supplicant.
Disorientation Stage 6 Verbal Expressions: DS6 Thanksgiving Praise Prayers	Prayers uttered within a context of disorientation the content of which is jubilant thanksgiving praise in full assurance of God's imminent salvation declared to the supplicant by the agency of a priestly or prophetic oracle.

4.5.3. Other Verbal Expressions Communicated to/before God and Humans

Having concluded our analysis on the development of these six subcategories of anthropological expressions of disorientation prosaic prayers of the OT (Genesis to Esther), we will now attempt a survey of other verbal expressions communicated to/before God and humans amidst disorientation. Particular attention is given here to verbal expressions amidst the death of a leading Israelite. The importance of including such verbal expressions can be heard once more in Olyan's words:

> Biblical representations of mourning the dead employ a distinct and particular vocabulary of mourning which is *also* used by other biblical texts to describe the ritual activity of petitioners and others who do not mourn the dead. In other words, the texts narrating the mourning rites of penitents, humiliated individuals, and persons seeking a divine revelation, among others, do not use a different vocabulary to describe their behaviour; rather, they utilize the vocabulary of mourning the dead.[93]

This thus necessitates viewing the vocabulary employed in death-related verbal expressions of disorientation as the prototypical vocabulary employed for non-death-related verbal expressions of disorientation to/before God and

---

93. Olyan, *Biblical Mourning*, 19; emphasis mine.

humans. Put differently, "Mourning the dead is, in other words, the model for other types of mourning."[94] In view of this, attention is now given to such death-related verbal expressions, not only because of the need to examine the full spectrum of verbal expressions amidst disorientation, but also because of the key role such verbal expressions will play in the dialectic correlation with other death-related vocabulary garnered from within both a Guyanese-Canadian and Vietnamese-Canadian culture.

4.5.3.1. Contrition and/or Confession

Observing his sister Miriam's skin breaking out in leprosy owing to her displeasure over Moses' Cushite wife (Num 12:1–10), Aaron intercedes on her behalf before Moses, saying, "Oh my lord, I beg you, do not account this sin to us, in which we have acted foolishly and in which we have sinned. Oh, do not let her be like one dead, whose flesh is half eaten away when he comes from his mother's womb!" (12:11–12). Hearing this cry, Moses goes before God and intercedes for his older sister, saying, "O God, heal her, I pray!" (12:13). Such a DS1 lament prayer, however, is met by, "But the LORD said to Moses, 'If her father had but spit in her face, would she not bear her shame for seven days? Let her be shut up for seven days outside the camp, and afterward she may be received again'" (12:14). "So Miriam was shut up outside the camp for seven days, and the people did not move on until Miriam was received again" (12:15).

The second occurrence of contrition is uttered by Achan as he says to Joshua, "Truly, I have sinned against the LORD, the God of Israel, and this is what I did: when I saw among the spoil a beautiful mantle from Shinar and two hundred shekels of silver and a bar of gold fifty shekels in weight, then I coveted them and took them; and behold, they are concealed in the earth inside my tent with the silver underneath it" (Josh 7:20–21). On account of his public confession, Achan indeed tells the truth and glorifies God.[95] Achan's declaration of guilt is nevertheless offered in the context of Joshua's DS1 lament prayer (7:7–9).

---

94. Olyan, 24.
95. Howard, *Joshua*, 197.

4.5.3.2. *Curse*

Only at the battle of Ai, during which Israel endured the casualties of thirty-six of their soldiers, do Joshua and the children of Israel discover Achan's sin, the very grounds for the deaths of the soldiers. Upon realizing his sin of coveting several items from the spoils of Jericho, items that were considered under the ban (חֵרֶם; Josh 7:1), things that were to be returned to the LORD because they belonged to him,[96] Joshua pronounces this curse on Achan: "Why have you troubled us? The LORD will trouble you this day" (7:25a).[97] Joshua's inquiry posed to Achan, according to David M. Howard, "is turned on its head by his next statement, an assertion that the Lord would bring trouble on Achan. Joshua used the same word for 'bringing trouble' here ('kr) that he had earlier used in warning the people against taking the devoted items, since doing so would bring trouble ('kr) on the entire camp (6:18)."[98] This curse was in keeping with the words of Yahweh spoken earlier to Joshua: "It shall be that the one who is taken with the things under the ban shall be burned with fire, he and all that belongs to him, because he has transgressed the covenant of the LORD, and because he has committed a disgraceful thing in Israel" (7:15). Of import here is the fact that Joshua's curse upon Achan is pronounced in the context of Joshua's DS1 lament prayer to God (7:7–9).

That Joshua curses Achan, however, should not be taken as "vindictiveness. Joshua acts in keeping with the divine command (v. 15); and God, the God of the covenant, acts in keeping with the covenant (cf. Ezek 16:59). A violation of the covenant causes covenant retribution. Physical death as punishment for sin was given prominence in OT times. This shows God's displeasure with sin."[99] Knowing that the spoils of war are considered holy to God and are thus to be wholly devoted to Yahweh (Josh 6:19), it is worth noting that, "If they are brought into the camp they contaminate the entire camp, so that it must be sanctified, made holy (7:13). Anyone who had come into contact with the goods was contaminated and had to be removed from that community

---

96. Hess, "Joshua," 36.

97. Among the coveted and stolen items are a beautiful mantle from Shinar, two hundred shekels of silver, and a bar of gold weighing fifty shekels, which Achan conceals in the earth of his tent with the silver underneath it (Josh 7:20).

98. Howard, *Joshua*, 198; "Ironically – and tragically – for Achan, God allowed the Israelites to take booty in the next victory, at the second battle of Ai (8:2). He could have had anything he wanted if he had only waited on God" (198).

99. Woudstra, *Book of Joshua*, 131.

to protect the community."[100] Achan and his family are thus removed from the community of God's covenant people who are called to be holy even as Yahweh their God is holy (see: Exod 19:5–6; Lev 11:44–45; 19:2; 20:7, 26).

Part of Achan's trouble from Yahweh thus involves the employment of Joshua and all Israel as his judicial instruments for exacting punishment upon Achan and all that belongs to him, including the things devoted to Yahweh, after which they stone and burn them, at a place they name the valley of Achor (7:25b–26). Robert L. Hubbard perceives that, "Even at the time the author wrote ('to this day'), people still called the spot 'Trouble Valley.' But Joshua's wordplay (v. 25) makes this particular heap a monument to 'double trouble' – the trouble that Achan caused Israel (i.e. defeat at Ai), and the trouble that Yahweh caused him (i.e. his execution)."[101] Put another way, "the stone heap at Trouble Valley forewarns 'potential Achans' within Israel's ranks to practice the fear of God by doing what he commands."[102]

4.5.3.3. Instructions (Assassination; Burying; Embalming; Holiness; For a Woman on Returning Home and Remarrying; and Transporting Cadaver for Burial)

4.5.3.3a. Instruction on Assassination

Second Samuel 4 records the assassination of Ish-bosheth the son of Saul at the hands of Rechab and Baanah, the sons of Rimmon the Beerothite (vv. 5–7). Thinking that they were doing something good in bringing the head of Ish-bosheth to him (v. 8), David, however, informs them of meeting the same fate.

> As the LORD lives, who has redeemed my life from all distress, when one told me, saying, "Behold, Saul is dead," and thought he was bringing good news, I seized him and killed him in Ziklag, which was the reward I gave him for *his* news. How much more, when wicked men have killed a righteous man in his own house on his bed, shall I not now require his blood from your hand and destroy you from the earth? (vv. 9–11)

---

100. Butler, *Joshua*, 228.
101. Hubbard, *Joshua*, 229.
102. Hubbard, 230.

Such rhetorical questions are then followed by David's instruction to assassinate Rechab and Baanah. "Then David commanded the young men and they killed them and cut off their hands and feet and hung them up beside the pool in Hebron. But they took the head of Ish-bosheth and buried it in the grave of Abner in Hebron (v. 12). David T. Tsumura notes that, "Unlike the case of Joab, there is no problem with executing the killers of Ishbosheth."[103] Bergen, however, adds that,

> David had rendered his judgment on Recab and Baanah; now it was time to act. To express the fact that Recab and Baanah died under divine curse (cf. Deut 21:22–23), David has his men "cut off their hands and feet" and then hang "the bodies by the pool in Hebron." By contrast, David showed respect for his murdered brother-in-law by burying Ish-Bosheth's head 'in Abner's tomb in Hebron.'[104]

While Ish-bosheth is given a proper burial, a burial of dignity, the cadavers of Rechab and Baanah are left publicly exposed and unburied, and thus viewed as one of humanity's worst indignities.[105]

4.5.3.3b. Instructions on Burying

In 1 Kings 13:31–32, an old prophet in Bethel instructs his sons as follows: "When I die, bury me in the grave in which the man of God is buried; lay my bones beside his [the man of God from Judah] bones." DeVries posits that in giving such an instruction to his sons, "The apparent reason is that he wishes to be sanctified in his death through contact with one who has proven to be holy."[106] As an alternative perspective, Paul R. House states that, "It is as if the old prophet has been on a quest to find a real word from God or as if he set out to be the personal tester of the man of God. Whatever his motives, and it is impossible to know them for sure, the old man is a mixture of curiosity, dishonesty, accuracy, and conviction."[107] For Mordechai Coogan,

---

103. Tsumura, *Second Samuel*, 92.
104. Bergen, *1, 2 Samuel*, 318.
105. Miller, "Funeral Customs," 821.
106. Simon DeVries, *1 Kings*, 171.
107. House, *1, 2 Kings*, 189.

however, such a burial instruction would mean that "it would be impossible to distinguish bone from bone."[108]

Whether or not the old Bethelite prophet's wish materializes, however, is not exactly known to the reader. What *is* known is that after Josiah inquires about the monument in Bethel, the men of the city inform him that "It is the grave of the man of God who came from Judah." (2 Kgs 23:17). The fact that no mention of the Bethelite prophet is made might thus suggest that the sons of the prophet had perhaps buried their father elsewhere. Otherwise, the bones of the Bethelite prophet and those belonging to the man of Judah have become indistinguishable so that both are spared desecration. As August H. Konkel points out, "The bones of the prophet are spared, along with those of the old prophet from Bethel, described here as from the territory of Samaria."[109]

4.5.3.3c. Instructions on Embalming

Concerning an embalming instruction, we are told that upon the death of his father Jacob (Israel), "Joseph commanded his servants the physicians to embalm his father" (Gen 50:2). While there is no such instruction for himself, Joseph is also embalmed in Egypt (50:26). Apart from Jacob and Joseph, no other OT Israelite undergoes embalming. Within the ancient Near East, embalming thus appears to have been an Egyptian practice.[110] Theologically speaking, "Embalming served to preserve the body of the deceased, but in Egypt the reason for doing so involved a lot of theology. They preserved the body so that it could be reinhabited by the spirit (*ka*) in the afterlife."[111] John H. Walton nevertheless remarks that, "Nothing in the text suggests that Joseph or his family had adopted the complex afterlife theology of ancient Egypt with its emphasis on rituals, spells, and other sorts of magic."[112]

4.5.3.3d. Instructions on Holiness

Offering strange fire before Yahweh resulted in immediate death for Nadab and Abihu by the consuming fire of Yahweh (Lev 10:12). "On the very first day of Aaron's high-priestly ministry his two eldest sons died for infringing

---

108. Cogan, *1 Kings*, 372.
109. Konkel, *1 & 2 Kings*, 637.
110. For more details on embalming, see Fisher, "Burial, Burial Customs," 388.
111. Walton, "Genesis," 137.
112. Walton, 137.

God's law."[113] Yet, as Gordon J. Wenham points out, "It may be assumed that they had the right to offer incense."[114] The production of incense occurs "by mixing aromatic spices together, which was then vaporized by putting them in a censer containing glowing lumps of charcoal, i.e. fire. According to Lev 16:12, these coals had to be taken from the altar."[115] While Wenham avers that "The reader would dearly love to know the precise nature of their sin," he also acknowledges, "What really mattered is stated next: it was fire *which he had not commanded them*."[116] Jacob Milgrom, however, posits that,

> The nature of Nadab and Abihu's sin is contained in the words "unauthorized coals" (*ēš zārâ*). The adjective *zārâ* "unauthorized" provides the clue. In contrast to Kora[h]'s incense offering, which was rejected because he was an *'îš zār* "an unauthorized person" (Num 17:5), Nadab and Abihu's incense offering was rejected because they utilized *ēš zārâ* "unauthorized coals."[117]

Milgrom further avers that, "Just as *qĕṭōret zārâ* 'unauthorized incense' (Exod 30:9, 39) means a composition other than that prescribed (Exod 30:34–36), so *ēš zārâ* 'unauthorized coals' implies that they were not the right kind." In other words, "This can only mean that instead of deriving from the outer altar (e.g., Lev 16:12; Num 17:11), the coals came from a source that was profane, or from outside, such as an oven."[118] Whatever the source may have been, however, the unauthorized coals ignite a strange fire, "which He had not commanded them" (Lev 10:1), thus resulting in the incineration of Nadab and Abihu.

Commenting on this tragic incident, Moses informs Aaron, saying, "It is what the LORD spoke, saying, 'By those who come near Me I will be treated as holy, and before all the people I will be honored'" (Lev 10:3). In other words, as Wenham points out, "Holiness (*qdsh*) is one of the great themes of Leviticus. The whole nation was called to be holy, but how much more responsibility rested on the priests whose duty was to perform the sanctifying

---

113. Wenham, *Book of Leviticus*, 153.
114. Wenham, 154.
115. Wenham, 155.
116. Wenham, 155; emphasis original.
117. Milgrom, *Leviticus 1–16*, 598; see also Wenham, *Leviticus*, 155.
118. Milgrom, 598.

rituals and to teach the people the way of holiness."[119] Nadab and Abihu's offering of strange fire unauthorized by Yahweh is thus an act of absolute defiance to their holy God. As priests of Yahweh, Nadab and Abihu should have known better than to administer their priestly duties before God whose eyes are "too pure to approve evil" (Hab 1:13). In Yahweh's holy presence, sin is not to be tolerated (Pss 5:5 [4]; 101:3–8; Isa 6:1–5; Hos 9:15).

Moses then gives this instruction to Aaron and his sons Eleazar and Ithamar: "Do not uncover your heads nor tear your clothes, so that you will not die and that He will not become wrathful against all the congregation. . . . You shall not even go out from the doorway of the tent of meeting, or you will die; for the LORD's anointing oil is upon you" (Lev 10:6–7). Aaron, Eleazar, and Ithamar are thus proscribed from joining "the customary rites of mourning."[120] While it is true that, "This rule normally applied just to the high priest (Lev 21:10); here it is extended to his sons as well. It is not explained why Eleazar and Ithamar could not join in mourning their brothers' deaths."[121] Wenham, however, conjectures that "Perhaps it was because Nadab and Abihu had not suffered a natural death, but a direct judgment from God. The surviving priests, even though they were brothers, had to identify themselves entirely with God's viewpoint and not arouse any suspicion that they condoned their brothers' sins."[122] Wenham further suggests, "Had they joined in the traditional customs of tearing their clothes, they might have been tempted in their grief to blame God for their brothers' deaths." Indeed, as Wenham observes, "Rare are men like Job, who can mourn the loss of relatives and praise God at one and the same time (Job 1:20–21)."[123] Furthermore, Moses commands Aaron,

> Do not drink wine or strong drink, neither you nor your sons with you, when you come into the tent of meeting, so that you will not die – it is a perpetual statute throughout your generations – and so as to make a distinction between the holy and the profane, and between the unclean and the clean, and so as

---

119. Wenham, *Book of Leviticus*, 155–156.
120. Wenham, 157.
121. Wenham, 157.
122. Wenham, 157.
123. Wenham, 157.

to teach the sons of Israel all the statutes which the LORD has spoken to them through Moses (Lev 10:8–11).

Thunderstruck by what has just transpired, these three priests instantaneously lose their appetite (though, of course, the goat of the sin offering had already been consumed by the fire of Yahweh [v. 16]). Yet, obediently, they remain silent at their post and continue to perform their priestly duties. Otherwise, they too could expect to feel the heat of Yahweh's consuming fire.

Interestingly enough, Yahweh issues a similar prohibition to Ezekiel upon the death of his wife: "Son of man, behold, I am about to take from you the desire of your eyes with a blow; but you shall not mourn and you shall not weep, and your tears shall not come. Groan silently; make no mourning for the dead" (24:16–17). In this case, his actions are to serve as a sign of what is to come from Yahweh upon the house of Israel (24:24). But as a priest himself (1:3), Ezekiel, as well as Aaron, Eleazar, and Ithamar, are acquainted with God's instructions for his appointed priests who serve before him. As long as the anointing oil is poured upon their heads and they are clothed in consecrated garments, they are prohibited from uncovering their heads, tearing their clothes, and approaching any dead person. Any such actions would only serve to defile them, and even worse, profane Yahweh's holy sanctuary (Lev 21:10–12). Since Yahweh is holy, his sanctuary, is to be treated as holy (21:3, 6). Therefore, any contact with and mourning for the dead while still wearing the anointed oil and priestly garments would mean that they are to be considered unclean and thus deserving of Yahweh's consuming fire. To avoid the thought of viewing Yahweh as sadistic, however, outside of performing their priestly duties without the anointing oil and priestly garments, mourning and defilement of themselves for their relatives is most certainly *permissible* (21:1–2), with the exception of the high priest, of course.[124]

Further to the verbal expression of instruction on holiness, in Numbers 16:36–38, Moses instructs Eleazar, the son of Aaron, the priest, to scatter the burning coals abroad, but to take up the censers out of the midst of the blaze, for they are holy; and hammer them into sheets for a plating of the altar, so that they might serve as a sign to the sons of Israel. The context of such an instruction comes in the wake of the consuming fire that devoured some

---

124. Cf. Fisher, "Burial, Burial Customs," 388.

two hundred and fifty rebellious men of Israel who opposed Moses the man of God. Korah, Dathan, and Abiram had risen up against Moses and said to him, "You have gone far enough, for all the congregation are holy, every one of them, and the LORD is in their midst; so why do you exalt yourselves above the assembly of the LORD?" (16:1–3). In humility, Moses falls on his face to the ground and then speaks to Korah and his company of men, "Take censers for yourselves, . . . and put fire in them, and lay incense upon them in the presence of the LORD tomorrow; and the man whom the LORD chooses shall be the one who is holy" (16:6–7). The next morning the earth opens its mouth and swallows up all the men belonging to Korah with their families and possessions (16:31–33). Korah's sons would survive the earthquake and supernatural burial (26:6). Next comes fire from Yahweh, which consumes the two hundred and fifty men who are offering the incense (16:35). Milgrom observes that while "Nadab and Abihu, died a similar death, when they also offered incense (Lev 10:1–2), their sins were nonetheless different. They were legitimate priests who offered illegitimate incense (strange fire). The 250 chieftains were illegitimate aspirants for the priesthood whose offering was legitimate."[125]

Eleazar is then tasked with the responsibility of taking up the censers out of the midst of the blaze and charred bodies, for they are holy to Yahweh. Then he is to scatter the burning coals abroad (16:36–37). "The coals from the collected censers were scattered outside the camp so as to not render others impure by contact with the remnants of the dead."[126] The censers are then to be hammered out as a plating for the altar serving as a constant reminder that no lay person is allowed to burn incense before Yahweh (16:40). Which means that, "Each of the 250 censers were hammered into thin sheets of bronze and then molded by hammer to the shape of the altar."[127]

4.5.3.3e. Instructions for a Woman on Returning Home and Remarrying

The first instruction of a woman to return home is recorded in Genesis 38 and occurs between Tamar and her father-in-law Judah. This instruction comes

---

125. Milgrom, *Numbers*, 138.
126. Cole, *Numbers*, 271.
127. Cole, 270.

on the heels of the deaths of Tamar's first and second husbands. On account of their rebellious act before Yahweh, both of her husbands die rapidly, their tragic deaths being a direct consequence of their sin against Tamar, and more so, Yahweh. "Then Judah said to his daughter-in-law Tamar, 'Remain a widow in your father's house until my son Shelah grows up'" (38:11a). The impetus behind such an instruction is heard in the following words: "For he [Judah] thought, 'I am afraid that he [Shelah] too may die like his brothers.'" Victor P. Hamilton comments that, "Judah's concern is not with Tamar but with his surviving son (v. 11b). Perhaps, thinks Judah, the fate of Er and Onan will overcome Shelah as well."[128] Which implies that "Judah is in danger of becoming like Er his firstborn – married, but with no male descendants. Judah does what he thinks is necessary to prevent the possibility. He declares Shelah ineligible, and he dismisses Tamar."[129]

Giving heed to her father-in-law's comforting instruction, "Tamar went and lived in her father's house" (38:11b). By complying with her father-in-law's instruction, "It remains in the balance whether Tamar will get her right; this seems to depend on Judah as hitherto it is he alone who has made all the decisions as father of the family,"[130] as Westermann remarks. As the narrative progresses, we discover that after Tamar realizes that she has been duped by her father-in-law, she returns the favor and dupes Judah (38:12–26). "The real action begins with Tamar seizing the initiative; she herself procures her right to have a son from her husband's family (vv. 12–23)." In coming to this realization, however, "Judah concedes the justice of her headstrong conduct (vv. 24–26)."[131] Which is to say that "Ironically, in trying to cover a small disgrace he was unaware that a much greater disgrace was being exposed – his disregard of levirate marriage [Deut 25:5–10]. Tamar thwarted Judah's attempt to pay his small pledge because she had been thwarted by his failure to keep his pledge of marriage to his youngest son."[132]

The second instruction of returning home is uttered by Naomi to her daughters-in-law, Ruth and Orpah: "Go, return each of you to her mother's

---

128. Hamilton, *Book of Genesis*, 437.

129. Hamilton, 437.

130. Westermann, *Genesis 37–50*, 52.

131. Westermann, 52.

132. Hartley, *Genesis*, 317.

house. May the LORD deal kindly with you as you have dealt with the dead and with me. May the LORD grant that you may find rest, each in the house of her husband" (Ruth 1:8–9). That Naomi instructs her two daughters-in-law to return to their mother's house "is surprising since widows normally returned to their 'father's house' (Tamar, Gen 38:11; cf. Lev 22:12; Num 30:17; Deut 22:21; Judg 19:2, 3)."[133] Observing that the phrase "occurs in contexts having to do with love and marriage," Hubbard avows that, "It seems likely, then, that Naomi here referred to some custom according to which the 'mother's house' – probably her bedroom, not a separate building – was the place where marriages were arranged."[134] Being young widows, Naomi therefore wishes both of her daughters-in-law well, that is, that they would remarry and be taken care of by their potentially new husbands in Moab.

More than this, "Naomi specifically sought *ḥeseḏ* for Orpah and Ruth from Yahweh . . . In this context, the kindness toward Naomi probably refers to their actions since their husbands died (v. 5). Though those deaths severed their social ties with Naomi, Orpah and Ruth had voluntarily stayed with her, indeed, even choosing to leave their own country to care for her in hers."[135] What is more, "As for their kindness to the dead, Naomi probably meant that their kindness to her in some unspecified way benefitted the dead; that is, loyalty to her was loyalty to the dead and vice versa. . . . In this case, human kindness has earned the possibility (even likelihood) of a God-given reward."[136]

Interestingly, while nothing else is known of Orpah who returns to Moab, supposedly to her mother's house, and even to her people and gods (1:15), Ruth travels to Bethlehem with Naomi, where she finds another Israelite man, Boaz, whom she marries. Boaz then becomes the father of Obed, who fathers Jesse, who fathers David, who thus becomes the paragon forebearer of Yahweh God in human form – the Lord Jesus Christ (4:1–21; cf. Matt 1:5–17).

---

133. Hubbard, *Ruth*, 102. The phrase of "mother's house" in lieu of father's house, has led LaCocque (*Ruth*, 43–51) to view the book of Ruth (along with Song of Songs) as being penned by a woman (44).

134. Hubbard, 102–103.

135. Hubbard, 104.

136. Hubbard, 104.

4.5.3.3f. Instructions on Transporting Cadaver for Burial

In regard to instructions on transporting the body of the deceased for burial, the first example comes from the mouth of Jacob (Israel) to his sons while in Egypt. In Genesis 49:29–30 we read, "I am about to be gathered to my people; bury me with my fathers in the cave that is in the field of Ephron the Hittite, in the cave that is in the field of Machpelah, which is before Mamre, in the land of Canaan, which Abraham bought along with the field from Ephron the Hittite for a burial site." Hamilton observes that, "Jacob is as sharp on his control of family history (vv. 29–32) as he is on his control of his family prophecy (vv. 1–28). He is clear both about the distant future of his family and its descendants (vv. 1–28), and his own immediate future (vv. 28–33). In particular, Jacob's mention of the land of Canaan (v. 30) is significant."[137] What is this significance? "By now in the Joseph story this expression has become 'the trump card of the narrator, who uses this card to impress on his readers that Israel really has to settle in the land of Canaan and in no other country.'"[138]

A chapter later, just prior to his death, Joseph instructs his brothers, "I am about to die, but God will surely take care of you and bring you up from this land [Egypt] to the land which He promised on oath to Abraham, Isaac and to Jacob . . . and you shall carry my bones up from here" (50:24, 25). Then, subsequent to the death of Nadab and Abihu by God's hand, Moses calls Mishael and Elzaphan, the sons of Aaron's uncle Uzziel, and says, "Come forward, carry your relatives away from the front of the sanctuary to the outside of the camp" (Lev 10:4).

4.5.3.4. Interrogation and Rejoinder

For these two verbal expressions, interrogation and rejoinder, we return to Leviticus 10:1–20. The context is the death of Nabab and Abihu by means of the consuming fire of Yahweh owing to their offering of strange fire before him (10:1–2). Upon inquiring about the goat of the sin offering that Eleazar and Ithamar were commanded to eat, Moses' anger is evoked by learning that it was not ingested (10:16–18). This sin offering, however, is not to be confused with the sin offering of the people (9:15), of which the priests were

---

137. Hamilton, *Book of Genesis*, 689.

138. Hamilton, 689; internal quote taken from Lemche, *Canaanites and Their Land*, 112.

forbidden to eat (4:13–21). Here, however, the goat of the sin offering could be eaten by the priests. At the same time, while Aaron, Eleazar, and Ithamar are allowed to eat the goat of the sin offering, this should not be considered a meal that is usually consumed during mourning (Jer 16:7; Hos 9:4). This goat of the sin offering was part of the sacrificial meal that the priests are allowed to eat (cf. Lev 6:26).

Questioning Eleazar and Ithamar, Moses asks, "Why did you not eat the sin offering at the holy place? For it is most holy, and He gave it to you to bear away the guilt of the congregation, to make atonement for them before the LORD. Behold, since its blood had not been brought inside, into the sanctuary, you should certainly have eaten it in the sanctuary, just as I commanded" (10:16–17). As a rejoinder, and speaking on behalf of himself and his sons, Aaron says, "Behold, this very day they [Eleazar and Ithamar] presented their sin offering and their burnt offering before the LORD. When things like these happened to me, if I had eaten a sin offering today, would it have been good in the sight of the LORD?" (10:19). Wenham remarks that, "Given the circumstances, Aaron's fear of eating 'most holy' things such as the meat of the purification offering was understandable."[139]

Upon hearing this response from Aaron, Moses expresses a sense of satisfaction: "It seemed good in his sight" (10:20). Which is to say that, "perhaps, God is more gracious to those who make mistakes because they fear him than those who carelessly and impudently enter his presence, as Nadab and Abihu did (cf. vv. 1–3)."[140] But while the sin offering was not eaten by Eleazar and Ithamar, it was nevertheless consumed in the fire (Lev 10:16), most likely by the fire of Yahweh that consumed their brothers Nadab and Abihu (10:2). After all, the offerings presented to Yahweh by fire are designated as God's food (21:6).

Upon the death of his unnamed son, "David arose from the ground, washed himself, and changed his clothes; and he came into the house of the LORD and worshiped. Then he came to his own house, and when he requested, they set food before him and he ate" (2 Sam 12:20). Bewildered at such actions, David's servants ask, "What is this thing you have done? While the child was alive, you fasted and wept; but when the child died, you arose

---

139. Wenham, *Leviticus*, 160.
140. Wenham, 160.

and ate food" (12:21). To which David replies, "While the child was still alive, I fasted and wept; for I said, 'Who knows, the LORD may be gracious to me, that the child may live.' But now he has died; why should I fast? Can I bring him back again? I will go to him, but he will not return to me'" (12:22–23). In furnishing such a rejoinder to his interrogators, "We may catch a glimpse of the fact that David was a *realistic* monotheist, trusting on the only God for his mercy."[141] Which is another way of saying that "David, whose life found its focus and fundamental motivations in God, explained his actions theologically."[142] By implication,

> The child's death did not mean that God was unjust or unloving; on the contrary, it meant that the divine word spoken through the prophet [Nathan] was trustworthy (cf. v. 14) – a fact that must have provided a measure of comfort to the king. The Lord's word had not changed, and the Lord himself had not changed; divine grace was just as real after the death as it had been before. Therefore, now that the child was gone David could and must get on with his life. Though David was now bereft of his son, the separation would be only temporary. There is to be heard a note of consolation in David's words "I will go to him."[143]

In life and in death, Yahweh gives and takes away, and thus he can be trusted and blessed, that is, worshiped (Job 1:21; 2 Sam 12:20).

Perhaps a bit more detail should be included here in light of the ongoing debate with regards to David's reactions. On the one hand, there are some readers who view David's countercultural reactions, as David A. Bosworth observes, "as wise, pious, and exemplary," while on the other hand, there are some readers who "find in this passage evidence of David's callous indifference to others and narcissistic concern for himself."[144] This bewilderment can be heard in the words of Bill T. Arnold who notes that, "The episode of the child's death and David's reversal of conventional mourning customs leaves interpreters perplexed (12:15–23)."[145] After all, in OT Israelite mourning cus-

---

141. Tsumura, *Second Samuel*, 198; emphasis original.

142. Bergen, *1, 2 Samuel*, 376.

143. Bergen, 376.

144. Bosworth, "Faith and Resilience," 692.

145. Arnold, *1 & 2 Samuel*, 537.

tom, "The normal period of mourning lasted seven days (1 Sam 31:13; cf. Gen 50:10)." Taking that into consideration, Arnold therefore makes the case that, "Since David assumes an attitude of mourning while he prays for the sick boy, he has already fulfilled the customary period of mourning proleptically."[146] Which therefore suggests that "David's cheerfulness is not as heartless as it might seem to contemporary readers,"[147] as Mary J. Evans remarks. Reasoning from this perspective, it creates the impression that David is no longer obligated to mourn another seven days following the death of his unnamed son. But taking exception to such an assumption, A. A. Anderson opines that, "It is equally unlikely that David mourned for the child proleptically,"[148] which is also the perspective held by the researcher.

That being said, one does wonder if there is a better perspective on David's countercultural grief reactions. From what one can observe, David's reversal of conventional mourning customs exhibits every sign of David having left his state of mourning and either returning to a state of normalcy, or even to a state of joy. This is made clear from Gary A. Anderson's statement that, "This joyous state meant that the mourner had to bathe, put on fresh clothes and scented oil, eat and drink, and even (according to some) resume sexual relations."[149] By doing each of these (see 2 Sam 12:13–25), David's mourning had thus turned into joy.

Observing that, "Grief looks different in different people, and people cope with grief in many ways," Bosworth avers that, "some coping strategies prove better than others: locating supportive people is preferable to abusing drugs and alcohol."[150] Citing the work of George A. Bonanno et al., he goes on to state that whereas there is considerable variation in individual behavior, researchers have observed four grief trajectories:

i. Resilience (which involves little or no loss of function in work, relationships, and practical tasks of living).
ii. Recovery (which involves some loss of function for a period of time followed by a gradual recovery).

---

146. Arnold, 537.
147. Evans, *1 & 2 Samuel*, 190.
148. Anderson, *2 Samuel*, 164.
149. Anderson, *Time to Mourn*, 50.
150. Bosworth, "Understanding Grief," 118.

iii. Prolonged grief (which involves extended loss of function and lack of recovery).

iv. Delayed grief (which involves little or no loss of function initially, but symptoms of grief later, and then followed by a prolonged or recovery trajectory).[151]

On the basis of this research, Bosworth proposes that, "While one may read David as cold hearted, the recognition of resilience opens another possibility: David may experience a resilient grief trajectory that does not reflect monstrous callousness or unconcern for his baby."[152] Which is to say that, "David continues to exhibit a capacity to continue with his life more or less as normal in spite of trauma, loss, or other adversity that might be expected to result in significant dysfunction."[153]

Bosworth further specifies that since resilience is best understood as the result of a process rather than an innate trait, one could speak of David's dual pathways to resilience:

i. David's external pathways (which includes the cause of death, David's large family, and his place in an ancient society with high infant mortality).

ii. David's internal pathways (which includes David's sense of personal agency and trust in God).[154]

Although David's external pathways doubtless play a significant role in his resilience amidst grief, it is more so his internal pathways, primarily that of his faith in Yahweh his God, that makes him resilient in times of adversity.[155]

So, while it is acknowledged here that there is an ongoing debate over the normativity of David's attitude toward grief following the death of his unnamed son with Bathsheba, here I follow Bosworth in contending that David's countercultural behavior should be viewed as one of *resilience*. That is, David's reactions exhibit "the human capacity to deal with, overcome, learn from, or

---

151. Bosworth, 118; cf. Bonanno, "Trajectories of Grieving," 287–307.

152. Bosworth, 119.

153. Bosworth, "Faith and Resilience," 692.

154. Bosworth, 700.

155. Bosworth, 692–693.

even be transformed by the inevitable adversities of life."[156] For this reason, "David need not be judged so harshly by scholars or presented as a normative model to bereaved parents. The description of David's behavior seems to be used in the Bible to characterize David, not to tell other parents how to mourn."[157] This argument is maintained throughout this book as I continue to reflect on each of David's countercultural, yet resilient, grief reactions.

4.5.3.5. Lament (Weeping and Elegy)

At the death of his first wife, Abraham weeps for Sarah (Gen 23:2). On the occasion of Jacob's death, Joseph and the Egyptians weep seventy days (Gen 50:1, 3). What is more, as the corpse of Jacob is being transported from Egypt to Israel, the funeral cortege (i.e. Joseph, all the servants of Pharaoh, the elders of his household, and the elders of the land of Egypt), pause for seven days at the threshing floor of Atad, which is beyond the Jordan, where they lament with a very great and sorrowful lamentation, and also mourn for Jacob (50:10). So great is this morning that the Canaanites say, "This is a grievous mourning for the Egyptians," for which reason the place is called Abel-mizraim (50:11). The longest recorded period of weeping in the OT is on behalf of the patriarch Jacob.

Moving to the priest, upon Aaron's death, the house of Israel weep thirty days for him (Num 20:29). Similarly, there is also a thirty-day period of weeping among the sons of Israel for the prophet Moses in the plains of Moab (Deut 34:8). And finally, at his death, David and the people with him weep for Abner (2 Sam 3:32).

According to Philip J. King and Lawrence E. Stager, "The announcement of death was followed by lamentation. . . . In addition to family members, professional mourners, generally women, were paid to lament during a funeral."[158] This is particularly observed in the words of Jeremiah: "Thus says the LORD of hosts, 'Consider and call for the mourning women, that they may come; and send for the wailing women, that they may come'" (9:17).

---

156. Luthar and Zelazo, "Research and Resilience," 513; cf. Bosworth, "Faith and Resilience," 697.

157. Bosworth, "Understanding Grief," 119; cf. Bosworth, "Faith and Resilience," 691–707.

158. King and Stager, *Life in Biblical Israel*, 372–373.

Laments, however, do not only constitute wailing and weeping, but can also include elegies, i.e. mournful songs. Amidst grief, five elegiac laments are located within the parameters of Genesis and Esther: three from David, one from an old prophet living in Bethel, and one from Jeremiah.

With regards to David's elegiac laments, the first and longest one is sung on the occasion of the death of Saul and Jonathan (2 Sam 1:19–27), the lyrics being thus:

> Your beauty, O Israel, is slain on your high places!
>> How have the mighty fallen!
> Tell *it* not in Gath,
>> Proclaim it not in the streets of Ashkelon,
> Or the daughters of the Philistines will rejoice,
>> The daughters of the uncircumcised will exult.
> O mountains of Gilboa,
>> Let not dew or rain be on you, nor fields of offerings;
> For there the shield of the mighty was defiled,
>> The shield of Saul, not anointed with oil.
> From the blood of the slain, from the fat of the mighty,
>> The bow of Jonathan did not turn back,
> And the sword of Saul did not return empty.
>> Saul and Jonathan, beloved and pleasant in life,
> And in their death they were not parted;
>> They were swifter than eagles,
>> They were stronger than lions.
> O daughters of Israel, weep over Saul,
>> Who clothed you luxuriously in scarlet,
>> Who put ornaments of gold on your apparel.
> How have the mighty fallen in the midst of the battle!
>> Jonathan is slain on your high places.
> I am distressed for you, my brother Jonathan;
>> You have been very pleasant to me.
> Your love to me was more wonderful
>> Than the love of women.
> How have the mighty fallen,
>> And the weapons of war perished!

Titled "The Song of the Bow," and written in the book of Jashar, this elegy is to be taught to the sons of Judah (1:17–18).

David's second elegy is occasioned by the death of Abner, cousin of Saul and commander-in-chief of Saul's army. Recorded in 2 Sam 3:33–34, the lyrics are thus:

> Should Abner die as a fool dies?
> Your hands were not bound, nor your feet put in fetters;
> As one falls before the wicked, you have fallen.

Then upon the death of his son Absalom, David pens his third elegy, the lyrics being: "O my son Absalom, my son, my son Absalom! Would I had died instead of you, O Absalom, my son, my son!" (18:33). This elegy is echoed once more in the words, "O my son Absalom, O Absalom, my son, my son!" (19:4).

In 1 Kings 13:29–30, an old prophet living in Bethel buries the man of God from Judah in his own grave. While mourning his death, the old prophet expresses his sorrow through the following elegiac lament: "Alas, my brother!"

Occasioned by the death of Josiah, not only does Jeremiah chant an elegiac lament, but together with Jeremiah, all the male and female singers speak and write about Josiah in their lamentations (2 Chron 35:25). Unfortunately, all such elegies or lamentations are lost to the reader.

Milton C. Fisher avers that, "Immediately following a death in a home the entire neighborhood was alerted to the sad event by the wail that was suddenly raised."[159] Which is to say, as J. B. Payne remarks, "Death was announced by a shrill cry, followed by a tumult of lamentation (2 Sam 1:12; 18:33; cf. Mark 5:38)."[160] Whereas the wives of the deceased mourn by themselves (Zech 12:12–14), it is the professional mourners (Amos 5:16), consisting mainly of women (Jer 9:17), who "occupied a prominent place"[161] during mourning. Payne further avers that, "Weeping, so natural in itself (Jer. 9:18), was supplemented by cries of 'Alas, alas' (Amos 5:16), 'Alas, my brother' (1 Kgs 13:30; cf. Jer 22:18; 34:5), and similar phrases, until self-control vanished."[162] Not surprisingly, Douglas J. Miller notes that, "In ancient Israel, groups of

---

159. Fisher, "Burial, Burial Customs," 386.
160. Payne, "Burial," 556.
161. Payne, 557.
162. Payne, 557.

paid mourners emerged who could wail on ritual cue. Much of the funeral services centered around these professional mourners who sang psalms and delivered elaborate eulogies for the dead (2 Chron 35:25; Jer 9:17–22)."[163]

4.5.4. Categorization of Death-Related Words

Based on the preceding survey, death-related verbal expressions to humans can be categorized as such:

Category	Description
Disorientation Stage 7 Verbal Expressions (Death-Related): DS7 Bereavement Vocabulary	Vocabulary associated with death, inclusive of which are Contrition and/or Confession; Curse; Instructions (Assassination; Burying; Embalming; Holiness; Returning Home and Remarrying; and Transporting Cadaver for Burial); Interrogation and Rejoinder; and Lament (Weeping and Elegy).

4.5.5. Summary

In the immediate section above, we surveyed several verbal expressions that were both communicated to/before God and humans, with emphasis placed on the latter, especially amidst the death of a leading OT Israelite. As such, the domain of anthropological expressions has now been extended to include both non-death-related and death-related verbal expressions communicated to or before God and humans, some of which will play a key role in chapter 5 where such verbal expressions will engage in a dialectical correlation with the verbal expressions garnered in chapter 3.

Having concluded our examination of the verbal anthropological expressions of disorientation within the prosaic section of the OT (Genesis to Esther), we now attempt a survey of the physical expressions communicated to or before God and humans amidst disorientation, both death-related and non-death-related.

---

163. Miller, "Funeral Customs," 821.

4.6. Physical Anthropological Expressions of Disorientation

Here we recall the words of Corless et al., for our understanding of physical expressions "which are comprised of physical signs, bodily expressions, and sensual aspects such as seeing and hearing. The manner in which the head is held (body language) is an example of a physical response, as is weeping. Sobbing, sighing, sudden, intense emotion, or other somatic, physical responses typically occur without intention."[164] Though Corless et al., have included the physical and the emotional expressions together, the two will be separated for the purpose of engendering a threefold typology of anthropological expressions – verbal, physical, and emotional. Having previously deliberated on the verbal expressions, we now move to examine the physical expressions communicated to/before God amidst a situation of disorientation. This implies that the physical expressions that accompany grief in the context of the death of a leading Israelite will also be included in the discussion. The importance of including such physical expressions can once again be heard in Olyan's words:

> Biblical representations of mourning the dead employ a distinct and particular vocabulary of mourning which is also used by other biblical texts to describe the ritual activity of petitioners and others who do not mourn the dead. In other words, the texts narrating the mourning rites of penitents, humiliated individuals, and persons seeking a divine revelation, among others, do not use a different vocabulary to describe their behaviour; rather, they utilize the vocabulary of mourning the dead.[165]

---

164. Corless et al., "Languages of Grief," 136.

165. Olyan, *Biblical Mourning*, 19. According to Dan 4, Nebuchadnezzar suffers from a temporary divine judgment of insanity (possibly lycanthropy) owing to his egotistic superciliousness. At the end of seven years, however, and *while* still dwelling like a beast of the field, Nebuchadnezzar raises his eyes toward heaven, and his reason returns to him; after which he blesses the Most High and praises him who lives forever (4:34). It might not be farfetched to say that had he not raised his eyes toward heaven in an act of humility and dependence upon the sovereign Lord, his insanity might not have been reversed. Psalm 123:1[2] declares, "To You I lift up my eyes, O You who are enthroned in the heavens!" (see also Ps 141:9 [8]; cf. 121:2 [1]). But since Nebuchadnezzar is not an Israelite, his posture of looking heavenward will not be included in our discussion.

That said, attention is next given to the physical expressions communicated to/before God amidst disorientation, followed by the emotional expressions.

4.6.1a. Anointing Oneself

After the death of his unnamed son, David anoints himself (2 Sam 12:20). Such an expression, however, seems ill-suited for the context of mourning. This is especially so in light of the question David's servants directed at him: "What is this thing you have done? While the child was alive, you fasted and wept; but when the child died, you arose and ate food!" (12:21). The fact that mention is made of David rising and eating food serves as a merism for everything he did in between. For that reason, David's anointing should be understood as a physical expression included in the servants' statement of bewilderment. Proffering the significance to his countercultural expression, David responds by saying, "While the child was *still* alive, I fasted and wept; for I said, 'Who knows, the LORD may be gracious to me, that the child may live.' But now he has died; why should I fast? Can I bring him back again? I will go to him, but he will not return to me" (12:22–23). "There is a note of consolation to be heard in David's words 'I will go to him.'"[166]

Nevertheless, 2 Samuel 13–14 tells us that after Absalom avenged his sister Tamar by killing Amnon for violating her, and knowing that King David's heart was inclined toward Absalom, "Joab sent to Tekoa and brought a wise woman from there and said to her, 'Please pretend to be a mourner, and put on mourning garments now, and *do not anoint yourself with oil*, but be like a woman who has been mourning for the dead many days" (14:1–2 [cf. 13:1–39]; emphasis mine).

As noted earlier, however, the fact that David anoints himself is indicative of David having left his state of mourning and either returning to a state of normalcy, or even a state of joy. This countercultural joy comes into view in the wake of his resilient grief trajectory, which is primarily grounded in David's faith in Yahweh his God. It should be noted here once more that David's choice to anoint himself is only meant to characterize David, not to tell parents how to mourn.[167]

---

166. Bergen, *1, 2 Samuel*, 376.

167. See also the discussion regarding David's mourning in section 4.5.3.4 on pp. 109-113.

4.6.1b. Blowing (Silver) Trumpets

Just prior to the battle between Israel, led by King Jeroboam, and Judah under King Abijah, we are told that even though Jeroboam set an ambush behind Judah, "When Judah turned around, behold, they were attacked both front and rear; so they cried to the LORD, and the priests blew trumpets" (2 Chron 13:13–14).

Such an expression should be understood against the backdrop of the words of Yahweh in Numbers 10:9, where Moses instructs the people of Israel, saying, "When you go to war in your land against the adversary who attacks you, then you sound an alarm with the trumpets, that you may be remembered before the LORD your God, and be saved from your enemies."[168] Cole identifies two types of trumpets employed by the people of Israel.

> The silver trumpets are to be distinguished from the ram's horn in function as well as appearance. The ram's horn (*šopār*) announced the Day of Atonement throughout the land (Lev. 25:9) and was used in the marching around Jericho (Josh. 6:2–21). The bright pitch of the silver trumpet called the people to march through the wilderness and was blown by Phineas in the battle against Midian (Num 31:6).[169]

Within the context of 2 Chron 13:14, it was the חֲצֹצְרוֹת (*hatsotseroth*) or the silver trumpets, and not the שׁוֹפָר (*sophar*) or the ram's horn that are blown by the priests as a clarion call to Yahweh for the purpose of divine intervention and victory over Judah's enemies. Yet Philip J. Budd probes, "In what sense can he need reminding?"[170] To which he responds, "It may be that this is a way of expressing man's complete dependence on God. From the perspective of faith God can never be taken for granted or exploited."[171] On a slightly different note, however, Cole remarks, "In the context of battle, the

---

168. It is worth mentioning here that the coupling of the blowing of trumpets and raising a war cry, which might be understood as shouting with a great shout, also played a key role in the fall of the wall of Jericho. Josh 6:20 says, "So *the people shouted*, and *priests blew the trumpets*; and when the people heard the sound of the trumpet, the *people shouted with a great shout* and the wall fell down flat, so that the people went up into the city, every man straight ahead, and they took the city" (emphasis mine). The trumpets blown in Josh 6:20, however, differ from those blown in 2 Chron 13:14.

169. Cole, "Numbers," 353.

170. Budd, *Numbers*, 1984), 108. This question is in reference to Num 10:9.

171. Budd, 108.

trumpets served as a prayer by which the covenant relationship between God and Israel was invoked, and thus reminded soldiers that God remembers and delivers his people."[172] Likewise, Milgrom suggests that "The trumpet blasts serve as a prayer whose efficacy is recorded in the war between Abijah and Jeroboam (2 Chron 13:12–16)."[173]

On that note, it can be said that Yahweh's ears are so attuned to the blowing of the silver trumpets, that upon hearing them, he immediately rouses himself to action for divine battle on behalf of his human-covenant partners who, rather than rely on their military prowess, resolve to acknowledge their dire need of his supernatural intervention and deliverance. This ritual of blowing silver trumpets interestingly occurs within the disorientation context of Judah's DS1 lament prayer.

4.6.1c. Burning

After discovering the plunderer guilty of stealing some of the devoted things belonging to Yahweh in Jericho, Joshua and all Israel take Achan, the silver, the mantle, the bar of gold, his sons, his daughters, his oxen, his donkeys, his sheep, his tent, and all things belonging to him to the valley of Achor (Josh 7:16–24). Once there, all Israel stones Achan and all things belonging to him; next, Israel burns them with fire (7:25).

As specified in 1 Samuel 31:10–13, following the death of Saul and his three sons (Jonathan, Abinadab, and Malchi-shua) at the hands of the Philistines, all the valiant men of Jabesh-gilead arise and walk all night. Arriving at their destination, the men take the body of Saul and his three sons from the wall of Beth-shan where they have been fastened. Upon their return to Jabesh, the men burn Saul and his three sons.[174]

Burning the dead, however, was not a common mourning ritual practiced among the OT Israelites. Payne notes that, "In contrast to the Greeks and Romans, whose custom was to cremate the dead . . . the Jews 'bury rather than burn dead bodies.'"[175] And as observed by Fisher, "Cremation of the

---

172. Cole, *Numbers*, 163.

173. Milgrom, *Numbers*, 75.

174. Interestingly, upon hearing that his daughter-in-law Tamar is guilty of prostitution, Judah's immediate reaction is thus: "Bring her out and let her be burned" (Gen 38:24; cf. Lev 21:9).

175. Payne, "Burial," 556; quote taken from Tacitus, *Histories*, v. 5.

bodies of Saul and his sons (1 Sam 31:12, 13) was also an exception to normal practice. The Roman historian Tacitus wrote that in contrast with Roman custom, Jewish piety required burying rather than burning of dead bodies. Under Mosaic law such burning was reserved as a sentence of judgment (Lev 21:9; Josh 7:25)."[176]

4.6.1d. Burying (and Purchasing Land)

With regards to what is otherwise referred to as interment, it is not surprising to observe that burying was the most conventional mourning ritual practiced among OT Israelites. Both Sarah and Abraham are buried in the cave of the field at Machpelah facing Mamre (that is, Hebron) in the land of Canaan (Gen 23:19; 25:9–10). Subsequent to giving birth to her second son, Ben-oni, who is later renamed Benjamin by his father Jacob, Rachel suffers severe labor, dies, and is buried on the way to Ephrath (that is, Bethlehem) (35:19). Although 35:29 says that Esau and Jacob buried their father Isaac, the location of this burial is not furnished. Ten chapters later, however, we read that Isaac, Rebekah, and Leah are also buried alongside Abraham and Sarah in the cave of the field of Machpelah before Mamre (49:13). The field at Machpelah was acquired by Abraham from Ephron the son of Zohar the Hittite (cf. 50:13). Serving as a burial site, this prime piece of land cost Abraham four hundred shekels (23:1–16). Although his death occurred in Egypt, Joseph's bones are later buried at Shechem, in the piece of ground that Jacob had procured from the sons of Hamor the father of Shechem for one hundred pieces of money (Josh 24:32). This is in keeping with Joseph's final request to his brothers to bury him in the land promised to Abraham, Isaac, and Jacob (Gen 50:24, 25).

Numbers 11:31–35 tells us that after complaining and grumbling for meat, the children of Israel finally receive what their stomachs crave greedily. But this also comes at a heavy price. After consuming their quail, Yahweh's anger is kindled against them, the result of which is a severe plague breaking out among them. The bodies of those who die are then buried in Kibroth-hattaavah (i.e. graves of the greedy), named as such on the grounds of the greed of the people.

Miriam, the sister of Aaron and Moses dies and is buried in the wilderness of Zin (20:1). Later, Aaron dies on Mount Hor and is buried in Moserah

---

176. Fisher, "Burial, Burial Customs," 388.

(Num 33:38–39; Deut 10:6). Of all the characters of the OT, Moses is the only person who receives a *divine* burial (the land of Moab; Deut 34:5–6). Moses' protégé, Joshua son of Nun, is buried in Timnath-serah, the territory of his inheritance, which is in the hill country of Ephraim, on the north of Mount Gaash (Josh 24:29–30; cf. Judg 2:9). Eleazar the son of Aaron, is buried at Gibeah of Phineas his son, which was given him in the hill country of Ephraim (Josh 24:33).

Among the judges that ruled Israel, Gideon is buried in the tomb of his father Joash, in Ophrah of the Abiezrites (Judg 8:32), Tola the son of Puah is buried in Shamir (10:2), Jair the Gileadite is buried in Kamon (10:5), and Jephthah the Gileadite is buried in one of the cities of Gilead (12:7). While Ibzan is buried in Bethlehem (12:10), Elon the Zebulunite is buried at Aijalon in the land of Zebulun (12:12). After his death in the temple of Dagon of Philistia, Samson's brothers and all his father's household come down, take up his body, and bury him between Zorah and Eshtaol in the tomb of Manoah his father (16:30–31). Interestingly, the burial places of Othniel, Ehud, Shamgar, and Deborah, are unspecified within the OT.

Upon his death, Samuel is buried at his house in his own city of Ramah (1 Sam 25:1; 28:3). David's commander Joab is buried at his own house in the wilderness (1 Kgs 2:34). After the man of God from Judah is killed by a lion, the old prophet of Bethel places the body of the man of God on his donkey, brings him back to Bethel, and buries him in his grave (1 Kgs 13:29–31).

Several kings are buried in the city of David: David (1 Kgs 2:10), Solomon (11:43), Rehoboam (14:31), Abijah (15:8), Asa (15:24), Jehoshaphat (22:50), Jehoram (2 Kgs 8:24), Amaziah (14:20–22), Azariah/Uzziah who is buried in the field of the grave, belonging to the kings (15:7, 2 Chron 26:23), Jotham (2 Kgs 15:38), Rehoboam (2 Chron 12:16), and Hezekiah (32:33). From Nehemiah 3:16, we learn that there are tombs of David, which perhaps is a reference to the field of the grave belonging to the kings (2 Chron 26:23). Likewise, with regards to their northern counterparts, there are a handful of kings who sleep with their fathers and are buried in Samaria: Omri (1 Kgs 16:28), Ahab (22:37), Jehu (2 Kgs 10:35), Jehoahaz (13:9), Jehoash (13:13), and Ahaz (16:20).

Outside of the normal burial custom in either the city of David or Samaria, we read that Baasha sleeps with his fathers and is buried in Tirzah (1 Kgs 16:6). Manasseh is buried in the garden of his own house, which is also known as the garden of Uzza (2 Kgs 21:18; 2 Chron 33:20). Amon son of Manasseh is also buried in his grave in the garden of Uzza (2 Kgs 21:26). Josiah dies in Megiddo but is then buried in Jerusalem in his own tomb (23:30).

It is worth noting here that while the Bible does not afford the reader a comprehensive view of all the mourning rituals practiced by the OT Israelites, it nonetheless alludes to some of the prohibitions relating to death. Since the children of Israel are considered a people holy to Yahweh their God, such prohibitions included not cutting oneself, nor shaving one's head for the sake of the dead (Lev 19:27–28; 21:5–6; Deut 14:1–2), for such were the practices of the pagan nations surrounding them.[177]

Having said that, "Placing the corpse in the ground or in a cave was the principal method of disposing of the dead. One of the worst indignities was to be left unburied or become 'food for beasts of prey' (Deut 28:26; 1 Kgs 11:15). If possible the deceased were to be buried on the day of death."[178] As a matter of fact, "In the ancient Near East generally, burial occurred within twenty-four hours of death."[179]

On the grounds of the desire for, or actual, burial of so many OT Israelites near their departed family members, it is hardly surprising for Fisher to aver, "A society's burial customs are a reflection of its spiritual views about death and the afterlife. . . . The ancient Hebrews emphasized a more spiritual concept of union or fellowship of the departed with generations gone before."[180] This can be observed in such phrases as "you shall go to your fathers in peace" (Gen 15:15; cf. 1 Kgs 13:22), "gathered to his people" (Gen 25:8, 17; 49:33), or "I will go to him" (2 Sam 12:23).

---

177. Why this proscription might be heard in Olyan's (*Biblical Mourning*, 110–123) statement: "In a word, shaving and laceration have the potential to become markers 'out of place', visible tokens of mourning on the bodies of those who have abandoned the mourning ritual stance and shifted to a posture of rejoicing" (123). What is more, "Such a mixing of mourning and rejoicing practices in the same ritual actor would blur the distinction between mourner and non-mourner, thereby obscuring the boundaries that separate the distinct ritual states and posing a threat to the continuity of the ritual order" (123).

178. Miller, "Funeral Customs," 821.

179. Arnold, *Genesis*, 386.

180. Fisher, "Burial, Burial Customs," 388.

4.6.1e. Chambering (Privacy/Isolation)

Following the death of David's son Absalom, "The king was deeply moved and *went up to the chamber over the gate* and wept. And thus he said as he walked, 'O my son Absalom, my son, my son Absalom! Would I had died instead of you, O Absalom, my son, my son!'" (2 Sam 18:33; emphasis mine). V. Philips Long notes that, "City gates had numerous rooms where commercial, civic, or military affairs could be conducted. David's retreat to one of the rooms afforded him a place where he could weep in relative privacy."[181] What is more, "His withdrawal from his position sitting in the gate to one of the rooms of the gate tower reflects the fact that he is 'shaken' by the news of Absalom's death, as his anguished fivefold repetition of 'my son,' and threefold repetition 'Absalom' aptly capture."[182]

Overcome with inconsolable grief, David not only voices one of his recorded elegies (cf. 1:19–27; 3:33–34; 19:4), but also "seeks isolation from others,"[183] as he leaves his company of ashamed combatants (of him, that is) to mourn alone in private within his chamber over the gate, "ironically situated 'between the sky and the earth' (v. 9), the same position in which Absalom had died."[184] Whether ironically or not, David's movement "into deep mourning"[185] causes him to move away from his joyful compatriots and into isolation in the chamber over the gate where he could mourn the death of his son Absalom. That he moves into the chamber over the gate might be attributed to it being "the nearest place he could be private."[186] Regardless of his personal feelings of grief, the text suggests that of all people, David should know better than to mix the ritual of mourning within that of rejoicing. In a context now dominated by rejoicing owing to Absalom's annihilation, mourning is thus deemed incompatible.[187] It is worth mentioning here, however, that David is

---

181. Long, "2 Samuel," 471.

182. Long, 471.

183. Bergen, *1, 2 Samuel*, 425.

184. Bergen, 425.

185. Evans, *1, 2 Samuel*, 216.

186. Tsumura, *Second Samuel*, 268.

187. See also Neh 8:9–12 for another example of the incompatibility of mourning in a context of rejoicing. But see Isa 22:12–14 for an example of the incompatibility of rejoicing in a context of mourning. For more on this issue, see discussion on pp. 191-199.

coerced into grieving privately, rather than being allowed to grieve publicly (cf. Job 2:11–13; Ezra 9:1–3; Neh 9:1–4).

4.6.1f. Changing Clothes

On the heels of losing his unnamed son, David "changed his clothes" (2 Sam 12:20). Which implies that David was wearing mourning clothes, perhaps sackcloth. That notwithstanding, David's servants cannot help but inquire of such a countercultural practice. "What is this thing you have done? While the child was alive, you fasted and wept; but when the child died, you arose and ate food" (12:19). The mere fact that he is asked by his servants to explain his unusual actions indicate that such expressions are unconventional amidst grief through death. Which implies that it would have been normal mourning practice for David to continue fasting and weeping in his mourning clothes during his time of grief following the death of his stillborn son. After all, had David not mourned the deaths of Saul (1:11–12) and Abner (3:31–35), and then later the deaths of Amnon (13:36–37) as well as Absalom (18:32–19:4)? But why not mourn his unnamed son? Here the same explanation as previously noted in 4.5.3.4 (pp. 109-113) applies, that is, in light of the fact that David has a high biblical hope of seeing his son again, David has moved from a state of mourning into a state of joy. This joy is owing to David's resilient grief trajectory, which is primarily grounded in David's faith in Yahweh his God. Noted here also is the fact that David's choice to change his clothes, that is, from mourning clothes to regular (royal) clothes, is meant to characterize David, not to tell parents how to mourn.[188]

4.6.1g. Covering Face and Head

In the midst of his DS2 imprecatory prayer against Ahithophel (15:31), David weeps while covering his head as he ascends the Mount of Olives, as do his entourage with him (15:30). In other words, "The group travelled in an attitude of mourning."[189] Moreover, as a continuation of the account of David's *unconventional* responses to his son Absalom's death in 2 Samuel 18:33, we read in 19:4 that, "The king *covered his face* and cried out with a loud voice,

---

188. For more details on this argument of David's grief trajectory of resilience, see pp. @@.
189. Firth, *1 & 2 Samuel*, 458.

'O my son Absalom, O Absalom, my son, my son!'" (emphasis mine).[190] Here, it seems as though David uses his hands to cover his face, which is similar to the act of placing one's hands on one's head, and which, according to 2 Sam 13:19 and Jer 2:37, seems to be a customary sign of mourning.

Nevertheless, overcome with inconsolable grief, David once more attempts to veil his sorrow in the midst of his company of joyful and victorious warriors (cf. 2 Sam 18:33), something that has now become visible, expressing itself upon his face. The anguish has become too unbearable for David the father and not just David the king. Little wonder the men in his company are covered with shame on account of David's dissonant behavior (19:5). In other words, from the perspective of Joab and his men, it is incumbent upon David to compose himself and get over or put aside his grief for his son Absalom during this joyous occasion. David's public grief is thus proscribed by Joab who reprimands David for not being emotionally strong so as to *rejoice* instead of *mourn* Israel's victorious battle over Israel's archnemesis at the time – Absalom (19:5–7). In other words, David's inconsolable grief keeps him from "recognizing the necessity of Absalom's death as a moral judgment as much as, or as well as, a political necessity."[191] Therefore, Absalom's death, from Joab's perspective, calls for merriment rather than mourning. As Olyan avers, "Victory in battle requires rites of rejoicing from the victors after the fact, as David learns in 2 Sam 19:1–9 (Eng. 18:33–19:8)."[192]

4.6.1h. Deep Moving (Trembling)

Subsequent to the death of David's son Absalom, we read that, "The king was *deeply moved* and went up to the chamber over the gate and wept. And thus he said as he walked, 'O my son Absalom, my son, my son Absalom! Would I had died instead of you, O Absalom, my son, my son!'" (2 Sam 18:33; emphasis mine). Here it should be noted that the words "deeply moved" do not quite convey the meaning of the Hebrew word רָגַז (*ragaz*). Tsumura avers

---

190. One wonders about Absalom's mother, Maacah's (1 Chron 3:2), response to this news of her son's death. Scripture, however, is silent on this matter.

191. Evans, *1, 2 Samuel*, 216.

192. Olyan, *Biblical Mourning*, 125. Similarly, in an effort to present her DS3 vow prayer to the LORD, Hannah separated herself both physically and ritualistically from the company of joyful Israelites at the sanctuary in Shiloh (1 Sam 1:9–11).

that the expression literally means, "trembling with emotion."[193] In other words, "David is simply convulsed with emotion."[194] Overcome with grief, David's body trembles uncontrollably, and this within a context of one of David's elegies.

4.6.1i. Donning and Removing of Widow's Clothes

Genesis 38:19 states that, subsequent to the deaths of her two successive husbands (Er and Onan; 38:6–10), Tamar the daughter-in-law of Judah "arose and departed, and removed her veil and put on her widow's garments" (38:19). Earlier, however, the text informs us that Tamar "removed her widow's garments" (38:14). Kenneth A. Mathews tells us that "The veil was a common ornamental garment of women, which accentuated her attractiveness and often signified an elevated status (cf. Isa 3:18–23)."[195] But whereas "the face might be veiled or the entire head draped with a veil"[196] during mourning, Tamar's veiling of her face is employed with an eye toward double-crossing her duplicitous father-in-law Judah (38:11–18). Interestingly enough, Mathews further notes that, "A woman's veil was not the garment of a harlot but of a betrothed woman. . . . Assyrian law forbid an unmarried woman from wearing a veil. The irony of the veil was that it not only hid her identity, but it also could have signaled that she had been given in pledge to another, namely, Shelah."[197] In connection with Tamar's widowed garments, however, the text remains silent as to its exact nature. Nevertheless, that Tamar removed and then donned widow's clothes "exhibits the depths of her humiliation . . . [for being] mistreated by the men of her family."[198]

4.6.1j. Donning Sackcloth

Second Samuel 3:31–32 says that, following the death of Abner, "David said to Joab and all the people who were with him, 'Tear your clothes and *gird on sackcloth* and lament before Abner" (emphasis mine). Futato states: "Sackcloth is a rough cloth typically made from camel hair, goat hair, hemp, or flax.

---

193. Tsumura, *Second Samuel*, 268.
194. Tsumura, 268.
195. Mathews, *Genesis 11:27 – 50:26*, 718.
196. Fisher, "Burial, Burial Customs," 387.
197. Mathews, *Genesis 11:27 – 50:26*, 718.
198. Mathews, 718.

Wearing sackcloth would be like wearing burlap. The physical discomfort of the sackcloth made it an appropriate external symbol of the internal discomfort associated with mourning. Thus, the wearing of sackcloth was often associated with mourning."[199] What is more, Joseph Blenkinsopp contends, "In keeping with the symbolism of diminution and death, the wearing of sackcloth (e.g., Job 1:21; Joel 1:8, 13; Jonah 3:5, 8) represented the shroud in which the corpse was wrapped."[200]

4.6.1k. Eating

Also found within the context of the death of David's unnamed son is his action of eating food (2 Sam 12:20). Such a countercultural response to death incited the following question from David's servants: "What is this thing you have done? While the child was alive, you fasted and wept; but when the child died, you arose and ate food!" (12:21). Bergen observes that, "David's servants were mystified by the king's actions and boldly asked him why he was 'acting this way' (v. 21). Whereas others rolled in the dust when a family member died, David had chosen to 'get up'; though others might fast (cf. Ezra 10:6), David ate."[201] The significance of David's countercultural expression can be heard in his optimistic response: "While the child was *still* alive, I fasted and wept; for I said, 'Who knows, the LORD may be gracious to me, that the child may live.' But now he has died; why should I fast? Can I bring him back again? I will go to him, but he will not return to me" (12:22–23).

In eating a meal, "he breaks his fast (cf. v.16) and eats ordinary food (as opposed to the food of mourners that he had earlier rejected . . . the verb 'ate' here is *'kl*, not *br*)."[202] K. A. Kitchen suggests that it was, "a breaking-fast meal [which] was possibly given to mourners."[203] Which indicates that secondary to regular food, there might have been a specific kind of food that was usually prepared and served to the immediate family members in mourning. Perhaps it was simply *bread* (לֶחֶם, *lehem*), but since it was served during a time of mourning, it might have assumed a different significance. In that case,

199. Futato, *Joy Comes*, 96.
200. Blenkinsopp, *Ezra–Nehemiah*, 295.
201. Bergen, *1, 2 Samuel*, 375.
202. Youngblood, "1 & 2 Samuel," 449.
203. Kitchen, "Burial and Mourning," 150.

it could then be referred to as the bread of mourners or bread of misfortune (Hos 9:4). If it were a mourning *meal*, however, it would have comprised the bread of mourners (2 Sam 3:35; Jer 16:7; Hos 9:4), otherwise the bread of men (Ezek 24:17, 22), in addition to the cup of consolation, which more than likely would have been wine (Jer 16:7; Hos 9:4).

Fisher notes, however, that any food preparation completed within the home of the deceased, was believed to be ceremonially unclean (Num 19:14, 15; Hos 9:4). The mourning meal would have been prepared outside of and subsequently brought into the home of the immediate family of the deceased. Those responsible for such preparations might be relatives, neighbors, and friends of the immediate family of the deceased. Ingestion of the mourning bread and imbibing of the consolation wine occurred, however, only after a period of fasting, which could last anywhere from one to several days (1 Sam 31:13; 2 Sam 1:12; 12:17, 20).[204]

By partaking of a meal immediately on the heels of his unnamed son's death, David moves swiftly from a state of mourning to a state of joy. And as noted by G. A. Anderson, "This joyous state meant that the mourner had to . . . eat and drink."[205] This lends credence to his hopeful words that he will go to his son. Once again, it is duly noted here that David's reactions of eating and drinking amidst grief, according to Bosworth, should be viewed, particularly in light of his faith in Yahweh, as responses of resilience.[206] And as previously noted, these responses are "used in the Bible to characterize David, not to tell other parents how to mourn."[207]

4.6.1l. Erecting Gravestones (Monuments)

Immediately after Jacob buries his beloved wife Rachel in Ephrath, that is, Bethlehem, he places a stone or pillar over her grave (Gen 35:19–20; cf. 48:7). As noted by Hamilton, "To memorialize Rachel, Jacob raises a *pillar* over her grave. This is the third time Jacob has attempted to commemorate some event or person, either glorious (28:18; 35:14) or tragic (35:20), by raising

---

204. Fisher, "Burial, Burial Customs," 388.

205. Anderson, *A Time to Mourn*, 50.

206. Bosworth, "Faith and Resilience," 692–693.

207. Bosworth, "Understanding Grief," 119. See section 4.5.3.4 (pages @@) for more details on this argument of David's grief trajectory of resilience.

a pillar."[208] It also appears as though "Some such identification of the burial place of Rachel was still known at the time of Samuel as can be seen from the fact that Samuel told Saul to look for the two men 'near Rachel's tomb' (1 Sam 10:2)."[209] First Samuel 10:2 presents a dilemma, however, when it says that Rachel's tomb is located in the territory of Benjamin at Zelzah, which is near Ramah.[210] This would therefore situate Rachel's tomb near Bethel (in lieu of Bethlehem) and thus about 16 km north of Jerusalem.[211] Jeremiah 31:15 supplies further corroboration for this site. "Thus says the LORD, 'A voice is heard in Ramah, lamentation and bitter weeping. Rachel is weeping for her children; she refuses to be comforted for her children, because they are no more.'" Based on this, some scholars have moved to conclude that the words "that is, Bethlehem" in Gen 35:20 should be considered an incorrect gloss.[212]

As specified by Kurt G. Jung, "Although these references do not determine the original location of the grave, they do point out that the Church very early accepted the present tomb as authentic."[213] Which thus suggests that in contradistinction to Bethel, more consideration should be given to Bethlehem as the correct locus of Rachel's tomb.

The fact that the editor notes that this pillar of Rachel's grave is still there to this day, lends itself to its easy identification. Which therefore suggests that perhaps an inscription of Rachel's name would have been written on the pillar. If it is true that, "A pillar was usually a large stationary stone monument with a symbolic meaning,"[214] then the fact that that stone was laid on top of the grave located in Bethlehem, seems to be intentional on the part of

---

208. Hamilton, *Genesis 18–50*, 386; emphasis original.

209. Sailhamer, "Genesis," 219. Noted here is the fact that Absalom also erected a pillar after his own name. However, this occurred during his lifetime the purpose of which was the preservation of his name since he had no son to preserve his name. The pillar is referred to as Absalom's Monument (2 Sam 18:18). If at the time of his death he had no son to preserve his name, then it implies that the expirations of his three sons (14:27) had already transpired, or that they were unwilling to perpetuate their father's name for reasons known only to them.

210. Cf. Scalise, "Rachel," 32.

211. Cf. Jung, "Rachel's Tomb," 32.

212. Cf. Jung, 32. The NT evangelist Matthew, however, implies Bethlehem as the burial place of Rachel (Matt 2:18).

213. Jung, 32.

214. Omanson and Ellington, *Handbook*, 1012. Perhaps this stone is what might be referred to as a standing stele, which usually included an inscription of some sort.

the editor to signal the key role that such a place would play in the history of the Israelites.[215]

Yet Rachel is not the only one who has a gravestone or pillar erected on top of her grave. Second Kings 23:17 furnishes additional information concerning the mysterious man of God from Judah when it says that a monument is erected on top of his grave. Thus, when Josiah and his men are undertaking a reformation throughout the land and come to the monument of the anonymous man of God from Judah, he says, "Let him alone; let no one disturb his bones" (23:18). What seems intriguing, however, is the fact that while the men are familiar with the monument, Josiah is not. Which begs the question: is there no inscription on the monument to assist Josiah in identifying the person whose bones lie buried below the monument?

Another leading OT Israelite with a gravestone on top of his grave is Absalom. However, his has more than one stone. In 2 Sam 18:17 we read that Joab and the people with him "took Absalom and cast him into a deep pit in the forest and erected over him a very great heap of stones." Note, however, that during his lifetime, Absalom had taken and set up for himself a pillar, which is in the King's Valley. The purpose of this pillar can be heard in his own voice: "I have no son to preserve my name. So he named the pillar after his own name, and it is called Absalom's Monument to this day" (18:18).

But one should not forget the rebellious Achan who caused Israel much trouble for pilfering the devoted things belonging to Yahweh, and thus, suffered death by stoning along with his entire family and all his belongings. Joshua 7:25–26a reads, "All Israel stoned them with stones; and they burned them with fire after they had stoned them with stones. They raised a great heap of stones that stands to this day" (cf. Deut 21:18–21).

As noted by Elizabeth Bloch-Smith, "Burial markers preserved the memory of the righteous, the sinner, and men without offspring."[216] Referencing all of the above names, as well as the king of Ai, and the five kings of the southern coalition (Josh 8:29; 10:26–27), Bloch-Smith further contends, "Monuments

---

215. This is to say nothing about the NT Israelites, and thus the Christians, who would recognize Bethlehem as the birthplace of the Messiah Jesus (Matt 2:1; Luke 2:4–7).

216. Bloch-Smith, "Burials," 787.

serving to perpetuate the memory of men without descendants, literally to 'memorialize the name,' have been associated with death cult activities."[217]

4.6.1m. Falling on and Kissing the Deceased

Upon the death of his father (Gen 49:33), Joseph not only falls or throws himself upon Jacob, but he also moves to kiss his father as well (50:1). Four chapters earlier, Yahweh tells Jacob, "I will go down with you to Egypt, and I will surely bring you up again; and Joseph will close your eyes" (46:4). Thus the reader is meant to understand that at the time of Jacob's death, his most loved son Joseph will be with him (37:3). It might also allude to "the custom of a near relative closing the eyes of the one who died with a fixed stare."[218] Falling upon his father and kissing him are therefore expressions demonstrating "the great bond between Jacob and Joseph, which has been the mainspring of the story since chap. 37."[219] In other words, such are expressions of affection assumed by loved ones. In fact, it is the oldest son or, failing him, the nearest of kin, in this case, Joseph, who would close the eyes of the dead, which appears to be "symbolic of the 'sleep of death' (Acts 7:60)."[220]

4.6.1n. Fasting

Perhaps one of the most common auxiliary expressions to prayers of disorientation is the physical expression of *fasting*. Upon being reprimanded by the prophet Nathan, from whom David also learns of the looming death of the child to be born as a consequence of his illicit affair with Bathsheba, "David inquired of God for the child; and David *fasted* and went and lay all night on the ground" (2 Sam 12:16; emphasis mine). A few verses later, after David is made aware of the death of the child, we read that his servants approach him asking, "What is this thing that you have done? While the child was alive, you *fasted* and wept; but when the child died, you arose and ate food" (12:21; emphasis mine). David then retorts by asserting, "While the child was *still* alive, I *fasted* and wept; for I said, 'Who knows, the LORD may be gracious to me, that the child may live.' But now he has died; why should

---

217. Bloch-Smith, "Burials," 787.

218. Fisher, "Burial, Burial Customs," 388.

219. Wenham, *Genesis 16–50*, 488.

220. Payne, "Burial," 556.

I *fast*? Can I bring him back again? I will go to him, but he will not return to me" (12:22–23; emphasis mine).[221] In these words, "There is to be heard a note of consolation in David's words 'I will go to him.'"[222]

Alongside David's presentation of his DS1 lament prayer to Yahweh (2 Sam 12:16), David fasts in the "hopes that the Lord might change his mind . . . to spare his son's life."[223] Or as Bergen indicates, "David's self-denial and self-abasement . . . may have been an effort to demonstrate to God that the child's recovery was more important to him than either food, comfort, or pride."[224]

James C. Vanderkam notes that, "Fasts and fasting receive fairly frequent mention in the Bible and could take the form of either personal or communal exercises. . . . Depriving oneself of food was regarded as a valuable religious exercise, one that many Jews appear to have practiced."[225] While fasting is not widely attested in the ancient Near Eastern context, J. A. Scurlock further maintains that its actual confirmation is in association with the ritual of *mourning*.[226] Further to this, in his comments on fasting, John Muddiman states that it is "the deliberate, temporary abstention from food,"[227] which was connected with the "rites of mourning, personal penance, or the reinforcement of supplicatory prayer."[228] Long also notes that fasting was likewise associated with ritual rites, such as that prescribed for the Day of Atonement (Yom Kippur).[229]

David's fast is therefore to be viewed as a mourning ritual, albeit not one done proleptically in anticipation of the impending death of his unnamed son, as A. A. Anderson proffers.[230]

---

221. While not discussed here, other examples of fasting within the context of OT prosaic prayers are recorded in 2 Chron 20:2–3; Ezra 8:23; Neh 9:1; Zech 7:3, 5; 8:19.

222. Bergen, *1, 2 Samuel*, 376.

223. Tsumura, *Second Samuel*, 195.

224. Bergen, *1, 2 Samuel*, 374.

225. Vanderkam, "Feasts and Fasts," 446; cf. 1 Sam 1:7; 2 Sam 3:35.

226. As cited in Long, "2 Samuel," 414.

227. Muddiman, "Fast, Fasting," 773.

228. Muddiman, 774.

229. Long, "2 Samuel," 414.

230. Anderson, *2 Samuel*, 164.

4.6.1o. Funeral Processioning

Following the death of Abner, David leads a funeral procession as he walks behind the bier and thereafter weeps at Abner's grave (2 Sam 3:31–32). The longest funeral procession, however, begins in the land of Goshen, Egypt, and ends in the cave of the field at Machpelah before Mamre. Part of this funeral procession involves the seven days of mourning for Jaco at the threshing floor of Atad, which is beyond the Jordan River. Eventually, Jacob is laid to rest alongside Abraham, Sarah, Isaac, Rebekah, and Leah (Gen 50:1–14; cf. 49:13). Arnold remarks that Jacob's funeral cortege "is the most elaborate funeral recorded in the Bible, parading the pomp and ceremony of Egypt itself, suitable for the patriarch whose life-story covers nearly half of Genesis."[231]

4.6.1p. Grieving/Mourning

The first person who is said to have mourned in the Bible is Abraham, who mourns on the occasion of the death of his first wife Sarah (Gen 23:2).[232] Judah mourns the death of his wife, the daughter of Shua (38:12). The entire nation of Israel gathers and mourns the death of the prophet Samuel (1 Sam 25:1; cf. 28:3). After receiving the news of Uriah's death, Bathsheba mourns for her husband (2 Sam 11:26). David and the people with him also mourn for his son Absalom (19:1–2). It is also here that the only occurrence of the emotive response of grief – "The king is *grieved* for his son" – comes to the fore within the borders of Genesis and Esther (19:2). The prophet at Bethel mourns for the man of God from Judah (1 Kgs 13:29–30; emphasis mine). But it is the patriarch Jacob for whom a caravan (comprised of Joseph, all the servants of Pharaoh, the elders of his household, and all the elders of the land of Egypt), pause for seven days at the threshing floor of Atad, which is beyond the Jordan, lament with a very great and sorrowful lamentation, and also mourn for Jacob (50:10). So great is this mourning that even the Canaanites exclaim, "This is a *grievous mourning* for the Egyptians," which is why the place is called Abel-mizraim (50:11; emphasis mine).

---

231. Arnold, *Genesis*, 386.

232. Abraham's second wife is Keturah (Gen 25:1). It is noted here that though not within the context of grief through death, Nehemiah mourns following his reception of the sad news that the wall of Jerusalem has been broken down and the gates have been burned with fire (1:1–11).

Hearing of the great distress and reproach that had fallen upon the remnant that had survived the captivity, and also about the broken wall of Jerusalem, as well as the gates being set on fire, Nehemiah not only presents to Yahweh his DS4 penitential prayer, but he also "sat down and wept and *mourned* for days" (1:4a; emphasis mine).

Within the OT Israelite culture, it was customary for close relatives and friends to visit the house of and mourn with the immediate family of the deceased (Job 2:11–13). During this time, it was also traditional for professional mourners to be hired (Jer 9:17–18). King and Stager note, "Mourning was part of the burial rite, a way of honoring the deceased. In addition to family members, professional mourners, generally women, were paid to lament during a funeral. . . . Mourning continued for a period of seven days."[233] Further to this, "The emphasis on mourning resulted from the Hebrew appreciation of human life and health, which was considered one of God's greatest gifts (Ps 91:16), and also from a view of human nature which affirmed embodied existence (Ps 16:9–11)."[234]

4.6.1q. Honoring (through Spice-Fire)

Second Chronicles 32:33 reads: "So Hezekiah slept with his fathers, and they buried him in the upper section of the tombs of the sons of David; and all Judah and the inhabitants honored him at his death." What would such an honor have been comprised of? As specified by Bloch-Smith, "The honor certainly entailed lamenting (1 Kgs 13:30; Jer 22:18) and offering sacrifices (Isa 57:7; 2 Chron 16:14)."[235]

According to 2 Chronicles 16:13–14, "Asa slept with his fathers, having died in the forty-first year of his reign. They buried him in his own tomb which he had cut out for himself in the city of David, and they laid him in the resting place which he had filled with spices of various kinds blended by the perfumers' art; and *they made a great fire for him*" (emphasis mine; cf. 1 Kgs 15:24). It is interesting to read in 2 Chronicles 21:18–19, however, that although he is buried in the city of David, though not in the tombs of the kings, no fire is made in honor of Jehoram. "So after all this the LORD

---

233. King and Stager, *Life in Biblical Israel*, 373.

234. Miller, "Funeral Customs," 821.

235. Bloch-Smith, "Burials," 786.

smote him in his bowels with an incurable sickness. Now it came about in the course of time, at the end of two years, that his bowels came out because of his sickness and he died in great pain. And his people made no fire for him like the fire for his fathers."

Speaking to Zedekiah, the prophet Jeremiah says, "You will die in peace; and as *spices* were burned for your fathers, the former kings who were before you, so they will burn *spices* for you; and they will lament for you, 'Alas, lord!'" (Jer 34:5). On the basis of 2 Chronicles 16:14 and Jeremiah 34:5, it is possible that the spices of various kinds blended by perfumers' art, which Asa places in his tomb prior to his death, are not the typical spices that are applied to a corpse. Rather, these spices are employed for the purpose of the great fire that is made in honor of Asa. As Ralph W. Klein avers, "A passage from Jeremiah [34:5] suggests that spices may have been the material that was burned."[236] Made of spices, the huge fire is thus not for cremation but rather, as the text says, in honor of Asa.

4.6.1r. Kneeling

While presenting his DS4 penitential prayer to God, Ezra the priest and scribe says, "I *fell on my knees*" (9:5; emphasis mine). While it is not unusual for humans to kneel before other humans (e.g., Gen 41:43), and before kings (e.g., 1 Kgs 19:18; Ps 95:7 [6]), Michael J. Brown submits that, "Kneeling frequently accompanies a request or supplication (e.g., 1 Kgs 8:54; 2 Chron 6:13)."[237] Brown further contends that, "Kneeling, or 'bowing,' or 'bending the knee,' (e.g., Isa 45:23; Phil 2:10), is a gesture of humility or reverence before a superior (Mark 10:17)."[238] Though he also affirms that the Israelites "prayed standing up," Brown nevertheless maintains that, "whenever it was done, kneeling was meant to underscore the seriousness of the situation."[239] Kneeling before Yahweh while uttering one's prayer in the context of disorientation can therefore be understood as a symbolic act of humility and impotence, and at the same time, an act of deep reverence and worship to Yahweh who is sovereign over all, and who alone can supply all one's needs.

---

236. Ralph W. Klein, *2 Chronicles*, 243.
237. Brown, "Kneel," 538.
238. Brown, 538.
239. Brown, 538.

4.6.1s. Lying on the Ground

Within the context of his DS1 lament prayer on behalf of his ill and unnamed son born through his clandestine relationship with Uriah's wife, Bathsheba, David "fasted and went all night and *lay on the ground*" (2 Sam 12:16; emphasis mine). Robert B. Chisholm tells us that, "This may be an echo here of David's sin. He had 'slept' (*shakab*) with Bathsheba (11:4); now he is 'lying' (*shakab*) on the ground before the Lord, confronted with the harsh consequences of his sin."[240]

Bergen avows that "David's self-denial and self-abasement probably should be interpreted as a demonstration of his remorse for the sins he had committed, carried out in an effort to gain a reprieve for his son. Alternatively, they may have been an effort to demonstrate to God that the child's recovery was more important to him than either food, comfort, or pride."[241] A chapter later, however, on the occasion of the death of his son Amnon at the avenging hands of Absalom and his servants for violating Tamar, David "tore his clothes, and *lay on the ground*" (2 Sam 13:31; emphasis mine), "in a classic expression of grief and distress (cf. Josh 7:6; 2 Sam 12:16)."[242]

4.6.1t. Offering Burnt Offerings and Peace Offerings

Judges 20:26 reads, "Then all the sons of Israel and all the people went up and came to Bethel and wept; thus they remained there before the LORD and fasted that day until evening. And they offered *burnt offerings* and *peace offerings* to the LORD" (emphasis mine). Such offerings accompany the sons of Israel's DS1 lament prayer. A burnt offering was a "Form of Israelite sacrifice in which a choice animal offered to make atonement for sin was completely consumed by fire."[243] Another term for peace offering is that of fellowship offering. Commenting on both offerings, Daniel I. Block states that, "The reference to offerings is especially telling, suggesting the Israelites may have finally come to realize that their covenant relationship with Yahweh is in doubt."[244]

---

240. Chisholm, *1 & 2 Samuel*, 429.

241. Bergen, *1, 2 Samuel*, 374.

242. Bergen, 385.

243. Elwell and Comfort, "Burnt Offering," 242.

244. Block, *Judges, Ruth*, 560.

4.6.1u. Offering Human Sacrifice

Although a ritual prohibited within Israel (Deut 12:31; 18:9–12; 2 Kgs 16:3; Ps 106:39 [38]; Jer 19:4–5), we read of a human sacrifice to Yahweh in Judges 11:39–40. "At the end of two months she returned to her father, who did to her according to the vow which he had made; and she had no relations with a man. Thus it became a custom in Israel, that the daughters of Israel went yearly to commemorate the daughter of Jephthah the Gileadite four days in the year." Jephthah thus fulfills his vow by sacrificing his one and only daughter as a burnt offering to Yahweh. Barry G. Webb comments that, "At the end of the two months she returns to her father, her submission complete. The time has come, and there is no word from heaven to stay Jephthah's hand (cf. Gen 22). So now quickly, without judgment, the narrator tells the deed." Which implies that,

> Only the narrator refers to the vow directly, by its name, but even here there is reticence: not, "he offered her up as a burnt offering," but (literally), "he did ('śh) to her his vow which he vowed (niḏrô 'ašer nāḏār)." The one of course implies the other, and given the wording of the vow itself, we are clearly meant to understand that Jephthah literally sacrificed his daughter.[245]

Further to this, Corrine L. Patton reasons, "The tragic irony of the text lies in the fact that his vow leads him to sacrifice the only heir to the inheritance he has worked so shrewdly to regain, his daughter . . . Jephthah has effectively disinherited himself."[246]

It is worth accentuating that the description of Jephthah's inhumane action appears to be used in the OT to characterize Jephthah, rather than to instruct other parents on the normativity of offering their child(ren) to Yahweh as a living sacrifice. "Stories like the sacrifice of Jephthah's daughter do not indicate that daughters were worthless, but in fact depend on the notion that they were cherished."[247] Which explains why Jephthah "tore his clothes," and cried out, "Alas, my daughter!" (Judg 11:35) – both expressions of deep grief and

---

245. Webb, *Book of Judges*, 333.

246. Patton, "From Heroic Individual," 41.

247. Bosworth, "Understanding Grief," 131.

love; after all, no one really grieves that which they do not love and cherish in some way or another.

Far from that being the case, such a ritual as that of sacrificing one's daughter (or son) remains categorically offensive and abominably grievous to Yahweh and to his holy people throughout the OT. Such a practice is never afforded a proper place within the OT Israelite cult. While the practice of offering one's daughter or son in the fire is meant to appease pagan deities, Yahweh God always relates to his people with grace and compassion (Exod 34:6; Lam 3:22), appeasing himself by means of the sacrifice of birds and animals (Lev 14:4; 16:15), and ultimately through his unique divine-human Son (Isa 53). After all, if each person bears the image of God (cf. Gen 1:26–27), why would Yahweh God take delight in prescribing the destruction of his innocent and godly image-bearers (cf. Ps 116:16 [15]; Lam 3:32–33)?

This, however, does not detract from the fact that Jephthah's inhumane sacrifice of his one and only daughter, as a burnt offering to Yahweh, is in fulfillment of his imprudent DS3 vow prayer to Yahweh. Such a humanly savage and divinely abominable act, (which not even Yahweh halts), nevertheless transpires within the context of the disorientation of enemy warfare (Judg 11:30–31).

4.6.1v. Outstretching Hands

Ezra 9:5 tells us that the priest and scribe "*stretched out my hands* to the LORD my God" (emphasis mine), while uttering his DS4 penitential prayer to God. The context of Ezra's disorientation expression is that of the postexilic people of Israel engaging once more in unlawful intermarriage (or more precisely, interreligious marriage) with the peoples of the land – the Canaanites, Hittites, Perizzites, Jebusites, Ammonites, Moabites, Egyptians, and Amorites. This physical posture of stretching or spreading out one's hands to Yahweh or to heaven (cf. Exod 9:29; 1 Kgs 8:22; Isa 1:15), according to John. D. W. Watts, "describes prayer," and in reference to Isaiah 1:15, "prayer in the particular sense of intercession."[248] Going even further, Hans Wildberger avers, "One prays by extending the hands, more specifically: the palms of the hands

---

248. Watts, *Isaiah 1–33*, 32.

extended upwards, so that the deity would allow them to be filled."[249] But one should ask: filled with *what*? Ross contends that praying with palms upwards is "a focused prayer, that is, a metonymy of adjunct because the gesture is accompanied by prayer. . . . The picture is that of the suppliant standing in the courtyard of the sanctuary with *uplifted hands* facing the Holy of Holies, where the LORD dwelt among his people, crying out for deliverance."[250] If this is the case, then Ezra is crying out with outstretched hands for Yahweh's deliverance in the form of forgiveness.

Interestingly, this expression is also observed in Psalms 63:5 [4] and 134:3 [2] as a form of blessing to Yahweh. In several cases throughout the OT (Job 11:13; Pss 28:3 [2]; 88:10 [9]; 143:7[6]; Lam 2:19), however, it appears within a context of disorientation, rather than of orientation or new orientation. Such an expression, as noted by Nancy deClaissé-Walford et al., "evokes the concept of God's presence. . . . an incarnational act signifying, as it were, the absence of God when in need but also a desire and faith in the nearness of God."[251] More specifically, this physical expression communicates a desire for Yahweh "to extend the power of divine presence in deliverance."[252]

The expression of stretching or spreading out one's hands to Yahweh or heaven, specifically the extension of one's palms turned upward, can therefore serve either as a symbolic action of supplication for divine presence in deliverance or for an offering of praise to Yahweh. Such a physical expression in the company of prayers uttered amidst a context of disorientation, as in the

---

249. Wildberger, *Isaiah 1–12*, 48. As noted earlier, each time a plague occurred in Exod 7:14 – 12:36, Pharaoh would acknowledge his sin and thereafter request Moses to petition God for its removal, and each time Moses would oblige him. What is particularly interesting, however, is that following the plague of hail, there is an absence of a Mosaic petition to God. Rather, we read thus: "So Moses went out of the city from Pharaoh, and *spread out his hands to the LORD*; and the thunder and the hail ceased, and rain no longer poured on the earth" (Exod 9:33; emphasis mine). Here, I've taken Moses' physical expression as his Hebraic Sign Language to Yahweh, especially in light of his speech impediment (cf. 4:10). A further example of this gesture is found in Exod 17:8–16 in the battle at Rephidim between Amalek and Israel when Moses once more lifts up his hands. In lieu of verbalizing his petition to Yahweh, one observes that whenever Moses lifts his hand, Israel gains the upper hand, while the lowering of his hands results in casualties. Interestingly there is no record of an articulated prayer of disorientation for deliverance from the lips of Moses, only that "his hands were steady until the sun set" (17:12). Yet, Yahweh understood that by the lifting of his hands, Moses was petitioning him for deliverance.

250. Ross, *Psalms*, 643; cf. 1 Tim 2:8.

251. deClaissé-Walford, *Book of Psalms*, 276.

252. deClaissé-Walford, 276.

case of Ezra 9:5, however, can be understood as a symbolic or incarnational act signifying God's absence and a desire to experience his divine nearness or touch, that is, his divine deliverance in the form of his compassionate acceptance and forgiveness.

4.6.1w. Paralleling Two Outstretched Bodies

This bodily expression of paralleling two outstretched bodies occurs in the life of two familiar prophets: Elijah and the son of the widow of Zarephath (1 Kgs 17:17–24), and Elisha and the son of the Shunammite woman (2 Kgs 4:18–37). In the case of Elijah, while presenting his DS1 lament prayer to Yahweh (17:20), *he stretched himself upon the child three times*, and called to the LORD and said, 'O LORD my God, I pray You, let this child's life return to him" (17:21; emphasis mine). Simon J. DeVries contends that, Elijah's action upon the child "is not magic, but a typical symbolic act familiar to the prophetic movement in Israel. It is an 'acted out' way of saying, 'Let his lifeless body be as my lively body,' and the prayer that accompanies it fortifies this symbol."[253] Paul R. House likewise avows that "Elijah stretches himself on the child, thereby seemingly transferring life from himself to the sick one."[254] Yet House also acknowledges, "Regardless of the method used, the important fact is that God raises the body from the dead. The child revives because Yahweh hears Elijah's plea, not because of the prophet's prowess. Yahweh is God, not Baal, not Elijah."[255]

In a similar fashion to that of Elijah, we are told that while bringing his DS1 lament prayer to Yahweh (2 Kgs 4:33), Elisha mirrors the lad as *"he went up and lay on the child, and put his mouth on his mouth and his eyes on his eyes and his hands on his hands, and he stretched himself on him"* (4:34a; emphasis mine). At such physical expressions, "the flesh of the child became warm" (4:34b). Thereafter, Elisha "returned and walked in the house once back and forth, and went up and *stretched himself on him*; and the lad sneezed seven times and the lad opened his eyes" (4:35; emphasis mine). Volkmar Fritz remarks that, "Elisha achieves the raising of the boy through prayer and body contact. The aspect of prayer indicates that it is Yahweh alone, as the Lord

---

253. DeVries, *1 Kings*, 222.

254. House, *1, 2 Kings*, 215.

255. House, 215.

of creation, who can give back life. The body contact confirms the share that the prophet has in this singular event: the life force of Elisha is passed on to the dead boy through his touch."[256]

Alternatively stated, "Elisha's work here proves the same points Elijah's healing demonstrated: the Lord controls death, and the Lord cares for the needy and hurting. This scene also shows that prophets not only are preachers of sin and repentance; they also are agents of God's healing mercy and kind compassion."[257] Small wonder that T. R. Hobbs observes, "What is important in the literary presentation of such incidents is not the miracle-working power attributed to Elisha, since the ability to perform miracles is not necessarily a sign of the power of God (cf. Exod 7:8–13)."[258] This is made all the more obvious as one witnesses "the narrator revealing a weakness on the part of Elisha during the performance of his most spectacular miracle, the raising of the Shunammite's son. Only on the third attempt is the miracle successful."[259] Rather than the miracle-working power of the prophet, "What is of great importance in these stories is the motivation of the miracle worker. Are the miracles an attempt at self-aggrandizement or do they have another purpose? In the case of Elisha in chap. 4, the motivation is the desire to respond to pressing human needs. The motivation is compassion."[260]

Motivated by the compassion of both prophets, such physical expressions communicated by Elijah and Elisha before Yahweh the unrivaled divine creator of life, in the context of the death of a child, are prophetic symbolic actions of transferring life from the living prophet to the dead child. But as noted above, such somatic and symbolic actions are not what necessarily effects the revivification of life, but rather, they serve as an auxiliary expression before Yahweh. The primary expression communicated to God, which effected the revivification of each child's life, is that of the prophets' DS1 lament prayer for the life of both lads to be restored. In both cases, the prayer is heard and answered as a means of demonstrating that it is Yahweh alone

256. Fritz, *1 & 2 Kings*, 252.

257. House, *1, 2 Kings*, 268.

258. Hobbs, *2 Kings*, 54.

259. Hobbs, 54.

260. Hobbs, 54.

who is not only compassionate to both Israelites and non-Israelites, but even more, that Yahweh alone is the creator and reviver of life.

4.6.1x. Placing in Coffin

Of all the Israelites who die inside or outside the promised land, it appears as though only Joseph the son of Jacob is placed in a coffin (אֲרוֹן, *aron*; Gen 50:26). Payne observes that, "Coffins were not employed in ancient Israel. The only one mentioned in the Bible is the sarcophagus (Heb. *ărôn*, 'box, chest,' Gen. 50:26) in which the embalmed body of Joseph was preserved in Egypt."[261] Here also the words of King and Stager are given due consideration: "To open the coffin or to remove the coffin from its resting place was tantamount to disturbing the rest of the dead."[262] If this is the case, rather than Egypt, it is Shechem that should be viewed as Joseph's final resting place (Josh 24:32), that is, the place where his bones are left undisturbed.

4.6.1y. Plucking Hair from Beard and Head

In the book that bears his name, Ezra the priest receives word from the princes concerning the abominations of the people of Israel, the priests, and the Levites who once again fail to separate themselves from the peoples of the lands. Thereafter, Ezra states that, "I tore my garment and my robe, and *pulled some of the hair from my head and beard*, and sat down appalled" (Ezra 9:3; emphasis mine), which is almost immediately met with Ezra's penitential prayer, otherwise referred to as a DS4 penitential prayer (9:5–15; cf. Neh 13:25).

H. G. M. Williamson avers that "Ezra's response should not be regarded as an expression of personal grief but rather as an attempt to act representatively on behalf of all the people."[263] Yet F. Charles Fensham states in no uncertain terms, "This is a gesture of grief."[264] Hannah K. Harrington adds that such an action is "a sign of sorrow and mourning, usually for the death of an individual but also a response to a great crisis."[265] Small wonder that Donna

---

261. Payne, "Burial," 557.

262. King and Stager, *Life in Biblical Israel*, 375.

263. Williamson, *Ezra, Nehemiah*, 132.

264. Fensham, *Books of Ezra*, 126.

265. Harrington, *Books of Ezra*, 234. Harrington further notes that, as a priest, Ezra "is not supposed to go into mourning or tear his sacred garments on account of the dead (Lev 21:10) . . .

Petter and Thomas Petter inform us that in such an act, Ezra "assumes the role of a mourner."[266] In other words, "Ezra engaged in ritual mourning that reflected extreme crisis. In the context it was meant to indicate repentance,"[267] as Leslie C. Allen observes.

Ezra's act of pulling out his own hair appears to be unique in the Bible. Blenkinsopp avers that the act of plucking hair from one's head is a "modified form of ritual shaving of the hair, a practice forbidden on account of its pagan connotations (Lev. 19:27; 21:5; Deut. 14:1)."[268] For a similar event, when confronted with the same issue, Nehemiah, instead of pulling out his own hair, plucks out the hair of the lawbreakers (Neh 13:25).

4.6.1z. Pouring Dirt on Oneself

The donning of sackcloth is usually completed in combination with that of pouring dirt (or dust or earth) upon oneself. Within the context of his DS4 penitential prayer, Neh 9:1 reads, "Now on the twenty-fourth day of this [seventh] month the sons of Israel assembled with fasting, in sackcloth and *with dirt upon them*" (emphasis mine). Blenkinsopp explains, "In keeping with the symbolism of diminution and death . . . the sprinkling of earth on the head (e.g., Josh 7:6; 1 Sam 4:12; 2 Sam 1:2; Job 2:12) stood for burial in the earth."[269] Fensham, however, comments that, "This was the general sign of mourning and of displaying the frailty of mankind."[270] Included here is the view that such an expression is a sign of "repentance,"[271] as Petter and Petter note. The act of pouring dirt upon one's head in the context of a DS4 penitential prayer can thus be understood as a mourning rite for burying one's sins in the earth, that is, an external authentication of internal contrition.

[thus] his clothes are not described as priestly vestments but are most likely his ordinary clothes" (234).

266. Petter and Petter, *Ezra–Nehemiah*, 212.

267. Allen, *Ezra, Nehemiah, Esther*, 74.

268. Blenkinsopp, *Ezra–Nehemiah*, 177.

269. Blenkinsopp, 295.

270. Fensham, *Ezra and Nehemiah*, 223. See also Harrington, *Ezra and Nehemiah*, 383; and Williamson, *Ezra, Nehemiah*, 310.

271. Petter and Petter, *Ezra–Nehemiah*, 394. See also Allen, *Ezra, Nehemiah, Esther*, 132.

4.6.1aa. Prostrating Oneself

In connection with his DS2 imprecatory prayer, and subsequent to Yahweh's favorable response through the Levite Jahaziel, "Jehoshaphat *bowed his head with this face to the ground*, and all Judah and the inhabitants of Jerusalem *fell down before the LORD, worshiping the LORD*" (2 Chron 20:18; emphasis mine). Amidst his DS4 penitential prayer to Yahweh, "Ezra was praying and making confession, weeping and *prostrating* himself before the house of God" (Ezra 10:1; emphasis mine).

S. J. Schultz and G. L. Knapp aver that yet "Another intensive manner of showing deep reverence or of appealing to a superior was by prostrating oneself, i.e. lying flat on the ground or kneeling with one's face and hands to the ground."[272] Culling support from such texts as Genesis 17:3, 17; Numbers 16:45; 20:6; Joshua 7:6; 1 Samuel 20:41; and 25:23, Schultz and Knapp further contend that, "Abject subjection was frequently involved and could be based either on genuine respect or on a fear of judgment."[273]

In Genesis 17:17, however, in falling on his face before God, Abram does *not* show abject subjection, genuine respect, or fear of judgment, for the text reads, "Then Abram *fell on his face and laughed*, and said, 'Will a child be born to a man one hundred years old? And will Sarah, who is ninety years old, bear *a child*?" (emphasis mine). According to Hamilton,

> Perhaps v. 17 means that *Abraham fell over laughing about God's most recent proposition*. Abraham is no expert on gynecology, but he knows that he and his wife are well beyond the parenting years. Much like Moses later on, Abraham believes that his circumstances limit the promises of God. God is ignoring some fundamental problems that in effect make his promises stillborn. So thinks Abraham. That Abraham had already fathered a child as recently as fourteen years ago (16:16) seems not to affect his thinking (emphasis mine).[274]

Abram therefore does not fall on his face with abject reverence for Yahweh. Rather, Abram communicates little to no faith in Yahweh's promise of being

---

272. Schultz and Knapp, "Postures; Attitudes," 912; other intensive manners include bowing, kneeling, and standing erect with head bowed (911–912)..

273. Schultz and Knapp, 912.

274. Hamilton, *Book of Genesis*, 477 (emphasis mine).

capable of fathering a son at the age of one hundred years as witnessed from his *laughter* (cf. 18:10–15). Yahweh's promise to Abram is thus one that he doubtless finds amusing.[275]

To be fair to Schultz and Knapp, however, falling on one's face before Yahweh in Numbers 16:45 is an act based on genuine respect and fear of divine judgment, though not for Moses and Aaron, but rather those opposed to them, i.e. all the congregation of the sons of Israel who grumbled against them (16:41). Which is why, on the instruction of Moses, Aaron makes expeditious atonement for the malcontents since Yahweh's wrath had already commenced in the form of a plague (16:46–50; cf. 20:6).

In the context of disorientation, the posture of falling prostrate or on one's face before Yahweh, which usually accompanies prayers of disorientation uttered to God, can thus be understood as both a deep reverence for God and fear of his wrath. In the context of orientation, as in Genesis 17:17, such an expression displays an absence of reverence for or faith in God. Generally speaking, however, prostrating oneself before God is to be considered a component of the "classic expression of grief and distress (cf. Josh 7:6; 2 Sam 12:16),"[276] as mentioned by Bergen.

4.6.1ab. Rising from the Ground

In 2 Samuel 12:20, following the death of his unnamed son, "*David arose from the ground*" (emphasis mine). This, however, is at dissonance with normal cultural mourning practices, which is observed in David's servants' question, "What is this thing you have done? While the child was alive, you fasted and wept; but when the child died, you arose and ate food!" (12:21). David then offers the following optimistic response: "While the child was *still* alive, I fasted and wept; for I said, 'Who knows, the LORD may be gracious to me, that the child may live.' But now he has died; why should I fast? Can I bring him back again? I will go to him, but he will not return to me" (12:22–23). In these words, Bergen tells us that, "There is to be heard a note of consolation in David's words 'I will go to him.'"[277]

---

275. In today's parlance, it would be like saying, *You've got to be kidding me, right, Yahweh?*

276. Bergen, *1, 2 Samuel*, 385.

277. Bergen, 376.

Bergen further remarks that, "Whereas others rolled in the dust when a family member died, David had chosen to 'get up.'"[278] Rising from the ground, rather than sitting *shiva*, is another example of how David exhibits a grief trajectory of resilience that is primarily grounded in his faith in Yahweh his God. Yet here also it is worth mentioning that such an action on David's part is only meant to characterize David, not to tell parents how to mourn.[279]

4.6.1ac. Sacrificing through Supernatural Fire (Building Altar, Making Trench, Arranging Wood, Cutting Ox, Laying Ox on Wood)

In his duel with the four hundred and fifty prophets of Baal on Mount Carmel, "Elijah took twelve stones according to the number of the tribes of the sons of Jacob . . . [and] with the stones he built an altar in the name of the LORD, and he *made a trench* around the altar, large enough to hold two measures of seed. Then he *arranged the wood* and *cut the ox* in pieces and *laid it on the wood*" (1 Kgs 18:30–34; emphasis mine). Making a trench, which would later be filled with water, arranging the wood, cutting the ox, and placing the ox on the wood, are secondary to that of the primary act of repairing or rebuilding Yahweh's altar, since the latter is done in the name of Yahweh (cf. Judg 21:4). This occurs within the context of Elijah's DS1 lament prayer.

Commenting on Elijah's act of rebuilding the altar for the purpose of sacrificing through supernatural fire, Iain W. Provan points out, "Strictly speaking, this represents the restoration of a 'high place'; and the authors of Kings are generally opposed to worship at such local shrines. They are even more opposed to idolatry, however, and it is unlikely that in a context where Israel has given itself over to idolatry, they intend us to think critically of Elijah for acting thus."[280] Which implies that "Centralization of worship of the LORD is ideal (cf. Deut 12), but any worship of the LORD is better than worship of Baal. And the LORD removes the altar, of course, after it has served its purpose (v. 38)!"[281]

---

278. Bergen, 376.

279. See also discussion in section 4.5.3.4 on p@@.

280. Provan, *1 & 2 Kings*, 141.

281. Provan, 142.

Bruce Chilton further observes, "Opposition to foreign cults and to degradations of Israel's worship especially concerns the early prophets."[282] It therefore comes as no surprise to read Chilton's further remarks that "Elijah symbolizes their confrontational stance in the context of Mount Carmel, where by supernatural means his sacrifice on the altar to Yahweh he repairs – carefully using the twelve stones that represent Israel (1 Kgs 18:30–32), prevails over the prophets of Baal (1 Kgs 18:17–40)."[283] Elijah's opposition to foreign cults and degradations of Israel's worship is further observed when Elijah "slays the prophets of Baal, much as Moses dealt with the idolaters of his time."[284] In the end, the purpose of this altar restoration is that of a supernatural animal sacrifice by fire from heaven in order to *prove* that, rather than Baal, it is indeed, "The LORD, He is God; the LORD, He is God" (18:39).

4.6.1ad. Separation from Foreigners

Nehemiah 9:2 reads thus: "The descendants of Israel *separated themselves from all foreigners*, and stood and confessed their sins and the iniquities of their fathers" (emphasis mine; cf. Ezra 10:3, 18–44). This occurs within the context of their DS4 penitential prayer. The issue at hand is that of mixed or intermarriage, or more precisely, interreligious marriages. While mixed marriages are not necessarily prohibited (cf. Gen 41:45; Num 12:1; Ruth 4:13), the peril of apostasy, nevertheless, lurks in proximity (cf. 1 Kgs 11:1–3). Edwin M. Yamauchi insists that "Though the actions of Ezra and later of Nehemiah may strike some readers as harsh, they were more than racial or cultural measures and were necessary to preserve the spiritual heritage of Israel."[285] Yamauchi further avers, "Both from the principle and from exceptions to the rule, warnings against intermarriage were clearly concerned not so much about racial miscegenation as about spiritual adulteration."[286] Yahweh's people are to be holy even as he is holy (Lev 11:44; 19:2; 20:7). Otherwise stated, since it was Yahweh their God who had delivered them from Babylonian exile, as he did for them while they were in Egypt, the children of Israel belonged exclusively

---

282. Chilton, "Altar," 116.

283. Chilton, 116.

284. Chilton, 116.

285. Yamauchi, "Ezra-Nehemiah," 420.

286. Yamauchi, 420.

to Yahweh their covenant God, and none other. That is, they were to have no other gods before Yahweh their God (Exod 20:1–3; Deut 5:1–7). To wallow in interreligious marriages, after all, would only lead the children of Israel down the wrong path of idolatry that ends in death, or at the very least, another exile, rather than in life in and through Yahweh their everlasting God (Deut 30:15–20). Ezra therefore takes drastic measures to rid sin from the company of Yahweh's covenant people, thus calling them back to be who they truly were, that is, Yahweh's covenant, holy, and image-bearing people who were to be a light to the nations, thus leading the nations to him, not the other way around (Isa 42:6; 49:6; 60:3).

4.6.1ae. Shedding Tears

Only one passage contains the expression of shedding tears within the bounds of Genesis and Esther, and that is in 2 Kings 20:5. The prophet Isaiah is told by Yahweh to return to Hezekiah, the leader of his people, and say to him, "Thus says the LORD, the God of your father David, 'I have heard your prayer, I have seen your *tears*; behold, I will heal you. On the third day you shall go up to the house of the LORD'" (emphasis mine). Peterman and Schmutzer speak of positive tears as those "tears that should be cried. That is, they are godly; they reflect love of people, grief over loss, and hatred of sin."[287] However, they also make note of the incongruity of such positive tears in averring that, "Ironically, positive tears may have a variety of negative causes. By negative we mean weeping that is incited by sin in its various manifestations: infidelity, betrayal, loss of loved ones through death, sexual abuse, social fragmentation, prejudice. Such tears may arise from abuse of power, arrogance, the crippling effects of disease or war, substance abuse, lack of love, violence, or deception."[288] In the case of Hezekiah, it is his tears, together with his DS1 lament prayer, that move God's compassionate heart, thus occasioning Hezekiah's healing.

4.6.1af. Sitting

The physical expression of sitting can occur within the context of a DS1 lament prayer (Gen 21:16; 1 Kgs 19:4), and also in silence (e.g., Job :2:13; Judg 20:26; Ezra 9:3; Neh 1:4). In fact, T. M. Gregory asserts, "Sitting in silence

---

287. Peterman and Schmutzer, *Between Pain and Grace*, 164.
288. Peterman and Schmutzer, 165.

is a trait associated with mourning in the OT (Judg 20:26; 2 Sam 12:16)."[289] Further to this, Judah J. Slotki comments, "The custom of mourners being seated (cf. Ps 137:1; Job 2:13) has survived among Jews, the bereaved sitting on low stools during the seven days of mourning."[290] Xuan H. T. Pham also points out that, "The initial loud weeping and wailing, accompanied by visible ritual gestures such as tearing clothes, strewing dirt on the head, gashing the body, and so on, was usually followed by a period of stunned silence."[291] The location for such a silent sitting can either be on an ash heap or on the ground (Job 2:13; Isa 47:1; Jonah 3:6).[292]

4.6.1ag. Spreading Out Letter

Threatening Hezekiah and the people of Judah, Sennacherib sends a letter to him via his messengers. Second Kings 19:14 reads, "Then Hezekiah took the letter from the hand of the messengers and read it, and he went up to the house of the LORD and *spread it out* before the LORD" (emphasis mine). This action occurs within the context of Hezekiah's DS1 lament prayer (19:15–19). Hobbs observes that "This is the first mention of letters in the diplomatic activity of this and the previous chapter."[293] What is more, "A letter would be the normal means of such discourse, and it would certainly reinforce the spoken words of the Assyrian delegation. Hezekiah's attitude is quite consistent. Having sought out the prophet and requested prayer, he is faced with an additional setback, so he enters the temple himself to pray."[294] Commenting on this expression, John N. Oswalt remarks, "It is not an attempt to inform God of something he does not already know but an expression of shock and outrage."[295] In other words, "Hezekiah does not merely wish to tell God about the offending document; he places it before him in its entirety, as if to say, 'Surely *this* cannot be left unanswered.'"[296] Rather than patiently wait for Isaiah to intercede before Yahweh on his behalf, Hezekiah's bold action of entering

---

289. Gregory, "Mourning," 304.

290. Slotki, *Daniel, Ezra, Nehemiah*, 183.

291. Pham, *Mourning in the Hebrew*, 29.

292. Pham, 28.

293. Hobbs, *2 Kings*, 277.

294. Hobbs, 277.

295. Oswalt, *Book of Isaiah*, 653.

296. Oswalt, 653.

into the temple and spreading out Sennacherib's letter before Yahweh is therefore to be understood as an expression of absolute urgency demanding divine intervention and deliverance. After all, it is Yahweh's name that is at stake. To wait any longer is to allow for the flourishing of Sennacherib's self-aggrandizements at the expense of Yahweh's honor. Such arrogance, however, must cease. Therefore, Yahweh must act swiftly to reclaim the fame of his glorious name. Hezekiah therefore spares no time, but urgently pleads with Yahweh to keep the content of Sennacherib's disrespectful letter spread out before him from becoming a devastating reality.

4.6.1ah. Standing

Prayers in the sanctuary of Yahweh in the context of disorientation can be uttered to God in a standing posture. While in the house of Yahweh at Shiloh, 1 Samuel 1:26 tells us that Hannah stands. Conversing with Eli the priest, "She said, 'Oh, my lord! As your soul lives, my lord, I am the woman who *stood* here beside you, praying to the LORD'" (emphasis mine). In the verses that follow, Hannah further explains to Eli that "For this boy I prayed, and the LORD has given me my petition which I asked of him. So I have also dedicated him to the LORD; as long as he lives he is dedicated to the LORD.' And he worshiped the LORD there" (1:27–28).

At the dedication of the temple, "Solomon stood before the altar of the LORD" and prayed to the LORD, God of Israel (1 Kgs 8:22). Within a context of disorientation, however, one does not only read, "The descendants of Israel separated themselves from all foreigners, and *stood* and confessed their sin and the iniquities of their fathers," but also, "Now on the Levites' platform *stood* Jeshua, Bani, Kadmiel, Shebaniah, Bani and Chenani, and they cried with a loud voice to the LORD their God" (Neh 9:1–4; emphasis mine). When the psalmist David asks, "Who may ascend into the hill of the LORD? And who may *stand* in His holy place?" (Ps 24:4 [3]; emphasis mine), John Goldingay remarks that, "Talk of standing rather than bowing down suggests that the questioners come not simply to worship but also to make request. They take the posture a suppliant takes before a king."[297] Observing that the posture of standing before Yahweh amidst a context of disorientation

---

297. Goldingay, *Psalms 1–41*, 358.

suggests supplication, it is hardly surprising that Hannah's standing posture occurs within the context of her DS3 vow prayer.

4.6.1ai. Tearing Clothes

After returning home from his victorious battle against the sons of Ammon, a victory granted by Yahweh in response to his DS3 vow prayer of sacrificing as a burnt offering whatever comes out of the doors of his house to meet him upon his return, Judges 11:35 reads, "When he saw her [his daughter] he *tore his clothes*" (emphasis mine). A similar physical expression is recorded in Joshua 7. In v. 5 we read, "The men of Ai killed about thirty-six of their men [Israelites] and chased them before the gate as far as Shebarim and struck them at the descent so that the hearts of the people melted and became as water." This is followed by "Then Joshua *tore his clothes* and fell on the earth on his face before the ark of the LORD until the evening, he and the elders of Israel. And they put dust on their heads" (7:6; emphasis mine).[298] Such an expression surfaces in the context of Joshua's DS1 lament prayer.

Just prior to his DS1 lament prayer, 2 Kgs 19:1 reads, "And when King Hezekiah heard *it* [the ominous news of Sennacherib's threat against Hezekiah and the people of Judah], "he *tore his clothes*, covered himself, with sackcloth and entered the house of the LORD" (emphasis mine). A few chapters later, when the book of the law is found and read to him, Josiah fears that the wrath of Yahweh might burn against him and the people of Judah on account of their fathers' sin. So, in 22:11, we read "When the king heard the words of the book of the law, he *tore his clothes*" (emphasis mine). Such an expression occurs within the context of Josiah's DS1 lament prayer. Approaching Yahweh with his DS4 penitential prayer after hearing of the abomination of intermarriage among the people of Israel and the priests and the Levites, Ezra says, "When I heard this matter, I *tore my garment and my robe*, and pulled some of the hair from my head and my beard, and sat down appalled" (Ezra 9:3, emphasis

---

298. It is noteworthy nonetheless to read the words of the prophet Joel as he admonishes the people of Israel, "And rend your heart and not your garments" (2:13), particularly since Yahweh is concerned about the circumcision of the heart (Deut 30:6; cf. Jer 24:7; Ezek 11:19; 36:26; Ps 51:10; Rom 2:25–29). Other occurrences of the physical expression of rending one's clothes can be found in Gen 37:29, 34; 44:13; 1 Sam 4:12; 2 Sam 15:32; 2 Kgs 18:37; Isa 36:22; Jer 41:5. Matthew 26:65 records that upon hearing Jesus' "blasphemous" words, the high priest rent his garment.

mine). And interestingly, on two occasions, David tears his clothes, once at the death of Abner (2 Sam 3:31), and then at the death of Amnon (13:31).

Commenting on this physical expression, Cole remarks that, "Tearing one's clothes was a form of self-debasing lament in the Old Testament."[299] And from our observations of the few aforementioned references on this physical expression, it is not surprising to read that the tearing of one's clothes "was widely practiced in the ancient Near East in mourning for the dead, in expressing sorrow over disease or plague, or in prefacing a prophetic lament of judgment against an individual or nation."[300]

4.6.1aj. Transporting Cadaver for Burial

According to Gen 50:5, Jacob requests that Joseph bury him in his grave, which he had dug for himself in the land of Canaan. So, after seventy days of weeping in Egypt, Jacob's embalmed body is transported from Egypt to the land of Canaan. His final resting place – the cave of the field of Machpelah before Mamre – was procured by Abraham himself along with the field for a burial site from Ephron the Hittite, even prior to going down to Egypt (50:13; cf. 23:16–20). In so doing, "The sons carry out their father's last wish. . . . Thus Jacob leaves one part of his family and joins another part of his family."[301]

Although his death occurs in Egypt, Joseph's *bones* are later transported by the children of Israel, and buried at Shechem, his final resting place, in the piece of ground that Jacob procured from the sons of Hamor the father of Shechem for one hundred pieces of money (Josh 24:32; cf. Exod 13:19). This is in keeping with his final request to his brothers to be buried in the land promised to Abraham, Isaac, and Jacob (Gen 50:24, 25). Hubbard comments, "Strikingly, through object-first word order the Hebrew throws the syntactical spotlight on the bones, not the burial. The generations between Jacob and the first settlers were buried either in Egypt or in the wilderness, so to highlight the bones underscores their symbolic significance."[302] This means that "They tangibly link the Israelite generation that realized the long-awaited promise

---

299. Cole, "Numbers," 362.

300. Cole, 362. Within a context of mourning for the dead, see 2 Sam 3:31–32 (Abner's death) and 13:31 (Ammon's death).

301. Hamilton, *Genesis 18–50*, 698.

302. Hubbard, *Joshua*, 594.

of land with the patriarchal generations who first received it."[303] In other words, "The box of long-carried and now-buried bones tucked into the earth symbolizes the long epic journey from Genesis to Joshua. Implicitly, those bones echo the last sound of one of the book's central themes, God's fulfillment to the patriarchs."[304] Indeed, "Not one of the good promises which the LORD had made to the house of Israel failed; all came to pass" (Josh 21:45).

Leviticus 10:1 reads, "Now Nadab and Abihu, the sons of Aaron, took their respective firepans, and after putting fire in them, placed incense on it and offered strange fire before the LORD, which He had not commanded them." And as one might expect in light of the holiness of Yahweh (10:3), "Fire came out from the presence of the LORD and consumed them, and they died before the LORD" (10:2). Beckoning Mishael and Elzaphan, the sons of Aaron's uncle Uzziel, the bodies of Nadab and Abihu (10:4), are then transported from the altar to outside the camp where they are presumably buried, even while still in their tunics (Lev 10:5). Wenham points out that, "We should have expected the brothers of Nadab and Abihu to have buried them; instead the task is delegated to Aaron's cousins Mishael and Elzaphan."[305] Wenham also observes that, "Their bodies are unclean and must be removed from the holy area into the realm of the unclean outside the camp (cf. 4:12, 21, etc.). They are treated like the useless parts of the sacrificial animals."[306] Even their tunics, "The garments that symbolized their high calling (8:13), were now used as shrouds for their ignominious burial."[307]

After his death in the temple of Dagon of Philistia, Samson's brothers and all his father's household come down, take him, transport him, and bury his corpse between Zorah and Eshtaol in the tomb of Manoah his father (Judg 16:30–31). Reading 2 Samuel 21:1–14, we learn that David goes and takes the bones of Saul and the bones of Jonathan his son from the men of Jabesh-gilead. His immediate reason for doing this is because the men of Jabesh-gilead had stolen the bones of Saul and Jonathan from the open square of Beth-shan, where the Philistines had hanged them on the day the

---

303. Hubbard, 594.
304. Hubbard, 594.
305. Wenham, *Leviticus*, 157.
306. Wenham, 158.
307. Wenham, 158.

Philistines struck down Saul in Gilboa. So, David transports the bones of Saul and the bones of Jonathan his son from there and gathers the bones of those who had been hanged in Gibeah, namely Rizpah's two sons (Armoni and Mephibosheth), and also the five unnamed sons of Merab the daughter of Saul. After being transported from Jabesh-gilead and Gibeah of Saul, their bones are finally buried properly in the country of Benjamin in Zela, in the grave of Kish the father of Saul.[308]

After the man of God from Judah is killed by a lion, the old prophet of Bethel places the man of God on his donkey, transports him back to Bethel, and buries him in his grave (1 Kgs 13:29–31). Ahab's body is transported from Ramoth-gilead to Samaria for burial (1 Kgs 22:37).[309] Amaziah's body is transported on horses from Lachish to Jerusalem for burial (2 Kgs 14:20–22). And even Josiah's lifeless body is transported in a chariot from Megiddo to Jerusalem for burial in his own tomb (23:30).

4.6.1ak. Turning Face to the Wall

Upon Hezekiah's becoming mortally ill, Isaiah the prophet sends these fateful words to him: "Thus says the LORD, 'Set your house in order, for you shall die and not live" (2 Kgs 20:1). Hezekiah, however, "turned his face to the wall and prayed to the LORD" (20:2). That he turns his face to the wall and prays to Yahweh might be indicative of Hezekiah's "desire for solitude, reflection or even mourning,"[310] as Lissa M. Wray Beal notes. What is more, House believes that it is Hezekiah's "refusal to accept this verdict as final."[311] So, rather than simply acquiesce to Isaiah's prophetic word, Hezekiah "does was he has done before when in jeopardy – he prays. Just as in the previous episodes, he asks the Lord to change what seems to be a logical sequence of events. This time, though, his petition also includes a change in what is, apparently, what God

---

308. King and Stager (*Life in Biblical Israel*, 319–381) tell us, "The bones of the dead were not to be disturbed" (375).

309. The next verse reads: "They washed the chariot by the pool of Samaria, and the dogs licked up his blood (now the harlots bathed themselves *there*), according to the word of the LORD which He spoke" (1 Kgs 22:38). The word of the LORD through the prophet Elijah the Tishbite was thus: "Have you murdered and taken possession? . . . In the place where the dogs licked up the blood of Naboth the dogs will lick up your blood, even yours" (21:19). Through Jezebel's wicked guile, her husband Ahab indirectly murdered Naboth and took possession of his family vineyard (21:1–16).

310. Beal, *1 & 2 Kings*, 481.

311. House, *1, 2 Kings*, 373.

intends to do."[312] Duly considered here is the fact that Hezekiah's physical expression occurs within the context of his DS1 lament prayer.

4.6.1al. Walking Barefooted

Upon discovering that he is among the conspirators with Absalom, David utters his DS2 imprecatory prayer to Yahweh against Ahithophel (2 Sam 15:31). In association with this prayer, we read, "David went up the ascent of the *Mount of Olives*, and wept as he went, and his head was covered and *he walked barefoot*" (15:30; emphasis mine). Not surprisingly then, Bergen tells us, "Covering the head and going about barefoot were both considered expressions of grief and despair in ancient Israelite society (Mic 1:8)."[313]

David therefore grieves over the fact that he is on the run for his very life owing to the fact that his own *trusted counselor* Ahithophel has chosen to entice his own *son* Absalom to conspire against him, with the aim of arrogating his divinely-appointed throne in Jerusalem (2 Sam 7:8). It is worth stating, however, that since Ahithophel is also mentioned in 2 Samuel 23:34 as the father of Eliam, and since Eliam is the father of Bathsheba, Ahithophel should arguably be viewed as the grandfather of Bathsheba (11:3). It is also noted that, later, Ahithophel counsels Absalom to enter into incestuous relationships with his father David's concubines (wives) *publicly*, thus making himself "odious to his father" (16:21). It would appear this was meant to be an act of retaliation against *David* for his *private* yet *coercive* affair with Ahithophel's granddaughter Bathsheba, along with the death of her husband Uriah, both of which he attempted to conceal (11:1–27). Perhaps cognizant of Ahithophel's indirect attempts to not only injure him, but even to take his life, David refuses to restrain himself from exploding with an outburst of words adjuring Yahweh to turn Ahithophel's counsel into foolishness (15:31). In other words, David's grief in the context of his fuming imprecatory prayer against Ahithophel might have come at a time when Ahithophel had also become odious to him.

---

312. House, 373.

313. Bergen, *1, 2 Samuel*, 405–406. See also Isa 20:2–4.

4.6.1am. Washing

Being made aware of the death of his son, David washes himself (12:20). Such an expression, however, runs counter to cultural norms. For this reason, David's servants inquire, "What is this thing you have done? While the child was alive, you fasted and wept; but when the child died, you arose and ate food!" (12:21). David then proffers the following optimistic response: "While the child was *still* alive, I fasted and wept; for I said, 'Who knows, the LORD may be gracious to me, that the child may live.' But now he has died; why should I fast? Can I bring him back again? I will go to him, but he will not return to me" (12:22–23). In these words, Arnold tells us that, "There is to be heard a note of consolation in David's words 'I will go to him.'"[314]

While it is true that David has mourned for his unnamed son seven days already, which has led some to consider his mourning as having been done anticipatorily.[315] In the act of washing himself, however countercultural it might have been at the time, David indicates that he has moved from a state of mourning to a state of joy. Gary A. Anderson's words confirm this understanding: "This joyous state meant that the mourner had to bathe."[316] The fact that David is able to move so quickly from a state of mourning to a state of joy implies that David has no contact with his son. Otherwise, it would have been compulsory for David to quarantine himself for seven days (Num 19:11) and he would have only been allowed to wash with water to purify himself on the third and on the seventh day. Only then would he have been clean, and allowed to re-enter society as a normal person, rather than as a mourner (19:12).

That David washes himself or bathes is another aspect of his behaviour showing that David's grief trajectory is one of resilience. Which is to say that while he is expected to remain in mourning for another seven days, or even to have significant dysfunction, David exhibits a capacity to continue with his life more or less as normal in spite of the loss of his unnamed son.[317] Such resilience, while undergirded by external circumstances such as the cause of death, David's large family, and his place in an ancient society with high infant

---

314. Bergen, 376.

315. Arnold, *1 & 2 Samuel*, 190.

316. Anderson, *A Time to Mourn*, 50.

317. Bosworth, "Faith and Resilience," 692.

mortality, is primarily grounded in his intrinsic circumstances, such as his sense of personal agency, and more particularly, his faith in Yahweh his God.[318]

4.6.1an. Worshiping God

Second Samuel 12:20 tells us that after being made aware of the sad news of the death of his unnamed son, David "came into the house of the LORD and *worshiped*" (emphasis mine). Lacking in conformity to cultural mourning practices, such an expression catches the attention of his servants who ask, "What is this thing you have done? While the child was alive, you fasted and wept; but when the child died, you arose and ate food!" (12:21). In other words, conventional mourning practice dictated that David continue sitting *shiva*, fasting, weeping, and wearing his mourning clothes (perhaps sackcloth) during his time of grief following the death of his stillborn son who goes un-named in the biblical text. Proffering the significance of his countercultural expression, David avows, "While the child was *still* alive, I fasted and wept; for I said, 'Who knows, the LORD may be gracious to me, that the child my live.' But now he has died; why should I fast? Can I bring him back again? I will go to him, but he will not return to me" (12:22–23). Bergen remarks, "There is to be heard a note of consolation in David's words 'I will go to him.'"[319]

In light of this, it is worth commenting briefly on two features inherent within David's counterintuitive actions. The first relates to David's worship "in the house of the LORD," which some have regarded as either anachronistic, since it refers to Solomon's temple,[320] or making use of a Jebusite cultic build-ing the locus of which was the threshing floor of Araunah, which Solomon later renovates and expands.[321] Tsumura points out that "The mention of 'the house of the LORD' (*bêt YHWH*) here has been considered anachronistic by several scholars. However, there is no reason to think that the author meant Solomon's temple; it was probably a tent shrine for the ark, which could be called a 'house' like the *bt* of El in Ugarit."[322]

---

318. Bosworth, 700. See also our previous discussion in section 4.5.3.4 on p@@.

319. Bergen, *1, 2 Samuel*, 376. Bosworth ("Understanding Grief," 117–138) avers that, "David finds comfort in the prospect of seeing his dead son in Sheol (2 Sam 12:23)" (128).

320. McCarter, *II Samuel*, 302.

321. As noted in McCarter, 302; Anderson, *2 Samuel*, 164.

322. Tsumura, *Second Samuel*, 197; Arnold, *1 & 2 Samuel*, 538–539. David's act of going into the house of Yahweh immediately following his unnamed son's death is indicative of the

Bergen, however, remarks that "In a manner appropriate for a priest (cf. Exod 30:20; cf. Ps 110:4) David first washed himself and then 'went into the house of the LORD and worshiped.' In losing his son, David sought more than ever to regain a deeper relationship with his Heavenly Father."[323] For this reason, "It is significant that David did not break his fast until after he had worshiped God; David's hunger for a right relationship with God exceeded his desire for culinary delights."[324] In other words, David's decision to worship Yahweh immediately after the death of his son whose survival he had inquired of God for, is a deep recognition that "he lives under Yahweh's greater authority."[325]

The second feature relates to a belief in the afterlife. King and Stager remark that "There existed in biblical Israel a belief in some form of afterlife, considered to be basically an extension of earthly life."[326] After expressing his frustration with his belief in divine retribution, that is, of the righteous being rewarded and the unrighteous being punished, Asaph finally concludes in Psalm 73:25–27 [24–26]:

> With Your counsel You will guide me,
>   And afterward receive me to *glory*.
> Whom have I in *heaven* but You?
>   And besides You, I desire nothing on earth.
> My flesh and my heart may fail,
>   But God is the strength of my heart and my portion
>   forever. (Emphasis mine)

Longman tells us, "Reading these verses in light of the fuller revelation of the afterlife that we have in the NT, many Christian readers have no doubt that these verses point to the heavenly realities."[327] Yet he acknowledges that, "in my opinion, scholars are too quick to deny that some places in the OT provide glimpses of this teaching that are more fully developed in the NT."[328]

---

fact that there is no prior contact with his son's body, a sin deserving of being cut off from Israel (Num 19:13).

323. Bergen, *1, 2 Samuel*, 375.

324. Bergen, 375.

325. Firth, *1 & 2 Samuel*, 429.

326. King and Stager, *Life in Biblical Israel*, 373.

327. Longman, *Fear of the Lord*, 188.

328. Longman, 188.

In other words, "while we cannot be certain, it seems to me that the psalmist is alluding to the idea that he will find his reward and the wicked will find their punishment, perhaps in this life, but certainly in the afterlife."[329]

In a similar vein, and even much earlier than Asaph, one hears Job exclaim in 19:25–27:

> As for me, I know that *my Redeemer lives*,
>> And at the last He will take His stand on the earth
>> .[עַל־עָפָר יָקוּם]
> Even after my skin is destroyed,
>> *Yet from my flesh I shall see God;*
> Whom I myself shall behold,
>> And whom my eyes will see and not another.
>> (Emphasis mine)

Eric N. Ortlund insists that, "Job literally says that his Redeemer will 'rise above the dust' or 'triumph over' it."[330] While it is true that עַל־עָפָר יָקוּם, *al-aphar yaqum* in 19:25 can be translated as "'he will stand on the dust,' since that verb [קוּם, *qum*] is used elsewhere for offering legal testimony, and 'dust' [עָפָר, *aphar*] can stand for the ground or the world more generally (see, e.g., Job 14:8, 19; 28:2)," it should be noted, however, that "dust is also a symbol for death and the grave in the book of Job (see 7:21; 17:16; 20:11, 26; 34:15; 40:13)."[331] Ortlund therefore maintains that the verb קוּם, *qum* "should be translated as 'rise above' or 'triumph over.' More than once it expresses God's action of self-exaltation to save his helpless people (see Pss. 3:8; 7:7; 9:22; 10:12; 12:6; 44:27; 68:2; 74:22; 76:10; 82:8)."[332] From this standpoint, "This means that when we hear of Job's Redeemer standing on the earth as a legal advocate, we should simultaneously hear Job confessing his hope that his Redeemer will 'rise above the dust' in the sense of triumphing over death."[333] Such an "Awareness of the multiple meanings in 19:25 also helps us to appreciate Job's statement that his Redeemer 'lives.' It is out of the power of his own indestructible life that Job's Redeemer triumphs over death to Job's

---

329. Longman, 188.

330. Ortlund, *Suffering Wisely and Well*, 108.

331. Ortlund, 108.

332. Ortlund, 108–109.

333. Ortlund, 109.

benefit."[334] This is further reinforced by the words that Job will see God and not another, that is, not a stranger (19:26–27). Seeing God therefore "means more than some distant glimpse; it means being caught up in God himself as Job is reunited in fellowship with him."[335] To speak of this physical reality another way, Job is not referring to a "vague, ghostly existence, like the shades in Sheol; when Job refers to his flesh (19:26) and his own eyes (19:27), he is speaking of embodied existence in God's presence after death. Although the hope of the resurrection is fully and clearly revealed only in the New Testament, it is hard for me to see how Job's hope here is any different."[336] In other words, "Job is here expressing the same rapturous hope that Christians feel when they read about seeing Jesus's face in Revelation 22:4."[337]

Here, however, a caveat is proffered by Herbert Brichto who cautions the reader from conflating a belief in afterlife with that of resurrection. Brichto contends that biblical belief prior to Daniel is limited to afterlife, while after Daniel, the biblical credo embraces resurrection to eternal life.[338] Therefore, by virtue of his belief in the afterlife, which is underpinned by his faith in Yahweh, his God, it is not difficult to understand why David could resume a normal life or transition into a joyous state of worshiping Yahweh so rapidly after losing his unnamed son. To put the matter differently, David's counter-cultural behavior of joyfully worshiping Yahweh, when expected to remain in a state of mourning the loss of his unnamed son, exhibits a grief trajectory of resilience, that is, a capacity to continue with his life more or less in spite of loss.[339] For this reason, Bosworth suggests that "David need not be judged so harshly by scholars or presented as a normative model to bereaved parents. The description of David's behavior seems to be used in the Bible to characterize David, not to tell other parents how to mourn."[340]

---

334. Ortlund, 109.

335. Ortlund, 109.

336. Ortlund, 110.

337. Ortlund, 110.

338. Brichto, "Kin, Cult, Land," 53. For more information on immortality in the house of Yahweh, particularly the temple, see Madigan and Levenson, *Resurrection*.

339. Bosworth, "Faith and Resilience," 692.

340. Bosworth, "Understanding Grief," 119. See pages 134–137 for more details on this argument of David's grief trajectory of resilience.

4.6.2. Categorization of Physical Expressions

Here an attempt is made to categorize the physical expressions in the context of the verbal expressions communicated to/before God amidst disorientation, both non-death-related and death-related, within the DS1–7 continuum. Within a DS1 lament context, several expressions come to the fore, namely blowing (silver) trumpets, fasting, lying on the ground, offering burnt and peace offerings, sacrificing through supernatural fire (building altar, making trench, arranging wood, cutting ox, laying ox on wood), shedding tears, sitting, spreading out letter, tearing clothes, and turning face to the wall. Only three expressions, covering head, prostrating oneself, and walking barefooted are found within a DS2 imprecatory context. The expressions of offering a human sacrifice, standing, and tearing one's clothes all appear within a DS3 vow context. Several expressions, such as kneeling, plucking hair from beard and head, pouring dirt upon oneself, separation from foreigners, sitting; and tearing one's clothes, are all located within a DS4 penitential context. With regard to the death-related rituals, one finds such physical expressions as anointing oneself, burning, burying (and purchasing land), chambering (privacy/isolation), changing clothes, covering face, deep moving (trembling), donning and removing widow's clothes, donning sackcloth, eating, erecting gravestones (monuments), falling on and kissing the dead, funeral processioning, grieving/mourning, honoring (through spice-fire), lying on the ground, placing in coffin, prostrating oneself, rising from the ground, sitting, transporting cadaver for burial, washing, and worshiping God. In light of this, we are now in a better position to categorize the physical expressions located within a context of disorientation within the OT (Genesis to Esther), which are both non-death-related (i.e. auxiliary expressions related to the DS1 Lament–DS6 Thanksgiving Praise Prayers), as well as death-related (DS7 Bereavement Vocabulary). Below is a table with the physical categories and their description.

Categories	Description
Disorientation Stage 1 Physical Expressions: DS1 Lament Rituals	Rituals associated with lament, including: Blowing (Silver) Trumpets; Fasting; Lying on the Ground; Offering Burnt and Peace Offerings; Paralleling Two Outstretched Bodies; Shedding Tears; Sacrificing through Supernatural Fire (Building Altar, Making Trench, Arranging Wood, Cutting Ox, Laying Ox on Wood); Sitting; Spreading Out Letter; Tearing Clothes; and Turning Face to the Wall.
Disorientation Stage 2 Physical Expressions: DS2 Imprecatory Rituals	Rituals associated with imprecation, including: Covering Head; Prostrating Oneself; and Walking Barefooted.
Disorientation Stage 3 Physical Expressions: DS3 Vow Rituals	Rituals associated with vow, including: Offering Human Sacrifice, Standing, and Tearing Clothes.
Disorientation Stage 4 Physical Expressions: DS4 Penitential Rituals	Rituals associated with penitence, including: Kneeling; Plucking Hair from Beard and Head; Pouring Dirt upon Oneself; Prostrating Oneself; Separation from Foreigners; Sitting; and Tearing Clothes.
Disorientation Stage 7 Physical Expressions (Death-Related): DS7 Bereavement Rituals	Rituals associated with death, including: Anointing Oneself; Burning; Burying (and Purchasing Land); Chambering (Privacy/Isolation); Changing Clothes; Covering Face; Deep Moving (Trembling); Donning and Removing Widow's Clothes; Donning Sackcloth; Eating; Erecting Gravestones (Monuments); Falling on and Kissing the Deceased; Funeral Processioning; Grieving/Mourning; Honoring (through Spice-fire); Lying on the Ground; Placing in Coffin; Rising from the Ground; Sitting; Transporting Cadaver for Burial; Washing; and Worshiping God.

4.6.3. Summary

At this juncture, we come to the end of our anthropological physical expressions communicated to/before God and humans amidst a context of disorientation inclusive of which was the death of a leading OT Israelite saint. These expressions will be added to the domain of anthropological expressions of disorientation along with their significance. Some of these expressions will play a key role in the dialectic correlation with the expressions garnered from within the Guyanese-Canadian and Vietnamese-Canadian cultures.

In the section that follows, we discuss the anthropological emotional expressions communicated to/before God and humans in the context of disorientation. Once again, the collection of this data is aimed at facilitating a dialectic correlation between biblical theology and pastoral theology. That is, a dialectic correlation between the verbal, physical, and emotional expressions conveyed to/before God from within a context of disorientation (i.e. the textual locus of the prosaic sections of the OT, namely Genesis to Esther), and that of the verbal, physical, and emotional expressions that surface amidst the phenomenon of grief among Christian leaders within a Guyanese-Canadian and Vietnamese-Canadian context. The objective of the entire endeavor, however, is the fostering of compassionate (liberative intercultural) pastoral care practices that are true to the gospel of God, and thus grief-transformative, rather than grievous.

4.6.4. Emotional Anthropological Expressions

Here, we recall the remark made by Corless et al., that physical responses within a context of grief "are composed of physical signs, bodily expressions, and sensual aspects such as seeing and hearing. The manner in which the head is held (body language) is an example of a physical response, as is weeping. Sobbing, sighing, sudden, intense emotion, or other somatic, physical responses typically occur without intention."[341] For the purposes of this book, however, a distinction is made between the physical and emotional expressions to provide a three-dimensional understanding of the anthropological expressions of disorientation communicated to/before God. In this section the emotional anthropological expressions communicated to/before God by leading Israelites within the OT are brought to the fore (both non-death-related

---

341. Corless, "Languages of Grief," 136.

and death-related). After all, "Every emotion, though horizontally provoked, nevertheless reflects something about the vertical dimension: our relationship with God,"[342] as Dan B. Allender and Tremper Longman insist. Some of these expressions will therefore play a key role within the dialectic correlation between biblical and pastoral theology in chapter 5.[343]

4.6.4a. Anger

After being made aware of the idolatry of the children of Israel, and making his way down Mount Sinai, we read in Exodus 32:19, "It came about, as soon as Moses came near the camp, that he saw the calf and *the* dancing; and Moses' *anger* burned, and he threw the tablets from his hands and shattered them at the foot of the mountain" (emphasis mine). This occurs just after his intercession on their behalf by means of a DS1 lament prayer to Yahweh (vv. 11–13). Within the bounds of Genesis and Esther, this emotive response of anger is only provoked here. Ellen van Wolde contends that, "Whenever the verb חרה is used [as in Exod 32:19], it obviously does not describe an emotion kept inside, but an erupting emotion followed by fierce discussions, rows or destructive actions, such as murder, destruction, crash."[344] She further observes that, "This feature, together with the location of anger in the nostrils or nose, lips, and tongue, and not a location in the belly, stomach, or chest . . . makes it plausible that the verb חרה denotes uncontrollable fury. Once aroused it immediately rises to the head and comes out of the nose and blows upon someone."[345] Little wonder she contends that, "Anger in the Hebrew Bible is related to the mouth, nose or face and expresses an uncontrollable fury in someone's head that leads prototypically to retributive actions."[346]

---

342. Allender and Longman, *Cry of the Soul*, 13–14.

343. See my Appendix 1 on the webpage: https://langhamliterature.org/9781839738401-appendix-1 which can be consulted for the full gamut of textual references associated with the emotional expressions that accompany prayers uttered within the lived context of disorientation, as well as those found in the context of the death of a leading Israelite.

344. van Wolde, "Sentiments as Culturally Constructed," 11.

345. van Wolde, 11–12.

346. van Wolde, 22. She also notes that only those instances of anger that start with and come from a person in a hierarchically higher position and are oriented towards someone in a lower position culturally are accepted (23). In the case of Exod 32, anger starts with and comes from Moses the leader of the people of Israel and is oriented towards the people of Israel. The only exception to her argument, however, as she notes, is Jonathan's expression of anger at his father Saul who desires to kill David (1 Sam 20:34). "Both the language of sentiment and

In light of this, is it not surprising that, following the shattering of the tablets, Moses' anger continues to manifest itself in his fierce discussion with Aaron (32:21–24), as well as his declaration calling for the slaughter of all those against Yahweh, which occasions the deaths of some three thousand men of the people of Israel that day (32:25–29).

4.6.4b. Appallment

Ezra 9 tells us that, after the scribe and priest hears of the mixed marriages, "I tore my garment and my robe, and pulled some of the hair from my head and my beard, and sat down *appalled*" (מְשׁוֹמֵם, *mešomem*; v. 3; emphasis mine). In other words, the news of the mixed marriages is something that Ezra finds disgusting. James A. Swanson comments, Ezra is deeply "horrified, terrified, dismayed, i.e. have an emotion or attitude of horror and great fear."[347] Which is another way of saying that this matter of mixed or contaminated marriages is not something that Ezra treats apathetically, and is in fact very revolting to this priest of Yahweh who desires that Yahweh's people be holy even as he is holy (9:1–2; cf. Exod 22:31; Lev 19:2; Deut 14:2). In other words, from Ezra's perspective, the people of Israel, the priests, and the Levites, should restrain themselves from such impure matrimonies (Exod 34:16) lest they contaminate themselves (Ps 106:35), turn away from Yahweh their God, and serve other gods, who are no gods at all (Deut 7:3–4).

Perceiving the potentially dangerous influence that a foreign wife is likely to have on her husband in enticing him away from his loyalty to Yahweh, Ezra is "extremely grieved."[348] Yet it should be noted that, "The term 'holy' [in the holy seed, Ezra 9:2] shows that the term 'seed' has nothing to do with racial prejudice. . . . It was a question of the living relation between the LORD and his people."[349] On the grounds of this spiritual infidelity with the potential for divorce from their holy God (Jer 3:8), Ezra finds unholy matrimonies a sacrilegious act, giving him cause to mourn deeply, as observed in both his penitential prayer as well as his physical outbursts (Ezra 9:3–15). In other words, Ezra is disgusted at such an unholy alliance among God's holy people,

---

the context of behaviour indicate the reversal of hierarchical roles in which Jonathan is not accepting his father's authority anymore" (16n28).

347. Swanson, שָׁמֵם, n.p.

348. Breneman, *Ezra, Nehemiah, Esther*, 150.

349. Fensham, *Books of Ezra and Nehemiah*, 125.

and fears what Yahweh might do in response. Since "emotional disgust frequently associates with impurity language, whether the issue is prohibited foods, various conditions involving genital discharge or skin ailments, . . . or disapproved behaviors,"[350] it is hardly surprising to read that Ezra's disgust manifests itself in his tearing of both his outer and inner garments, thus exposing the intensity of his appallment.

Interestingly, this emotive response of being appalled or disgusted comes to the fore only once, in the context of Ezra's passionate DS4 penitential prayer (Ezra 9:6–15). Such an emotive response surfaces in the company of Ezra's physical expressions of tearing his garment and robe, pulling some of his hair from his head and beard, sitting down (9:3), falling on his knees, and stretching out his hands to Yahweh his God (9:5).

4.6.4c. Dismay

When the sons of Moab, the sons of Ammon, and some of the Meunites make war against Jehoshaphat, Jahazial the son of Zechariah twice instructs all Judah and the inhabitants of Jerusalem and King Jehoshaphat, "Do not fear or be *dismayed*" (2 Chron 20:15, 17; emphasis mine). This implies that along with fear, *dismay* is also a present emotive response, which only occurs alongside Jehoshaphat's imprecatory prayer (20:6–12). On account of the supernatural deliverance that they are about to experience the following day at the hands of Yahweh who is with them, the effect of dismay is to be viewed as incompatible for the people of the living and ever-present *God* (20:17; cf. Deut 31:6, 8; Josh 1:5). Yahweh's people are therefore not to abandon their hope in God their divine warrior, who will fight with and for them.

According to Allender and Longman, otherwise referred to as despair, the affect of dismay "is the refusal to struggle. It deadens our heart to the hope that we will be rescued, redeemed, and happy."[351] In other words, "Despair refuses to hope . . . Despair vocalizes the core question: *Is God good, or will he leave me in isolation? Will he offer his presence to others and leave me alone?*"[352] However, with the following reassuring words from Jahaziel, God puts their dismay to rest: "You *need* not fight this battle; station yourselves, stand and

---

350. Kazen, "Disgust in Body," 103.

351. Allender and Longman, *Cry of the Soul*, 48.

352. Allender and Longman, 48–49; emphasis original.

see the salvation of the LORD on your behalf, O Judah and Jerusalem. . . . for *the LORD is with you*'" (2 Chron 20:17; emphasis mine). Interestingly, on account of such reassuring words, their dismay or despair gives way to such wondrous joy that they find themselves incapable of restraining themselves from offering their jubilant thanksgiving praise to Yahweh even *before* the battle is fought and the victory won (20:18–19, 21–22). Nevertheless, dismay is an emotion displayed prior to the oracle of salvation delivered to them by the agency of Jahaziel, and this in connection with a DS2 imprecatory prayer.

4.6.4d. Displeasure / Distress / Oppressed in spirit

Numbers 11:10–15 gives the account of the children of Israel grumbling over the food that God is providing for them miraculously on a daily basis. Dissatisfied with their daily manna, otherwise referred to as the bread of angels (Ps 78:26 [25]), the children of Israel weep throughout their families, each man at the doorway of his tent, thus greatly kindling the anger of Yahweh (Num 11:10). As Moses records, "They weep before me, saying, 'Give us meat that we may eat!'" (11:14). Unable to fulfill their selfish desire, however, "Moses was *displeased*" (11:10; emphasis mine).

Interestingly, the Hebrew text reads, וּבְעֵינֵי מֹשֶׁה רָע, *ube'ene Moše raʿ*, translated and in Moses' eyes, [it was] evil.[353] Milgrom thus asks: "Is the referent of 'it' the people's complaint or the Lord's actions? That is, with whom did Moses side – with God, that the people's complaint was evil, or with the people in their complaint against God?"[354] Milgrom responds: "Moses' own discomfiture with God in the following verse indicates that he concurred with Israel that the Lord had dealt ill with it."[355] Timothy R. Ashley, however, adds, "As the following verses indicate, Moses does not react against the people's rejection of God's provision but against the people for making his job as leader more difficult, and against Yahweh for giving him the task as leader."[356]

Being the leader of such a great number of people so overwhelms Moses that he directs his affect of displeasure or distress at both the people of Israel *and* Yahweh. The burden of supplying God's people with food affects Moses

---

353. See also Ashley, *Book of Numbers*, 210.
354. Milgrom, *Numbers*, 85.
355. Milgrom, 85.
356. Ashley, *Numbers*, 210.

to the point that he even petitions Yahweh to take his life. Moses's emotive response of displeasure or distress, nevertheless, occurs within his DS1 lament prayer recorded in 11:11–15.

On account of his persistent idolatry, Manasseh is taken into captivity. But 2 Chronicles 33:12 reads, "When he was in *distress*, he entreated the LORD his God and humbled himself greatly before the God of his fathers" (emphasis mine). That the Hebrew word used here appears in the Hiphil infinitive construct (וּכְהָצֵר, *ukehatser*), suggests that the situation in which Manasseh finds himself causes him distress.[357] In his distressing situation of being treated like a subdued animal,[358] he petitions God in humility. "Manasseh's plea issues from a contrite heart, for he 'humbled himself [*kn'*] greatly (33:12). This word signifies true repentance . . . For this reason, the report of Manasseh's repentance and prayer of forgiveness is reminiscent of the language of God's promise to King Solomon to restore those who 'humble themselves and pray' (2 Chron 7:14)."[359] As such, Manasseh's distress is located within the context of his DS4 penitential prayer.

After hearing of Yahweh's regret in making Saul king of his people Israel, 1 Samuel 15:11 reads, "And Samuel was *distressed*" (emphasis mine). Interestingly, the Hebrew text reads: וַיִּחַר לִשְׁמוּאֵל, *wayyichar lišmuel*, which Tsumura translates, "Samuel was angry." Yet he notes, "It suggests that the prophet of the Lord feels God's inner feelings, the divine pathos, violently."[360] His reference to divine pathos comes from Abraham J. Heschel, who observes that the experience of Samuel is "a fellowship with the feelings of God, a *sympathy with the divine pathos*, a communion with the divine consciousness, which comes about through the prophet's reflection of, or participation in, the divine pathos."[361] Bergen, however, posits, "First of all, God was 'grieved' [*nhm*] that he 'made Saul king' . . . The employment of the term suggests that the Lord was deeply concerned – or as H. V. D. Parunak asserts, 'suffered

357. See BDB 864 where the word means "*make narrow* for, *press hard* upon, and *cause distress* to."

358. Dillard, *2 Chronicles*, 268.

359. Hill, *1 & 2 Chronicles*, 482.

360. Tsumura, *First Samuel*, 396; cf. van Wolde, "Sentiments as Culturally Constructed," 11–12, 22.

361. Heschel, *Prophets: An Introduction*, 26; emphasis original.

emotional pain' – regarding choices Saul made of his own volition.'"[362] Clearly there is some kind of emotional pain within the heart of God and that of Samuel's.

As is observed from these passages of Scripture, within the parameters of Genesis and Esther, this emotive response of distress, appears in a variety of Hebrew words. Additionally, while distress is awakened in most cases amidst a DS1 lament prayer, it is also observed within the context of a DS4 penitential prayer.

Despite that, 1 Samuel 1:10–11a reads: "She [Hannah], greatly *distressed*, prayed to the LORD and wept bitterly. She made a vow and said . . ." (emphasis mine). The Hebrew text reads, מָרַת נָפֶשׁ, *marat nepheš*, translated *bitter of soul*. The bitterness in Hannah's soul manifests itself in her bitter weeping (וּבָכֹה תִבְכֶּה, *ubakoh tibkeh*). In the process of such great distress, "Hannah's agony finally finds words,"[363] even as she presents her DS3 vow prayer to Yahweh, which accompanies her standing posture.

In addition to this, Bergen maintains that the phrase "bitterness of soul" is "a phrase used elsewhere to characterize the psychological pain experienced by one who has been deprived of a child through death (cf. Ruth 1:13, 20; 2 Kgs 4:27; Zech 12:10) or who is experiencing great personal physical suffering (cf. Job 3:20; 7:11; 10:1; Isa 38:15)."[364] He also observes, "Relief from this sort of pain is never pictured in the Hebrew Bible as coming from a human being; in each case divine intervention was the only remedy. Wisely, Hannah also went to the Lord for help."[365]

Later, as Eli the priest wrongfully accuses Hannah of drunkenness, Hannah responds, "No, my lord, I am a woman *oppressed in spirit*; I have drunk neither wine nor strong drink, but I have poured out my soul before the LORD" (1 Sam 1:15; emphasis mine). Tsumura translates the phrase קְשַׁת־רוּחַ, *qešat ruach*, as "struggling in spirit."[366] Comparing the expression oppressed or struggling in spirit with the determinedness of Sihon in Deuteronomy 2:30, Takamitsu Muraoka, however, posits that Hannah is "firmly determined to

---

362. Bergen, *1, 2 Samuel*, 170; see Parunak, "Semantic Survey of NḤM," 519.

363. Tsumura, *First Samuel*, 117.

364. Bergen, *1, 2 Samuel*, 68.

365. Bergen, 68.

366. Tsumura, *First Samuel*, 121.

take up the matter with her God."[367] Possessing an oppressed spirit or struggling spirit, "Hannah here takes her refuge in the Lord, bringing her problem directly to her God by prayer."[368] Within the bounds of Genesis and Esther, only here does the emotive response of an oppression within one's spirit appear within the context of a DS3 vow prayer to Yahweh (cf. Prov 31:2).

4.6.4e. Embarrassment and Shame

Upon the confession of his sins and the sins of his people, Ezra declares, "O my God, I am *ashamed* and *embarrassed* to lift up my face to You, my God, for our iniquities have risen above our heads and our guilt has grown even to the heavens" (Ezra 9:6; emphasis mine). The elicitation of the emotive response of embarrassment only occurs here within the bounds of Genesis and Esther, and this within a DS4 penitential prayer.

That being said, as Ezra and the family heads return to Jerusalem, Ezra seeks Yahweh's protection for the journey, but admits, "For I was *ashamed* to request from the king troops and horsemen to protect us from the enemy on the way, because we had said to the king, 'The hand of our God is favorably disposed to all those who seek Him, but his power and his anger are against all those who forsake Him'" (8:22; emphasis mine). Within the parameters of Genesis and Esther, only here does the emotive response of shame surface amidst a DS1 lament prayer (8:21, 23). As noted in Ezra 9:6, however, the emotive response of shame comes to the fore amidst his DS4 penitential prayer.

Ezra therefore feels ashamed in the holy eyes of God. Allender and Longman add that shame "is one of our deepest fears: We will be isolated and mocked forever. It is a taste of hell – the experience of being caught without defense or cover and condemned to unrelenting humiliation."[369] In other words, "Shame is feeling exposed as ugly beyond words. Nothing else cuts to the core so personally as shame does."[370] In fact, "Shame drains us of our energy and withers our desire to exist."[371] What is more, "Its typical posture is

---

367. Muraoka, "1 Sam 1,15 Again," 98–99.

368. Tsumura, *First Samuel*, 121.

369. Allender and Longman, *Cry of the Soul*, 51.

370. Allender and Longman, 51.

371. Allender and Longman, 51.

eyes downcast, shoulders slumped, heart disengaged."[372] Small wonder then that Ezra finds it difficult to even look up to Yahweh. Interestingly, along with his DS4 penitential prayer, Ezra tears his garment and robe, pulls some of the hair from his head and beard, and sits down appalled (9:3), falls on his knees and stretches out his hands to Yahweh his God (9:5), ashamed and embarrassed that he cannot lift up his face to Yahweh his God (9:6).

4.6.4f. Fear (Divine and Human)

The emotion of fear is elicited toward God and humans. Thus, we read in Exodus 3:6, "Then Moses hid his face, for he was *afraid* to look at God" (emphasis mine), and this within a DS1 lament prayer (3:13). The rationale behind Moses' fear of looking at God, however, is heard in the words of God in 33:20: "You cannot see My face, for no man can see Me and live!"

For an example of the fear of a human being, after sojourning with Laban, Jacob prepares to reunite with his older twin brother and rival Esau. While he camps in Manahaim (Gen 32:2), he sends messengers before him to Esau in the land of Seir, the country of Edom (32:3), commanding them, "Thus you shall say to my lord Esau: 'Thus says your servant Jacob, 'I have sojourned with Laban, and stayed until now; I have oxen and donkeys and flocks and male and female servants; and I have sent to tell my lord, that I may find favor in your sight'" (32:4–5). Returning from their meeting with Esau, the messengers tell Jacob, "We came to your brother Esau, and furthermore he is coming to meet you, and four hundred men are with him" (32:6). At this the reader is informed, "Then *Jacob was greatly afraid* and distressed; and he divided the people who were with him, and the flocks and the herds and the camels, into two companies; for he said, 'If Esau comes to the one company and attacks it, then the company which is left will escape'" (32:7–8; emphasis mine). What is more, in his DS1 lament prayer to Yahweh his God, Jacob does not hesitate to acknowledge his fear.

> "O God of my father Abraham and God of my father Isaac, O LORD, who said to me, 'Return to your country and to your relatives, and I will prosper you.' I am unworthy of all the lov-ingkindness and of all the faithfulness which You have shown

---

372. Allender and Longman, 51.

to Your servant; for with my staff *only* I crossed this Jordan, and now I have become two companies. Deliver me, I pray, from the hand of my brother Esau; for *I fear him*, that he will come and attack me *and* the mothers with the children. For You said, 'I will surely prosper you and make your descendants as the sand of the sea, which is too great to be numbered'" (emphasis mine).[373]

Allender and Longman aver that, "fear energizes us to flee. It quickens our retreat. It makes any movement forward into battle seem absurd. Fear triggers a dilation of the pupils, as if our eyes are opening wide enough to take in all the data necessary to avoid destruction."[374] They further observe that in fear, "Our stomach tightens, heaviness descends, and sweat glands release moisture to 'cool' down the physical machine, so that it doesn't burn up. The body is prepared for flight and hiding. As fear increases, the body is prepared to shut down and curl up. At its extreme, terror is immobilizing."[375]

On the whole, the fear of another human, which is likely to cause one to flee, is aroused within the context of a DS1 lament prayer within the parameters of Genesis and Esther (Exod 14:10; 1 Sam 7:7; 28:5; 1 Kgs 19:3; 2 Kgs 19:3; Neh 2:2). So also, the fear of God appears within the context of Moses' DS1 lament prayer. However, in only one case, as the sons of Moab, the sons of Ammon, and the Meunites wage war against him, Jehoshaphat's fear is evoked within the context of his DS2 imprecatory prayer (2 Chron 20:15, 17).

4.6.4g. Grief

Following on the heels of the death of his son Absalom, 2 Samuel 19:2 reads, "The king is *grieved* for his son" (emphasis mine). According to Bosworth, "Grief is more than bereavement; it encompasses a range of losses and trauma. Grief responses may occur in connection to any serious threat to a valued relationship (both the seriousness of the threat and the importance of the relationship are determined in the culturally-embedded mind of the person who appraises them)."[376] Although he admits "there is no fixed sequence,

---

373. For other examples, see 1 Sam 28:6; 2 Chron 20:2–3.

374. Allender and Longman, *Cry of the Soul*, 46.

375. Allender and Longman, 46.

376. Bosworth, "Understanding Grief," 126–127.

grieving behaviors can be organized into 'stages,' beginning with numbness, then protest, despair, and finally detachment / reorganization."[377]

Wayne E. Oates, however, posits at least six quantitative kinds of grief: (i) anticipatory (a double grief, that is, the grief of a person dying with a long-term grief over his or her gradual loss of life due to a terminal illness and the grief of the family and close friends of the dying); (ii) sudden or traumatic (with little or no warning and which can lead to shock, alarm, disbelief, panic, hastening back to hyperactive work, or grieving alone); (iii) chronic sorrow or no end grief (also called "the death of a dream" grief); (iv) near miss grief (in which a person narrowly escaped being killed); (v) pathological grief (the shock of a sudden death unhinges the judgment and behavior of a severely shocked family member or an intense desire to be near God but it is complicated by the complaint that God does not care, does not hear, or does not exist; (vi) tragic sense of life grief (arises from the sense of being limited in our care of others and the sense of being subject to death ourselves).[378] Against the backdrop of this outline, it is likely that David experiences a sudden or traumatic grief, which manifests itself, at least in one way, by his desire to grieve alone.[379] As 2 Samuel 18:33 reads, "The king was deeply moved and went up to the chamber over the gate and wept."

4.6.4h. Guilt

The affect of guilt comes to the fore in Ezra 9:6 after Ezra catches wind of the news from the princes that the people of Israel, the priests, and the Levites have not separated themselves from the peoples of the lands. Instead, they have encouraged interreligious marriages between their sons and daughters and those of the Canaanites, Hittites, Perizzites, Jebusites, Ammonites, Moabites, Egyptians, and Amorites (Ezra 9:1–2). A few verses later we read, "O my God, I am ashamed and embarrassed to lift my face to You, my God, for our iniquities have risen above our heads and our *guilt* has grown even to the heavens" (9:6; emphasis mine; cf. 9:7). As such, the emotive response of guilt is evoked amidst Ezra's DS4 penitential prayer.

---

377. Bosworth, 127–128.
378. Oates, *Grief, Transition, and Loss*, 20–25.
379. Oates, 21.

According to Susan Krauss Whitbourne, "Guilt is, first and foremost, an emotion . . . it's more accurate to think of guilt as an internal state. In the overall scheme of emotions, guilt is in the general category of negative feeling states. It's one of the 'sad' emotions, which also include agony, grief, and loneliness."[380] Looking at guilt "From a cognitive point of view, guilt is an emotion that people experience because they're convinced they've caused harm. In cognitive theory, the thoughts cause the emotions. The emotion of guilt follows directly from the thought that you are responsible for someone else's misfortune, whether or not that's the case."[381] Applying this cognitive theory, Whitbourne proposes five types of guilt: (i) guilt for something you did; (ii) guilt for something you didn't do, but want to; (iii) guilt for something you think you did; (iv) guilt that you didn't do enough to help someone; and (v) guilt that you're doing better than someone else.[382]

In the case of Ezra, guilt is elicited not necessarily because of what *he* has done, but because of what the people of Israel and the priests and the Levites have done. They have not separated themselves from the peoples of the lands, and in fact have taken some of their daughters as wives for themselves and for their sons. In doing so, the holy race intermingles with the peoples of the lands and contaminates itself. As a priest himself and an Israelite, Ezra doubtless sees himself as inextricably connected to this rebellious community of people. As Fensham notes,

> A great sin had been committed, a sin which ran contrary to the law of God. Ezra identified himself with this sin, although he and the exiles who had returned with him did not commit it. In a certain sense Ezra accepted solidarity with his people. He became mediator for them as Moses did after the golden bull was worshipped at Sinai (cf. Exod 32:33ff).[383]

In identifying himself and standing in solidarity with his people, Ezra brings his DS4 penitential prayer to Yahweh and pleads for his merciful forgiveness (9:6–15).

---

380. Whitbourne, "Definitive Guide to Guilt," para. 2.

381. Whitbourne, para. 4.

382. Whitbourne, para. 7–17.

383. Fensham, *Ezra and Nehemiah*, 125.

4.6.4i. Sadness

Upon hearing of the condition of the city of Jerusalem, and taking up the wine and giving it to king Artaxerxes, as was his custom as the cupbearer, the king asks Nehemiah, "Why is your face so *sad* though you are not sick?" (Neh 2:1–2a; emphasis mine). According to king Artaxerxes, "This is nothing but *sadness* of heart" (2:2b; emphasis mine). Fensham maintains that Nehemiah's sadness is really a depression. At a time when everyone is rejoicing, Nehemiah is depressed.

> All the people were enjoying the party. Why should this cupbearer spoil the party? *Why are you so depressed?* Literally "Why is your face so bad?" The word translated depressed (plural of *ra'*, which was used in v. 1) has a great variety of meanings. It is always associated with something unpleasant, bad, or wicked. In this case the inner feeling of Nehemiah was reflected in his outward appearance. The term depressed is the best translation of this phenomenon . . . The last expression speaks of a sad heart (Heb, *rōa' lēḇ*).[384]

Clearly Nehemiah is "unhappy about something."[385] Nehemiah's sadness stems from the city of Jerusalem being desolated and the gates being consumed by fire (2:3). Within the bounds of Genesis and Esther, this is the only occurrence of the emotive response of sadness within the context of a DS1 lament prayer (1:11).

4.6.4j. Tender-heartedness

After finding the book of the law and reading it, Josiah not only weeps before Yahweh, but in 2 Kings 22:19–20, we read these words from Huldah the prophetess concerning him: "Thus says the LORD God of Israel, '*Regarding* the words which you have heard, because your *heart was tender* and you humbled yourself before the LORD when you heard what I spoke against this place [Judah] and against its inhabitants that they should become a desolation and a curse, and you have torn your clothes and wept before Me, I truly have heard you,' declares the LORD" (emphasis mine).

---

384. Fensham, 159–160.
385. Fensham, 160.

Mordechai Cogan and Hayim Tadmor note, "*since you took fright.* Heb. *rak lĕbābĕkâ*, lit. 'your heart was soft.' This idiom is used in parallel to verbs of fear and timidity; cf. Deut 20:3, Isa 7:4, Jer 51:46, 2 Chron 13:7. Here it describes Josiah, overcome by the warnings in the book of the Law read to him."[386] Only here does this tender-hearted emotive response occur within the bounds of Genesis and Esther, and contiguous to a DS1 lament prayer.

4.6.4k. Troubled Heart

After taking a census of Israel and Judah, David is convicted of his sin. "Now David's *heart troubled* him after he had numbered the people" (2 Sam 24:10; emphasis mine). The Hebrew reads, "וַיַּ֤ךְ לֵב־דָּוִד֙ אֹת֔וֹ" *wayyak leb-david oto* translated *but David's heart struck him.* This is another way of saying that David was conscience-stricken.[387] It is therefore not surprising that David's emotive response is elicited within the context of his DS4 penitential prayer. Within the bounds of Genesis and Esther, this is the only place that the emotive response of a troubled or conscience-stricken heart is elicited.

4.6.5. Categorization of Emotions

At this juncture an attempt is made to categorize the emotions that have just been discussed, both non-death-related and death-related. With regard to the non-death-related emotions, one observes that of the twelve emotions explored above, half were found in the context of a DS1 lament prayer. These emotions are anger, displeasure or distress, fear of God and humans, sadness, shame, and tender-heartedness. It should be pointed out, however, that the fear of humans can also be found within the context of a DS2 imprecatory prayer (only once; 2 Chron 20:15, 17), distress can also occur within the context of a DS3 vow prayer (only once; 1 Sam 1:10–11), and distress and shame can also be located within the context of a DS4 penitential prayer. While dismay occurs within the context of a DS2 imprecatory prayer, such emotions as appallment, embarrassment and shame, guilt, and a troubled heart were found within the context of a DS4 penitential prayer. Finally, the emotion of grief was found in a death-related context. Below is a table with the aforementioned categories and their description.

---

386. Cogan and Tadmor, *II Kings*, 284.
387. McCarter, *II Samuel*, 510.

Categories	Description
Disorientation Stage 1 Emotional Expressions: DS1 Lament Feelings	Feelings associated with lament prayer, including: Anger; Displeasure / Distress; Fear of God and Humans; Sadness; Shame; and Tender-heartedness.
Disorientation Stage 2 Emotional Expressions: DS2 Imprecatory Feelings	Feelings associated with imprecatory prayer, including: Dismay and Fear of Humans.
Disorientation Stage 3 Emotional Expressions: DS3 Vow Feelings	Feelings associated with vow prayer, including: Distress / Oppressed in spirit.
Disorientation Stage 4 Emotional Expressions: DS4 Penitential Feelings	Feelings associated with penitential prayer, including: Appallment; Embarrassment and Shame; Distress; Guilt; and Troubled or Conscience-stricken Heart.
Disorientation Stage 7 Emotional Expressions (Death-Related): DS7 Bereavement Feelings	Feelings associated with death, including: Grief.

4.6.6. Summary

In this section the emotional anthropological expressions communicated to/ before God amidst disorientation, both non-death-related and death-related, were explored. Further to this, an attempt was made to categorize these emotions, especially considering the categorization of the verbal anthropological expressions communicated to/before God amidst disorientation (i.e. prayers).

4.7. Domain of Anthropological Expressions of Disorientation Prayers and Their Auxiliaries

In consideration of all that has been completed within this chapter, the domain of anthropological expressions of disorientation (verbal, physical, and emotional) within biblical theology can thus be generated as follows:

Verbal Anthropological Expressions	
Categories	**Description**
Disorientation Stage 1 Verbal Expressions: DS1 Lament Prayers	Prayers uttered within a context of disorientation at the heart of which is a cry for help; it is occasionally accompanied by the stinging lament question of "Why?" or even simply groans, and sometimes wailing or weeping.
Disorientation Stage 2 Verbal Expressions: DS2 Imprecatory Prayers	Prayers uttered within a context of disorientation that call for a divine judgment or curse upon one's enemies.
Disorientation Stage 3 Verbal Expressions: DS3 Vow Prayers	Prayers uttered within a context of disorientation wherein a promise is made to God that is predicated on a favorable answer from him, that is, "If . . . then."
Disorientation Stage 4 Verbal Expressions: DS4 Penitential Prayers	Prayers uttered within a context of disorientation the content of which is penitence over one's (in) direct sins.
Disorientation Stage 5 Verbal Expressions: DS5 Confidence Prayers	Prayers uttered within a context of disorientation in confident anticipation of God's readiness to answer favorably, something of which has been (in)directly disclosed to the supplicant.
Disorientation Stage 6 Verbal Expressions: DS6 Thanksgiving Praise Prayers	Prayers uttered within a context of disorientation the content of which is jubilant thanksgiving praise in full assurance of God's imminent salvation declared to the supplicant by the agency of a priestly or prophetic oracle.
Disorientation Stage 7 Verbal Expressions (Death-Related): DS7 Bereavement Vocabulary	Vocabulary associated with death, including: Contrition and/or Confession; Curse; Instructions (Assassination; Burying; Embalming; Holiness; Returning Home and Remarrying; and Transporting Cadaver for Burial); Interrogation and Rejoinder; and Lament (Weeping and Elegy).

Physical Anthropological Expressions	
Categories	**Description**
Disorientation Stage 1 Physical Expressions: DS1 Lament Rituals	Rituals associated with lament, including: Blowing (Silver) Trumpets; Fasting; Lying on the Ground; Offering Burnt and Peace Offerings; Paralleling Two Outstretched Bodies; Shedding Tears; Sacrificing through Supernatural Fire (Building Altar, Making Trench, Arranging Wood, Cutting Ox, Laying Ox on Wood); Sitting; Spreading Out Letter; Tearing Clothes; and Turning Face to the Wall.
Disorientation Stage 2 Physical Expressions: DS2 Imprecatory Rituals	Rituals associated with imprecation, including: Covering Head; Prostrating Oneself; and Walking Barefooted.
Disorientation Stage 3 Physical Expressions: DS3 Vow Rituals	Rituals associated with vow, including: Offering Human Sacrifice, Standing, and Tearing Clothes.
Disorientation Stage 4 Physical Expressions: DS4 Penitential Rituals	Rituals associated with penitence, including: Kneeling; Plucking Hair from Beard and Head; Pouring Dirt upon Oneself; Prostrating Oneself; Separation from Foreigners; Sitting; and Tearing Clothes.
Disorientation Stage 7 Physical Expressions (Death-Related): DS7 Bereavement Rituals	Rituals associated with death, : Anointing Oneself; Burning; Burying (and Purchasing Land); Chambering (Privacy/Isolation); Changing Clothes; Covering Face; Deep Moving (Trembling); Donning and Removing Widow's Clothes; Donning Sackcloth; Eating; Erecting Gravestones (Monuments); Falling on and Kissing the Deceased; Funeral Processioning; Grieving/Mourning; Honoring (through Spice-fire); Lying on the Ground; Placing in Coffin; Rising from the Ground; Sitting; Transporting Cadaver for Burial; Washing; and Worshiping God.

Emotional Anthropological Expressions	
Categories	**Description**
Disorientation Stage 1 Emotional Expressions: DS1 Lament Feelings	Feelings associated with lament prayer, including: Anger; Displeasure / Distress; Fear of God and Humans; Sadness; Shame; and Tender-heartedness.
Disorientation Stage 2 Emotional Expressions: DS2 Imprecatory Feelings	Feelings associated with imprecatory prayer, including: Dismay and Fear of Humans.
Disorientation Stage 3 Emotional Expressions: DS3 Vow Feelings	Feelings associated with vow prayer, including: Distress / Oppressed in spirit.
Disorientation Stage 4 Emotional Expressions: DS4 Penitential Feelings	Feelings associated with penitential prayer, including: Appallment; Embarrassment and Shame; Distress; Guilt; and Troubled or Conscience-stricken Heart.
Disorientation Stage 7 Emotional Expressions (Death-Related): DS7 Bereavement Feelings	Feelings associated with death, including: Grief.

In chapter 5, some of this data will facilitate a dialectic correlation between biblical theology and pastoral theology. Of particular interest are those expressions conveyed to/before God in the life setting of grief within the textual locus of the prosaic sections of the OT (Genesis to Esther). Together with those expressions that surfaced amidst the phenomenon of grief among Christian leaders from within a Guyanese-Canadian or Vietnamese-Canadian context, a dialectic correlation will be set in motion. To reiterate, the objective of this endeavor is that of fostering compassionate (liberative intercultural) pastoral care practices that lend their aid toward mitigating and transforming grief, thus making it manageable and even redemptive, rather than complicated.

CHAPTER 5

Dialectic Correlation of Anthropological Expressions of Disorientation:
Biblical and Pastoral Theology

5.1. Introduction to Dialectic Correlation of Anthropological Expressions of Disorientation Between Biblical and Pastoral Theology

This chapter employs a dialectic correlation between the multivalent anthropological expressions of disorientation communicated to/before God by contemporary Christian pray-ers amidst their lived experience of grief, with those conveyed to/before God by ancient OT Israelites amidst grief and recorded within the prosaic limits of Genesis to Esther. The practices examined within this chapter are rooted in biblical theology and conversant with those practices present within pastoral theology. Particular attention, however, is afforded those expressions that help to sustain the bereaved as part of their coping and sustaining mechanism amidst their grief.[1]

On account of this, an examination of the practices that have emerged during grief, from within the Guyanese-Canadian and Vietnamese-Canadian contexts, will participate in a critical, theological reflection with the practices

---

1. Lartey, *In Living Color*, 64.

of the OT Israelites, the objective of which is attending to those practices that are grief-transformative, rather than grievous. Which means that, even though it is an expression of love rather than despair, grief needs mitigation to facilitate the continuous abundant living of the bereaved (John 10:10).

5.1.1. Dialectic Correlation of Anthropological Expressions among Israelite OT, Guyanese-Canadian, and Vietnamese-Canadian Leaders

What follows is the collective expressive domain of the anthropological expressions of disorientation culled from within each of the three contexts (Israelite OT [Genesis to Esther], Guyanese-Canadian, and Vietnamese-Canadian). These expressions are as follows:

Verbal Anthropological Expressions	
Categories	Description
Disorientation Stage 1 Verbal Expressions: DS1 Lament Prayers	Prayers uttered within a context of disorientation at the heart of which is a cry for help; it is occasionally accompanied by the stinging lament question of "Why?" or even simply groans, and sometimes wailing or weeping.
Disorientation Stage 2 Verbal Expressions: DS2 Imprecatory Prayers	Prayers uttered within a context of disorientation that call for a divine judgment or curse upon one's enemies.
Disorientation Stage 3 Verbal Expressions: DS3 Vow Prayers	Prayers uttered within a context of disorientation wherein a promise is made to God that is predicated on a favorable answer from him, that is, "If . . . then."
Disorientation Stage 4 Verbal Expressions: DS4 Penitential Prayers	Prayers uttered within a context of disorientation the content of which is penitence over one's (in) direct sins.
Disorientation Stage 5 Verbal Expressions: DS5 Confidence Prayers	Prayers uttered within a context of disorientation in confident anticipation of God's readiness to answer favorably, something of which has been (in)directly disclosed to the supplicant.

Categories	Description
Disorientation Stage 6 Verbal Expressions: DS6 Thanksgiving Praise Prayers	Prayers uttered within a context of disorientation the content of which is jubilant thanksgiving praise in full assurance of God's imminent salvation declared to the supplicant by the agency of a priestly or prophetic oracle.
Disorientation Stage 7 Verbal Expressions (Death-Related): DS7 Bereavement Vocabulary	Vocabulary associated with death, including Contrition and/or Confession; Curse; Instructions (Assassination; Burying; Embalming; Holiness; Returning Home and Remarrying; and Transporting Cadaver for Burial); Interrogation and Rejoinder; and Lament Elegies and Loud Cries for Help/Wailing/Weeping/Screaming/Shouting; Promise; Sharing Stories of Each Other's Grief.

Physical Anthropological Expressions	
Categories	**Description**
Disorientation Stage 1 Physical Expressions: DS1 Lament Rituals	Rituals associated with lament, including: Blowing (Silver) Trumpets; Fasting; Lying on the Ground; Offering Burnt and Peace Offerings; Paralleling Two Outstretched Bodies; Shedding Tears; Sacrificing through Supernatural Fire (Building Altar, Making Trench, Arranging Wood, Cutting Ox, Laying Ox on Wood); Sitting; Spreading Out Letter; Tearing Clothes; and Turning Face to the Wall.
Disorientation Stage 2 Physical Expressions: DS2 Imprecatory Rituals	Rituals associated with imprecation, including: Covering Head; Prostrating Oneself; and Walking Barefooted.
Disorientation Stage 3 Physical Expressions: DS3 Vow Rituals	Rituals associated with vow, including: Offering Human Sacrifice, Standing, and Tearing Clothes.
Disorientation Stage 4 Physical Expressions: DS4 Penitential Rituals	Rituals associated with penitence, including: Kneeling; Plucking Hair from Beard and Head; Pouring Dirt upon Oneself; Prostrating Oneself; Separation from Foreigners; Sitting; and Tearing Clothes.

Categories	Description
Disorientation Stage 7 Physical Expressions (Death-Related): DS7 Bereavement Rituals	Rituals associated with death, including: Anointing Oneself; Avoiding Food and People (Silence and Solitude)/Isolation; Bearing the Cost of the Funeral; Burning; Burying (and Purchasing Land); Celebrating the Life of the Deceased Annually with Lots of Food; Celebrating the Life of the Deceased through a Eulogy, a Shared Meal, and Singing Psalms, Hymns, and Songs of the Spirit to the Lord, such as Upbeat Songs or Bhajans, while also Proclaiming an Evangelistic Message of Hope in the Lord Jesus Christ alone, and the Comforting Presence of the Holy Spirit; Chambering (Privacy/Isolation); Changing Clothes; Composing Vietnamese Songs and Poems; Covering Face; Deep Breath; Deep Moving (Trembling); Donning and Removing Widow's Clothes; Donning Sackcloth; Eating; Embracing the Deceased's Cadaver; Erecting Gravestones (Monuments); Fainting; Falling on and Kissing the Deceased; Funeral Processioning; Grieving/Mourning; Keeping Memorabilia; Keeping Wake (with Kweh-kweh); Kissing the Deceased; Honoring (through Spice-fire); Lying on the Ground; Lying Down on the Casket/Hitting Oneself; Placing in Coffin; Reading through the Bible; Rising from the Ground; Sitting; Sitting Beside the Tomb while Thinking about the Lost Loved One; Transporting Cadaver for Burial; Visiting the Grave and Carrying Flowers; Washing; Wearing a White Band; Worshiping God; and Writing Letters of Comfort to the Bereaved.

Emotional Anthropological Expressions	
Categories	**Description**
Disorientation Stage 1 Emotional Expressions: DS1 Lament Feelings	Feelings associated with lament prayer, including: Anger; Displeasure / Distress; Fear of God and Humans; Sadness; Shame; and Tender-heartedness.
Disorientation Stage 2 Emotional Expressions: DS2 Imprecatory Feelings	Feelings associated with imprecatory prayer, including: Dismay and Fear of Humans.
Disorientation Stage 3 Emotional Expressions: DS3 Vow Feelings	Feelings associated with vow prayer, including: Distress / Oppressed in spirit.
Disorientation Stage 4 Emotional Expressions: DS4 Penitential Feelings	Feelings associated with penitential prayer, including: Appallment; Embarrassment and Shame; Distress; Guilt; and Troubled or Conscience-stricken Heart.
Disorientation Stage 7 Emotional Expressions (Death-Related): DS7 Bereavement Feelings	Feelings associated with death, including: Anger/Heartbreak/Shock; Confusion/Depression; Comfort/Joy/Happiness; Grief; Pain/Sadness/Sorrow/Listlessness/Guilt/Regret; Stress/Bogged Down/Mourning.

While each of these expressions is of significant import, of particular interest are the pastoral practices that have aided in the mitigation of grief within the context of death. The following is a list of ancient OT Israelite expressions observed amidst a context of grief over the death of a leading Israelite: (i) Burning and/or Burying; (ii) Chambering (Isolation); (iii) Donning Mourning Clothes (Widow's Clothes and/or Sackcloth); (iv) Elegiac Lament/Dirge and Weeping Lament; (iv) Fasting / Eating; (v) Mourning / Grief; (vi) Worshiping. The Guyanese-Canadian and Vietnamese-Canadian grief expressions will be conversant with those gleaned from within the OT Israelite context for the purpose of determining whether or not these expressions are faithful to the gospel of God, that is, helpful (transformative) or harmful (complicated). The goal of course is that of generating compassionate (liberative intercultural) pastoral care expressions that are transformative and even redemptive of grief, thus sustaining the bereaved and restoring their souls.

5.1.1a. Burning and/or Burying

As was noted earlier, burning was not a common mourning ritual practiced among the OT Israelites. Neither does one observe it within the NT. As Payne remarks, "In contrast to the Greeks and Romans, whose custom was to cremate the dead . . . the Jews 'bury rather than burn dead bodies.'"[2] Within the OT, and throughout the time of Christ's first advent and earthly ministry, it was commonplace to have caves or tombs for burial, and within a garden. John 19:38–42 tells us that after being given permission to remove his body from the cross for burial, Joseph of Arimathea, a secret disciple of Jesus, along with Nicodemus, took Jesus' body, bound it in linen wrappings with the spices (a mixture of myrrh and aloes), as was the burial custom of the Jews, and placed the body of Jesus in the tomb that was in a garden. Thus, even Jesus himself was buried in a sepulcher cave, which appeared to have been a single-chamber cave. But by the time of Jesus, sepulcher caves were coated with lime making them easily recognizable and thus avoided so as not to contaminate the living.[3] In light of Christ's own burial, it is not surprising to know that among Christians of both Guyanese-Canadian and Vietnamese-Canadian cultures, burial is the more generic option. While GL5 spoke of "announcing the death and burial of the deceased," VL3 spoke of "head[ing] to the cemetery to bury my brother." In fact, according to F. L. Cross, "Burial is the traditional Christian method of disposing of the dead."[4] This, however, raises the question of the appropriateness of burning as an option for Christians today.

Since burning is particularly practiced among non-Christians, burying has been deemed more appropriate for Christians. But it is worth pointing out that Christians are not called to imitate Christ in *everything* that he said and did. Wright maintains, "For when we speak about Christian discipleship as 'Christlikeness', *we do not mean that we are obliged to imitate every detail of Jesus' earthly life in first-century Galilee.* Often we work back from the stories of Jesus to a composite picture of his character, attitudes, priorities, values, reactions and goals. Then we seek to be 'Christlike' by reflecting what we know to have been true of Jesus in the choices, actions and response we have

---

2. Payne, "Burial," 556; quote taken from Tacitus, *Histories*, v. 5.

3. Editors of Encyclopaedia Britannica, "Burial: Death Rite," para. 4.

4. Cross, "Burial Services," 255.

to make in our own lives."[5] With reference to the acronym WWJD (What Would Jesus Do?), Wright suggests that, "a rather simplistic tag, but it does embody a valid ethical stance, even if it usually needs a lot of hard thinking and working out in our very ambiguous circumstances (and usually more than most people are prepared to do)."[6]

As a disciple or follower of Christ, Christians are called to imitate Christ. As Paul says, "Have this attitude in yourselves which was also in Christ Jesus" (Phil 2:5). The literary context suggests that such an attitude is one of humility (2:6–8), for which reason God the Father highly exalted Christ the incarnate Son as Lord over all (2:10–11; cf. Prov 3:34; 29:23; Matt 23:12). At the same time, Paul also urged, "Be imitators of me, just as I also am of Christ" (1 Cor 11:1). If by this Paul meant doing exactly as Jesus did, it seems fair to say that one should expect him to have abstained from food offered to idols, as would have been the case with Christ as part of his perfect fulfillment of the law (cf. Matt 5:17–19). Paul, however, remarked, "But food will not commend us to God; we are neither the worse if we do not eat, nor the better if we do eat" (1 Cor 8:8). Small wonder that he could say elsewhere, "I know and am convinced in the Lord Jesus that nothing is unclean in itself" (Rom 14:14), and thus, "All things indeed are clean" (14:20). Yet Paul asserted, "The faith which you have, have as your own conviction before God. Happy is he who does not condemn himself in what he approves" (14:22).

Reasoning from this equivalent analogy, it might be safe to contend here that if one approves of burying, good. If another approves of burning, this is also good. For in doing either, both done with thanksgiving to God, is done for the Lord (cf. 14:5–9). By doing so, no judgment is passed on the one who chooses to burn in lieu of bury, or vice versa, for all Christians will stand before the judgment seat and give an account to God (14:10–12). And if there is no condemnation for anyone who is in Christ Jesus, then on judgment day, one should not expect the verdict in Christ's court of law to be annulled (Rom 8:1; cf. John 5:24).

Although one might consider the fact that Jesus was buried rather than burned, on the one hand, this might have been in keeping with the Jewish practice of burial as a means of distinction from the Greeks and Romans

---

5. Wright, *Old Testament Ethics*, 37–38; emphasis mine.

6. Wright, 38.

who burned their dead. But on the other hand, and even more specifically, in preference to burning, Jesus' burial appears to have served as a fulfillment of God's word in Ps 16:11 [10], "For You will not abandon my soul to Sheol; nor will You allow Your Holy One to undergo decay." According to Peter C. Craigie and Marvin E. Tate,

> *Sheol* was conceived as a kind of underworld; the word is trans-lated in G as *hades* (ἅδη). In Sheol, persons were believed to exist in a form of semi-life, at rest, yet not in joy, for they had not the fullness of life which made possible the riches of relationship with the living God. Death was thus to be dreaded. . . . in the state of Sheol there would be neither memory of God, nor the praise and worship of God.[7]

And in agreement with Paul, these words from Ps 16:11 [10] applied not to David, but to one greater than David, that is, David's greatest son Jesus Christ whom God raised from the dead (Acts 13:35–38).

The same, however, cannot be said of Christians. For it is appointed for all humans to die once, and after this, to stand before the judgment seat of Christ the righteous and just Judge of all the earth, the living and the dead (Heb 9:27; cf. John 5:22, 27; Acts 10:42; 17:31; 2 Tim 4:1; 1 Pet 4:5). Avoiding decay is thus not a possibility for any Christian. Preferring therefore to bury the dead will eventually lead to decomposition, which occurs swiftly upon burning the dead. The end – putrefaction – is still the same for both, albeit for a short while. Purification and transformation of our earthly bodies into bodies of immortality and imperishability will transpire at the appearing of Christ Jesus our Savior and Judge (1 Cor 15:42–57; Phil 3:20–21).

Further to this, as noted by Miller, within the early church, "Because pagans often desecrated Christian tombs and burned bodies, however, Christians began to affirm that any form of disposal was acceptable – no method could impede the resurrection."[8] Either burning or burial therefore seems reasonably acceptable for all those who are in Christ Jesus. Even if more non-Christians practice it, there is *nothing sinful* in Christians adopting the ritual of cremation. And apart from the high cost of a burial, "Cremation is

---

7. Craigie and Tate, *Psalms 1–50*, 93.
8. Miller, "Funeral Customs," 821.

becoming more popular in the West and may become more widely practiced because of the increasing scarcity of land for grave sites."[9]

It therefore seems that the choice is left to the believer in Christ whether to be burned or buried. Burning should not be viewed as somehow less dignifying than burying. Especially when the finances and the land for grave sites are becoming more and more difficult to obtain, coercing followers of Christ to bury rather than burn their dead seems more grief-complicating than grief-transforming. Consequently, *both* burning *and* burying appear to be helpful and transformative grief practices for Christians of all cultures. Both take death seriously, and both offer comfort to the bereaved. Yet one should not be favored over another because one might be deemed sinful, for both are acceptable when viewed from God's perspective with thanksgiving, particularly in light of the resurrection that is a matter of fact for all those who are in Christ, their resurrection, and their life (John 11:25).

When accomplished with thanksgiving to God, and to the Lord (cf. Rom 14:5–9), both burning and burying are grief-transformative and embodying of the gospel of God since they both serve the purpose of honoring the dead while comforting the bereaved, both of whom have been created in the image of God, and thus endowed with dignity. And even if it is *impossible* for one to either burn or bury, (e.g., in the case of a person going missing at sea without resurfacing), we can still trust that God will perform the necessary funeral rites (as in the case of Moses [Deut 34:5–6]). Ultimately, at the second advent of Christ, all the dead in Christ will be raised in glory and power, their bodies fully transformed from perishability to imperishability, and from natural to spiritual, that is, completely dominated by the Spirit of the true and living God, just as it is at present with Christ's body (1 Cor 15:42–57; Phil 3:20–21; 1 John 3:2). Grounded in such confidence, all Christians can therefore exclaim: Thanks be to God who gives us victory over death, burial, and burning, through our Lord Jesus Christ (1 Cor 15:57).

5.1.1b. Chambering (Privacy/Isolation)

Following the death of David's son Absalom, 2 Sam 18:33 tells us that, "The king was deeply moved and went up to the chamber over the gate and wept. And thus he said as he walked, 'O my son Absalom, my son, my son Absalom!

---

9. Miller, 820.

Would I had died instead of you, O Absalom, my son, my son!'" Overcome with grief, David's body begins to tremble uncontrollably. Prohibited from grieving the death of his son Absalom in the company of his joyful soldiers who are *celebrating* Absalom's demise, however, David is forced into isolation to mourn alone in his private chamber.

Similarly, we learned from VL1 that "In my culture . . . The father never cries in front of the family, but alone; he tries to be strong." VL4 also noted that, "Grieving is not approvable in our culture. Men are encouraged to show strength and courage in pain and sorrow. People withdraw when they grieve. They would like to vent their pain and sorrow, but only to their trusted friends or relatives. People also cry. Women tend to cry more than men." While ministering to the bereaved, especially during a funeral service, GL2 noted that, "Yes, I may be crying before, or after with the family. But at the time of the service, when I'm called upon to be a pastor, a minister, in that role, God gives me the grace to be able to do these things. And especially when the family members are all around you, even hugging you, or leaning on you for support, you have to be strong and stand up there."

In his article "Aspects of Men's Sorrow," Zylla acknowledges, "Research shows that men are more likely than women to avoid emotional expression in response to a loss or to be less willing to talk about their loss."[10] From his own personal research on the autobiographical works of C. S. Lewis (*A Grief Observed*), Henri J. M. Nouwen (*A Letter of Consolation*), and Nicholas Wolterstorff (*Lament for a Son*), Zylla discovered a few insights into how one might think about gender roles in grief. "The lifeworld of grieving men takes new form with the loss of their loved one. There is a rupture in their lived world but also continuity. This forces an internal creative response of taking on parts of the loved one within one's self and expressing the features of that person – even if it means changing their own self of self."[11] Zylla especially references the work of J. A. Cook whose research involved a qualitative study of fifty-five fathers who had lost their child to cancer within the previous five years. Four major mourning strategies were found helpful in allowing

---

10. Zylla, "Aspects of Men's Sorrow," 846–847; cf. Cook, "Dad's Double Binds," 285–308; Littlewood, *Aspects of Grief*; Staudacher, *Men and Grief*.

11. Zylla, "Aspects of Men's Sorrow," 847.

these fathers to "handle upsetting feelings without disclosing them to other people,"[12] which were:

1. Thinking about something else (i.e. cognitive blocking whereby the person deliberately thinks about practical, concrete details of their day-to-day lives).[13]

2. Reason/reflection (i.e. a rational reflection on the situation that caused the death of their child and a rather intentional focusing on the details of painful memories and failures rather than blocking them from consciousness).[14]

3. Doing something else (i.e. deflecting the pain of the grief by doing other things, which were divided into two orders: one was distracting themselves from their own mourning, and the other was allowing their child's death to serve as a catalyst especially for engagement in community involvements).[15]

4. Solitary reflectiveness (i.e. expressions of grief as part of a private and solitary experience, partly because of the internal pressure to be strong for others who were affected by the loss, and partly because of social scripting).[16]

Zylla observed that Lewis, Nouwen, and Wolterstorff each also practiced at least one of these mourning strategies as part of the process of handling their grief.[17]

Feelings of guilt, with its not-too-distant friend of regret, can also be an emotion that creeps into the context of grief, even when grief is expressed in private. Commenting on David's grief expressions at the funeral of Absalom, Arnold observes, "David's powerful sense of loss ('If only I had died instead of you,' 18:33) towers over the landscape of this narrative, turning the army's spectacular military achievement into defeat (19:2). His anguish 'my son' is repeated five times in 18:33 (and another three times in 19:4) and reflects David's inconsolable attempt to fathom the loss." Arnold adds, "He seems to

---

12. Cook, "Dad's Double Binds," 294.

13. Cook, 295.

14. Cook, 297.

15. Cook, 298–299.

16. Cook, 290.

17. Zylla, "Aspects of Men's Sorrow," 849–852.

gather the past, with all his sins and those of his family, into this one defining moment of sorrow. When all is said and done, David cannot begin to resolve the incompleteness of his loss."[18] David presumably has regrets and thus feels a sense of guilt. Small wonder that Joseph Bayly acknowledges that "Guilt is another natural response to death's wound."[19] Likewise, it was GL5 who noted that moments of being alone and pondering memories of the lost loved one might lead one to "start thinking about what you could have done, and what you should have done. All these things come back in grief, and you feel regret, and you feel guilty. These are the emotions that you pass through and you get depressed."

In his monograph *On Caring*, Milton Mayeroff states,

> In caring I commit myself to the other; I hold myself out as someone who can be depended on. If there is an acute break within this relationship because of my indifference or neglect, I feel guilty, as if the other were to say, "Where were you when I needed you, why did you let me down?" This guilt results from my sense of having betrayed the other, and my conscience calls me back to it. The more important this particular other is to me, the more pronounced is my guilt.[20]

Further, Mayeroff affirms that

> Like pain, guilt tells me that something is wrong; if it is felt deeply, understood, and accepted, it provides me with the opportunity to return to my responsibility for the other. That return does not necessarily reinstate the relationship as it existed prior to the break; rather, it often makes for a deeper seriousness and awareness of my trust. It is like almost losing something through indifference, and by this near-loss realizing more deeply how precious it actually is to me. I do not resume caring simply to overcome guilt, but I overcome guilt by renewed caring.[21]

---

18. Arnold, *1 & 2 Samuel*, 596.
19. Bayly, *Last Thing*, 46.
20. Mayeroff, *On Caring*, 45.
21. Mayeroff, 45.

But one does wonder what happens in the context of the loss of a loved one and thus the inability of the caregiver to offer further care. In other words, what does the caregiver do with that pronounced guilt within? Margaret Stroebe et al., affirm that, "People often wish that they could have done things differently following the death of a loved one; this can make them feel guilty. For example, bereaved persons may think that they should have done more to prevent the death or to have lived up to their expectations in their prior relationships with the deceased."[22] Within the context of grief, guilt has been defined as "a remorseful emotional reaction in bereavement, with recognition of having failed to live up to one's own inner standards and expectations in relationship to the deceased and/or the death."[23] However, from their longitudinal investigation among participants of bereaved spouses (thirty widows and thirty widowers), Stroebe et al., realized that "self-blame was associated with grief at the initial time-point and with its decline over time."[24]

Even Bayly states, "All of us hurt the person we love, one way or another: we say sharp words, are inconsiderate and impatient, act selfishly . . . In life we have a chance to straighten things out with, 'I'm sorry, please forgive me,' with gifts and surprises and special acts of love. Death closes the door on making amends, opens the door to a flood of 'If only . . .' thoughts."[25] Nevertheless, Bayly also counsels, "If we feel guilty, we must find forgiveness. We can't say 'I'm sorry' to the one who has died, but we can say it to God (Psalm 51:4, 10, 11)."[26]

Rather than allow it to become overwhelming, guilt can be channeled elsewhere, as the mourner chooses to extend care to others who might be alive and in need of it, though not for the purpose of overcoming guilt, which has already been removed by the ever-efficacious lifeblood of Jesus Christ, once for all (Heb 9:14). Eugene Khan suggests that, "The solution to self-pity is to feel pity for someone else and move in the direction of helping that person."[27] In doing so, it is likely that "Our thoughts will no longer be on what might have been, nor on visiting a cemetery plot or keeping a room

---

22. Stroebe, "Guilt in Bereavement," para. 1.

23. Li, "Guilt in Bereavement," 166.

24. Stroebe, "Guilt in Bereavement," e96606, para. 42.

25. Bayly, *Last Thing*, 46–47.

26. Bayly, 48.

27. In Bayly, 48–49.

'just as it was the last time he was in it,' nor on 'what she'd like us to do,' nor on one's own pains and fears of death. We will be freed from bondage to the past to move in a meaningful forward direction."[28] In fact, even after losing their three children, Bayly admits, "In ministering to the healing of others, my wife – and I – found healing."[29]

Zylla also notes that, "Although men may not demonstrate strong emotions in loss and may suppress or contain the powerful emotions of grief, these recognitions begin to take root – grief isolates."[30] In other words, "Grief is powerfully isolating. . . . loneliness is inevitable."[31] In the same vein, Allender and Longman aver that "Inevitably, a loss of hope leads to loneliness: the absence or loss of relationship. Loneliness is isolation from those who mean the most to us."[32] Cole, however, remarks,

> Most people feel lonely after a significant loss, especially the loss of a person with whom they spent a lot of time. When I served as a pastor, I heard widows and widowers speak frequently of feeling lonely after the spouse died. Several of these people confirmed, in different ways, what one woman said after her husband of fifty-two years died: "The nights are the worst. I dread going to bed because that's when the loneliness becomes almost unbearable." I also listened to those who had lost children, friends, and colleagues, and social outlets speak of their loneliness and the pain it caused. We feel lonely because we miss what we once had but have now lost. But sometimes feelings of loneliness are also tied to our fears and anxieties about living with our loss.[33]

Writing from his own twin experience of grief having lost both of his wives,[34] J. Oswald Sanders avows that, "One of the most prolific creators of loneliness is the natural grief and sorrow that accompany bereavement. In

---

28. Bayly, 49.

29. Bayly, 49.

30. Zylla, "Aspects of Men's Sorrow," 846.

31. Zylla, 846.

32. Allender and Longman, *Cry of the Soul*, 142.

33. Cole, *Good Mourning*, 13.

34. After the passing of his first wife, Sanders remarried, but also lost his second wife.

the early stages of that shattering experience, the sense of loss of the loved one is so pervasive that the grieving person cannot believe the sun will shine again. It seems quite outside the bounds of possibility that one could ever again face life with any semblance of enjoyment."[35]

Yet a significant loss can lead to a desire to be left alone in silence and solitude. Bayly captures it quite accurately as he enumerates some of the natural responses to death, listing first a "Desire to be alone, or to have social contacts severely restricted."[36] At some point, however, the mourning individual will realize that it is not good for them to be alone for the remainder of their lives (cf. Gen 2:18). Life must go on, and that without the deceased. The community of pastoral caregiving Christians therefore becomes a primary resource for the mourner to continue along life's journey together, and not alone (2 Cor 1:3–4). It is therefore necessary that the grieving person move, when they feel comfortable to do so, from a place of isolation into a space of communal silence and solitude. Eventually, that silence will be broken, and words will return so that communal communication can persist, and the burden of grief can be borne. That is, weeping, or more precisely mourning, can be reciprocated (Rom 12:15). Otherwise, the mourner will find the words of Earl A. Grollman to be true: "Pain suffered in solitude is more difficult to bear than anguish that is shared."[37]

What is worse, however, is that of being the object of isolation, which might be referred to as social degradation, where the mourner is forced to isolate themselves from the company of *happy* people. A clear biblical example of this is observed in 2 Samuel 19:5 where David is forced into isolation by Joab and his men amidst his expressions of grief at Absalom's funeral.[38]

---

35. Sanders, *Facing Loneliness*, 67.

36. Bayly, *Last Thing*, 45.

37. Grollman, "What You Always Wanted," 31.

38. Here it should be noted that men's grief is not *always* done in private. David is coerced to express his grief privately. However, there are occasions in Scripture when men grieve publicly, as in the case of Jacob's son upon the rape of their sister Dinah by Shechem son of Hamor (Gen 34:1–7); Job's public grief in the company of his three friends (Job 2:11–13); Ezra's public display of grief over the mixed or interreligious marriages among the people of God (Ezra 9:1–3); the communal grief expressed by Nehemiah and the sons of Israel over their sins and the iniquities of their fathers (Neh 9:1–4); and Jesus at the tomb of his friend Lazarus in the company of several mourners (John 11:35), and then again in the company of throngs of people who assembled to see him experience an imminent and shameful death on a cross all while enduring the spiritual desolation of being forsaken by God the Father (Matt 27:46); etc.

Sadly, Dana G. Cable observes that, "Today mourning is regarded by some as morbid, even pathological. We want the bereaved to express their grief in *private*."[39] For that matter, "We make all kinds of efforts to encourage them to do so. Such statements as *You are doing so well*, *You have to be brave for the children*, and *Big boys don't cry*, effectively discourage outward signs of mourning. We even go so far as to suggest that the loss is easily replaceable, as in the statement, *You're young, you can have another baby*."[40] Cable further perceives that

> Much of this response is a function of our own discomfort with death and our lack of knowledge of what to say to grievers. We do not like to see people sad, and we attempt to cheer them up. Therefore, we communicate the subtle message that if someone wants our company and support, they should "be happy." If they start to speak of the dead, we try to change the subject. If that doesn't work, *we begin to avoid them*. It doesn't take long for them to get the message: "Don't show your grief to me." In turn, they withdraw, or learn how to cover up their real feelings when they are with us.[41]

Since its appearance on the pages of the edited volume *Living with Grief* some twenty plus years ago, the perceptive comments of Cable still appear to ring true today. Such an attitude of negativity towards others who might be grieving and mourning, which can be considered as characteristics of affliction, has seen minimal change, if any at all. This is especially witnessed in Zylla's recent assertion that "When we encounter the suffering of others, we do not readily enter into that suffering as much as we might think. In subtle ways we fail to acknowledge the full implications of the situation."[42] Further to this, "Often, suffering includes this social experience of being shamed, ridiculed, accused, or attacked."[43] This has given rise to Zylla's identification of the three types of social suffering that are inter-related, and which deepen the experiences of social degradation: "abandonment (the deep disappointment

---

39. Cable, "Grief in the American Culture," 62; emphasis mine.
40. Cable, 62–63; emphasis original.
41. Cable, 63; emphasis mine.
42. Zylla, *Roots of Sorrow*, 93.
43. Zylla, 62–63.

of the withdrawal of support of others), rejection (the alienation from the community where companionship of life is refused), and forsakenness (the anticipation of love and acceptance is fully disappointed and, in its place, one experiences scorn or forsakenness itself)."[44]

Challenging the community of God to act compassionately rather than indifferently, Zylla states, "Before we can fully live into our mandate as the compassionate community of God [i.e. moving toward suffering rather than away from it, and thus entering into the suffering of others with active help] we must come to terms with the source of our indifference to the suffering of others,"[45] by which is meant "the failure to either see, to acknowledge or to act on behalf of others."[46] One way of acting on behalf of others in their suffering is by moving into the context of grief so as to be with and sit in solidarity with those who mourn. As Nicholas Wolterstorff suggests,

> Death is awful, demonic. If you think your task as comforter is to tell me that really, all things considered, it's not so bad, you do not sit with me in my grief but place yourself off in the distance away from me. Over there, you are of no help. What I need to hear from you is that you recognize how painful it is. I need to hear from you that you are with me in my desperation. To comfort me, you have to come close. *Come sit beside me on my mourning bench.*[47]

Perhaps someone in the throes of grief can find comfort in the following prayer by Edward Musgrave Blaiklock. Blaiklock wrote this prayer in support of those who experience loneliness amidst sorrow and grief, the likeness of which he experienced at the passing of his wife Kathleen Minnie Mitchell. "Father, we pray for all lonely people, especially for those who, coming home to an empty house, stand at the door hesitant, afraid to enter. May all who stand in a doorway with fear in their hearts, like the two on the Emmaus road, ask the Living One in. Then, by His grace, may they find that in loneliness they are never alone, and that He peoples empty rooms with His presence."[48]

---

44. Zylla, 62–63.

45. Zylla, 12.

46. Ford, *Sins of Omission*, 12.

47. Wolterstorff, *Lament for A Son*, 34; emphasis mine.

48. Blaiklock, *Kathleen*, 41.

5.1.1c. Donning Mourning Clothes (Widow's Clothes and/ or Sackcloth)

According to Gen 38:14, after the deaths of her two successive husbands (Er and Onan), Tamar the daughter-in-law of Judah donned widow's clothes. Second Samuel 3:31–32 says that, following the death of Abner, David, Joab, and all the people with them, clothe themselves in sackcloth. Larry G. Herr comments, "It most frequently refers to a garment worn during times of mourning or sorrow (Gen. 37:34; Ps. 30:11 [MT 12])."[49]

While it was not mentioned, it is customary for Guyanese-Canadians to wear all black to a funeral. It was noted by VL3, however, that, "There is a traditional Vietnamese way of dealing with grief. During the funeral service, whereas in Vietnam the immediate bereaved family wear all white, the mourners in Canada wear black clothing with a white band around their head and/or their arm." Explaining the significance behind this ritual, VL3 further elucidated, "This traditional white band is to be worn for an entire year as a sign of mourning and as a symbol of the loss of life or the ashes of the deceased." Also implied in such a year-long physical expression is the silent truth that *grief* is not terminated upon the completion of the committal (burial or cremation) of the deceased. Alternatively stated, wearing the traditional white band throughout the rest of the year following the death of a close family member is to suggest the implicit statement that even when the dead is long gone and no longer physically present, grief *still* persists.

At this juncture we are reminded of the words of Hoang who noted that, "After the funeral, family members wore a small piece of black or white fabric on their clothes everyday to signify that they were in mourning."[50] Hoang further remarked that this piece of fabric would usually be worn for two years. "On the second anniversary, these clothes would be burned to signify that the mourning period was over."[51] And according to Hoang, "The burning of the mourning clothes signifies the incorporation of the bereaved into the normal

---

49. Herr, "Sackcloth," 256.
50. Hoang, "Death Rituals," para. 21.
51. Hoang, para. 21.

course of life."[52] Yet Hoang also affirmed that, "The deceased's memory is not erased and the family still observes the anniversary of the death each year."[53]

One might therefore contend that wearing sackcloth or mourning clothes rooted within one's culture can be understood as something helpful rather than harmful. When worn amidst grief, mourners continue to testify to the reality that grief is not something that vanishes with the invisibility of the body of the deceased to either interment or incineration. But even while it persists, grief can be transformed in the wearing of such mourning clothes as it signals to outsiders that the mourner is still in a period of grief, and thus should be respected, especially when there is a tendency for some to coerce mourners to get over their grief as soon as possible to move on with their lives. Grief becomes complicated when people are told to move on with their lives quickly following the death of their loved ones. By wearing their culture's customary mourning clothes for a specific period, and in so doing keep the memories of the deceased alive, the bereaved can indeed move on with their lives, one step at a time, rather than expeditiously. Doing so will permit them a time to process their grief rather than hurry it along, which can make matters worse for the bereaved. The possibility for grief to be transformed increases as the bereaved is respectfully allowed time to grieve (Eccl 3:4), and this, even by means of wearing of their cultural mourning clothes. Even Jesus told his disciples, "Truly, truly, I say to you, that you will weep and lament, but the world will rejoice; you will grieve, but your grief will be turned into joy. . . . Therefore you too have grief now; but I will see you again, and your heart will rejoice, and no one *will* take your joy away from you" (John 16:20, 22). By inference, patience with those who need time to process their grief even as they wear their grief clothes, can be viewed as an act of compassion that embodies the gospel of God (1 Thess 5:14).

5.1.1d. Elegiac Lament/Dirge and Weeping Lament

We saw in 4.5.3.5. how Abraham wept for Sarah, Joseph and the Egyptians for Jacob, Israel for Aaron and Moses, and how David wept for Abner. Similarly, it was remarked by VL2 that "When a close relative like a mother, a father, husband, or wife, passes away, the bereaved who have been closely bonded

---

52. Hoang, para. 22.

53. Hoang, para. 22.

with the deceased, will lament that death for a long time." At the death of VL2's mother, VL2 stated, "We lament in silence." Likewise, GL1 noted, "It is normal for people to wail and weep so much that they actually pass out. It is normal sometimes for people to scream and shout virtually at the top of their lungs all while beating their chest. It is not uncommon to hear loud wails from those stricken by grief. You see that at some funerals. But it has a deep emotional impact."

Weeping lament was also observed in GL3's understanding of grief as that of "An outward expression of an inward feeling," which was further supplemented by, "The word grief means to me that you have a loss, and there is something to lament over that is beyond your control." In addition to this, GL3 averred, "You lose a part of you, or a part of your relationship with loved ones and friends, and you cannot help them, so you grieve. . . . It's a loss that you lament over." Sharing the example of the loss of a sister, GL3 further stated "There is always an empty space, an empty chair there, and you lament over that." For GL3, grief in the form of lament includes weeping and shedding of tears.

Laments, however, do not only constitute wailing and weeping, but can also include dirges and elegies, which are mournful songs. We have already seen this in the biblical text, and analyzed five elegiac laments within the bounds of Genesis to Esther amidst grief in section 4.5.3.5.

VL5 remarked, "Vietnamese people grieve for our loved ones who passed away for a long period. At the time of the funeral, family and relatives usually show deep grief as loud crying, talking to the [deceased] loved one." Similarly, GL1 noted, "People in the Guyanese culture are not afraid to express their emotion and especially among Indian people, old Indian people who were Hindus. They will just express it, and sometimes they will express it in singing. Wailing singing would be like a funeral dirge. They might express it by saying things related to the past. They might repeat words told them by the deceased." To this GL1 further stated, "I was at one funeral where a lady said to the deceased, 'I know you used to tell me that my family is ugly, and your family is nice. Yeh, that's true, you know. But you're taking all your niceness with you right now." When such humor surfaces, GL1 remarked, "You probably have to put your hand on your mouth" in an effort to restrain oneself from bursting into laughter.

When asked what range of expressions of grief are normal responses within the Guyanese-Canadian culture, it was GL1 who acknowledged, "Well, there are all kinds of expression. There's tears, there's wailing, there's mourning. People can faint. It is normal for people to faint and have to be revived in our culture. It is normal for people to wail and weep so much that they actually pass out. It is normal for people to scream and shout virtually at the top of their lungs all while beating their chest. You see that at some funerals. But it has a deep emotional impact." Such emotional impact has to do with love for the deceased, which can be heard in the words of GL1: "In terms of the significance, I think it is the culture that people grew up in, and what they saw that is just what they continue to do, especially among Indian people. Indian people felt that if you do not do that, you were not actually showing that you love that person. And it would come over to their family that you really didn't care about that person." In other words, according to GL1, "So in many cases, the wailing, the weeping, the fainting, were ways of telling their people that we also love this person. If they didn't do something like that, it might be conceived that they didn't really love the person."

This reminds us, as we have already observed in 4.5.3.5., that in the OT, death was announced by a loud cry and much lamentation through tears and cries. Within the NT, wailing is evoked at the death of a synagogue official's daughter. Mark 5:38 reads, "They [Jesus, Peter, James, and John] came to the house of the synagogue official; and He saw a commotion, and people loudly weeping and wailing." Weeping also surfaces at the death of Dorcas (Tabitha) of Joppa, a disciple of Christ and a woman abounding in the deeds of kindness and charity. Requesting his presence in Joppa, Acts 9:39 tells us that Peter travelled from Lydda to Joppa where he was taken into the upper room where all the widows stood and wept while they showed him all the tunics and garments that Dorcas used to make during her time with them. Following the death of Lazarus, Jews visited the home of Mary and Martha to console them during their grief. As Jesus advanced towards Bethany, the village of Mary and Martha, we observe that the consoling Jews came along with Mary when she approached Jesus and together, they wept with her (John 11:33). Upon seeing this, Jesus was so deeply moved in spirit and troubled that we are told in no uncertain terms, "Jesus wept" (11:35). Is it any wonder that when Paul wrote his letter to the Romans, he admonished the believers to be united in their sincere love for each other by rejoicing with those who rejoice, and weeping with those who weep (Rom 12:15)?

While it can evoke wailing or weeping, it is not uncommon for grief to also inspire eulogies and elegies. It is not unusual for most funerals to include a formal eulogy of the deceased with many informal eulogies by family and friends during a wake night or viewing, or even days leading up to or following the death of a person. In fact, "the funeral is the last opportunity to publicly present someone's characteristic personality."[54] Eulogies can take the form of elegies, that is, funeral songs or dirges or poems written and sung and recited in memory of the deceased. For VL1, "especially since Vietnamese music is sad music, the composition of songs and poems" become essential expressions that aid in the coping of grief.

Within our contemporary society, while it is common for the bereaved to write a eulogy, finding such elegiac poems and songs is a rather rare expression. Especially since it has served as a coping mechanism for the Vietnamese people, thus transforming their grief, which embodies the gospel of God (Rev 2:8–11; cf. Jer 29), such a practice can be reclaimed for our contemporary Christian appropriation.

5.1.1e. Fasting

Upon the death of the tribe of Benjamin, the sons of Israel fasted (Judg 20:26). The tribe of Benjamin, however, was destroyed at the hands of the sons of Israel on account of their sin of abusing the body of the concubine of a Levite (Judg 19). The valiant men of Jabesh-gilead also fasted following the death, burning, and burial of Saul and his three sons. Their fast lasted seven days (1 Sam 31:32). Interestingly, David fasted for seven days prior to the death of his son through his clandestine relationship with Bathsheba the wife of Uriah (2 Sam 12:15–18). As a mourning ritual, fasting was one of the initial reactions to grief among OT Israelites, and this especially "at times of extraordinary grief, as at the death of an only son (Jer 6:26; Amos 8:10; Zech 12:10)."[55]

GL5 stated that, "For some Guyanese, as a means of respecting the dead, no rank food like meat or fish, is consumed during the time of grief." It is also possible for those in grief to engage in an involuntary fast. Thus, in the

---

54. van Tongeren, "Individualizing Ritual," 127.
55. Payne, "Burial," 557.

words of GL5, "Your stomach doesn't accept anything." Upon receiving the sad news of the death of two sisters and three nephews at sea while crossing from Vietnam to Canada, VL1 remarked, "When I realized this, for eight years, I prayed and questioned God, 'Why has this happened to me and my family?' I even went to the Prayer Garden in Oshawa and prayed and fasted for answers from God."

Westermann comments, "No worship observance in ancient Israel is as well known to us as is the special rite of lamentation, often called a 'fast' (*sôm*)."[56] What is more, "Since it was always anticipated by a special crisis, fasting had to be announced in preparation for the rite. The community had to be called together for it, and that meant the entire people, including women and children (cf. the summons to community laments in Ezek 21:12; Joel 2:16; Jonah 3:5)."[57] Further to this, "Part of the observance of a fast included purification of the worshipers (Joel 1:14), abstinence, and garments of mourning. Above all, girding on sackcloth (Isa 22:12; Jer 4:8; 6:26), sprinkling one's head with dust and ashes (Josh 7:6; Neh 9:1), gestures of humiliation and entreaty, and 'weeping before the Lord' (Judg 20:23–26)."[58] And as specified by Gunkel, "The holy act of 'fasting before YHWH' (Jer 36:9) characteristically arises from the withholding of food and drink (Deut 9:9, 18; Judg 20:26; 1 Sam 7:6; Isa 58:3; Neh 9:1 Jonah 3:7; Esth 4:16) in precise contrast to the joyous festivals in which the consumption of the sacrificial meat before YHWH plays such an important role."[59]

In a similar vein, Clarence B. Bass observes, "In the OT the fast was regarded as an act of self-renunciation designed to mollify God's wrath and move him to act in gracious disposition. In times of emergency, the people fasted to persuade God to spare them from impending calamity."[60] Otherwise stated, by performing the ritual act of fasting, "One hoped especially that the plight of the helpless would move God."[61] In the case of David, his fast was employed in "hopes that the Lord might change his mind . . . to spare

---

56. Westermann, *Psalms: Structure, Content*, 30.
57. Westermann, 30.
58. Westermann, 30.
59. Gunkel and Begrich, *Introduction to the Psalms*, 83.
60. Bass, "Fast, Fasting," 781; cf. Jer 14:12 and Isa 58:1–10 for an abuse of fasting.
61. Gunkel, *Introduction to the Psalms*, 83.

his son's life."[62] To put the matter another way, "David's self-denial and self-abasement . . . may have been an effort to demonstrate to God that the child's recovery was more important to him than either food, comfort, or pride."[63]

Voluntarily or not, fasting is observed to be part of the cycle of processing one's grief. When fasting is inhibited, grief can become complicated. Fasting, however, is not forever. There will come a time when fasting needs be broken, and a consistent intake of food commenced for the healthy development of the body, which is from God, and should be cared for as part of one's self-love, and love for God (cf. Eph 5:29). Otherwise, complications can arise, leading to another unnecessary death, and with it, compounded grief for other bereaved relatives. When properly done, fasting can thus embody the gospel of God, and thus be both an expression that is transformative of grief, and helpful rather than hurtful to the bereaved.

5.1.1f. Grieving / Mourning

We noted in 4.6.1. how several OT Israelites engaged in the ritual of mourning their dead and how within the OT Israelite culture, it was customary for close relatives and friends to visit the house of and mourn with the immediate family of the deceased. During this time, it was also customary for professional mourners to be hired (Jer 9:17–18). In terms of its significance, "The emphasis on mourning resulted from the Hebrew appreciation of human life and health, which was considered one of God's greatest gifts (Ps 91:16), and also from a view of human nature which affirmed embodied existence (Ps 16:9–11)."[64]

While there is nothing unusual about mourning, different cultures mourn differently. As noted by VL2, "Last year my mother passed away in the hospital. Since my younger sister was living with my mother for a long time, she was deeply attached to her, she was the one who mourned much. She cried in loud tears expressing her love for my mother, embracing her still warm body." For VL3, "Emotionally, from time to time, when I am driving alone, I would cry remembering my dad sitting beside me, and what he said. I usually don't tell anyone about this because it's my way of mourning for my dad

---

62. Tsumura, *Second Samuel*, 195.
63. Bergen, *1, 2 Samuel*, 374.
64. Miller, "Funeral Customs," 821.

by myself." VL3 further noted that while mourners wear black clothing in Canada, it is more traditional for Vietnamese to wear a white band around their head or arm for an entire year as a sign of mourning, as a symbol of the loss of life, or as a symbol of the ashes of the deceased.

For GL1, mourning is itself an expression of grief. In fact, "the culture believes that you should grieve, and that you should mourn the loss of a loved one. The cultural belief is that you should pull together at that time, and do your very best in expressing your final respects for the deceased." However, there is comfort in mourning, as noted by GL5's reference to Matt 5:3, which reads, "Blessed are those that mourn for they shall be comforted." Thus it is not surprising to hear GL5 further avow, "God is the God of all comfort. You know that he is the only One who can bring you through, and give the strength at the time of your great loss. And he's the only One that you can depend on and lean upon at this time. And you know that you have the full assurance that God is not going to forsake you, and let you down, because he promises in his word to bring you that comfort and to be there." Which is why GL5 further asserted, "So you turn to him because he is your only source of comfort. You have family and friends that are there to comfort and surround you, but God is the ultimate comfort that you turn to. So you lean mostly on him."

Privately or publicly, mourning should be expressed, otherwise it can become complicated, adding sorrow upon sorrow. Billman and Migliore contend, "The capacity to grieve deeply is a mark of psychological maturity, rooted in the processes that are essential to human life and development. The inability to mourn diminishes human life."[65] From this perspective, Billman and Migliore can go on to affirm that within the Christian tradition, grief and mourning are inclusive within lament.[66] Sadly, much of our Western culture has denied and minimized our expression of grief with all its emotions. One ramification of this is the opening of wounds amidst grief that have been expanded and grown from cracks to chasms, leaving Christian mourners "less and less human, empty Christian shells with painted smiley

---

65. Billman and Migliore, *Rachel's Cry*, 82.

66. Billman and Migliore, 82.

faces. For some, a dull, low-level depression descends upon us, making us nearly unresponsive to all reality."[67]

J. LeBron McBride avows that, "Some of the symptoms of an unresolved grief reaction can be clinical depression lasting more than one and one half years after the loss, prolonged isolation, emotional numbing, continuing compulsive overactivity without a sense of loss, profound identification with the deceased, and extreme and persistent anger."[68] Likewise, John Bowlby points out that much of the anxiety, depression, and personality disturbance observed within clinical practice may very well be attributed to pathological or disordered mourning.[69] Alternatively termed complicated bereavement disorder (CBD) or complicated grief (CG), Deborah Khoshaba maintains,

> Grieving the loss of a loved one tears open our hearts, our lives, and seems to make time stand still, as we search for ways to make sense of the loss and what it means to our whole lives. We cry, eat more or less, can't sleep, long for our loved ones and wonder how we will ever be able to live without them. This is all normal in simple grief. . . . However, for some people, acute grief can gain a foothold and become a chronic, debilitating mental health condition that worsens over time, rather than gets better. This is called complicated grief.[70]

Allowing one to grieve their loss might therefore serve as a healthy step toward preventing the onslaught of complicated grief and the subsequent need for professional treatment. However, it is equally important to keep in mind that "Pre-existing mental health conditions, multiple stressors, emotional dependency, or substance abuse issues complicate the grieving process and increase the likelihood of complicated bereavement disorder that may necessitate professional treatment."[71] If it does reach that point, however, it is crucial for the Christian mourner to know that they should not be ashamed to seek out professional help. That said, however, Khoshaba also perceives that:

---

67. Scazzero, *Emotionally Healthy Spirituality*, 139.

68. McBride, *Spiritual Crisis*, 97.

69. Bowlby, *Attachment and Loss*, 23.

70. Khoshaba, "About Complicated Bereavement Disorder," para. 2.

71. Khoshaba, para. 3.

CG do not adequately mourn the loss of the loved one because they haven't faced the reality of the loss. Preoccupation with the deceased and exclusion of activities and relationships that fall outside this preoccupation gives them enough subconscious pleasure to keep them stuck in the grieving process. They are feeling most certainly. But, their feelings emphasize more a wish to keep the person alive than an acceptance that the person is gone."[72]

In other words, depression can result from the mourner's inability to let go of the deceased loved one, which is another natural response to death wherein people feel bound to the one who has died.[73]

In his *Ministry of Lament: Caring for the Bereaved*, Gene Fowler employs Therese A. Rando's proposed six-stage mourning processes as a conversation partner[74] with that of the form or structure of a typical lament psalm as a way to extend pastoral care. In this connection:

i.   recognizing the loss corresponds to the address to God.
ii. reacting to the separation corresponds to the complaint.
iii. recollecting and reexperiencing the deceased and the relationship corresponds to the confession of trust.
iv. relinquishing the old attachments to the deceased and the old assumptive world corresponds to the petition.
v.   readjusting to move adaptively into the new world without forgetting the old corresponds to the words of assurance.
vi. reinvesting corresponds to the vow of praise and thanksgiving.[75]

Through this dialogue, Fowler characterizes those who are rewriting their bereaved life story as contemporary psalmists of lament. Fowler commends this ministry of lament to pastors and congregations in hopes that they will learn from contemporary psalmists of lament what it is like to grow in relationship to God during the course of rewriting their bereaved life story.

---

72. Khoshaba, para. 13.
73. Bayly, *Last Thing*, 47.
74. Rando, *Treatment of Complicated Mourning*, 44–60.
75. Adapted from Fowler, *Ministry of Lament*, 43–149.

As psalmists, they become poets who cry out to God for help in prayer. They experience complaint, bringing the awfulness of their suffering to light, facing their alienation from God, and wrestling with the perennial human questions about suffering. They also reach the point of confessing trust in God's reliability, not by avoiding complaint but by facing it. They make specific petitions for help, and they experience assurance that God heard their prayer and will act. They know what it means to be grateful to God in the aftermath of all that has happened, and they genuinely respect, admire, and appreciate God, which we see in their praise.[76]

In a world wracked with grief, it is hoped and prayed that the ministry of lament will continue to find a prominent place where it may serve to bring comfort and healing and sustainability to all who grieve.

5.1.1g. Shedding Tears

Only one expression of shedding tears was found within the bounds of Genesis to Esther, and that in 2 Kings 20:5. In this passage of Scripture, the prophet Isaiah is told by Yahweh to return to Hezekiah, the leader of his people, and say to him, "Thus says the LORD, the God of your father David, 'I have heard your prayer, I have seen your *tears*; behold, I will heal you. On the third day you shall go up to the house of the LORD'" (emphasis mine).

Here we are also reminded of the words of VL3 that, "Emotionally, from time to time, when I am driving alone, I would cry remembering my dad sitting beside me, and what he said." VL4 also added, "People also cry. Women tend to cry more than men." And according to VL5, "From a Vietnamese point of view, my understanding of grief is that of a deep cry . . . Vietnamese people grieve for our loved ones who passed away for a long period of time. At the time of the funeral, family and relatives usually show deep grief as loud crying." For GL5, "Crying is the most common one [expression]. When you don't cry, it's grieving within your inner being, and it makes you sad." During the funeral, staring at the body of their eldest brother, GL1 stated, "When I

---

76. Fowler, 148–149.

saw him, his body, I released my grief by crying and expressing it in tears, and I felt so much better."

Peterman and Schmutzer speak of positive tears as those "tears that should be cried. That is, they are godly; they reflect love of people, grief over loss, and hatred of sin."[77] However, they also make note of the incongruity of such positive tears in averring that, "Ironically, positive tears may have a variety of negative causes. By negative we mean weeping that is incited by sin in its various manifestations: infidelity, betrayal, loss of loved ones through death, sexual abuse, social fragmentation, prejudice. Such tears may arise from abuse of power, arrogance, the crippling effects of disease or war, substance abuse, lack of love, violence, or deception."[78]

It is an irrefragable reality known the world over that death brings with it the shedding of tears. Yet, as Thomas and Habermas remark, "Crying is one of God's ways of helping us release the intensity of our pain."[79] However, Judith Kay Nelson, relying on the attachment theory proposed by John Bowlby, recently developed a comprehensive theory of crying. Nelson asserts that "Crying is above all a relationship behavior, a way to help us get close and not simply a vehicle for emotional expression or release. We do not cry because we need to get rid of pain, but because we need connection with our care givers – literal, internal, fantasized, or symbolic – in order to accept and heal from our pain and grief."[80]

Shedding tears then appears to be a cathartic response to grief. Bottling one's tears, rather than pouring them into God's bottle (Ps 56:9 [8]), might only serve to complicate rather than mitigate grief. Therefore, shedding tears should be encouraged as a means of mitigating one's grief, and sustaining the bereaved.

5.1.1h. Worshiping God

We noted in 4.6.1an. that according to 2 Samuel 12:20, following the death of his unnamed stillborn son, "David arose from the ground, washed, and anointed *himself*, and changed his clothes; and *he came into the house of the*

---

77. Peterman and Schmutzer, *Between Pain and Grace*, 164.
78. Peterman and Schmutzer, 165.
79. Thomas and Habermas, *Enduring Your Season*, 239.
80. Nelson, *Seeing Through Tears*, 6.

LORD and worshiped. Then he came to his own house, and when he requested, they set food before him and he ate" (emphasis mine). Worshiping God was also found to be a common practice among both Guyanese-Canadians and Vietnamese-Canadians amidst their grief. According to GL5, wake prayer services will be held in memory of the deceased. Such services usually involve singing hymns and songs to bring comfort. Such songs or hymns would be "the favorite hymns of the person while he or she was alive." Also noted by GL5 is that "You sing sacred hymns and songs of comfort and healing such as: 'O God Our Help in Ages Past,' 'Happy the Home When God is There,' and 'The Lord's My Shepherd.' And if the person who died is of an East Indian descent, we usually sing bhajans at the wake and funeral. One of the most common bhajans is 'Yishu Ne Kaha: Jiwan Ki Roti,' which means, 'Jesus said: I am the bread of life.'"

When it comes to worshiping God amidst grief within the Vietnamese-Canadian context, it was noted by VL2 that "We commemorate the life of the deceased one devoted to God by holding a solemn ceremony with one's family and others, either in the church, or in the funeral home. During the funeral service we worship God with meaningful songs, prayer, and witnessing to unbelievers [through preaching]." The impetus for such worship can be heard in VL2's affirmation of VL2's mother being in the very hands of God, that is, Christ, in whose presence VL2's mother had gone to be: "After a while, I gathered my brothers and sisters together in the hallway of the hospital and reminded them that the most important thing was my mother had put her faith in God through the blood of Christ. Her life was in God's hands. We believe in the eternal life that God has promised to those who put their faith in him. Since we are believers in Christ, we believe we will meet our mother again."[81]

Having this hope fuels Vietnamese-Canadian believers to proclaim an evangelistic message at every funeral service for the salvation of their souls. Just as the Lord had sent ships to rescue them so that they were and are able

---

81. Eternal life (*zōē aiōnios*) can be defined primarily as "The life of the age (*aiōn*) to come, resurrection life, which believers in Christ enjoy in advance because of their union with one who is already risen from the dead. In the Gospel of John that meaning is certainly present, but eternal life here [in John 3:15] is the very life of God which resides in the eternal Word ('in him was life') and is communicated by him to all believers" (Bruce, *Gospel of John*, 89; see also Carson, *Gospel According to John*, 202–203).

to find refuge in such places as America and Canada, according to Minh Van Lam, "The Lord Jesus Christ . . . also wants to save our souls."[82] Indeed, for Jesus himself asked, "For what does it profit a man to gain the whole world, and forfeit his soul?" (Mark 8:36). Souls are saved only through the proclamation of the gospel (good news) of Jesus Christ (Mark 8:35). Yet Stephen J. Nichols warns, "The idea of proclaiming merely by our presence is never a substitute for using words. The saying, often attributed to Saint Francis, 'Preach Christ and if necessary use words,' may sound good, but actually makes no sense. It runs entirely counter to the model of Christ himself. He used words, a lot."[83] As the apostle Paul states, "How then will they call on Him in whom they have not believed? How will they believe in Him whom they have not heard? And how will they hear without a preacher? How will they preach unless they are sent? Just as it is written, 'How beautiful are the feet of those who bring good news of good things!'" (Rom 10:14–15).

Central to this good news is the person of Jesus Christ (Mark 1:1). As the last Adam, yet unlike the first Adam, Jesus Christ lived an earthly life of perfect obedience to God the Father in heaven, a prerequisite for being the only One suitable to bear upon himself the sin of all humanity, and with it, the fierce wrath of God. Thus, in his sacrificial death, Jesus Christ paid in full the atoning price for our sins – past, present, and future – and satisfied the righteous requirement of God's holy law. It is therefore no accident then that when he saw Jesus Christ, John, the son of Zacharias and Elizabeth (Luke 1:57–63), exclaimed to the crowd nearby, "Behold, the Lamb of God who takes away the sin of the *world*!" (John 1:29; emphasis mine). On account of Jesus's once-for-all sacrifice for the purification of all sinful humanity (Heb 1:1–3; 9:11–14), not only does God the Father refuse to count humanity's sins against those who trust only in his beloved Son Jesus Christ for their salvation (2 Cor 5:19), but simultaneously, he also withdraws his wrath from over their heads (Rom 8:1; cf. John 3:36; 5:24). On the grounds of this act of love wherein God the Father sent his beloved Son to be the propitiation of the world's sins (1 John 4:10), slaves to sin from every tribe, language, people, and nation can thus be spiritually transformed into blood-bought, born-again (or born from above), beloved, children of God with all the rights and

---

82. Lam, *God's Miracles*, 160.

83. Nichols, *Welcome to the Story*, 143.

privileges thereof: the privilege of boldly and confidently addressing God in the same manner as the Lord Jesus Christ, as "Abba! Father!" (Gal 4:4–6; cf. Mark 14:36), and also the right to the eternal and universal inheritance of the kingdom of Christ and God (Eph 5:5; Rev 5:6–10). As John R. W. Stott aptly stated, "Evangelical Christians believe that in and through Christ crucified God substituted himself for us and bore our sins, dying in our place the death we deserved to die, in order that we might be restored to his favor and adopted into his family."[84] To put this beautifully good news another way, like the rainbow (Gen 9:12–17), the cross of Christ is the universal sign of God's covenant with the world signifying that his war with the world is over, if only they would believe in his beloved Son Jesus Christ, and him alone, for their eternal salvation (John 3:16–17; 14:6). As Bekele D. Anshiso avers, "In a nutshell, the major purpose of Jesus's death was to reveal himself to the whole world and to save those who confess him as God's Son."[85] For even though the wages of our sin is death (Rom 6:23), "God was bearing all the cost and penalty of our sin *in his own self*. God took all the terrible consequences of sin and suffered for them himself in the person of God the Son."[86]

As joyful ambassadors of Christ then, born-again Christians herald this beautifully good news in the hope that many will eagerly come to repentance and share in the joy of eternal life, which is found nowhere else but in the reconciling knowledge of God in Christ our mediator (2 Cor 5:18–20; 1 Tim 2:5-6; Heb 7:25). It is therefore on account of this truth that these Vietnamese-Canadian believers enthusiastically affirm that there is nothing more important in life than having an intimate relationship with God the Father in Christ the incarnate Son through the Spirit who offers the free and unmerited gift of eternal life to *all* who will simply ask (John 3:16; 11:25–26; Rom 10:9–10).

True biblical hope from sin and death for any mortal, however, is predicated on God's amazing grace alone through faith in Christ alone (John 14:6; Rev 1:17–18). So, like the apostle Peter, these Vietnamese-Canadian believers insist, "there is salvation in no one else; for there is no other name under heaven that has been given among men by which we must be saved" except

---

84. Stott, *Cross of Christ*, 13.

85. Anshiso, *Jesus's Identification*, 207.

86. Wright, *To the Cross*, 131; emphasis original.

in the name of the crucified-yet-resurrected Lord Jesus Christ (Acts 4:12; 1 Cor 15:20). Or as Alister E. McGrath asserts, "The resurrection of Jesus . . . establishes and undergirds the Christian hope. This has both *soteriological* and *eschatological* implications."[87] Which means that, "At the *soteriological* level, it enables the death of Christ upon the cross to be interpreted in terms of God's victory over death and a coalition of allied forces and powers. At the *eschatological* level, it gives both foundation and substance to the Christian hope of eternal life."[88] This genuine hope in the crucified-yet-resurrected Christ thus enables the believer in Christ "to observe the power of death in terms of its empty future and in the knowledge of its, not God's, sure defeat. It can tolerate, therefore, the agonizing presence of the power of death as 'on the way out,' and be confident that evil will not have the final say over God's creation."[89] This message of hope is central to what is proclaimed in the hope that unbelievers would gladly become believers in the Lord Jesus Christ, thus sharing in his resurrection to eternal life (1 Cor 15; Phil 3:7–11, 20–21) in his glorious presence of exceeding worshipful joy (Jude 24).

But worship, even through the proclamation, or even reading the word of God, also brings comfort to the bereaved. As Cole avers, worship draws the bereaved more deeply into the Christian story. "This story tells of how God, especially known in the person of Jesus, comforts, heals, renews, and restores health, wholeness, relational well-being, and spiritual vitality. . . . Living with this story shapes how we feel and think about life and death, and also our hopes for the future."[90] Further, "On occasions of loss, we are invited to perceive our experience and need in light of the Christian faith, its support, and its hope. To that end, worship and reading [and hearing] Scripture draw us into the Christian story, keep us there, and sustain us with its promises."[91]

Cole also states that worship can even foster connections to God and others within the community of faith for the bereaved. Being a member of a church therefore "provides for strong connections to God and to other persons."[92] By participating in the rituals of the church, such as reading the

---

87. McGrath, *Christian Theology*, 314; emphasis mine.
88. McGrath, 314; emphasis original.
89. Beker, *Suffering and Hope*, 121–122.
90. Cole, *Good Mourning*, 76.
91. Cole, 77.
92. Cole, 77.

Bible together, praying together, etc., the bereaved can "live the Christian story together. In living this story with one another, we find ourselves bound to God, each other, and the world in ways that only come with sharing a worshipful life."[93] By virtue of this communal worship, "living your faith with others *will* enrich your life."[94]

At the same time, Cole also avows that worship moreover transports the bereaved to spiritual and emotional places where mourning can occur. It is in "creating and cultivating new 'places' or 'spaces' for mourning that we find comfort, rest, encouragement, and hope."[95] It is also likely that the bereaved may "find a deeper connection with God, other people, and the Christian story."[96]

5.2. Summary

While each of these expressions of grief are generally commonplace among all cultures, there are certain grief expressions that were observed within both the Guyanese-Canadian and Vietnamese-Canadian cultures, but which were not discussed, because they do not overlap between the two aforementioned contemporary cultures. These practices (five to be exact) would be considered distinctly intercultural and hopefully transformative of grief, thus sustaining the bereaved. These five redemptive mourning practices will thus be explicated in chapter 6.

---

93. Cole, 78.
94. Cole, 79.
95. Cole, 79–80.
96. Cole, 80.

Compassionate Intercultural Pastoral Care Practices for Coping with Grief

6.1. Reflective Practice or Compassionate Pastoral Care Responses

Based on our discussion in the previous chapters, this chapter consequently proposes and explores five compassionate pastoral care practices that are liberative and intercultural in their approach. It is hoped that these five compassionate practices will sensitize pastoral caregivers to their multivalent significance within our intercultural society, and also challenge them to explore further ways people define, express, experience, and adapt to the phenomenon of grief.[1] Drawing upon theories and practices from different cultures (and with respect to this book, the Guyanese and Vietnamese cultures), the underlying premise of the liberative intercultural pastoral care framework is "equal respect for all cultures and all people as bearing the image and likeness of God."[2] Which is to say, "The *modus operandi* of intercultural pastoral care and counseling has entailed respectful dialogue between participants from different geographic and social locations in which each purports to learn from the other."[3] The essential principle here is, "If all people are cre-

---

1. Doka and Davidson pursued a similar line of research in their edited volume *Living with Grief*, albeit not from a biblical and pastoral theological position, as is the case of this current project.

2. Lartey, "Postcolonializing Pastoral Theology," 80.

3. Lartey, 80.

ated in and bear the image of God then all have a contribution to make in the presentation of the God of all creation and in the care of all humanity. It goes without saying that if there is to be genuine intercultural interaction among pastoral practitioners, there indeed needs to be recognition and respect for each participant's cultural and religious heritage."[4] This is all the more significant in light of the fact that "The colonial project with its inherently oppressive and de-facing characteristics in relation to cultures different from itself has left partners in intercultural interaction who originate from the former colonies unable to truly engage the colonizers and the descendants from an equal epistemological and political base."[5] As a consequence of this, "Participants in the intercultural dialogue whose origins lie on the side of the formerly colonized need the uplifting strength and empowerment of their own resources in order to be enabled to relate to the descendants of the colonizers on an equal or at least more fulsome and authentic footing."[6] It is therefore hoped that respect will be extended to both the Guyanese and Vietnamese cultures, moderately represented here in this book, as legitimate intercultural dialogue participants.

Liberative intercultural pastoral care encompasses six functions: healing, sustaining, guiding, reconciling, liberating, and empowering. Of import to a discussion on the phenomenon of grief is the function of *sustaining*. Lartey avers that, "When death has actually occurred, no amount of denial, natural as it is, is going to reverse it. It is in such circumstances that the art of *sustaining* is called for."[7] Viewed negatively, "Sustaining goes beyond resignation. It is not about maintaining a stoic silence or a cynical resolution."[8] Considered positively, however, "To be sustained is to find strength and support, from *within* and *without*, to cope adequately with what cannot be changed. It has to do with a transformation of a situation by traversing through it, and is more to do with attitude than escape."[9] In this light, Lartey urges that, "Pastoral caregivers give support in such times not by promising a favorable outcome or better times, but by enabling and facilitating coping mechanisms within

---

4. Lartey, 80.
5. Lartey, 80.
6. Lartey, 81.
7. Lartey, *In Living Color*, 63–64; emphasis mine.
8. Lartey, 64; emphasis mine.
9. Lartey, 64.

them. Or else by helping them draw upon sustaining forces outside them-selves, within their immediate social or cultural circumstances."[10] Liberative intercultural pastoral care is thus inductive, collective, and inclusive as it seeks to be present empathically in the concrete experiences of the bereaved, even those whose voices have been muted by external oppressive voices.[11] For this reason, it allows the bereaved the complete freedom to express in their own way, the length and breadth and height and depth of their grief experience.[12] Here also the knowledge and understanding of the divine and the human are enriched,[13] even while communal spaces are cultivated wherein all God's people can be safe, nurtured, and empowered to grow by the power of God's Spirit into the image of God's unique Son, Jesus Christ (Eph 4:15–16).[14]

What follows in this chapter are five compassionate (liberative intercul-tural) pastoral care practices that endeavor to help and sustain others amidst their situation of grief, each of which is couched within rituals. As specified by Elaine J. Ramshaw, "A ritual proper is a relatively formalized, corporate, symbolic act of ritualization. Ritualization is a much wider phenomenon, including all the aspects of our biosocial behavior that are patterned, repeti-tive, conventionalized."[15] Which implies that, "Without ritualization we would have to plan every action from scratch and analyze the meaning of every interaction. . . . All ritualization, then, is about the ordering of experience."[16] Or as Donald Capps asserts, rituals "help persons become better oriented in the world."[17]

When it comes to formal corporate rituals, as opposed to everyday ritual-ization, it is important to note that "healthy rituals order experience flexibly. The greater formalization is necessary due to the corporate nature of the event, the symbolic weight it must bear, and the tradition it must pass on."[18] Which means that "all ritualization communicates some sort of meaning. . . . Formal

---

10. Lartey, 64.

11. Lartey, 125.

12. Lartey, 125.

13. Lartey, *Pastoral Theology*, 98.

14. Lartey, *Postcolonializing God*, 121.

15. Ramshaw, *Ritual and Pastoral Care*, 23.

16. Ramshaw, 23.

17. Capps, *Life Cycle Theory*, 116.

18. Ramshaw, *Ritual and Pastoral Care*, 24–25.

rituals carry the core meanings of the social group performing them, the meanings which determine the group's worldview."[19] This is enacted "through the use of symbols which have many layers of significance as a wooden cross or the act of giving bread or the community's forming a circle, [wherein] we express the deepest meanings we know of, and often meanings deeper than we consciously know."[20] It is no accident then that "The human need to make sense of experience is universal and fundamental. Faced with the biggest questions of life and death, love and evil, the origin and destiny of the human race and the universe, we cannot pin down an answer in logical formulas."[21] In those moments, "We turn to symbolic expressions of our trust in that which grounds the goodness in our experience and shapes the tradition which we make our meanings."[22] Or as someone once said, "When words are inadequate, have a ritual."[23]

It would be a mistake, however, to think that a symbol should only serve as a vehicle for meaning. Such was the definition Geertz proposed when he sought to define a symbol as "any object, act, event, quality, or relation which serves as a vehicle for conception – the conception is the symbol's meaning."[24] Challenging this definition, however, Talal Assad contends that, "the symbol is not an object that serves as a vehicle for a conception, *it is itself the conception*."[25] Symbol is therefore equivalent to meaning. For support, Asad leans on the work of Marcel Mauss, particularly Mauss' "Techniques of the Body."

According to Mauss, "The body is man's first and most natural instrument. Or more accurately, not to speak of instruments, man's first and most

---

19. Ramshaw, 25.

20. Ramshaw, 25.

21. Ramshaw, 25.

22. Ramshaw, 25.

23. Anonymous; noted in Wolfelt, *Creating Meaningful Funeral Ceremonies*, 13.

24. Geertz, *Interpretation of Cultures*, 91.

25. Asad, *Genealogies of Religion*, 30; emphasis original. Cf. Bell (*Ritual: Perspectives and Dimensions*, 72–83) who remarks that, "ritual is more complex than the mere communication of meanings and values," and therefore suggests that "it is a set of activities that construct particular types of meanings and values in specific ways" (82). She therefore avoids proffering a universal definition for ritual since she is opined to believe that such an act can "obscure how and why people produce ritualized actions" (82). For this reason, she affirms that "Ritual, or ritualization, may be best defined in culturally specific ways since cultures, and even subcultures, differentiate among their actions in distinctive ways" (82).

natural technical object, and at the same time technical means, is his body."[26] In his comment on this statement, Asad remarks that, "By talking about 'body techniques,' Mauss sought to focus attention on the fact that if we were to conceptualize human behavior in terms of learned capabilities, we might see the need for investigating how these are linked to authoritative standards and regular practice."[27] For Mauss, "these techniques of the body are the ways in which from society to society men know how to use their bodies."[28] It is here that Mauss' notion of the *habitus*, that Latin word, which emphasizes the social nature of embodied action, comes into play.

For Mauss, "These habits do not vary just with individuals and the imitations; they vary especially between societies, educations, proprieties and fashions, and prestiges. In them we should see the techniques and work of collective and individual practical reason rather than, in the ordinary way, merely the soul and its repetitive faculties."[29] In this way, as Asad notes, "The concept of *habitus* invites us to analyze the body as an assemblage of embodied aptitudes, not as a medium of symbolic meanings."[30]

By virtue of this fact, the human body should not be viewed simply as the passive recipient of "cultural imprints, and still less, as the active source of natural expressions that are clothed in local history and culture."[31] On the contrary, the human body should be viewed "as the developable means for achieving a range of human objectives, from styles of physical movement (e.g., walking), through modes of emotional being (e.g., composure), to kinds of spiritual experience (e.g., mystical states)."[32]

Reasoning from this, it can thus be concluded that a ritual should be understood not as a symbolic action that communicates an idea, but, though complex, an embodied action that emerges from socio-cultural aptitudes

---

26. Mauss, "Techniques of the Body," 104.

27. Asad, *Genealogies of Religion*, 75.

28. Mauss, "Techniques of the Body," 97.

29. Mauss, 101. Interestingly, Mauss did not chose the French word most familiar to him: *habitude* (habit or custom).

30. Asad, *Genealogies of Religion*, 75.

31. As noted in Asad, 76; here, Asad refers to Mary Douglas' interpretation of Mauss in *Natural Symbols*.

32. Asad, 76; in this way, Mauss seems to avoid the Cartesian dualism of the mind and objects of the mind's (body) perception that has dominated Western thought (as also noted by Rodney A. Werline, my external doctoral examiner, through personal correspondence).

that humans acquire and develop.[33] By means of habituated performance, rituals are socially acquired and culturally shaped, rather than individual or universal in form.[34] Which is to say that ritual is the way in which humans properly function, move, and relate to each other within culture.[35] Rituals, as embodied practices (including language in use), therefore form a precondition for varieties of religious experience,[36] even that of grief and mourning. Alternatively stated, rituals, as embodied practices, become "a means of entering into communion with God,"[37] even the God who grieves and mourns with those find themselves in the crucible of bereavement (cf. John 11:35).

"Care for the dead is a universal human phenomenon which manifests itself in diverse cultures and religions in varied customs and rituals surrounding death."[38] This infers a willingness to embrace grief as one's own, as well as the grief of others, in a life marked by prophetic engagement, the courage to risk compassionate involvement, and communion with God who grieves with us.[39] That each of these practices is understood as ritualistic does

---

33. As noted by Werline through personal correspondence; even the action of bringing a meal to a grieving family is not symbolizing a detached ideal of love, but rather, the action *is an embodied act of love* (emphasis Werline).

34. Farnell, "Techniques of the Body," 2.

35. As noted by Werline through personal correspondence.

36. Asad, *Genealogies of Religion*, 76–77; cf. Bell, *Ritual*, 72–83, wherein she notes, "A practice approach to ritual will first address how a particular community or culture ritualizes (what characteristics of acting make strategic distinctions between these acts and others) and then address when and why ritualization is deemed the effective thing to do" (81). In this respect, "The goal of ritualization is completely circular: the creation of a ritualized agent, an actor with a form of ritual mastery, who embodies flexible sets of cultural schemes and can deploy them effectively in multiple situations so as to restructure those situations in practical ways. Among the most important strategies of ritualization is the inherent flexibility of the degree of ritualization invoked" (81). Ritual as practice therefore involves "a basic shift from looking at an activity as the expression of cultural patterns to looking at it as that which makes and harbors such patterns" (82).

37. Mauss, "Techniques of the Body," 122. Yet, Asad also contends that the perspective on ritual as embodied symbolic activity is nonetheless an historically shaped organization of power. Asad therefore cautions against the normative application of concepts that are the historical products of a Christian history and Christian organizations of power (Asad, *Genealogies of Religion*, 27–79). See also Bell (*Ritual*, 72–83) who avers that, rather than viewing "ritual as the vehicle for the expression of authority, practice theorists tend to explore how ritual is a vehicle for the construction of relationships of authority and submission" (82).

38. van Tongeren, "Individualizing Ritual," 117.

39. Adapted and changed from Zylla's, *Roots of Sorrow*, 167; Zylla acknowledges that these have been adapted and changed from a proposal first put forward by Westerhoff, *Spiritual Life*, 30.

not necessarily assume a need of our own, but rather, "God's invitation."[40] Yet as Victor White points out, "God's command to us to worship him is a concession to our needs."[41] Which infers that "whatever else we do together, the core of our communal identity is enacted in our worship. . . . The more widely and actively people participate in a ritual, the more they experience it as their own, as part of their identity, and the more connected they tend to feel with the other participants."[42] And as Ramshaw indicates, "the pastor's role is to assist the people's creative task, through her knowledge of the church's liturgical tradition and the people's ritual needs."[43] At the same time, lest we forget, it is important to emphasize that "The normative aim of the liturgy is not human comfort but the glory of God."[44] But in light of the fact that God has chosen to make his dwelling with humans, implies that "God has chosen to link divine glory and human need. The incarnational heart of our theology is what opens the way to a consideration of the human side of the religious experience."[45] It is therefore in their religious experience that humans encounter God, and that they do this through rituals.

According to Romeo Vitelli, "It is safe to say that grief is universal. Everybody experiences loss, whether it's the loss of a loved one, the ending of a romantic relationship, or any sort of a serious setback in life. The process of dealing with that grief often involves mourning 'rituals' that vary across different times and cultures."[46] By virtue of this, Vitelli asserts, "How mourners respond emotionally to a death can also be carefully controlled by mourning rituals."[47] Vitelli further contends, "Though rituals can be highly formal, such as the kind of rituals seen in many religions, they can also be informally created by people needing to find a way to come to terms with

---

40. Ramshaw, *Ritual and Pastoral Care*, 16.

41. As quoted in Hovda, *Dry Bones*, 59.

42. Ramshaw, *Ritual and Pastoral Care*, 30.

43. Ramshaw, 22; here she also notes that "*liturgy* etymologically means the work of the people, not the work of the pastor. The pastor's work is to midwife the labor of the people of God. She presides, leads, directs, and organizes, all to help the people of God do their work. She coaches them in the various skills necessary to their work" (emphasis original).

44. Ramshaw, 22.

45. Ramshaw, 22–23.

46. Vitelli, "Can Rituals Help Us," para. 1, 2.

47. Vitelli, para. 3.

grief."[48] This implies that "Since people who have suffered some kind of loss often feel as if their lives are out of control, using rituals can help restore that feeling of control and, in turn, make it easier for them to cope with grief."[49] From research conducted among both participants and non-participants of rituals, it has been observed that, "The evidence to date suggests that using rituals, whether formal rituals associated with many religions or the informal rituals we can create ourselves, can help people regain some feeling of control in their lives as well as cope with loss."[50] So, bearing in mind "the devastating impact that grief can have on physical and mental health, relying on rituals can play an important role in alleviating the deep grief of loss as well as the more mundane losses we all experience."[51]

The necessity for rituals become all the more important when the church is called upon "to answer certain generic needs, [for example], the need to shape communal grief."[52] And as one funeral director notes in relation to immigrants embedded in traditional communities: "The more the community is involved and the more the family is involved in this event, the more meaningful [it becomes]."[53]

When it comes to ritual with regards to the dying, Ramshaw notes, "The type of ritual expression appropriate would vary widely according to the personality and religious style of the dying person, and the circumstances of the death."[54] Ramshaw also finds that "A number of people writing about the process of dying have observed that often the patient comes to terms with the fact that she is dying before the family does."[55] On such occasions, "she then finds it difficult to 'let go' because she senses that her family is not ready to let go. In such cases, the use of a rite of commendation with the family may be a way of their giving her permission to die."[56]

---

48. Vitelli, para. 5.

49. Vitelli, para. 5.

50. Vitelli, para. 14.

51. Vitelli, para. 14.

52. Ramshaw, *Ritual and Pastoral Care*, 55.

53. As quoted in Laderman, *Rest in Peace*, 165.

54. Ramshaw, *Ritual and Pastoral Care*, 67.

55. Ramshaw, 67–68.

56. Ramshaw, 68.

Further to this, "When a death is foreseen, the ritual care of the dying person's circle of friends and/or family can start before death. One of the ways to use ritual as the focus for beginning the grieving process is to plan the funeral ahead of time."[57] In fact,

> Many families have found it a deeply moving experience to plan the funeral or memorial service together. It can be a time for family members and friends to say some of the things to the dying person that otherwise might not be said until the wake or funeral: what they value most about her, what their favorite memories are, why they would want to sing a certain song.[58]

At the same time, it is worth pointing out that "For the circle of friends and family closest to the person who dies, the funeral is not likely to be able to help them 'work through' or resolve their grief, unless the death was long-expected and most of the grief has been worked through before death occurs."[59] In actual fact, "For many people, the most the funeral can do is get them out of the initial state of shock, numbness, and denial, and *into* grief, that is, to help them into rather than through or out of grief."[60] Or as Alan D. Wolfelt states, "The funeral is a ritual of ending, but it only marks the beginning of the healing process."[61] For this reason, "the crucial moments for the family and close friends are usually the signs of finality: the closing of the casket, the lowering of the casket into the ground, the first shovel of dirt."[62] It is very likely that during such moments, "The mourners will seesaw between denial and acceptance for a long time to come, but ritual honesty and care for healthy grieving require that the funeral state clearly that the one they mourn is gone from this world forever."[63] Rituals consequently serve to sustain the bereaved so that they are able to cope well with their grief.

It is thus against this background that the following five compassionate pastoral care practices are developed, each of which are liberative and

---

57. Ramshaw, 69.
58. Ramshaw, 69–70.
59. Ramshaw, 71.
60. Ramshaw, 71; emphasis original.
61. Wolfelt, *Creating Meaningful Funeral Ceremonies*, 15.
62. Ramshaw, *Ritual and Pastoral Care*, 71.
63. Ramshaw, 71.

intercultural in their approach.[64] Couched in rituals, these compassionate practices have been deemed worthy of embodying with an eye toward the mitigation of grief, transforming it so that it becomes redemptive, and in the process, sustains and restores the soul of the mourner:

1. Bearing the Funeral Expenses of the Poor – Extending Offers of Help

2. Composing and Singing Sad (and Joyful Theopoetic) Songs and Poems of Lament – Finding Emotional Catharsis through Music

3. Incorporating Indigenous Christian Devotional Songs (e.g., Bhajans) in the Wake/Funeral Liturgy – Tapping into the Cultural Liminal Memory of a Deep Experience of Faith

4. Celebrating the Life of the Deceased through Dancing and Singing Upbeat Gospel Songs – Spiritual Rejoicing for Having Arrived Home in Heaven

5. Connecting Personal Grief Stories to God's Sacred Story – Experiencing Hope in the Crucified-yet-Resurrected Christ

6.1a. Bearing the Funeral Expenses of the Poor – Extending Offers of Help

It was VL1 who commented that, within the Vietnamese culture, "People also visit and go out with the bereaved. They also give a love gift in an envelope to the bereaved."[65] In a similar vein, it was observed as being commonplace among Guyanese of an East Indian heritage – (but not quite as much among those of an Amerindian, African, Chinese, or European heritage) – of willingly bearing the *entire* cost of the funeral for the poor.[66] GL1 remarked,

---

64. As noted above in the conclusion of chapter 5, these five compassionate pastoral care practices are deemed liberative intercultural on account of the fact that they do not overlap between the following two cultural groups: Guyanese-Canadian and Vietnamese-Canadian.

65. Nothing, however, was said of paying for the funeral expense in full.

66. It should be noted here that East-Indian Guyanese Christians would come forward voluntarily asking the pastor how they can offer their help. By inference, no solicitation is involved. It appears that by approaching the pastor to offer help even without the mourner's knowledge, the secret giver gives to the poor without allowing their left hand to know what their right hand is doing (Matt 6:3). There are times when giving was done openly, as in the case of the financial donation from the Gentile churches for the Jerusalem church (Acts 11:27–30; Rom 15:26; 1 Cor 16:1–3; 2 Cor 8–9). Great care should be taken, however, to reduce the public

"Generally, especially among the Indian people more than anyone else, they will chip in to pay without being asked to pay for the funeral. They would be willing to join in and help to pay for the expenses. They would come and ask, 'Can I help?' But you will find this almost exclusively among the Indians." Ince-Carvalhal perceives that, "Often seeing the love, affection and sentiment that others feel can provide a great support network and a sense of togetherness, pride and kindred spirit."[67] Considering the high funeral costs in Canada, such benevolent monetary aid from without the bereaved but within their immediate social or cultural circumstance, doubtless serves to assuage their financial burden, and thus sustain them amidst their grief.[68]

The impetus for Christian generosity in helping to offset the financial needs of others, even their funeral expenses, especially among the less fortunate believers, is also observed in the OT, particularly in 1 Kings 13:1–34. In this passage of Scripture, we learn that there was a man of God from Judah whom Yahweh sent to Bethel for a prophetic ministry. It was his mission to announce to Jeroboam the coming of a son to be born of the house of David, namely Josiah. At the end of his oracle, Jeroboam requested that the man of God return with him to the king's house. Jeroboam's request was however declined as the man of God was admonished, "You shall eat no bread, nor drink water, nor return by the way which you came." (v. 9). As such, the man of God "did not return by the way which he came to Bethel" (v. 10).

As the narrative unfolds, we learn that the man of God was sitting under an oak tree. It is here that an old prophet from Bethel finds him and requests that he returns with him to Bethel. Once again, the man of God explains, "I cannot return with you, nor go with you, nor will I eat bread or drink water with you in this place. For a command came to me by the word of the LORD, 'You shall not eat bread, nor drink water there; do not return by going the way which you came'" (vv. 16–17). But when the old prophet from Bethel said, "I am also a prophet like you, and an angel spoke to me by the word of the LORD, saying, 'Bring him back with you to your house, that he may eat

---

knowledge of one's financial help "so that your giving will be in secret; and your Father who sees *what is done* in secret will reward you" (6:4).

67. Ince-Carvalhal, "Unfortunate Reality of Grieving," para. 5.

68. Lartey, *In Living Color*, 64.

bread and drink water,'" the man of God "went back with him, and ate bread in his house and drank water" (vv. 18–19).

On account of his disobedience, as the man of God made his way back to Judah, "a lion met him on the way and killed him" (v. 24) tearing his body to pieces and throwing it on the road (v. 26). Eventually the old prophet of Bethel caught wind of this fatal news, trekked to the place where the cadaver was left lying on the road, took it up, laid it on his donkey, and brought it back to Bethel. Here, the old prophet buried the man of God in his *own* grave, that is, "in the family sepulchre,"[69] and mourned his death, even while lamenting, "Alas, my brother!" (v. 30).

Within the NT, the extension of a helping hand is observed in Jesus' parable of the Good Samaritan (Luke 10:25–37). To set the stage for the parable, a discourse commences between Jesus and an expert in the Mosaic law. Intending to test Jesus, the lawyer said, "Teacher, what shall I do to inherit eternal life?" (10:25). In typical rabbinic fashion, Jesus responded by questioning him, "What is written in the Law? How does it read?" (10:26). By way of a summary statement of the law of God in the OT (with its many individual commandments), the lawyer retorted, "You shall love the Lord your God with all your heart, and with all your soul, and with all your strength, and with all your mind; and your neighbor as yourself" (10:27). Applauding his insight, Jesus remarked, "You have answered correctly; do this and you will live" (10:28). In other words, he passed the test. But intending to justify himself, the lawyer inquired, "And who is my neighbor?" (10:29). At this point, Jesus commenced the parable of the Good Samaritan.

> A man was going down from Jerusalem to Jericho, and fell among robbers, and they stripped him and beat him, and went away leaving him half dead. And by chance a priest was going down on that road, and when he saw him, he passed by on the other side. Likewise a Levite also, when he came to the place and saw him, passed by on the other side. But a Samaritan, who was on a journey, came upon him; and when he saw him, he felt compassion, and came to him and bandaged up his wounds, pouring oil and wine on *them*; and he put him on his own beast,

---

69. Cogan, *1 Kings*, 372.

and brought him to an inn and took care of him. On the next day he took out two denarii and gave them to the innkeeper and said, 'Take care of him; and whatever more you spend, when I return I will repay you.' (10:30–35)

After narrating this parable to the lawyer, Jesus tested him with this question: "Which of these do you think proved to be a neighbor to the man who fell into the robbers' *hands*?" (10:36). When the lawyer responded, "The one who showed mercy toward him," Jesus remarked, "Go and do the same" (10:37).

Darrell L. Bock comments that, "Love for one's neighbor is often seen as a summary of the law."[70] As an expert in the law of Moses, this lawyer who attempted to test Jesus, would have been familiar with the teaching in Judaism, which recognized that if humans were created in God's image, then a love for God was confirmed by a love for one's fellow humans.[71] Some of the Jews, however, developed at least two ways in which to outwit this demonstrative love for a fellow human: (i) The isolationist approach, which could be described as "I want to be left alone, so I will not involve myself with others."[72] (ii) The restrictionist approach, which seeks to define and thus restrict who one's neighbor is.[73] In the parable of the Good Samaritan, the lawyer appears to have attempted the restrictionist approach. In contradistinction to him, however, "In Jesus' parable of the Good Samaritan, the Samaritan sees that the man on the side of the road is in need of help and he stops with active help. This is the essence of the compassionate response: *to move into the suffering of others with active help*."[74]

At the heart of extending a helping hand in bearing the cost of the funeral expenses of the poor, whom Christians are called to remember (Gal 2:10),[75] so as to alleviate their need, is the fundamental human concern for the shalom or wellbeing and dignity of every person, even the dying person. The

---

70. Bock, *Luke 9:51 – 24:53*, 1026.

71. See Derrett, *Law in the New Testament*, 223–224.

72. Bock, *Luke 9:51 – 24:53*, 1026.

73. Bock, 1026; Bock, however, does not use the term *restrictionist approach*, but simply gives a description of this second approach.

74. Zylla, *Roots of Sorrow*, 100.

75. See also Deut 15:7, 9, 11; 24:14, 15; 1 Sam 2:8; 2 Sam 12:3–4; Isa 10:2; 58:7; Job 29:12; Jer 2:34; 5:28; Zech 7:10; Luke 4:18; 7:22; 14:13; 16:20–22; 18:22; 19:8; Jas 2:2–6.

dignity of every person, even and especially the poor, finds its underpinning in the fact that every person is made in the very image and likeness of God (Gen 1:26–27; 5:1; 9:6; Ps 139:14–17 [13–16]; Jas 3:9). As Sarna asserts, "the resemblance of man to God bespeaks the infinite worth of a human being and affirms the inviolability of the human person."[76] This is further enriched by the fact that: (i) Jesus himself became poor for us ("For you know the grace of our Lord Jesus Christ, that though He was rich, yet for your sake He became poor, so that you through His poverty might become rich" [2 Cor 8:9]); and (ii) In Jesus' declaration in his Sermon on the Mount as of first importance, "Blessed *are* you *who* are poor, for yours is the kingdom of God" (Luke 6:20; cf. Matt 5:3). Turning a blind eye to the poor then is at the same time a turning of a blind eye to God whose preference is for the poor and to whom the inheritance of the kingdom of God belongs (Matt 25:31–40).[77]

While it is true that burdens are lifted at Calvary, to borrow the words of John M. Moore, this ought never negate the compassionate act of extending a helping hand in bearing the burdens of another, and in the case of grief, that of covering the funeral expense of the bereaved poor. Compassionate generosity meets the needs of others, especially the poor, because they are in need of help – *our* help – the help of fellow brothers and sisters in Christ who *also* bear God's image. By virtue of the fact that liberation theology extends preferential option for the poor, Gustavo Gutiérrez avers that, "The commitment to the poor is not 'optional' in the sense that a Christian is free to make or not make this option, or commitment, to the poor, just as the love we owe to all human beings, without exception is not 'optional.'"[78] Simply put, "an option for the poor is an option for the God of the kingdom whom Jesus proclaims to us."[79]

Yet, as Gutiérrez points out, "The ultimate reason for commitment to the poor and oppressed is not to be found in the social analysis we use, or in human compassion, or in any direct experience we may have of poverty. These are all doubtless valid motives that play an important part in

---

76. Sarna, *Genesis*, 12.

77. For more on this topic, see Anshiso, *Jesus's Identification*.

78. Gutiérrez, *Theology of Liberation*, xxvi.

79. Gutiérrez, xxvii.

our commitment."[80] Rather, our commitment as Christians to the poor "is grounded, in the final analysis, in the God of our faith. It is a theocentric, prophetic option that has its roots in the unmerited love of God and is demanded by this love."[81] Yet this love and preferential option for the poor that is demanded of Christians finds it underpinning in the fact that God's unmerited love is directed toward those who are his image bearers, and thus are endued with inherent dignity and worth. But such inherent worth can only be a reality if these are created beings of the One who is of ultimate worth, and that One is none other than Yahweh the God of the Bible, the Creator of heaven and earth and everything therein. This infers that out of his goodness and love, God creates humans in his image and likeness, and in this divine act, God endues each person with inherent dignity and worth. Human dignity, even and especially the inherent dignity and worth of the poor, is thus never divorced from God's goodness and love.

It is therefore by virtue of the worth and dignity of the poor, a worth derived from God their Creator, that, "The Father's goodness and love reaches out to the simple and the unimportant, [especially the poor and the forgotten], and gives them preference."[82] Puebla puts it more precisely: "The poor merit preferential attention, whatever may be the moral or the spiritual situation in which they find themselves. Made in the image and likeness of God to be his children, this image is dimmed and even defiled. That is why God takes on their defense and loves them."[83]

This however does not negate the fact that, "solidarity with the poor and the starving, which leads to an ongoing transformation of history and requires behavior to this end, is the fruit of the gratuitous love of God."[84] The fruit of God's gratuitous love will thus confirm itself in the lives of God's image-bearing children in Christ (John 1:12–13) as they take their stand in solidarity with the poor amidst their grief, especially for the purpose of extending a helping hand in bearing their funeral expenses, thus validating their inherent dignity and worth.

---

80. Gutiérrez, xxvii.
81. Gutiérrez, xxvii.
82. Gutiérrez, *On Job*, xiii.
83. In Gutiérrez, xiii.
84. Gutiérrez, 99.

Furthermore, the fact that humans, both male and female, are created in the image of God implies not only that humans are like God, but also that humans represent God. Therefore, as God's representatives, the heart of God's compassionate character (Exod 34:6) is revealed in the Christian's compassion toward the poor (Luke 15:20). As a matter of fact, Scripture states that, "One who is gracious to a poor man lends to the LORD, and He will repay him for his good deed" (Prov 19:17). Little wonder that the kingdom of heaven is granted to those who feed the hungry, satiate the thirsty, extend hospitality to the stranger, clothe the naked, and visit the sick and the imprisoned. "The King will answer and say to them, 'Truly I say to you, to the extent that you did it to one of these brothers of Mine, *even* the least *of them*, you did it to Me'" (Matt 25:34–40). To this, one might add the bearing of the funeral expenses of those who are poor (cf. 27:57–61) on account of God's gratuitous and unmerited love for those who bear his image.

Supported by the magnanimous generosity of God the Father in Christ the Son, Christians are encouraged here to perceive the needs of our less fortunate brothers and sisters amidst grief and standing in solidarity with them by extending a helping hand in bearing the cost of their funeral expenses. Empowered by the Spirit (Gal 5:22–26), such an external coping mechanism from a Guyanese Christian perspective will doubtless mitigate the grief of and sustain the bereaved, while confirming our legitimacy as God's image-bearing children and Christ's disciples (John 13:34–35).[85]

6.1b. Composing and Singing Sad (and Joyful Theopoetic) Songs and Poems of Lament – Finding Emotional Catharsis through Music

Here we recall the words of VL1 who noted that amidst grief, it is helpful to "Compose songs and poems, since Vietnamese music is sad music." It

---

85. It is worth pointing out here that as Christians, we not only bear the name of Christ, but if Christ is the replacement of God's temple (John 2:19, 21), and thus the locale of God's name – Yahweh (cf. Deut 12:5), then it follows that we who are in Christ and are also the temple of God (1 Cor 3:16; 6:19–20; 2 Cor 6:16; Eph 2:19–22) bear that name (Yahweh) as well. And bearing the name of God well is synonymous with our imaging forth God to the world, even through our acts of compassion, a tangible example being the extension of a helping hand to bear the cost of the funeral expenses of the poor. For more on bearing God's name, see Imes, *Bearing God's Name*.

is believed that the beginning of modern Vietnamese song can be traced "to a performance by Nguyen Van Tuyen of his original compositions in Hanoi on June 9, 1938."[86] This is not to say that prior to him there were no other composers, but "Tuyen's performance marks the first public, reviewed presentation of original songs."[87] In more recent years, such songs "have come to be called nhac tien chien, or pre-war music."[88] The rationale behind such an designation can be heard in the following words: "This appellation probably came about as an imitation of the genre named tho tien chien, or pre-war poetry, the name used in South Vietnam after 1954, where the poetry remained very popular."[89] However, Jason Gibbs makes note of the fact that "Some Northern musician I met questioned the usefulness of the name 'pre-war songs.' One asked, 'Which war? We've fought so many wars.' One politically correct designation I heard for these songs was 'dong am nhac lang man truoc Cach Mang Thang Tam' or the 'current of romantic songs before the August Revolution.'"[90] All things being equal, however, Gibbs maintains that, "Whatever their designation, these songs continue to be popular among Vietnamese, both overseas and in Vietnam, especially among the older generation."[91] As a matter of fact, "They are regularly performed at the concert hall of the Hoi Nhac Si Viet Nam (Vietnamese Association of Musicians) in Hanoi under the appellation nhac truc tinh or lyrical music. When this Association in 1994 presented a festival commemorating 50 years of Vietnamese song, these songs were well represented."[92]

The ethos of these "Nhac tien chien songs carry with them an air of nostalgia, perhaps nostalgia for an era when Vietnam was still unified, the era preceding nearly 20 years of civil war."[93] One of the best representations of the genre of *nhac tien chien* can be observed in the song "Giot Mua Thu" or "Autumn Rain Drops" by Dang The Phong.[94]

---

86. Gibbs, "Nhac Tien Chien," para. 9.
87. Gibbs, para. 9.
88. Gibbs, para. 23.
89. Gibbs, para. 23.
90. Gibbs, para. 24.
91. Gibbs, para. 24.
92. Gibbs, para. 24.
93. Gibbs, para. 25.
94. For the lyrics to this song along with the English translation, see Gibbs, para. 27–52.

As in the case of the Vietnamese people, the composition of sad songs and poems are equally observed within the OT Israelite context, two examples being the books of Job and Lamentations. Job's laments are written in the context of the loss of his children and his livestock. And following on the heels of the destruction of Jerusalem by the cruel hands of King Nebuchadnezzar circa 586 BCE, Jeremiah penned his lament song.

But within the narratival bounds of the OT (i.e. from Genesis to Esther), one also recalls five elegiac laments: three from David, one from an old prophet living in Bethel, and one from Jeremiah which we analyzed in section 4.3.5.3.

Most often referred to as lament poems or prayers or songs, their primary locale is that of the Psalter or the book of Psalms. Westermann notes that, "Each psalm had a long and extensive prehistory. Only at the very end was it fixed in written form and included in the collection. It was first prayed, sung, and spoken by many extremely different kinds of people. Only later, at the point where these many voices were gathered in worship, did it receive the form that is normative for all and accessible to all."[95] In short, "This process of liturgical shaping of the psalm took many generations."[96] In his article, "Belting Out the Blues as Believers: The Importance of Singing Lament,"[97] however, Robert S. Smith observes, "A careful reading of the Psalter reveals that a large number of the psalms were intended, by their authors, to be sung. This is clear, firstly, from the content of those psalms in which we find exhortations to sing (e.g., Pss 9:11; 30:4; 68:4) or from calls to join the psalmist in singing the Lord's praise (e.g., Pss 34:3; 95:1–2; 118:24). It is also apparent from the historical information contained in the titles of a number of psalms (e.g., Pss 7, 18)."[98] Further to this, Smith contends that, "if not from the point of composition, certainly by the time of the Psalter's compilation, a plethora of musical designations and liturgical directions are embedded in the psalm titles."[99]

---

95. Westermann, *Psalms*, 15.
96. Westermann, 15.
97. Smith, "Belting Out the Blues," 89–111.
98. Smith, 90.
99. Smith, 91.

Little wonder that Paul instructed, "be filled with the Spirit, speaking to one another in psalms and hymns and spiritual songs, singing and making melody with your heart to the Lord; always giving thanks for all things in the name of our Lord Jesus Christ to God, even the Father" (Eph 5:18–20). And again, "Let the word of Christ richly dwell within you, with all wisdom teaching and admonishing one another with psalms *and* hymns *and* spiritual songs, singing with thankfulness in your hearts to God" (Col 3:16). Such gratitude, however, usually comes by way of grief. As Westermann notes, "In Israel, all speaking to God moved between two poles. There is no petition, no pleading from the depths, that did not move at least one step (in looking back to God's earlier saving activity or in confession of confidence) on the road to praise. But there is also no praise that was fully separated from the experience of God's wonderful intervention in time of need, none that had become a mere stereotyped liturgy."[100] Joy does come in the morning, but sometimes after a very long night, or many long nights of weeping (Ps 30:6 [5]; 6:7 [6]).

John Dickson writes, "The Bible does not overrule the question of pain. Nor does it discourage it. It invites us to come with anguished muscles fully flexed and say, 'My God, why?'"[101] Further, Dickson avers, "I suspect that even faithful church-going folk might feel awkward echoing the sentiment of Psalm 22 (and many others like it).[102] Many suppose that the only response to suffering is the one found in the very next psalm, the more famous Psalm 23: 'The LORD is my shepherd, I lack nothing.'"[103] However, Dickson contests such a theological perspective as he asserts, "the presence of Psalm 22 in the Bible, immediately before Psalm 23, is a reminder that sometimes the cry, 'My God, why?' is just as spiritually valid as the affirmation 'The LORD is

---

100. Westermann, *Praise and Lament*, 154.

101. Dickson, *Life of Jesus*, 95.

102. For one such example, see the Introduction of Harrichand, "Recovering the Language of Lament," 101. Allender and Longman (*Cry of the Soul*, 29–39) also state that, "Some believers cringe from this language of desperation and rage, even though they have the model of the psalmist. 'The psalmist didn't have Christ, but we do, so we can't be lonely, angry, or afraid!' But this is presumption, not faith. The laments of the Psalms encourage us to risk the danger of speaking boldly and personally to the Lord of the universe" (37). Lament psalms can thus be viewed as an invitation from God to question him with our Why's? or How long's? as part of our worship language. "God invites us to bring before Him our rage, doubt, and terror but He intends for us to do so as part of our worship. This is the kind of emotional struggle we must engage in if we are to fathom the nature of God's heart for us" (37).

103. Dickson, *Life of Jesus*, 95.

my Shepherd.'"[104] To put the matter another way, "One does not get to resurrection except through crucifixion."[105]

With good reason, Brueggemann likewise remarks, "The use of these 'psalms of darkness' may be judged by the world to be *acts of unfaith and failure*, but for the trusting community, their use is *an act of bold faith*, albeit a transformed faith . . . it insists that the world must be experienced as it is and not in some pretended way. . . . it is bold because it insists that all such experiences of disorder are a proper subject for discourse with God."[106] Otherwise referred to as the psalms of complaint, such psalms "are powerful expressions of the experience of disorientation. They express the pain, grief, dismay, and anger that life is not good. (They also refuse to settle for things as they are, and so they assert hope.)"[107] What is more, in praying and singing these psalms of disorientation, "Such daring honesty, at God's throne of mercy, is the only route to transformative well-being. That is the secret of the laments that cannot be hid."[108] Likewise, Sigmund Mowinckel asserts, "The psalms of lamentation trust God to do great things, and expect great things from him. Without him no rituals and 'sacred' words are of any use."[109] The ritualistic act of lamenting therefore finds it underpinning in *God*, the one whom the lamenter trusts.

What is of particular interest here is the fact that the lament songs have "a pronounced and well-recognized ability to console,"[110] and by extension sustain the bereaved amidst grief. According to Ruth Bright, especially amidst the "difficulty of finding words to express one's emotions,"[111] it is "Music that reaches into the person's inner depths more easily than words. . . . and helps to resolve tension and conflict."[112] Smith remarks that, "This provision is seen most powerfully in the practice of singing therapy, where singing is used to

---

104. Dickson, 95.

105. Fowler, *Ministry of Lament*, 76.

106. Brueggemann, *Message of the Psalms*, 52; emphasis original. For Brueggemann, Ps 22 is a psalm of darkness or disorientation.

107. Brueggemann, *Praying the Psalms*, 19.

108. Brueggemann, *From Whom No Secrets*, 93.

109. Mowinckel, *Psalms in Israel's Worship*, 203.

110. Smith, "Belting Out the Blues," 101.

111. Bright, "Music Therapy," 497; one might think of such emotional expressions as anger, confusion, depression, heartbreak, pain, remorse, sadness, shock, and sorrow.

112. Bright, "Music Therapy," 483.

assist those suffering trauma to release suppressed emotions, and, by so doing, to help them 'process the truth and reality behind their inner pain.'"[113] It was even remarked by Martin Luther that, "Next to the Word of God, music deserves the highest praise. She is a mistress and governess of those human emotions . . . which control men or more often overwhelm them. . . . Whether you wish to comfort the sad, to subdue frivolity, to encourage the despairing, to humble the proud, to calm the passionate or to appease those full of hate . . . what more effective means than music could you find."[114]

Ramshaw maintains, "All pastoral care can be described as the effort to help people make connections between their personal story and the sacred stories carried by the community. In the context of post-mortem ritual, this means that we together with the bereaved find forms (words, actions, pictures, musical expressions) of both lament and hope that resonate with them in their particular struggle."[115] Ramshaw further avers, "Mourners have many needs that are best met by music. Music affects, calls out, expresses and enables people to share strong feelings. A ritual feels suited to a particular loss when the music speaks to what these mourners are feeling, helping them move towards pain while also sustaining them with beauty and the possibility of joy."[116] In other words, "music connects with our emotions, expresses and evokes them, and makes them humanly liveable."[117] Small wonder that Ramshaw observes that, "If we ask people what stands out in their memory about a particular funeral or memorial service, what touched or moved them most, very rarely will they refer to any spoken words. Occasionally they will mention a ritual action (the folding of the flag with hone, the spreading of the pall with tender care), but most often they talk about music."[118] Which implies that, "Music not only helps us express difficult emotions, it also articulates or gives structure to inchoate responses."[119]

Rather than suppress all grief and complaint, as some contemporary funerals have managed to do, "we need to remember that biblical faith is not

---

113. Smith, "Belting Out the Blues," 103; cf. Bright, "Music Therapy," 469.
114. Luther, "Preface to Georg Rhau's," 323.
115. Ramshaw, "Personalization of Postmodern," 177.
116. Ramshaw, 176.
117. Ramshaw, "Singing at Funerals," 206.
118. Ramshaw, 206.
119. Ramshaw, 206.

defined by suppressing one's doubts and protests, but by addressing one's trust and doubt and praise and protest to God as if it mattered supremely to do so."[120] Interestingly enough, it is in such an act, that is, "It is in the dark struggles with God that we are surprised by His response to our anger and fear. What we receive from Him during our difficult battle is not what we expect. Instead, we find that He wants our passionate involvement and utter awe in the mystery of His glorious character."[121] Which is to say, rather than "hide behind trite spiritual platitudes," it is in such lament and protest against God that one learns to trust and "love God."[122]

Not surprisingly, Wolfelt avers that post-mortem rituals should help mourners begin to grieve not by avoiding pain, but rather by "moving toward the pain of loss."[123] Which is another way of saying that "While the emotional needs of the bereaved perhaps should not be the controlling factor in the shape of the liturgy, it might be argued that they should receive more attention."[124] One helpful ritual that can be engaged by the bereaved in bringing their emotions to the fore in worship is that of ancient Israel's psalms of lament, which "do not bid us to share the sufferer's hate, but rather, the sufferer's pain by allowing that pain to be expressed."[125] Otherwise stated, psalms of lament "allowed for the expression of a wide range of human emotion: not merely affirmation and joy but doubt, fear, and even hostility. The liturgy not only acknowledged the reality of such emotions, but sanctioned their expression in community: defined their limits, gave them form, and guided them in meaningful directions."[126] Noted here, however, is that "While none of the psalms are funeral liturgies, they are concerned with the various manifestations of 'death' and rarely even with mortality (e.g., Ps. 90)."[127] By taking into consideration the form of the hymn or psalm of lament, Herbert Anderson perceives that

---

120. Ramshaw, *Ritual and Pastoral Care*, 33.

121. Allender and Longman, *Cry of the Soul*, 38.

122. Allender and Longman, 36.

123. Wolfelt, *Creating Meaningful Funeral Experiences*, 18.

124. Bailey, *Biblical Perspectives on Death*, 107.

125. Hopkins, *Journey through The Psalms*, 93.

126. Bailey, *Biblical Perspectives on Death*, 106.

127. Bailey, 107.

The structure of lament has implications for many aspects of the ministry of care and for the link between the Bible and pastoral care. The structure of lament is an alternation between resistance and relinquishment, between protesting against injustice and trusting in the mystery of God. Resistance without relinquishment ends in bitterness and relinquishment without resistance leads to quiet powerlessness in the face of evil. The language of lament gives voice to mute pain and creates community of the suffering ones. The recovery of the language and structure of lament may be the most important aspect of connecting the Bible and pastoral care for our time.[128]

By employing the form or structure of the psalm of lament, one is able to "give structure to emotionally charged experiences," and when accompanied by music, one's song or psalm of lament becomes a "powerful aid to the process of mourning."[129] Small wonder that Jeremy S. Begbie calls this "representative concentration," as he maintains that, "in music, emotionally significant bodily movements are embodied in a concentrated (musical form), in such a way that the music can represent us and concentrate us emotionally as we are drawn into its life."[130] In this respect, "music can enable a more concentrated emotional engagement with the object or objects with which we are dealing."[131]

Futato adds, when reading the songs of lament, one immediately feels their pathos.[132] In other words, "Feelings of grief, loneliness, perplexity, anger, frustration, abandonment, despair, and more come to expression in the lyrics of these songs. Through the songs of lament the Holy Spirit teaches us, among other lessons, that it is okay to be brutally honest with ourselves

---

128. Anderson, "Bible and Pastoral Care," 208–209.

129. Begbie, "Faithful Feelings," 349. Agreeing with Kübler-Ross, Brueggemann ("Formfulness of Grief," 263–275), notes that, "the grief and death process tends to follow a fairly regular form . . . Thus it is important that Kübler-Ross has been able to establish the agenda that this human experience is inevitably *formful* and no technical claim to the contrary can deny that" (267; emphasis original). See also Capps, *Biblical Approaches*, 73–92, for the helpful role the form of a lament psalm plays in pastoral counseling.

130. Begbie, "Faithful Feelings," 349.

131. Begbie, 349.

132. Futato, *Joy Comes*, 50.

and with God when the days are dark and the nights are cold."[133] The fact that the songs of lament were composed for the purpose of being sung, and not only prayed, or read, or proclaimed, is essential in light of the fact that such songs, put to music, are efficacious enough to heal and console. In this way, the song of lament accompanied by music and thus sung, "highlights its God-given capacity of assisting us in the honest articulation of sorrow, the effective processing of pain and the awakening of genuine hope."[134] As remarked by Logan C. Jones, "the psalms of lament do not dismiss or deny or seek to avoid sorrow. On the contrary, they allow a grieving person to move more fully into the valley of the shadow; knowing on different levels, that no matter what, God is indeed present in the sorrow."[135]

As a matter of fact, "The Psalms [of lament] help us understand that every emotion is a theological statement. All feelings reveal our attempt to maneuver into a position of regaining access to the pleasures and perfection of God. All dark emotions are rooted in our *reactive* response (flight) to being out of the Garden and our *aggressive* response (fight) to regain access to Eden."[136] One can aver it is "In the darkness of our emotional wrestling with God that we grow in our understanding of Him."[137] Further, "In the most peculiar fashion, He chooses to reveal His perfect heart by analogy with human emotion that is stained by depravity. If we are to comprehend more richly the heart of God, it is imperative that we seek to understand our internal world."[138] The lament psalms therefore "propel us into the deepest questions about ourselves, about others, and about God. As we let them expose the depths of our emotion, they will lead us to the God who reveals Himself in the midst of our struggles."[139] Catharsis is therefore mediated through one's worshipful songs or psalms of lament to God.

When put to music, indigenous Vietnamese Christian songs of lament therefore serve as a cathartic tool in releasing dark or negative emotions

---

133. Futato, 50–51.

134. Stenhouse, "Psalms of Lament," 194–195.

135. Jones, "Psalms of Lament," 47.

136. Allender and Longman, *Cry of the Soul*, 34; emphasis original.

137. Allender and Longman, 39.

138. Allender and Longman, 39.

139. Allender and Longman, 39.

that need not be suppressed within the mourner.[140] The state of rest or the restoration of the soul and spirit of the bereaved "can be reached only after the mourning and/or lamenting is over."[141] Which means that "Emotional relief is not possible without a sharing of the trauma,"[142] and this to God, who extends healing by his wounds (Isa 53:5; cf. Matt 8:17). To conceal one's wounds, that is, to suppress or put a lid on one's dark or negative emotions, is to cover our own wounds, and thus refuse God's wounded healing, to our own detriment. This is all the more important when one realizes that the Christian God does *not* identify himself with the healthy, but rather with the sick, the broken, the wounded (Mark 2:17). As Dietrich Bonhoeffer put it, "Matthew 8:17 makes it quite clear that Christ helps us, not by virtue of his omnipotence, but by virtue of his weakness and suffering."[143] As a matter of fact, "Identifying with the suffering of Jesus in particular may help us place more trust in God as we mourn,"[144] even musically.

But as the mourner musically laments their situation of grief to/before God, such negativity is accepted by God as part of one's healing process. "Music makes a difference. Songs can clarify our thinking or release our emotions from the deep well of the soul . . . We do not always experience life as well ordered. Our lives are not always well oriented. 'Disorientation' better describes life at times. The laments or songs of disorientation were written for times such as these."[145] As Smith puts it, "in such a place of dislocation and disorientation, singing praise can be (or at least feel) either impossible or inappropriate."[146]

Indigenous Vietnamese Christian songs of lament therefore express the mourner's emotions, akin to the psalms of lament, and of which Smith believes "Calvin's list of 'distracting emotions' clearly indicates that the lament psalms were uppermost in his mind as he penned these oft-quoted words."[147]

---

140. Pham, *Mourning in the Hebrew Bible*, 38.

141. Pham, 22.

142. Oates, *Grief, Transition, and Loss*, 28.

143. Bonhoeffer, *Letters and Papers*, 361.

144. Cole, *Good Mourning*, 73.

145. Futato, *Joy Comes*, 1, 5.

146. Smith, "Belting Out the Blues," 93.

147. Smith, 93. Here Smith (89–111) refers to Calvin's words: "I have been accustomed to call this book, I think not inappropriately, 'An Anatomy of all the Parts of the Soul;' for there is not an emotion of which anyone can be conscious that is not here represented as in a

Just as tears were never meant to be restrained but rather released so as to be collected in God's bottle (Ps 56:9 [8]), negative or sad emotions were also not meant to be repressed, but rather released to/before God, even in lyrical writing, thus making it cathartic. In this act of lamenting through song, rather than moving away from God, the Vietnamese Christian mourner is thus encouraged to move toward God, before whom they might pour out their heart, recognizing that God alone has the balm to heal the broken-hearted and bind up their wounds (147:4 [3]).

As poetry, the psalms of lament are especially concerned "with experience."[148] Laurence Perrine states, "Poetry takes all life as its province. Its primary concern is not with beauty, not with philosophical truth, not with persuasion, but with experience."[149] The lament psalms are therefore, "depictions of the psalmists' experiences of suffering."[150] Composing one's sad songs and poems, as appears to be conventional among the Vietnamese people, therefore necessitates taking into account one's life experiences of grief.[151] Such sad songs and poems not only comprise life's tragic experiences, but like the psalms of lament, *God* is to be consider as their center point. Even what might be considered the *darkest* psalm of the Psalter (a Disorientation Stage 1 Verbal Expression: DS1 Lament Prayer, or a pure lament prayer) commences with, "O LORD, the God of my salvation" (Ps 88:2 [1]; cf. 88:7 [6], 19 [18]). The Vietnamese Christians can thus lead the charge in the composition of such sad or lament poems in expressing their grief, yet not without assuming a *theopoetic* posture. For it is through their sad songs and poems or psalms of lament, they "become witnesses to the possibility of sustaining a relationship with the God from whom we do not have to hide anything, even our worse thoughts and feelings."[152] This is all the more important as one considers that

---

mirror. Or rather, the Holy Spirit has here drawn to the life all the griefs, sorrows, fears, doubts, hopes, cares, perplexities, in short, all the distracting emotions with which the minds of men are wont to be agitated" (93).

148. Villanueva, "Preaching Lament," 66.

149. Perrine, *Sound and Sense*, 9.

150. Villanueva, "Preaching Lament," 66.

151. Interestingly, Fowler (*Ministry of Lament*, 1–4) notes that "The many ways that people share with others their mourning and their spiritual life demonstrate that ultimately we all are psalmists of lament" (4). In addition, "Those who practice the ministry of lament stand with the bereaved during difficult times" (147).

152. Fowler, *Ministry of Lament*, 149.

not only are Vietnamese a marginalized community, but "the poetic" is also a "marginalized epistemology."[153]

Theopoetics first appeared, according to L. B. C. Keefe-Perry, "in the form of *theopoiesis*, used by Stanley Romaine Hopper in a 1971 speech."[154] Theopoetics since that time "has served as a noun referring to a particular devotional quality of a text, a genre of religious writing, and a postmodern perspective on theology."[155] A working definition provided by Keefe-Perry is that theopoetics would be "the study and practice of making God known through text."[156] Additionally, when "Used as an adjective, a theopoetic text is one that reveals some aspect of the divine."[157] Yet at a broader level, the meaning of the term is found in its very etymology, where *theo* and *poiein* combine to mean "a means of making God, of shaping experience of the divine, and the study of ways in which people come to know the Spirit."[158] Zylla has contributed to this area of scholarship and has penned a number of poems that have now been put into book form. Zylla has also issued the clarion call for Christians suffering in affliction to put words to pen and to create writing that makes God known through the medium of theopoetics.[159] There is, however, a caveat for the potential poet, proffered by Gutiérrez:

> God is first contemplated when we do God's will and allow God to reign; only after that do we think about God. To use familiar categories: contemplation and practice together make up the *first act*; theologizing is a *second act*. We must first establish ourselves on the terrain of spirituality and practice; only subsequently is it possible to formulate discourse on God in an authentic and respectful way. Theologizing done without the mediation of contemplation and practice does not meet the requirements of the God of the Bible.[160]

---

153. Common, "What Do People Mean," n.p.
154. Keefe-Perry, "Theopoetics: Process and Perspective," 579.
155. Keefe-Perry, 579.
156. Keefe-Perry, 579.
157. Keefe-Perry, 579.
158. Keefe-Perry, 579–580.
159. Zylla, "What Language," 135–136, 138, 140–142.
160. Gutiérrez, *On Job*, xiii.

Which is to say that before any attempt is made to speak of God and one's experience of grief poetically, the theopoet should begin with silent attention before God so as to reflect on one's grief and God's presence (or apparent absence). Only after this long silence before God, this "absolute, unmixed attention,"[161] which is the "posture of prayer,"[162] can the potential theopoet venture to write truthfully of grief and God. In a similar vein, Zylla avows, "If we are to speak meaningfully of the deeper experiences of God in our lives and in the lives of our congregations, we need to pay careful attention to how language may express the depth dimension of our searching. Poetic language moves to the depth dimension."[163] In this respect, Zylla proposes three movements when it comes to capturing this depth dimension in poetic language:

(i) *Numinous Silence as Our Orientation.* "Numinous is the word we use for this unspoken longing. It beckons us to recognize that the deepest search we carry as human beings is our search for communion with God."[164] Which is another way of saying that "Mystery is the basis for our fundamental orientation in theopoetic pastoral theology."[165]

(ii) *Radical Engagement of Complexity – Ministry as Disorientation.* Amidst the complexity of life, Christians are called by God to walk in step with the Holy Spirit, the silent Shepherd of our souls, and to "enter into the affliction of others with God's compassion and the tenderness of Jesus Christ."[166] Which means that, "Our vocation is to be shepherds of the subtle persistence of hope."[167]

(iii) *Ministry as Reorientation: The Birth-Hour of a New Clarity.* This is where the hard work of theopoetic articulation commences, and where the word of God governs the movement. Here, "The silence of the first movement of prayer and the radical engagement with the real-life experiences of ministry are brought into conversation with the Word of God."[168] In other

---

161. Weil, *Gravity and Grace*, 170.

162. Zylla, "What Language," 134.

163. Zylla, "What Language," 130–131.

164. Zylla, 132. To this we may add, even the God who hides himself (Isa 45:15).

165. Zylla, "What Language," 132. For Zylla's poem "Numinous Faith" see "What Language," 135–36.

166. Zylla, 137. For Zylla (*Virtue as Consent*, i–158), "Virtue is compassion: to suffer with," which finds expression in his poem "Pati Cum," the Latin phrase from which compassion is derived (vi, 128).

167. Zylla, 138. For Zylla's poem "Longings," see "What Language," 138.

168. Zylla, 139.

words, theopoetic articulation "is the task of pastoral theological reflection,"[169] otherwise referred to as, "the climatic crescendo that comes only after the word has been eaten, assimilated, lived."[170] As Christians, "called to speak from the depths as 'one speaking the very words of God' (1 Pet 4:11), we are compelled . . . to theopoetic articulation."[171]

Ann Weems' *Psalms of Lament* comprises fifty lament poems penned on account of the pointless death of her son Todd less than an hour after celebrating his twenty-first birthday on August 14, 1982.[172] Weems asserts that, "This book is for those who weep and for those who weep with those who weep."[173] Brueggemann believes that it is through Weems' "wounded words we may be healed"[174] for such "utterance is *cathartic*."[175] Crucial then to the task of mourning is attention to the questions of meaning that usually develop in the face of death, questions when voiced, result in healing to the grieving soul. Owing to such a cathartic nature of such lament utterance, I hereby proffer my first theological poem:

> In the dark night of my soul,
>   I searched aimlessly about,
> Searching for my imminent heavenly Father,
>   Only to find a transcendent God!
> Where have you gone, O dear heavenly Father?
>   Why have you left me all alone in the dark?
> Will You ever return to me?
>   Me, the one who calls you, *Abba*?[176]

---

169. Zylla, 139.

170. Zylla, 139.

171. Zylla, 139. For Zylla's poem "Baptism," see 140–142.

172. Weems, *Psalms of Lament*, xix. At the time of its publication in 1995, Weems confessed, "and still I weep" (xix).

173. Weems, xix.

174. In Weems, xvii.

175. In Weems, xv; emphasis mine. See also Lamb (*God Behaving Badly*, 157–179) who experienced a very low point in his life while pursuing his doctoral studies and admitted to taking a long walk along the canal in Oxford and lamenting to God. "I vented my frustration at God, asking him why this was happening to me, how long this would go on and where he was. While I didn't receive any clear divine response immediately, afterward I felt better. *The act of lamenting was cathartic*" (162; emphasis mine).

176. This is my first theological lament poem, which was penned at 5:17 a.m. on March 27, 2015.

The composition and singing of theopoetic sad or lament songs and poems, should not be an end in itself. Taking the Psalter as our reference, we observe that it begins with a preponderance of lament but ends on a note of praise. In the middle there are songs that alternate between lament and praise, and praise and lament, but the end is always praise. "The balance between disorientation and orientation/reorientation in the final book of the Psalter is a clear reminder for the enduring need for both."[177] Vietnamese Christian theopoetic sad songs and poems of lament should thus also consider this reality especially in light of the future hope of glory in Christ their living hope (Col 1:27; 3:4; 1 Pet 1:3; 1 John 3:2). Conducted this way, "hymns of lament can house the questions and pain of tragic loss, as well as the hymns of resurrection hope."[178]

The words of Rolf A. Jacobson are helpful: "Cognitive dissonance theory holds that the thoughts of individuals need to be consistent and harmonious."[179] For this reason, "When a person holds two or more inconsistent thoughts, that person experiences a cognitive dissonance . . . The person will try to resolve this uncomfortable cognitive dissonance, and some of the ways of doing so are: (i) Changing attitude; (ii) Adding new thoughts; and (iii) Changing behavior."[180] Employing the theory of cognitive dissonance liturgically, Jacobson reasons that "the tension between the words that we place in worshipers' mouths and the internal emotional state of the worshipers can be put to creative pastoral and theological use."[181]

Jacobson draws upon Brueggemann's sequence of orientation – disorientation – reorientation in relation to the psalms, and employs them liturgically. But rather than matching expression to experience, as Brueggemann does, Jacobson argues that "an expression that is precisely contrary to present experiences may be introduced in order to initiate a change in experience."[182] From this perspective, if a person is in a place of orientation, Jacobson suggests that the pastor and worship leader "place words of disorientation in the mouth of the congregation by using a lament psalm liturgically. The pastoral goal

177. Boda, "Varied and Resplendid Riches," 75.

178. Ramshaw, "Personalization of Postmodern," 176.

179. Jacobson, "Burning Our Lamps," 92.

180. Jacobson, 92.

181. Jacobson, 92.

182. Jacobson, 98n7.

here would be to introduce a dissonant cognition of disorientation into an oriented person's mind in the hopes that this new thought would eventually be a catalyst that would cause the person to add new cognitions and new attitudes."[183] In this (dis)connection, "Rather than judging sufferers or fearing them, compassion and love might take seed."[184] On a similar note, Swinton insists that, "Lament does not belong only to those who are suffering. Lament is a practice that the body of Christ must learn together in times of happiness and tragedy so that it can deal faithfully with times of sadness, brokenness, and disappointment."[185] Which is to say, "We need to learn how to lament for and with our brothers and sisters in Jesus so that, when it's our turn to suffer, we (and all of us together) know how to embody the language of lament."[186]

In the same spirit, when a mourner finds herself in a place of disorientation, "psalms of reorientation [can be] placed in the mouths of the disoriented in order to introduce new cognitions."[187] So, for example, if the mourner is thinking of being abandoned and alone, they will find it helpful to employ the familiar words of Psalm 23:5 [4]: "Even though I walk through the valley of the shadow of death, I fear no evil, for You are with me; Your rod and You staff, they comfort me."[188] In so doing, this ritual of placing the words

---

183. Jacobson, 95.

184. Jacobson, 96. Here, we might note, by way of an example, the words of Swinton (*Finding Jesus*, 71–116): "If Jesus is our joy, then that joy is inevitably and inextricably imbedded and embodied within Jesus's body, that place of reciprocity, mutuality, and burden bearing. When our brother or sister in Jesus struggles to hold on to the great joy of Jesus, other brothers and sisters hold it for him or her, not in a way that is judgmental – 'If you can't feel Jesus in the way that I do, then you are spiritually less than I am. You'd better work out what sin you have committed'" (87). Rather than a expressing a spirit of condemnation, brothers and sisters in a place of orientation or new orientation can hold out the great joy of Jesus in a spirit of compassion that says, "OK, for now it feels like Jesus has abandoned you. Jesus knows what it feels like to be abandoned. At this moment in time, you don't feel the way I feel, but I desperately want to help you hold on to the possibility that God exists, and the possibility that God loves you, and the possibility that joy might be closer than you think. I know that's not how you feel, but it remains a possibility, and I want to hold that for you" (87). And one of the best ways of expressing this spirit of compassion tangibly is by sitting in the darkness with those who find themselves in the place of disorientation. As Swinton states, "I want to sit with you in this darkness (as best I can), and I want to say that I love you and that God loves you and that we can wait together. The storm will pass. Let me hold joy for you for a little while" (87).

185. Swinton, *Finding Jesus*, 86–87.

186. Swinton, 87.

187. Jacobson, "Burning Our Lamps," 96.

188. Here, it should be noted that צַלְמָוֶת, *tsalmawet*, is one word in the Hebrew text, and is translated "deep darkness," rather than the usual "shadow of death," which requires splitting

of reorientation into the life of the mourner can in some measure "create new life for the sufferer, [and] evoke new horizons. In the words of the New Testament, they raise the dead."[189]

On those grounds, the words of reorientation, or rather new orientation spiritual songs sung to the Lord,[190] which speak powerfully of God's redeeming love and comforting presence, can bring a disoriented mourner to a place of healing and sustainability. There might be times of returning to disorientation of course, but eventually the bereaved will move to a place of new orientation in Christ. For it is only in Christ that the bereaved is guaranteed genuine comfort amidst mourning (Matt 5:4), even as Christ shepherds, guides, and comforts the bereaved, supplying them with springs of the water of life, and wiping every tear from their eyes (Rev 7:17; cf. Ps 23:4 [3]).

What is being encouraged here is the composition of theopoetic songs and poems, of both lament *and* praise, and putting them to music before God as a means of catharsis amidst grief. Stated another way, the theological songs and poems of lament *and* praise, accompanied by music, will serve as an efficacious medium whereby those in the throes of grief can find consolation and restoration for their distressed soul, and thus, the transformation of their grief. Such wounded words have the potential of healing even those who grieve with those who grieve. As Henri Nouwen put it, "A Christian community is therefore a healing community, not because wounds are cured and pains are alleviated, but because wounds and pains become openings or occasions for a new vision. Mutual confession then becomes a mutual deepening of hope, and shared weakness becomes a reminder to one and all of the coming strength."[191] Such mutual confession advocated here is mediated through the compassionate theopoetic poems and songs of both lament and praise to God who accepts them both as legitimate language of his faithful followers.

---

the word into two, thus forming צֵל, *tsal* and מָוֶת, *mawet*. And according to Longman (*Psalms*, 133–137) "The former rendering has been considered more likely" (135).

189. Jacobson, 97.

190. Preference is here given to the words "new orientation" rather than reorientation since the mourner never returns to the exact place of orientation.

191. Nouwen, *Wounded Healer*, 100.

6.1c. Incorporating Indigenous Christian Devotional Songs (e.g., Bhajans) in the Wake/ Funeral Liturgy – Tapping into the Cultural Liminal Memory of a Deep Experience of Faith

Distinct among the Guyanese of East Indian heritage is singing spiritual or devotional Christian songs in Hindi during a wake or funeral. Such Christian devotional Hindi songs are better referred to as *bhajans*. As noted by GL5, "And if the person who died is of an East Indian descent, we usually sing bhajans at the wake and funeral."

Even amid disorientation, spiritual or devotional songs can also be heard coming from the lips of the children of Israel. We see this especially in 2 Chronicles 20:18–19. Surrounded by enemies who have caused him distress, "Jehoshaphat bowed his head with *his* face to the ground, and all Judah and its inhabitants of Jerusalem fell down before the LORD, worshiping the LORD. The Levites, from the sons of the Kohathites and of the sons of the Korahites, stood up to praise the LORD God of Israel, with a loud voice." Referred alternatively to as a DS6 thanksgiving praise prayer, the content of their songs of praise expressing their devotion to the LORD, even in the heart of a situation of distress, can be heard in the following lyrics: "Give thanks to the LORD, for His lovingkindness is everlasting" (v. 21; see also 1 Chron 16:34, 41; 2 Chron 5:13).[192]

With respect to indigenous East Indian Guyanese spiritual or devotional songs, James G. Lochtefeld states that a bhajan literally means "sharing," but it can also refer to "any song with a religious theme or a spiritual idea, originating from within a regional language from the Indian subcontinent."[193] Guy Beck notes that the bhajan, which describes a devotional song sung to a deity, is derived from the Sanskrit word *bhaj*, meaning to share or partake, and is thus relative to the term *bhakti*, meaning devotion.[194] "Bhakti is also the name for a Hindu tradition which focuses on personal, loving devotion to God.

---

192. Even in the midst of death, such lyrics can also be appropriated by Christians as part of their grief liturgy in joyful gratitude for the victory that is already theirs all because of Christ who graciously imparts abundant and eternal life to them amidst death (cf. John 11:25–26; Eph 2:1–9).

193. Lochtefeld, *Illustrated Encyclopedia of Hinduism*, 97.

194. Beck, "Religious and Devotional Music," 254.

Bhajans were developed within the bhakti tradition by medieval poets such as Ramananda, Surdas, Kabir, Tukaram, and Mira Bai."[195]

From a Hindu perspective, "Bhajan singing may be done individually but is more commonly a communal affair. Songs often tell stories and in general celebrate the presence or close communion of the god or lament the god's absence. It is the singing of the words that increase their power. By singing of love to one's god, a purification takes place. The purification then leads to a mystical union,"[196] according to Terry Muck. Describing this mystical union, Harold Coward and David Goa aver that both "Lover and believer become one in ecstatic song."[197] What is more, Muck remarks that since each singer and listener of a bhajan are paradoxically separate from and identical with *Brahman*, the all-encompassing reality, it is believed that such a paradox can be resolved through bhajan singing.[198] Observed by T. R. Sharma, bhajan singing takes a person through four stages of devotion:

- Ordering of religious devotion.
- Instrumental devotion attainable by special external efforts.
- Emotional devotion resulting from spontaneous inward feeling.
- Loving devotion, maintained reciprocal devotion.[199]

Dating back to the early nineteenth century, however, such devotional songs to God began taking a new shape and content. Hindu bhajans started assuming a Christian perspective giving particular reverence to Christ. Today, bhajans sung by Guyanese-Canadian Christians of East Indian heritage, during a wake or a funeral, affirm a devoted love to and belief in the one, true, and living God, who bestows eternal life to all who believe in his Son Jesus Christ (John 3:36).

Adapted from Hindu bhajans, Christian bhajans have thus been especially favored by Hindu-background Christians. Especially when there is difficulty adapting to "Western hymns set to Western melodies," Hindu-background Christians "may struggle to adapt to the foreignness of music in their church."[200]

---

195. Burbank, "Bhajans," A2.

196. Muck, "*Psalm*, Bhajan, *and* Kirtan," 11.

197. Coward and Goa, *Mantra: Hearing the Divine*, 61.

198. Muck, "*Psalm*, Bhajan *and* Kirtan," 11.

199. Sharma, "Psychological Analysis of Bhakti," 89.

200. Burbank, "Bhajans," A1.

Owing to this, "they are more stirred to reverence by their own traditional style of devotional music, a genre called *bhajan*."[201] In other words, a Christian bhajan written and sung in the traditional style of devotional music taps into the cultural liminal memory of a deep experience of faith. As Ramshaw put it, "music strongly evokes the past."[202] Small wonder John Bell points out that "All of us can similarly revisit our past via songs which root us in that past . . . We are creatures of our past. We cannot be separated from it, and although we cannot always remember it, songs will unexpectedly summon portions of it into mind."[203] It is not surprising to hear Ramshaw also aver, "When in deep grief, spoken words often bounce off us, but words we sing resonate within us."[204] By virtue of this, Christian devotional songs such as bhajans access a former Hindu's affective memory, resulting in them bringing memories of their former spirituality in Hinduism, while simultaneously (re)directing rather correctly a deep reverence for the one, true, and living God who alone bestows eternal life on the dead and the living (John 11:25–26; cf. 1 Cor 8:4–6).

Employing such indigenous Christian devotional songs as a bhajan in the church as a means of expressing one's reverence to Christ, however, has not come without opposition. The two main objections proposed by critics are: its Hindu origin and its old-fashionedness.[205] Yet, Ray Burbank maintains that such critics have not only failed "to assess the theological validity of the actual content of Christ-centered bhajans,"[206] but have also failed to realize that "even bhajans can be adapted in instrumentation and melody and yet remain truly bhajan."[207] As such, Burbank insists that "Indigenous, Christ-centred bhajans in India can be used not only for the cultivation of reverent worship among Hindu-background Christians but also as an instructional means of conveying biblical truth to Christ-followers." To this we might add not only India, but Guyana, Canada, and wherever Hindu-background Christians reside today.

---

201. Burbank, A1.

202. Ramshaw, "Singing at Funerals," 206.

203. Bell, *Singing Thing*, 39.

204. Ramshaw, "Singing at Funerals," 207.

205. Burbank, A1–A2.

206. Burbank, A1.

207. Burbank, A2.

Amidst grief, such Christ-centered bhajans can also reinforce the biblical truth concerning Christ and his gracious gift of eternal life to all who trust in him. Eternal life, described by Jesus Christ, is knowledge of the only true God, and Jesus Christ whom he has sent (John 17:3; cf. 1 John 2:24–25). As GL5 noted, one of the most prominent bhajans that is sung during the liturgy of wakes and funerals is that of "Yishu Ne Kaha: Jiwan Ki Roti," which means, "Jesus said: I am The Bread of Life."

The lyrics of this bhajan take the worshipper through the "I am" sayings of Jesus in John's Gospel. These are: John 6:35 ("Jesus said, 'I am the bread of life; he who comes to Me will not hunger, and he who believes in Me will never thirst.'"); John 10:11 ("I am the good shepherd; the good shepherd lays down His life for the sheep."); John 14:6 ("Jesus said, 'I am the way, and the truth, and the life; no one comes to the Father but through Me.'"); John 10:9 ("I am the door; if anyone enters through Me, he will be saved, and will go in and out and find pasture."); John 11:25–26 ("Jesus said to her [Martha], 'I am the resurrection and the life; he who believes in Me will live even if he dies, and everyone who lives and believes in Me will never die.'"); and John 8:12 ("Then Jesus again spoke to them, saying, 'I am the Light of the world; he who follows Me will not walk in the darkness, but will have the Light of life.'").

From beginning to end, this bhajan is infused with the lifegiving gospel message of Jesus Christ who identified himself as "I am!" (John 8:58; cf. 1:1–3; 10:30), a clear reference to the God of the OT who introduced himself to Moses by the name "I AM" (Exod 3:14). Each stanza echoes an emphatic asseverative or truth statement from the lips of Jesus himself, the only one who could say with all honesty, "because I live, you will live also" (John 14:19). Bhajans such as "Yishu Ne Kaha: Jiwan Ki Roti," thus reinforce the living hope of Hindu-background Christians in their promised resurrection to eternal life, which is predicated upon Jesus the Christ, the Son of God (John 20:30–31), the living One, the One who was dead, and who is now alive forevermore (Rev 1:18). And in so doing, the bereaved is sustained amidst their grief.

Which is why such Christ-centered bhajans should not be marginalized in favor of our more popular Western Christian music. Room should be allowed for such Christ-centered cultural expressions to God within our intercultural evangelical settings. Christopher D. Hale thus remarks, "by and large, a bhajan is 'live' and sung in the context of a *satsang*, or religious meeting where a preacher expounds Scripture with bhajans interspersed throughout keeping the devotees actively involved."[208] Sung in the context of a *satsang*, or religious meeting, or a wake, or a funeral, a Christian bhajan can thus be "conducive to biblical meditation. First, there is the exposition of the passage by the preacher which enlightens the understanding through the Holy Spirit. Then there is the repetition of the Biblical thought through the singing of the bhajan and the thought goes from the mind into the heart and touches the emotions and the will."[209] When employed within the liturgy of a wake or funeral, Christ-centered bhajans can therefore serve to fortify the faith of Hindu-background Christians who continue to hold fast to the solid biblical truth that Christ has indeed conquered death and promised life eternal (John 11:25–26). At the same time, Christ-centered bhajans can serve as a welcomed evangelistic tool for Hindu-background Christians attempting to reach their exisiting Hindu family and friends. Small wonder that Hale asserts,

> What we need, then, is for people to begin learning and using the traditional forms and arranging them musically using a combination of Indian and Western instruments. By and large, the first part must be done by Indian poets and Indian musicians. Foreigners can help especially with the packaging because of their access to quality electronic musical equipment and their familiarity with its use. With God's help, there is much that can be done with music to communicate the message of the Gospel.[210]

Though Hale makes the case for only *Indian* poets and *Indian* musicians learning and using the traditional bhajan forms, here I make the case for *all* East Indian background poets and musicians, including those of an East Indian Guyanese heritage, to collaborate with Western evangelical musicians to put bhajans to music. However, it must be noted that "Those who wish to sing bhajans with Hindu friends must do the hard work of learning the songs well enough to be able to genuinely worship Jesus while singing them."[211] But as Burbank asserts, "The way bhajans engage the heart and mind helps the truths of God's word penetrate a person's heart. When a believer helps a Hindu friend learn Yeshu [Jesus] bhajans that sing of the atonement,

---

208. Hale, "Reclaiming the Bhajan," 16.
209. Hale, 17.
210. Hale, 17.
211. Burbank, "Bhajans," A10.

the incarnation, the salvation in Jesus's name alone, and the living water of Christ, the Hindu experiences Christ in a way that allows him or her to 'see' Christ more clearly."[212]

At the same time, if such Christ-centered bhajans are indeed powerful to traverse the mind to the heart so that even the emotions and will are touched, then the bereaved can continue to sense Christ's ever-abiding presence and glorious return for them (John 14:1–6, 13–16, 18, 19; cf. Matt 28:20; Heb 13:5), which will sustain them amidst their grief. What is more, such Christ-centered evangelistic bhajans will aid in the transformation of grief as Hindu-background Christians observe, by God's amazing and irresistible grace, their Hindu family and friends take the bold step of faith out of the dominion of darkness and into the kingdom of God's beloved Son (Col 1:13; cf. 1 Pet 2:9). Taking this step of salvific faith from death to life (John 3:16–17; 5:24) will doubtless occasion further and even complete joy for grieving Hindu-background Christians (1 John 1:1–4), whose sole object of worship is the triune God revealed most vividly in God the Son, Jesus Christ (Heb 1:1–4), in whom alone is life (John 1:1–4).

6.1d. Celebrating the Life of the Deceased through Dancing and Singing Upbeat Gospel Songs – Spiritual Rejoicing for Having Arrived Home in Heaven

When it comes to grief, what appears to be distinctly cultural from an African-Guyanese-Canadian perspective, is the incorporation of the ritual *Kweh-kweh*, which encompasses singing upbeat gospel songs such as "Mansion Over the Hilltop." On a similar note, such upbeat songs can also be heard breaking loose from the mouths of the Levites, particularly those of the sons of the Kohathites, and also those of the sons of the Korahites, even as they stood up to harmoniously doxologize Yahweh the God of Israel with a loud voice (2 Chron 20:19). Expressed amid a situation of disorientation, the lyrics of such an upbeat song of thanksgiving praise, which also happens to be a DS6 thanksgiving praise prayer, are euphonically voiced along the following lines:

---

212. Burbank, A10.

"Give thanks to the LORD, for His lovingkindness is everlasting" (v. 21; see also 1 Chron 16:34, 41; 2 Chron 5:13).[213]

In her article "Come to My Kwe-Kwe," Richards-Greaves speaks of the evolution of the traditional African-Guyanese *Kweh-Kweh* ritual underscored by multiple interpretations of authenticity,[214] which is being re-enacted annually in New York for the purpose of bringing together the African-Guyanese-American community "for one night of performance, unification, and community building."[215] But more than this, she also notes that, "like African Guyanese in Guyana, expatriates in the United States who are nostalgic for their former homeland, as well as those who seek to reconstruct differential ethnic identities in the new homeland, are increasingly embracing traditional *kwek-kweh*."[216] So on the one hand, these US African-Guyanese expatriates possess a nostalgia for their *immediate* former homeland of Guyana, and on the other hand, they also possess a nostalgia for their *distant* former homeland of Africa.

But as observed within the African-Guyanese Canadian context, the *Kweh-Kweh* ritual, which includes the upbeat song "Mansion Over the Hilltop," alludes to another homeland – a *future* homeland called *heaven* (Phil 3:20–21; Heb 11:15–16). So, while the African-Guyanese can look back with nostalgia for their two former homelands (Africa and Guyana), they can also look forward with greater nostalgia for their forthcoming homeland, their permanent homeland called heaven. As Jesus himself promised his disciples, "In My Father's house are many dwelling places; if it were not so, I would have told you; for I go to prepare a place for you. If I go and prepare a place for you, I will come again and receive you to Myself, that where I am, *there* you may be also" (John 14:2–3). Singing such songs with reference to this future homeland of heaven therefore enables the transformation of grief as

---

213. While this upbeat doxological song of thanksgiving praise can be understood as a battle cry voiced in the context of a warfare (see Jonker, *1 & 2 Chronicles*, 231), Christians can also appropriate these lyrics as part of their grief liturgy in grateful and joyful anticipation of the victory that Christ their Redeemer has already wrought over death on their behalf (cf. 1 Cor 15:54–57).

214. Richards-Greaves, "Come to My 'Kwe-Kwe'," 93; she employs the spelling kweh-kweh when referring to the traditional (wedding-based) kweh-kweh, and Come to my Kwe-Kwe when discussing the re-enactment of the ritual (93n1).

215. Richards-Greaves, 87.

216. Richards-Greaves, 93.

they remind the bereaved that the deceased is beyond question, in a better place, in that mansion over the hilltop, to borrow the language of the upbeat gospel song penned by Ira F. Stanphill.[217] For such Guyanese-Canadians of an African heritage, "to be absent from the body [is] to be at home with the Lord" (2 Cor 5:8; cf. Phil 1:21). This calls for immediate celebration of the life of the deceased in Christ, which has crossed over the rolling Jordan today, and entered into the Promised Land of heaven, to appropriate the words of the African spiritual writer Erskine Peters. In other words, death is merely a dark vale through which the deceased in Christ pass in order to reach the other side, the side of ultimate joy in the presence of their Lord and Savior Jesus Christ (John 16:20–22; Jude 1:24–25; cf. Ps 16:11).[218] Small wonder that Oates asserts, "The funeral itself is a time of mourning and a time of celebration of the life of the deceased with the accent on the celebration."[219]

Also, if the *Kweh-kweh* ritual within the African-Guyanese Canadian context still retains any connection to its traditional function as a medium for matrimonial instruction for soon-to-be-married couples, then it is from this mansion over the hilltop that the currently bereaved person[220] can anticipate the return of their groom – the Lord Jesus Christ (John 14:1–6; Rev 19:7). At Christ's return, an extravagant meal will be shared among the invited guests in the kingdom of God (Luke 14:15). *Kweh-kweh* ritual within an African-Guyanese Canadian context therefore anticipates this grander wedding, inclusive of which is that lavish meal. "Blessed are those who are invited to the wedding supper of the Lamb!" (Rev 19:9; cf. Luke 14:15).

---

217. Here, it should be noted that Stanphill used the KJV, which renders the Greek word μοναί, *monai* as mansions instead of rooms or dwelling places.

218. This statement has been adapted from Keller (*On Death*, 75–96) who states that, "And if we die, it is merely a dark door into ultimate joy" (79).

219. Oates, *Grief, Transition, and Loss*, 27. Note also the words of Keller (*On Death*, 35–74), who says, "At a funeral service (as opposed to a memorial service), we are literally in the presence of death. There is a dead body in that coffin. While people have many reactions to being in the presence of death, there are two opposite mistakes we can make: One is to despair too much; the other is to shrug it off and not learn what we should from it. Neither will be of much benefit to you" (69). As a corrective to such erroneous reactions, Keller thus encourages us "To do as the Bible tells us to do: We should grieve, yet we should have hope; we should wake up from our denial and discover a source of peace that will not leave us; and finally, we should laugh and sing" (69).

220. All Christians collectively belong to the church of Jesus Christ, which is also referred to the bride of Christ (John 3:29; Matt 25:1–13; Eph 5:22–33; Rev 21:2, 9–10; 22:17).

So, while it is true that there is "A time to weep and a time to laugh; A time to mourn and a time to dance" (Eccl 3:4), for Guyanese-Canadians of African heritage, weeping and laughing, as well as mourning and dancing, can occur within the *same* life setting of grief. Grounded in the firm belief that the spirit or soul is immediately transported into the very presence of Christ upon death, and thus simultaneously takes up new residence in heaven (Luke 23:43; Phil 1:23), it is therefore not uncommon to see those in grief among Guyanese-Canadians of African heritage actually express joy *amidst* mourning. They are, as the apostle Paul puts it: "sorrowful yet always rejoicing" (2 Cor 6:10). Sorrow and grief do not have to be somber, but celebratory as well.

On several occasions the Bible speaks of the performance of dancing. After crossing the Red Sea, Exodus 15:20 tells us, "Miriam the prophetess, Aaron's sister, took the timbrel in her hand, and all the women went out after her with timbrels and with dancing." There was even dancing at the foot of Mount Sinai, but not to God. Rather it was to a golden calf, which Aaron made from the gold of the people, saying, "This is your god, O Israel, who brought you up from the land of Egypt" (Exod 32:4, 19). First Samuel 18:6 reads, "It happened as they were coming, when David returned from killing the Philistine, that the women came out of all the cities of Israel, singing and dancing, to meet King Saul, with tambourines, with joy and with musical instruments." When the ark of God was brought to Jerusalem, we read in 2 Samuel 6:14, "And David was dancing before the LORD with all *his* might, and David was wearing a linen ephod" (cf. 6:16). One psalmist invites the sons of Zion to "Let them praise His name with dancing; let them sing praises to Him with timbrel and lyre" (Ps 149:4 [3]). The final psalm, 150:5 [4]) reads, "Praise Him with timbrel and dancing; praise Him with stringed instruments and pipe." And while Lamentations 5:15 reads, "The joy of our hearts has ceased; our dancing has been turned into mourning," Psalm 30:12 [11]) says, "You have turned for me my mourning into dancing; You have loosed my sackcloth and girded me with gladness."

Richards-Greaves notes, "*Kweh-kweh* music includes singing and often dancing and playing musical instruments. *Kweh-kweh* singing is a communal enactment, performed in Creolese (Guyanese Creole language) in call-and-response form. . . . address[ing] a wide range of conjugal matters."[221] As a com-

---

221. Richards-Greaves, "Come to My 'Kwe-Kwe,'" 87.

munal act, "participants sing *kweh-kweh* songs in the communal circles, they perform the ritual dance, composed of choreographed stomping, shuffling, and kicking of the feet, contorting the upper body, and in the case of women, swaying maxi skirts from side to side."[222] During the *Kweh-kweh* ritual, "While the contact of the feet against the floor or ground offers rhythmic accompaniment to the singing, drums and makeshift instruments, like bottles and spoons and buckets and sticks, provide the primary musical instruments."[223]

Kimerer LaMothe in her article "Dancing in the Face of Death," speaks of the dance piece *Santuario* (Sanctuary) that was inspired by the deadly shootings of forty-nine people at the Pulse nightclub in Orlando, Florida on June 11, 2016. Speaking of her experience as an observer of this dance piece by the Philadelphia based company, Kun-Yang Lin/Dancers, LaMothe avers, "Dance has agency in its ability to stir and catalyze acute awareness of pain and a loving, whole human response to it at the same time. The very movements that make our pain evident, visceral, and communal are the same movements that exercise our only hope of acting otherwise."[224] LaMothe adds, "At one level, a dance tells a story, in this case, loosely acting out a tragic event, not literally, but in an abstract, symbolic manner. Yet dance is never just telling a story. Because there, in front of you, are bodily selves – whole humans – beautiful, strong, lithe, expressive bodily selves. And they are moving. They are pouring their attention, their time, their energy, their love into making these kinetic images. The pain they depict bleeds out in their sweat and our tears."[225] Small wonder LaMothe asserts, "dancing serves, perhaps uniquely, to buoy and nurture humanity in the face of tragedy."[226]

If looking back on a tragic event by means of a symbolic dance appears to have some redemptive quality to it as it fosters communal support for the wounded thus furnishing a sense of buoyancy amidst grief, how much more is symbolic dancing to upbeat gospel songs? Without factoring God into the frame, dancing as a symbolic expression of a tragic event, will nevertheless fall short of *full* redemption. With the inclusion of God within one's worldview,

---

222. Richards-Greaves, 87.

223. Richards-Greaves, 87.

224. LaMothe, "Dancing in the Face," para. 16.

225. LaMothe, para. 11–12.

226. LaMothe, para. 2.

however, tragedy is made bearable, grief is made manageable, and the bereaved can continue to live an abundant life on account of the confident hope that such tragedy and grief find their answers in Christ. Only in Christ, the God who suffers for us and with us, can the bereaved really find sustainability amidst grief (Matt 5:4). Comforted truly by God that is predicated upon the future hope of eternal life with him who *will* terminate death, mourning, crying, pain, and tears (Rev 21:4), grieving Christians can employ dance as a symbolic expression as they look back *and* forward, not only to the tragedy of the deceased, but more so to the crucified-yet-resurrected Lord Jesus Christ who is the only sure hope who redeems *all* tragedies.

Jürgen Moltmann states it more specifically when he says, "The history of the suffering, forsaken and crucified Christ is so open that the suffering, forsakenness and anxieties of every loving man or woman find a place in it and are accepted. If they find a place in it and are accepted, it is not in order to give them permanence, but in order to transform and heal them."[227] Put another way, "In Christ's death on the cross, God took evil, sin and rejection of himself, transforming it into goodness, grace and election in the sacrifice of his infinite love. All evil, all sin, suffering and damnation is 'in God'. They have been endured by him, abolished in him, transformed by him. These are 'the benefits of his passion' for us."[228] Only in Christ and Christ alone, the God who suffers for and with us, is death swallowed up in victory (1 Cor 15:54). With the apostle Paul, grieving Christians can thus joyfully exclaim, "'O death, where is your victory? O death, where is your sting?' The sting of death is sin, and the power of sin is the law; but thanks be to God who gives us the victory through our Lord Jesus Christ (15:55–57). Moltmann, in *The Crucified God*, emphasized it like this:

> The death of Jesus on the cross is the *centre* of all Christian theology. It is not the only theme of theology, but it is in effect the entry to its problems and answers on earth. All Christian statements about God, about creation, about sin and death have their focal point in the crucified Christ. All Christian statements about history, about the church, about faith and sanctification, about the future and about hope stem from the crucified Christ.

227. Moltmann, *Experiences of God*, 75.

228. Moltmann, 79.

The multiplicity of the New Testament comes together in the event of the crucifixion and resurrection of Jesus and flows out again from it. It is one event and one person. . . . Thus the centre is occupied not by 'cross and resurrection,' but by *the resurrection of the crucified Christ*, which qualifies his death as something that has happened for us, and *the cross of the risen Christ*, which reveals and makes accessible to those who are dying his resurrection from the dead.[229]

The problems of tragedy, death, and grief therefore find their answers on earth in the God made flesh, God the Son Jesus Christ. To furnish answers to life's most difficult questions while rejecting any discussion on the resurrection of the crucified Christ *and* the cross of the risen Christ will undoubtedly fail to touch the mind and heart of the bereaved. As Bonhoeffer asserted, "Only the suffering God can help us."[230] In the God who suffers for and with us are we made alive by grace through faith in Christ (Eph 2:1–9). Stated positively, life is a sure guarantee for all those who place their faith in Christ precisely because Christ lives forevermore without any possibility of dying (John 11:25–26; 14:19). Tragedy, death, and grief are therefore transformed in the crucified-yet-resurrected Lord Jesus Christ. Or else, the cross without the resurrection of Christ "is quite simply a tragedy and nothing more than that."[231] But as Paul stated, "For I delivered to you as of first importance what I also received, that Christ died for our sins according to the Scriptures, and that He was buried, and that He was raised on the third day according to the Scriptures" (1 Cor 15:3–4). In Christ, death will be abolished, and all will be made alive (15:22, 26).

African-Guyanese-Canadian Christians stand firm on these biblical truths as they dance to upbeat gospel songs even in the midst of tragedy as a symbolic expression of one's love for the deceased and for Christ in whose heavenly presence the deceased now resides (2 Cor 5:8). "For when we use a symbol, we do not speak; we let an object or gesture speak for us. This is precisely how we proceed in the liturgy; symbolic language is the language

---

229. Moltmann, *Crucified God*, 204; emphasis original.

230. Bonhoeffer, *Letters and Papers*, 361.

231. Moltmann, *Experiences of God*, 53.

of a love that transcends words."[232] As a symbolic gesture of love, *Kweh-kweh* dancing accompanied by upbeat gospel songs amidst grief are undergirded by the theological truths of Scripture, which speak of a loving God who alone offers redemption in the crucified-yet-resurrected Lord Jesus Christ. It is this Christ who is in the process of making all things new (Rev 21:5), inclusive of which is the liberation from death, mourning, crying, and pain (21:4). Only in Christ can our tragedies and griefs be truly and fully redeemed.

For some folks, dancing to and singing upbeat gospel songs might very well be countercultural. But says Nouwen, "when we have finally found the anchor place for our lives within our center we can be free to let others enter into that space created for them, and allow them to dance their own dance, sing their own song, and speak their own language without fear. Then our presence is no longer threatening and demanding, but inviting and liberating."[233]

Within an African-Guyanese-Canadian context of grief, *Kweh-kweh* dancing to and singing upbeat gospel music appears therefore to be a mixture of confidence and thanksgiving to the loving God who alone furnishes redemption for all sinners and innocent sufferers. Like the psalms of thanksgiving, such dancing and singing joyfully acknowledges the good things that God has done on behalf of the believers, both deceased and bereaved, even their redemption. In this *Kweh-kweh* celebration, the bereaved are granted the opportunity to share their sorrows and their joys, their defeats and their victories, their doubts and their faith, their selves, and their God.[234] During this celebratory time, it is acknowledged that God has indeed been loyal to the deceased, delivering them from the troubles of life, and has now taken them to be with him forever in glory land, beyond the Jordan, in the Promised Land of heaven. As such, *Kweh-kweh* dancing and singing upbeat gospel songs in thanks and praise to God, serves as a sign of one's positive outlook on life that is heralded by God's messengers, and grounded in God's redemptive acts in support of his people, as recorded in the Bible. Just as God redeemed his people Israel from the cruel bondage in Egypt, so too he has already redeemed his people from the bondage of death, even though this redemption awaits it actualization at the parousia of the Lord Jesus Christ (Rom 8:18–25).

---

232. Gutiérrez, *On Job*, xiv.

233. Nouwen, *Wounded Healer*, 98.

234. Cf. Futato, *Joy Comes*, 80.

Kweh-kweh dancing and singing are almost certainly bound to have holistic healing properties amidst grief. With their eyes transfixed upon Jesus, the author and perfecter of their faith, who for the joy set before him endured the cross, despising the shame, and has sat down at the right hand of the throne of God (Heb 12:2), Guyanese-Canadians of African heritage, can lay aside every encumbrance, even the burden of grief, and the sin which so easily entangles, and run with endurance and joy, the race set before them (12:1). In other words, they follow the exhortation of Paul in rejoicing in the Lord always (2 Cor 6:10; 7:4; Phil 4:4). As such, when it comes to mourning, based on the confident belief that the departed soul or spirit is with Jesus the crucified-yet-resurrected Lord and King, dancing and singing in celebration of a life well lived for God's renown, can definitely serve as a powerful tool in the transformation of grief.

6.1e. Connecting Personal Grief Stories to God's Sacred Story – Experiencing Hope in the Crucified-yet-Resurrected Christ

Here we are reminded of the words of VL2 following the death of VL2's mother: "I gathered my brothers and sisters together in the hallway of the hospital and reminded them that the most important thing was my mother had put her faith in God through the blood of Christ. Her life was in God's hands." In other words, "We believe in the eternal life that God has promised to those who put their faith in him. Since we are believers in Christ, we believe we will meet our mother again." VL2 also stated, "We reminded ourselves of all the good things she had done, and the good life she had lived. We needed to encourage one another to keep on with her legacy of love, dedication to the family, and faithfulness to God, which she adopted in her later years." In such comments one observes that each bereaved person had a grief story to tell of their mother, but their personal grief stories were connected to God's grand sacred story. In this connection, each mourner, being a believer in Christ, found hope: "Since we are believers in Christ, we will meet our mother again." And in so doing, they are able to sorrow with hope.

Affirming his belief in the reality of heaven, Lam recalls a snippet of the last days in the life of a gentleman who was a non-Christian but who made the decision to follow Christ just prior to his cancer-related death.

> Mr. Nguyen, forty-one years old, was sick with nose cancer. As he lay in the hospital, he accepted the Lord Jesus Christ. The next Saturday, his wife called [me] to come see him because he was dying. He was dead for eleven minutes but came back to life. I drove to see him the next day, and he told me that on the previous night he had gone to a very beautiful place and met his father, who had died four months prior. When I asked him if he was afraid of death, he said no.

Lam's knowledge of Mr. Nguyen (and other Vietnamese Christians who have had visions of heaven, e.g., Mr. Tran and Mrs. Vo), and hearing them speak of heaven the ways in which they did (i.e. as a beautiful place full of diamonds) furnished him ample evidence that "they had seen it. This gave me a strong trust in God's miracles. They guaranteed me that I've been saved and am God's child, who inherits heaven."[235] In the case of Mr. Nguyen, heaven is a place where he will see his father again.

In the OT, one also hears such a note of hope sounded from the lips of David in the story of the death of his and Bathsheba's unnamed son. "While the child was still alive, I fasted and wept; for I said, 'Who knows, the LORD may be gracious to me, that the child may live.' But now he has died; why should I fast? Can I bring him back again? *I will go to him*, but he will not return to me" (2 Sam 12:22–23; emphasis mine). The words "I will go to him" collectively sound an echo of hope from the perspective of David.[236] Otherwise stated, "There is to be heard a note of consolation in David's words 'I will go to him.'"[237] With this hope, David is able to move from a state of mourning to a state of normalcy, or even a state of joy. This is made clear from the words of Anderson, "This joyous state meant that the mourner had to bathe, put on fresh clothes and scented oil, eat and drink, and even

---

235. Lam, *God's Miracles*, 200. For Mr. Tran, heaven "was so beautiful," while for Mrs. Vo, heaven is "full of diamonds" (200).

236. Similarly, in Job 14:14, Job asked, "If a man dies, will he live *again*?" The resounding answer to that question is heard very emphatically in these hopeful words from the mouth of Job: "Even after my skin is destroyed, yet from my *flesh* I shall see God" (19:26; emphasis mine). Such a hope is grounded in the life of Job's Redeemer. As Job himself acknowledged, "As for me, I know that my Redeemer lives, and at last He will take His stand on the earth" (19:25).

237. Bergen, *1, 2 Samuel*, 376.

(according to some) resume sexual relations."[238] By doing each of these (see 2 Sam 12:13–25), David's grief narrative is thus transformed from one of sorrow to one of hopeful joy, which is primarily grounded in David's faith in Yahweh his God.[239]

Each person has a story to tell, and every story is equally significant because every person is sacred to God (Gen 1:26–27; 5:1; 9:6; Ps 139:14–17 [13–16]; Jas 3:9). At the same time, no one story is *more* important than another. All stories of all peoples are significant, even and especially the stories of faithful believers in the Lord Jesus Christ. Although the deceased is no longer physically present with us, the story of their life remains a significant part of the community of faith. Compassionate pastoral care will make room for such stories of the departed believer to be shared and appreciated.[240]

Equally important here are the words of Hopkins, who asserts, "Pastoral care and counseling, at its heart, is about *storytelling*."[241] This means that, "Stories center the pastoral care encounter, offering points of reflection for self-perception and understanding. Pastoral caregivers do not engage in 'extreme makeovers' of the psyche, but rather help organize and frame our understanding of ourselves, the world, the way we speak about it, and the way we relate to God."[242] Speaking of her constructive experience during a workshop at a denominational evangelism conference she attended where stories were shared, Hopkins offers the following description: "The stories of our experience of God and of community formed the core of our Christian self-identity and bound us together in that workshop. Our shared stories were 'privileged and imaginative acts of self-interpretation' that invited our pastoral caring for one another."[243] Yet one wonders what would happen if such a pastoral care practice would take root in, and become part of the life of the local faith community of Christ's followers so that it becomes a ritual

---

238. Anderson, *Time to Mourn*, 50. See 2 Sam 12:24 for David's resumption of sexual relations with his wife Bathsheba.

239. It should be noted here once again that while it is possible for one to read David's unconventional grief expressions as cold-hearted, it is also possible that David exhibits a capacity to grieve resiliently – see also discussion in section 4.5.3.4 on p@@.

240. See also Ramshaw, "Personalization of Postmodern," 177.

241. In Hopkins and Koppel, *Grounded in the Living Word*, 6; emphasis mine.

242. In Hopkins and Koppel, 6.

243. In Hopkins and Koppel, 6; see also Hopkins, *Journey through The Psalms*, 1–2. Internal quote taken from Anderson and Foley, *Mighty Stories, Dangerous Rituals*, 5.

of great import for pastoral care? Such a compassionate pastoral care practice is what is being advocated here.

Stories of the departed faithful believer in the Lord Jesus Christ can inspire contemporary Christians to imitate our brothers and sisters in Christ who have gone before us as they help us to keep our eyes on Jesus Christ, the author and perfecter of our faith (Heb 12:1–2). On the flip side, the sharing of stories of the deceased can also elevate the status of the deceased faithful believer to that of a *god*. Knowledge of such a subsisting undercurrent should serve as a warning for every Christian sharing their story of their deceased loved one. Avoiding this danger zone therefore compels the mourner to temper each rendition of the story of the faith of the deceased with that of the story of the faithfulness of God. Care should therefore be taken to avoid idealizing and idolizing such familial persons that the story of our faithful high priest, the Lord Jesus Christ, appears to pale in comparison. It is essential to the life of the Christian mourning storyteller to acknowledge explicitly or implicitly during the storytelling that there is only one God who exists as three persons: Father, Son, and Holy Spirit, from whom the deceased derives their very existence (Acts 17:28). It should then follow that the deceased is *never* to be viewed as being on par with the triune God. The mere fact that they're deceased should be indicative of the reality that the deceased is *not* to be idolized, especially in the form of ancestral worship, or even bordering on, the divine (Exod 20:3–5; Lev 26:1; Deut 4:15–19).

Though a necessity in our grief process, stories of our deceased loved ones ought to be subservient to the story of the gospel of Jesus Christ without which there would be no story of faith. Thus, Zylla's remark, "Pastoral theology has always attempted to bridge the complex world of experience with the deepest roots of the gospel."[244] All our faithful stories fall under the umbrella of God's grand metanarrative and his dealings with this world that he created by his word *ex nihilo*, that is, out of nothing (Heb 11:3). Without the metanarrative of God's story, the stories of our deceased loved ones possess little to no meaning at all. Faith and hope thus thrive rooted in God's metanarrative. As Paul M. Beckingham maintains,

---

244. Zylla, "What Language," 129.

Faith is a journey of discovering ultimate value – and we are all on it. Some choose to ground their experience under the umbrella of truth that is God's story, outlines in His dealings with His biblical people. When I read my own narrative, and weigh the text of my life, I deliberately place it within that meta-narrative, or the overarching story of the nature of God – His acts of love in dealing with His people. The writings of those biblical authors record His tender involvement with His world. Hope grows as we read our own story in that light, and against the backdrop of this bigger story in which we find ourselves. Our story is caught up within it as it becomes part of the ultimate resolution of our pain, and healing for our brokenness. This is the hope towards which God is moving us, if we will let Him.[245]

This is especially true in the light of the faith chapter of Heb 11 which foreshadows Hebrews 12. In the former, the writer shares his rendition of the stories of the multiple giants of the faith, but in the latter, he ultimately cautions and challenges the faithful readers and hearers of his letter to fix their eyes upon the Lord Jesus Christ, who is none other than the author or pioneer and perfecter of their faith (Heb 12:2). Stated alternatively, the legacy of the faith of the human deceased loved one, profound as it may be, is always hinged upon, and thus subordinate to, the faith of Jesus Christ, the One of whom Scripture emphatically refers to as our "merciful and faithful high priest in all things pertaining to God" (2:17). Like the faith chapter in the sermonic letter of Hebrews, while the faith of each of the giants of the faith are ascribed ample recognition for their faith in the Lord, it is the Lord Jesus Christ who is always the main character of faith. Mourning storytellers should never lose sight of Jesus Christ who is the point of every story (see Mark 1:1; Luke 24:44–49; John 5:39). Of utmost importance then to the mourner is the acknowledgement that, naked the deceased came from their mother's womb, and naked they shall return. Yahweh gave and Yahweh has taken away. Blessed be the name of Yahweh (Job 1:21). The accent therefore falls *not* on the deceased loved one, but on Yahweh who loves the deceased

---

245. Beckingham, *Walking Towards Hope*, 145.

perfectly, and has thus received the deceased into glory (Pss 8:5–9 [4–8]; 73:24–25 [23–24]; Luke 23:43; Acts 7:55–56).

Therefore, in speaking of the deceased loved one, although strongly encouraged as part of the grief and healing process, it is much more important to stress, as a Christian, that the life of the deceased is wrapped up in the life of the faithful One, with whom there is no variation or shifting shadow (Jas 1:17), and of whom the Scripture says, "Jesus Christ *is* the same yesterday and today and forever (Heb 13:8). It is this faithful One who brought the deceased into existence, privileged them with a lifespan (short or long; 70 is the average number proffered in Ps 90:11 [10]), and thereafter, carried them back into the arms of father Abraham (Luke 16:23), and more so, at home with him (2 Cor 5:8). Further to this, "Jesus Christ [is] the faithful witness, the firstborn of the dead" (Rev 1:5a). And as a consequence of this historical reality, those whom Jesus Christ has released from "sins by His blood" (1:5b), even the faithful deceased loved one, will doubtless be guaranteed a place among the second-born of the dead in Christ who is the resurrection and the life (John 11:25; 1 Cor 15:20–23; Rev 20:4–6).

At the same time, acquainted with grief in their own lives, communal compassionate pastoral caregivers become fellow wounded healers. Rather than the unwounded (e.g., Job's friends), it is the wounded healers who are virtually always in a better position to heal the wounded. As Nouwen avers, "Making one's wounds a source of healing, therefore, does not call for a sharing of superficial pains, but for a constant willingness to see one's own pain and suffering as rising from the depth of the human condition that we all share."[246] At the same time, there is the probability that the deceased is known within the community of pastoral caregivers, and if that is the case, then they too can join in the sharing of their own stories of the faithful one who is now deceased, as a way to encourage the immediate mourner.

But even when the communal pastoral caregivers share an acquaintance with the deceased and are thus able to relate their stories of the deceased with the mourning loved one(s), it is also ultimately the story of the only perfectly faithful One who died and rose again that needs to be highlighted

---

246. Nouwen, *Wounded Healer*, 94–95. Contra "walking wounded," a term Calvin Morris uses to characterize those who deny their woundedness and vulnerability, and yet who walk around as wounded caregivers seeking to help others. As noted in Wimberly, *Recalling Our Own Stories*, 13.

by all pastoral caregivers (John 14:19; Rev 1:17–19). And this for the very fact that it is the story of the life of Jesus Christ that gives credence to the story of the life of the faithful deceased. Bereft of the story of God's faithful Son, Jesus Christ, and his death and triumphant resurrection, ascension, and coronation to the right hand of God the Father (Eph 1:19–23), the faith stories of the deceased carry very little significance. Apart from the rising Sun of Righteousness who brings healing on his wings (Mal 4:2) to shine upon those who sit in darkness and the shadow of death (Luke 1:79; cf. Isa 9:2), the stories of the dead remain simply that, dead, lifeless, and lacking in vigor to inspire the living faithful witness of Christ who is called to live for the glory of God in every possible way (1 Cor 10:31).

So, while one may share the stories of the faithful human deceased loved one, it is of chief importance that the story of the faithful divine-human Son of God, God the Son, Jesus Christ, be shared even more and above all. Sharing the story of the deceased human loved one can thus serve as an evangelistic tributary that flows from the mouth of the mourner into the river of God's metanarrative, pointing fellow humans ultimately to the living hope of the world, namely Jesus Christ, the unique Son of God the Father (Rom 15:12; 1 Pet 1:3; 3:15; 1 John 3:3). It is therefore in sharing the story of both the faithful human who has joined the great cloud of witnesses of and to the faithfulness of God (Heb 12:1), and more crucially the story of the faithful divine-human Son of God, Jesus Christ, that faith can leap in the heart of an unbeliever, and all this only by the grace of God (Eph 2:8–9).

The story of the deceased therefore serves as helpful segue into the ultimate framework of the grand metanarrative of God, within which the story of the deceased finds its true meaning,[247] and in so doing, the mourning storyteller

---

247. Similarly, Newbigin (*Gospel in a Pluralist*, 14–26) states, "The way we understand human life depends on what conception we have of the human story. What is the real story of which my life story is part?" (15). MacIntyre (*After Virtue*, 204–25) also maintains that "I can only answer the question 'What am I to do?' if I can answer the prior question, 'Of what story do I find myself a part?'" (216). Bartholomew and Goheen (*Drama of Scripture*, 15–27) affirm, "In order to understand our world, to make sense of our lives, and to make our most important decisions about how we ought to be living, we depend upon some story . . . Individual experiences make sense and acquire meaning only when seen within the context or frame of some story we believe to be the true story of the world: each episode of our life stories finds its place there" (18). As such, "biblical Christianity claims that the Bible alone tells the true story of our world . . . In other words, the Bible provides us with the basic story that we need in order to understand our world and to live in it as God's people" (20, 21). Otherwise stated in the words of Wright (*Christian Origins*, 38–43) "The whole point of Christianity is that it

acknowledges themself as a living testimony and witness of and to the faithfulness of God (cf. Luke 24:48; Acts 1:8; 1 Cor 1:9). In a nutshell then, the grand metanarrative of God can be drafted along these lines:

> After God created the world and human rebellion marred it, God set out to restore what he had made: "God did not turn his back on a world bent on destruction; he turned his face toward it in love. He set out on the long road of redemption to restore the lost as his people and the world as his kingdom." The Bible narrates the story of God's journey on that long road of redemption. It is a unified and progressively unfolding drama of God's action in history for the salvation of the whole world.[248]

To which we may add: and this only through God incarnate, Jesus Christ (the King). Storytelling then from the lips of the mourner concerning the deceased loved one and follower of Jesus Christ, although encouraged as part of the grieving and healing pastoral care process, should *never* take precedence over the story of God's grand metanarrative, of whom Jesus Christ is the central character. And if Carrie Doehring is correct in stating, "Caregiving involves constructing meaning and practices that can deepen a sense of connection with God/the sacred and the web of being that includes self, others, and all of creation,"[249] then what better place to find meaning with each of these than in God's grand metanarrative, at the heart of which is Jesus the crucified-yet-resurrected, reigning, and returning Lord, Master, and King?

Edward P. Wimberly, in his *African American Pastoral Care*, suggests that "Indeed, the metaphor 'indigenous storyteller' still remains powerful for giving guidance to constructive approaches for recreating village functions in contemporary black churches."[250] The origin of this metaphor can be heard in the following words: "Eschatological indigenous African American

---

offers a story which is the story of the whole world. It is public truth" (41–42). Sire (*Universe Next Door*, 15–24) also states that a ministry of the Christian is that of "encouraging people to think in terms of worldviews, that is, with a consciousness of not only our own way of thought but also that of other people, so that we can first understand and then genuinely communicate with others in our pluralistic society" (17).

248. Bartholomew and Goheen, *Drama of Scripture*, 11–12; internal quotation from Contemporary Testimony Committee of the Christian Reformed Church, *Our World Belongs to God*, paragraph 19.

249. Doehring, *Practice of Pastoral Care*, 180.

250. Wimberly, *African American Pastoral Care*, x.

storytelling is an artistic and imaginative practice of meaning-making that, although derived from necessity [amidst slavery], focused on God's presence. What grief and sorrow African Americans experienced in the present was, in all actuality, being ameliorated or improved by God's glorious, unfolding story."[251] What is more, "They witnessed God creating a new world that was present but not yet. They encountered what the Gospel stories were telling them about the coming of a new age called the kingdom of God."[252] And as a consequence of this, "through their own creative encounters with God, they created an imaginative set of practices known as storytelling that form a master narrative or eschatological plot 'best exemplified in the stories of the exodus of the Hebrew children from Egypt and of the resurrection of Jesus from the dead.'"[253]

This indigenous storytelling approach to grief has a story line to it, which Wimberly refers to as the "eschatological plot."[254] It is this eschatological plot that "envisions hope in the midst of suffering and oppression, because God is working out God's purposes in life on behalf of persons. The eschatological plot takes suffering and oppression very seriously without minimizing their influence in life. Yet despite the prevalence of suffering and oppression, God's story of hope and liberation is unfolding."[255] What then is the goal of this indigenous storytelling or narrative approach to pastoral care? According to Wimberly, especially within the black church, it is that of "link[ing] persons in need to the unfolding of God's story in the midst of life. The African American pastor has narrated, and continues to narrate, stories that help people catch a glimpse of hope in the midst of suffering."[256] Which is another way of saying that "It is by identifying with the story that Christians have linked themselves to purposeful directions in life, despite suffering and pain."[257]

Wimberly therefore proposes the "Telling and retelling [of] stories from the Bible, from our faith communities, and from our everyday lives as people of faith evoke concrete images and memories that propel us into imaginatively

---

251. Wimberly, xii.
252. Wimberly, xii.
253. Wimberly, xii.
254. Wimberly, 4.
255. Wimberly, 4.
256. Wimberly, 4–5.
257. Wimberly, 5.

recreating our village connections."[258] So in the case of the death of a parish-ioner, an African pastor "trained lay people to share stories from their own lives to encourage the bereaved to share their stories of hurt and pain. He informed them that a brief story from the lives of the caregivers could assist the bereaved to review their relationships with the deceased and enable feel-ings of bereavement to be expressed. The pastor warned them, however, to tell their stories in ways that kept the bereaved person's needs for grieving central."[259] In the process of sharing their stories of bereavement in their own lives the caregivers "included testimonies of God's presence in the midst of death."[260] What is missing from this pastoral encounter, however, is that of the bereaved *not* being given another chance to retell their grief story in light of the grief stories of the lay caregivers. It would have been helpful for the bereaved to retell their grief story, especially after being reminded of such a story that is part and parcel of God's grander redemptive story of the Bible, which encompasses the ongoing and ever-abiding presence of God amidst grief, even in and through the presence of the caregivers. Subsequently, this shared support system would have a common faith story, which, when shared, would hold out hope in tragedy.[261]

Together with the wake and funeral, the African pastor made a concerted effort to include "Images of God's presence in the lives of those who were bereaved in Scripture [which] held out hope for developing new life sce-narios. The liturgy of the funeral gave the message that God will assist you in fashioning a new story without the presence of the deceased."[262] In other words, "Through the funeral and wake, they could encounter the spacious resources of God's story of grace and hope."[263] Wimberly's reflection on this method of storytelling, inclusive of which is story-listening, as well as story-retelling, as a way of offering hope to the bereaved, is summarized in the following statement:

---

258. Wimberly, x–xi.
259. Wimberly, 36.
260. Wimberly, 38.
261. Wimberly, 38.
262. Wimberly, 38.
263. Wimberly, 38.

Essential to the narrative understanding of caring ministry to the bereaved is the envisioning of the funeral and the caring as being linked to God's unfolding drama in our lives. God's unfolding story is a drama made up of episodes, scenes, chapters, and a plot. The funeral and the ministry of caring in God's name are miniplots in the midst of God's unfolding macroplot. The macroplot of God involves death and rebirth made possible by Jesus Christ. The salvation drama is made up of dying with Christ and rising with Christ. Therefore, in ministry to the dying and the bereaved, the task is to draw the people into God's salvation drama of death and rebirth.[264]

Of import here is the fact that compassionate storytelling *necessitates* compassionate story-listening, on the part of both the immediately bereaved and the previously bereaved lay caregivers. Otherwise, there will be a breakdown in the narrative cycle. This process of compassionate storytelling, story-listening, and then story-retelling within God's grander kingdom story of the defeat of sin and death through the triumphal resurrection of Jesus Christ, and thus liberation, healing, and wholeness,[265] "reinforces relational ties that sustain grieving persons in integrity."[266]

Interestingly, Caitlin Vieira also notes, "To healthily grieve, we take all the time we need. Do not let anyone tell you when you should be 'over it'. . . . Accept support when offered – there's no need to put on a brave face. Talk regularly about the loss with those closest to you."[267] In other words, talk about your grief stories. Vieira then goes on to add, "There are things that we can do for others who are grieving. We can ask about their feelings and be present."[268] What Vieira means by this is spelled out in the following words: "Be good listeners. You can ask them to share good memories of the loss they experienced."[269] Compassionate grief storytelling therefore also implies compassionate grief story-listening. At the same time, Vieira also offers the

---

264. Wimberly, 39.
265. Wimberly, 19.
266. Wimberly, 13.
267. Vieira, "Grief and Mental Health," para. 12.
268. Vieira, para. 13.
269. Vieira, para. 13.

following caveat: "If they do not want to speak, just visit them. Of course, everyone is busy and have their own lives so if you can't be with them daily, make simple phone calls."[270]

From a Christian perspective, however, compassionate pastoral care is deprived of its efficacy where only storytelling and story-listening are present. Compassionate pastoral care necessitates both storytelling and story-listening, but accompanied by story-retelling in light of God's grander redemptive story. By telling and retelling one's grief story, in collaboration with the grief stories of other lay Christians, and this in connection to the metanarrative of God's sacred or redemptive story, the grieving person is sustained in integrity, and finds hope. Compassionate storytelling and listening to each other's grief stories, together with the compassionate act of story-retelling, are empty without the inclusion of God's grander salvific story, which does not minimize, but rather embraces death and grief. Yet God's redemptive story encompasses a subsequent resurrection triumph after death, and as such, serves as the most powerful tool in the transformation of grief. The reason being is that it holds out a sure and certain hope for the bereaved so that they are able "to see reality the way it is shaped by God's hand and teachings."[271] The story of the bereaved therefore does not end with *death*. Rather, since the final word in God's metanarrative is *life* (Isa 25:8; Rev 21:4), the personal stories of every grieving born again child of God ends on a note of *life*. By virtue of the fact that Christ is "the resurrection and the life" (John 11:25; 14:19; 20:30–31), and the Christian's "living hope" (1 Pet 1:3; 1 John 3:3), the Christian mourner can confidently concur with N. T. Wright that, "Resurrection means bodily life *after* 'life after death', or, if you prefer, bodily life after the *state* of 'death.'"[272]

6.2. Summary

This section presented and developed five ways pastoral care practitioners can lend aid to those in grief so that the bereaved might be able to handle and transform their grief. These five compassionate (liberative intercultural)

---

270. Vieira, para. 13.

271. Wimberly, *African American Pastoral Care*, 19.

272. Wright, *Christian Origins*, 108–109; emphasis original.

expressions were deemed worthy of transforming grief and thus sustaining the bereaved:

1. Bearing the Funeral Expenses of the Poor – Extending Offers of Help
2. Composing and Singing Sad (and Joyful Theopoetic) Songs and Poems of Lament – Finding Emotional Catharsis through Music
3. Incorporating Indigenous Christian Devotional Songs (e.g., Bhajans) in the Wake/Funeral Liturgy – Tapping into the Cultural Liminal Memory of a Deep Experience of Faith
4. Celebrating the Life of the Deceased through Dancing and Singing Upbeat Gospel Songs – Spiritual Rejoicing for Having Arrived Home in Heaven
5. Connecting Personal Grief Stories to God's Sacred Story – Experiencing Hope in the Crucified-yet-Resurrected Christ

From this list it is observed that each of these five compassionate pastoral care practices are both liberative and intercultural and couched within ritual. By virtue of this, "The hope for the church's life is that we might all live the truth of the mutuality of service in love so well that we enact it unconsciously in our liturgies, transforming them into rituals of liberation for individuals and for the world."[273] What is more, it is also hoped that these compassionate (liberative intercultural) pastoral care practices will sensitize pastoral caregivers in their God-empowered endeavors to bring healing and sustainability to those in grief, and with God-centered, cultural integrity.

---

273. Ramshaw, *Ritual and Pastoral Care*, 114.

CHAPTER 7

Conclusion

7.1. Summary

Anthony C. Thiselton maintains that "God created humankind because God loves us and chose to reach forth, as it were, out of himself, to create beings 'other' than himself, to commune with them and to enjoy fellowship with them."[1] In some measure, this communion and fellowship involve what is referred to as prayer, that is, the dialogic encounter between the divine and the human. Recognizing what Henry A. Murray and Clyde Kluckhohn refer to as the "Trinitarian" formulation of personhood in regards to pastoral care, which is constructed on the premise, "Every human person is in some respects (a) like all others, (b) like some others, and (c) like none other,"[2] has spurred the two central theological questions addressed in this book. Question number one was: within the prosaic sections of the OT (Genesis to Esther), does the potential exist for one to discover, in association with lament and praise, various modes of expression communicated during the lived context of disorientation to/before God (verbal, physical and emotional) by faithful pray-ers? Encouraged by the first, question number two was: amidst the phenomenon of grief, and in association with lament and praise, does the possibility exist

---

1. Thiselton, *Systematic Theology*, 102.

2. Murray and Kluckhohn, *Personality in Nature*, 15; cf. Lartey, *In Living Color*, 34. The following Guyanese proverb seems fitting to note: "All cassava get same skin but nah all taste de same way." Translated from creole English, "Though people may look alike because of their mode of dress, they are different in their ways." In this book, such a difference can be seen from the diverse verbal, physical, and emotional expressions conveyed to/before God especially amidst disorientation/affliction of which grief is a phenomenon.

for one to discover other modes of expression communicated during the lived context of grief to/before God (verbal, physical, and emotional) within a contemporary Christian intercultural context outside-yet-inside of the West (i.e. principally among Canadian immigrants from Guyana and Vietnam)?

In addressing these two central theological questions, the prosaic prayers of the OT, which are literarily positioned within the parameters of Genesis to Esther, and situated within the lived context of disorientation, were investigated for the purpose of attending to their multivalent anthropological expressions (i.e. verbal, physical, and emotional) and significance to/before God within an Israelite OT context. At the same time, several expressions (i.e. verbal, physical, and emotional) and their significance were also observed within a contemporary intercultural Guyanese-Canadian and Vietnamese-Canadian context. Below is an itemization of the full gamut of anthropological expressions otherwise referred to as the *Anthropological Expressive Domain of Disorientation* from within the three contexts.

Verbal Anthropological Expressions	
Categories	**Description**
Disorientation Stage 1 Verbal Expressions: DS1 Lament Prayers	Prayers uttered within a context of disorientation at the heart of which is a cry for help; it is occasionally accompanied by the stinging lament question of "Why?" or even simply groans, and sometimes wailing or weeping.
Disorientation Stage 2 Verbal Expressions: DS2 Imprecatory Prayers	Prayers uttered within a context of disorientation that call for a divine judgment or curse upon one's enemies.
Disorientation Stage 3 Verbal Expressions: DS3 Vow Prayers	Prayers uttered within a context of disorientation wherein a promise is made to God that is predicated on a favorable answer from him, that is, "If . . . then."
Disorientation Stage 4 Verbal Expressions: DS4 Penitential Prayers	Prayers uttered within a context of disorientation the content of which is penitence over one's (in)direct sins.

Categories	Description
Disorientation Stage 5 Verbal Expressions: DS5 Confidence Prayers	Prayers uttered within a context of disorientation in confident anticipation of God's readiness to answer favorably, something of which has been (in)directly disclosed to the supplicant.
Disorientation Stage 6 Verbal Expressions: DS6 Thanksgiving Praise Prayers	Prayers uttered within a context of disorientation the content of which is jubilant thanksgiving praise in full assurance of God's imminent salvation declared to the supplicant by the agency of a priestly or prophetic oracle.
Disorientation Stage 7 Verbal Expressions (Death-Related): DS7 Bereavement Vocabulary	Vocabulary associated with death, inclusive of which are: Contrition and/or Confession; Curse; Instructions (Assassination; Burying; Embalming; Holiness; Returning Home and Remarrying; and Transporting Cadaver for Burial); Interrogation and Rejoinder; and Lament Elegies and Loud Cries for Help/Wailing/ Weeping/Screaming/Shouting; Promise; Sharing Stories of Each Other's Grief.

Physical Anthropological Expressions	
Categories	Description
Disorientation Stage 1 Physical Expressions: DS1 Lament Rituals	Rituals associated with lament, inclusive of which are: Blowing (Silver) Trumpets; Fasting; Lying on the Ground; Offering Burnt and Peace Offerings; Paralleling Two Outstretched Bodies; Shedding Tears; Sacrificing through Supernatural Fire (Building Altar, Making Trench, Arranging Wood, Cutting Ox, Laying Ox on Wood); Sitting; Spreading Out Letter; Tearing Clothes; and Turning Face to the Wall.
Disorientation Stage 2 Physical Expressions: DS2 Imprecatory Rituals	Rituals associated with imprecation, inclusive of which are: Covering Head; Prostrating Oneself; and Walking Barefooted.
Disorientation Stage 3 Physical Expressions: DS3 Vow Rituals	Rituals associated with vow, inclusive of which are: Offering Human Sacrifice, Standing, and Tearing Clothes.

Categories	Description
Disorientation Stage 4 Physical Expressions: DS4 Penitential Rituals	Rituals associated with penitence, inclusive of which are: Kneeling; Plucking Hair from Beard and Head; Pouring Dirt upon Oneself; Prostrating Oneself; Separation from Foreigners; Sitting; and Tearing Clothes.
Disorientation Stage 7 Physical Expressions (Death-Related): DS7 Bereavement Rituals	Rituals associated with death, inclusive of which are: Anointing Oneself; Avoiding Food and People (Silence and Solitude)/Isolation; Bearing the Cost of the Funeral; Burning; Burying (and Purchasing Land); Celebrating the Life of the Deceased Annually with Lots of Food; Celebrating the Life of the Deceased through a Eulogy, a Shared Meal, and Singing Psalms, Hymns, and Songs of the Spirit to the Lord, such as Upbeat Songs or Bhajans, while also Proclaiming an Evangelistic Message of Hope in the Lord Jesus Christ alone, and the Comforting Presence of the Holy Spirit; Chambering (Privacy/Isolation); Changing Clothes; Composing Vietnamese Songs and Poems; Covering Face; Deep Breath; Deep Moving (Trembling); Donning and Removing Widow's Clothes; Donning Sackcloth; Eating; Embracing the Deceased's Cadaver; Erecting Gravestones (Monuments); Fainting; Falling on and Kissing the Deceased; Funeral Processioning; Grieving/Mourning; Keeping Memorabilia; Keeping Wake (with Kweh-kweh); Kissing the Deceased; Honoring (through Spice-fire); Lying on the Ground; Lying Down on the Casket/Hitting Oneself; Placing in Coffin; Reading through the Bible; Rising from the Ground; Sitting; Sitting Beside the Tomb while Thinking about the Lost Loved One; Transporting Cadaver for Burial; Visiting the Grave and Carrying Flowers; Washing; Wearing a White Band; Worshiping God; and Writing Letters of Comfort to the Bereaved.

Emotional Anthropological Expressions	
Categories	**Description**
Disorientation Stage 1 Emotional Expressions: DS1 Lament Feelings	Feelings associated with lament prayer, inclusive of which are: Anger; Displeasure / Distress; Fear of God and Humans; Sadness; Shame; and Tender-heartedness.
Disorientation Stage 2 Emotional Expressions: DS2 Imprecatory Feelings	Feelings associated with imprecatory prayer, inclusive of which are: Dismay and Fear of Humans.
Disorientation Stage 3 Emotional Expressions: DS3 Vow Feelings	Feelings associated with vow prayer, inclusive of which is: Distress / Oppressed in spirit.
Disorientation Stage 4 Emotional Expressions: DS4 Penitential Feelings	Feelings associated with penitential prayer, inclusive of which are: Appallment; Embarrassment and Shame; Distress; Guilt; and Troubled or Conscience-stricken Heart.
Disorientation Stage 7 Emotional Expressions (Death-Related): DS7 Bereavement Feelings	Feelings associated with death, inclusive of which are: Anger/Heartbreak/Shock; Confusion/ Depression; Comfort/Joy/Happiness; Grief; Pain/ Sadness/Sorrow/Listlessness/Guilt/Regret; Stress/ Bogged Down/Mourning.

The fact that there was such a plethora of grief expressions only reaffirms the reality that grief is handled differently by different people. Of course, there were a few expressions that overlapped and thus were considered universal. Despite that, grief is never always processed the same, even by peoples of the same culture. Grief takes time; often longer than one night (Ps 30:6 [5]). As such, the bereaved should be allowed to grieve without being coerced to get over it. Such coercion has the potential to make matters worse, complicating rather than mitigating one's grief. As part of embodying the gospel of God, Christians should endeavor to draw near to those who grieve to grieve *with* them, while also rejoicing with them when they rejoice (Rom 12:15; 1 Cor 12:26). At the same time, however, as was observed in this book, depending on the cultural context, some will *grieve* amidst grief (cf. Eccl 3:4), while others will *rejoice* amidst grief (cf. 2 Cor 6:10; 7:4). Cultural sensitivity is therefore encouraged at *all* times.

Recognizing each of these expressions, however, involved the employment of the *Renewed Form Criticism* in relation to the OT prosaic prayers of disorientation and their auxiliary expressions within the Israelite OT context of distress, and the *Liberative Intercultural Praxis* coupled with the *Hermeneutical Phenomenology* regarding the expressions communicated to/before God amidst grief within both a contemporary Guyanese-Canadian and Vietnamese-Canadian context. As to the operationalization of the *Revisionist Method of Mutual Critical Correlation*, following their discovery, each of these expressions was placed in a dialectic correlation with the others thereby producing expressions that were deemed worthy of mitigating grief. Subsequent to this, through the application of *Ritual Theory*, five compassionate (liberative intercultural) pastoral care practices, couched within rituals, were proposed owing to their potential to mitigate grief making it manageable to sustain the bereaved while restoring their soul (Ps 23:4a [3a]). These were:

1. Bearing the Funeral Expenses of the Poor – Extending Offers of Help
2. Composing and Singing Sad (and Joyful Theopoetic) Songs and Poems of Lament – Finding Emotional Catharsis through Music
3. Incorporating Indigenous Christian Devotional Songs (e.g., Bhajans) in the Wake/Funeral Liturgy – Tapping into the Cultural Liminal Memory of a Deep Experience of Faith
4. Celebrating the Life of the Deceased through Dancing and Singing Upbeat Gospel Songs – Spiritual Rejoicing for Having Arrived Home in Heaven
5. Connecting Personal Grief Stories to God's Sacred Story – Experiencing Hope in the Crucified-yet-Resurrected Christ

It is my hopeful prayer that these five compassionate liberatitive intercultural pastoral care practices for coping with grief, which are couched in ritual, will find a home within our Christian churches where they might be engaged for the purpose of fostering sustainability for those within a life context of grief. While each of these rituals has the potential of becoming "a procrustean bed," according to Ramshaw, "When a religious community is fully alive, its traditional ritual patterns are more like water flowing on land, taking the contours of each particular piece of earth it sinks into, enlivens, and transforms. It is such living water that people need in the desert of grief."[3]

In light of the foregoing work, I proffer a working definition of disorientation. Disorientation can be defined as a distressful situation that encompasses, yet is not limited to, physical pain, psychological anguish, social degradation, and spiritual despondency.[4] Disorientation is also three-dimensional in its anthropological (i.e. human) expressiveness as it incorporates the verbal (e.g., confidence, lament, thanksgiving praise, sharing stories of each other's grief, etc.), the physical (e.g., anointing oneself, burning, burying, worship, etc.), and the emotional (e.g., anger, comfort, guilt, joy, etc.). When viewed from this perspective, not only does disorientation probe the depth-dimension of affliction, but does so with an eye toward compassionate pastoral care responses that mitigate and transform it, and thus sustain the afflicted while restoring their soul.

7.2. Projected Potential Studies Relative to Expressions of Disorientation

Taking into consideration that not all the prosaic sections of the OT wherein disorientation is experienced were examined, a potential study could identify the multifaceted anthropological expressions of disorientation from within such contexts. Another potential study could be the anthropological expressions of disorientation from within the *poetic* portions of the OT where disorientation is experienced. This would further expand the expressive domain of anthropological expressions of disorientation. At the same time, biblical theology could continue to engage in dialectic correlation with pastoral theology examining multiplex anthropological expressions from non-Western cultures (African, Asian, First Nations, etc.). Both differences and similarities in anthropological expressions of disorientation would thus be observed. Subsequently, the universal church of Jesus Christ will continue to learn and employ other additional compassionate pastoral care practices for coping with grief and restoring the soul of the bereaved.

---

3. Ramshaw, "Personalization of Postmodern," 177–178.

4. Here, disorientation is viewed as being synonymous with affliction in its four dimensions as proposed by Zylla (see *Roots of Sorrow*, 54–67).

From a heavenly perspective, the question concerning expressions that *God* has communicated to his people in the midst of his affliction, can be given attention. For example, on several occasions when the children of Israel rebelled against God, Scripture says that God's *emotive* anger burned against his people (Num 12:9; 32:13; Isa 5:25). In Numbers, the consequence of his burning anger resulted in the almost forty years of restless wandering in the wilderness, so that finally, their corpses littered the wilderness (Num 14:32–35; cf. 32:13; Deut 2:7; Ps 107:4). Another example comes from the fact that when God's anger is kindled, he also *verbalizes* that he will forsake his people and even hide his face from them (Deut 31:17–18; cf. Ps 104:29; Isa 8:17).[5] Constructing an expressive domain of divine expressions might help correlate what verbal and physical expressions occur at the elicitation of certain affects.

As I come to the close of this book, I quote this short story concerning the reality and impact of the resurrection of our Lord Jesus Christ.

> An atheist committed disciple of the "truth" of Communism, once gave a speech to an enormous crowd in the former Soviet Union. He mocked the Christian faith, saying it was all mere fantasy. It was not Jesus but the program of Marx and Lenin that was destined to bring history to its appointed purpose. The atheist was eloquent and withering in his scorn for Christianity. When he finished, an Orthodox priest asked if he could say just two words in reply (his two Russian words are translated by three words in English). The priest shouted, "*Christ is risen!*" and the crowd roared back the response carried with them from childhood: "*He is risen indeed!*" For a world so twisted by evil and enslaved by sin, what other message could there be? *Christ is risen*. In the resurrection of Jesus Christ, a new world is dawning. The night of evil has ended. The light of God will fill the whole earth again. The resurrection stands at the center of the Christian faith.[6]

---

5. Interestingly, upon the recognition of their sin, Adam and Eve hide themselves from God (Gen 3:8, 10).

6. Bartholomew and Goheen, *Drama of Scripture*, 165.

Underpinning the confident hope of eternal life for humans deserving of death (Ezek 18:4, 20; Rom 6:23a) is the resurrection of the crucified Christ and the cross of the risen Christ. Christ then is humanity's only living hope (1 Pet 1:3). Death and grief are swallowed up in the resurrection of Christ, so that all who exercise their faith in Christ have died and their lives are now hidden with Christ in God (Col 3:3). When Christ, who is their life, is revealed, then they also will be revealed with him in glory (3:4).[7] In the meantime, grieving Christians can endeavor to sustain other grieving Christians (2 Cor 1:3–4), thus restoring their souls, especially the poor and marginalized, through the instrumentality of bearing their funeral costs, composing and singing sad (and joyful theopoetic) songs and poems of lament, incorporating indigenous Christian devotional songs (e.g., bhajans) into their wake or funeral liturgy, celebrating the life of the deceased through *Kweh-kweh* dancing and singing upbeat gospel songs, and connecting one's personal grief story with God's sacred story (metanarrative). At the same time, consideration should be given to the biblical truth of our present griefs being unworthy of comparison with the future glory to be revealed to us (Rom 8:17–18), even the reflection of the glory of our Lord and Savior Jesus Christ (2 Cor 3:18; 1 John 3:2), when all suffering, death, and grief will be forever reversed and given way to imperishability, immorality, and eternal joy in God's glorious presence (1 Cor 15:50–57; Rev 21:1–4; cf. Ps 16:11). As C. S. Lewis beautifully states,

> He said (in the Bible) that we are "gods" and He is going to make good on His words. If we let Him – for we can prevent Him, if we choose – He will make the feeblest and filthiest of us into a god or goddess, a dazzling, radiant, immortal creature, pulsating all through with such energy and joy and wisdom and love as we cannot now imagine, a bright stainless mirror which reflects back to God perfectly (though, of course, on a smaller scale) His own boundless power and delight and goodness. The process

---

7. To some degree, we might think of this theological truth as a stack of three Russian dolls, which separate at the middle, top from bottom, to reveal a smaller figurine of the same kind inside, which has, in turn, another figurine inside of it. Here, God the Father would be considered as the first or outer figurine, Christ as the inner figurine, and born-again Christians as the second inner figurine.

will be long and in parts very painful, but that is what we are in for. Nothing less. He meant what He said.[8]

With an ever-watchful eye toward this resplendent and holy reality, it is therefore my hopeful and fervent prayer that even in the throes of grief, Christians living within an intercultural society (like that of the Greater Toronto Area) may continue to express themselves legitimately before our triune God verbally, physically, and emotionally, even while adjuring him, saying, *Maranatha! Come, Lord Jesus!* (1 Cor 16:22; Rev 22:20).

---

8. Lewis, *Mere Christianity*, 205–206. Theologically speaking, this is referred to as *Christoformity*, which can be described as the work of the Holy Spirit of God and Christ in conforming the beloved born-again and adopted children of God the Father in heaven to the image of the unique Son of God, the Lord Jesus Christ (Rom 8:29; 1 Cor 15:48–49; 2 Cor 3:18; Gal 4:19; 1 John 3:2), whose character is that of perfect love, joy, peace, patience, kindness, goodness, faithfulness, gentleness, self-control (Gal 5:22–23), etc.

Bibliography

Allen, Leslie C. *Ezra, Nehemiah, Esther*. UBCS. Grand Rapids: Baker, 2003.

Allender, Dan B., and Tremper Longman III. *The Cry of the Soul: How Our Emotions Reveal Our Deepest Questions About God*. Colorado Springs: NavPress, 1994.

Anderson, A. A. *2 Samuel*. WBC 11. Dallas: Word, 1989.

Anderson, Gary A. *A Time to Mourn, A Time to Dance: The Expression of Grief and Joy in Israelite Religion*. University Park: The Pennsylvania State University Press, 1991.

Anderson, Herbert. "The Bible and Pastoral Care." In *The Bible in Pastoral Practice: Readings in the Place and Function of Scripture in the Church*, edited by Paul Ballard and Stephen R. Holmes, 195–211. London: Darton, Longman, and Todd, 2005.

Anderson, Herbert, and Edward Foley. *Mighty Stories, Dangerous Rituals: Weaving Together the Human and the Divine*. San Francisco: Jossey-Bass, 1998.

Anderson, Ray S. *Dancing with Wolves while Feeding the Sheep: Musings of a Maverick Theologian*. Eugene: Wipf & Stock, 2002.

Anshiso, Bekele Deboch. *Jesus's Identification with the Marginalized and the Liminal: The Messianic Identity in Mark*. Carlisle: Langham Academic, 2018.

Arbuckle, Gerald A. *Culture, Inculturation, and Theologians: A Postmodern Critique*. Collegeville: Liturgical Press, 2010.

Arnold, Bill T. *Genesis*. NCBC. New York: Cambridge University Press, 2009.

———. *1 & 2 Samuel*. NIVAC. Grand Rapids: Zondervan, 2003.

Asad, Talal. *Genealogies of Religion: Discipline and Reasons of Power in Christianity and Islam*. Baltimore: Johns Hopkins Press, 1993.

Ashley, Timothy R. *The Book of Numbers*. NICOT. Grand Rapids: Eerdmans, 1993.

Bailey, Lloyd R., Sr. *Biblical Perspectives on Death*. OBT. Philadelphia: Fortress, 1979.

Balentine, Samuel E. *Prayer in the Hebrew Bible: The Drama of Divine-Human Dialogue*. OBT. Minneapolis: Fortress, 1993.

———. "Suffering and Evil." In *NIDB* 5:391.

Bartholomew, Craig G., and Michael W. Goheen. *The Drama of Scripture: Finding Our Place in the Biblical Story*. Grand Rapids: Baker Academic, 2004.

Bass, Clarence B. "Fast, Fasting." In *Baker Encyclopedia of the Bible*, edited by Walter A. Elwell, 2:780–781. Grand Rapids: Baker, 1988.

Bayly, Joseph. *The Last Thing We Talk About: Help and Hope for Those Who Grieve*. Elgin, IL: David C. Cook, 1992.

Beck, Guy. "Religious and Devotional Music: Northern Area." In *South Asia: The Indian Subcontinent: The Garland Encyclopedia of World Music*, edited by Alison Arnold, 246–258. New York: Routledge, 2000.

Becking, Bob. "Review of Mark J. Boda, Praying the Tradition: The Origin and Use of Tradition in Nehemiah 9." *Review of Biblical Literature*, 2000. *http://www. bookreviews.org*.

Beckingham, Paul M. *Walking Towards Hope: Experiencing Grace in a Time of Brokenness*. Pickering: Castle Quay, 2005.

Begbie, Jeremy S. "Faithful Feelings: Music and Emotion in Worship." In *Resonant Witness: Conversations between Music and Theology*. Calvin Institute of Christian Worship Liturgical Studies, edited by Jeremy S. Begbie and Steven R. Guthrie, 323–354. Grand Rapids: Eerdmans, 2011.

———. *Resounding Truth: Christian Wisdom in the World of Music*. London: SPCK, 2007.

Beker, J. Christiaan. *Suffering and Hope: The Biblical Vision and the Human Predicament*. Grand Rapids: Eerdmans, 1994.

Belcher, R. P., Jr. "Suffering." In *Dictionary of the Old Testament: Wisdom, Poetry and Writings*, edited by Tremper Longman III and Peter Enns, 775–781. Downers Grove: InterVarsity, 2008.

Bell, Catherine. *Ritual: Perspectives and Dimensions*. New York: Oxford University Press, 1997.

Bell, John. *The Singing Thing: A Case for Congregational Song*. Chicago: GIA, 2000.

Bellinger, W. H., Jr. *Leviticus, Numbers*. UBCS. Grand Rapids: Baker, 2001.

Bergen Funeral Service Inc. "Funeral Customs of Guyana." No pages. Online: http://bergenfuneralservice.blogspot.com/2013/12/funeral-customs-of-%20 ritan.html.

Bergen, Robert D. *1 & 2 Samuel: An Exegetical and Theological Exposition of Holy Scripture*. NAC 7. Nashville: B&H, 1996.

Billings, J. Todd. *Rejoicing in Lament: Wrestling with Incurable Cancer and Life in Christ*. Grand Rapids: Brazos, 2015.

Billman, Kathleen D., and Daniel L. Migliore. *Rachel's Cry: Prayer of Lament and Rebirth of Hope*. Cleveland: United Church, 1999. Reprint, Eugene, OR: Wipf & Stock, 2006.

Blaiklock, Edward Musgrave. *Kathleen: A Record of a Sorrow*. Grand Rapids: Zondervan, 1980.

Blenkinsopp, Joseph. *Ezra–Nehemiah: A Commentary*. Philadelphia: Westminster, 1988.

Bloch-Smith, Elizabeth. "Burials." In *ABD* 1:785–789.

Block, Daniel I. *Judges, Ruth: An Exegetical and Theological Exposition of Holy Scripture*. NAC 6. Nashville: B&H, 1999.

Blum, Eberhard. "*Formgeschichte* – A Misleading Category? Some Critical Remarks." In *The Changing Face of Form Criticism for the Twenty-First Century*, edited by Marvin A. Sweeney and Ehud Ben Zvi, 32–45. Grand Rapids: Eerdmans, 2003.

Blumenthal, David R. *Facing the Abusing God: A Theology of Protest*. Louisville: Westminster John Knox, 1993.

Bloesch, Donald G. *The Struggle of Prayer*. Colorado Springs: Helmers & Howard, 1988.

Bock, Darrell L. *Luke 9:51 – 24:53*. BECNT. Grand Rapids: Baker Academic, 2008.

Boda, Mark J. *After God's Own Heart: The Gospel According to David*. The Gospel According to the Old Testament. Phillipsburg: P&R, 2007.

———. "Form Criticism in Transition: Penitential Prayer and Lament, *Sitz im Leben* and Form." In *Seeking the Favor of God, Vol. 1: The Origin of Penitential Prayer in Second Temple Judaism*, edited by Mark J. Boda et al., 181–192. SBLEJL 21. Atlanta: SBL; Leiden: Brill, 2006.

———. "Prayer." In *Dictionary of the Old Testament: Historical Books*, edited by Bill T. Arnold and H. G. M. Williamson, 806–811. Downers Grove: InterVarsity, 2012.

———. "Prayer as Rhetoric in the Book of Nehemiah." In *New Perspectives on Ezra-Nehemiah: History and Historiography, Text, Literature, and Interpretation*, edited by Isaac Kalimi, 279–296. Winona Lake: Eisenbrauns, 2012.

———. *The Heartbeat of Old Testament Theology: Three Creedal Expressions*. Grand Rapids: Baker Academic, 2017.

———. *Praying the Tradition: The Origin and Use of Tradition in Nehemiah 9*. BZAW 277. Berlin: de Gruyter, 1999.

———. "'Uttering Precious Rather Than Worthless Words': Divine Patience and Impatience with Lament in Isaiah and Jeremiah." In *Why? . . . How Long? Studies on Voices of Lamentation Rooted in Biblical Hebrew Poetry*, edited by Leann Snow Flesher et al., 83–99. London: Bloomsbury T. & T. Clark, 2014.

———. "Varied and Resplendid Riches: Exploring the Breadth and Depth of Worship in the Psalter." In *Rediscovering Worship: Past, Present, Future*, edited by Wendy J. Porter, 61–82. Eugene: Pickwick, 2015.

———. "Words and Meanings: ידה in Hebrew Research." *WTJ* 57 (1995): 277–297.

Boda, Mark J. and Phil C. Zylla. "A Catalytic Study of the Range of Emotion in Biblical Lament." Paper: Society of Biblical Literature, Bible and Practical Theology, San Antonio, TX, November 2016.

Boling, Robert G. *Joshua: A New Translation with Notes and Commentary.* AYB 6. New Haven: Yale University Press, 2008.

Bonanno, George A., et al. "Trajectories of Grieving." In *Handbook of Bereavement Research and Practice: Advances in Theory and Intervention,* edited by Margaret Stroebe et al., 287–307. Washington: American Psychological Association, 2008.

Bonhoeffer, Dietrich. *Letters and Papers from Prison.* Enlarged ed. Edited by Eberhard Bethge. New York: Touchstone, 1997.

———. *Life Together: The Classic Exploration of Christian Community.* New York: HarperOne, 1954.

———. *Psalms: The Prayer Book of the Bible.* Minneapolis: Augsburg Fortress, 1970.

Bosworth, David A. "Faith and Resilience: King David's Reaction to the Death of Bathsheba's Firstborn." *CBQ* 73 (2010): 691–707.

———. "Understanding Grief and Reading the Bible." In *Mixed Feelings and Vexed Passions: Exploring Emotions in Biblical Literature,* edited by F. Scott Spencer, 117–138. Atlanta: SBL, 2017.

Bowlby, John. *Attachment and Loss, Vol. III: Loss, Sadness, and Depression.* New York: Basic, 1980.

Breneman, Mervin. *Ezra, Nehemiah, Esther: An Exegetical and Theological Exposition of Holy Scripture.* NAC 10. Nashville: B&H, 1993.

Brichto, Herbert. "Kin, Cult, Land, and Afterlife – A Biblical Complex." *Hebrew Union College Annual* 44 (1973): 1–54.

Bright, Ruth. "Music Therapy in Grief Resolution." *Bulletin of the Menninger Clinic* 64 (1999): 481–498.

Brown, Michael Joseph. "Kneel." In *NIDB* 3:538.

Brown, Sally A. "When Lament Shapes the Sermon." In *Lament: Reclaiming Practices in Pulpit, Pew, and Public Square,* edited by Sally A. Brown and Patrick D. Miller, 27–37. Louisville: Westminster John Knox, 2005.

Brown, Sally A., and Patrick D. Miller, eds. *Lament: Reclaiming Practices in Pulpit, Pew, and Public Square.* Louisville: Westminster John Knox, 2005.

Brown, William P. "Psalms, Book of." In *NIDB* 4:661–680.

Broyles, Craig C. "Lament, Psalms of." In *Dictionary of Old Testament: Wisdom, Poetry, and Writings,* edited by Tremper Longman III and Peter Enns, 385–399. Downers Grove: InterVarsity, 2008.

———. *Psalms.* UBCS. Grand Rapids: Baker, 2012.

Bruce, F. F. *The Gospel of John.* Grand Rapids: Eerdmans, 1983.

Bruckner, James K. *Exodus.* UBCS. Grand Rapids: Baker, 2008.

Brueggemann, Walter. *From Whom No Secrets Are Hid: Introducing the Psalms*, edited by Brent A. Strawn. Louisville: Westminster John Knox, 2014.

———. *Great Prayers of the Old Testament*. Louisville: Westminster John Knox, 2008.

———. "Lament as Antidote to Silence." *Living Pulpit* 11.4 (2002): 24–25.

———. *Praying the Psalms: Engaging Scripture and the Life of the Spirit*. 2nd ed. Eugene, OR: Cascade, 2007.

———. "The Costly Loss of Lament." *JSOT* 11 (1986): 57–71.

———. "The Formfulness of Grief." *Interpretation* 31 (1977): 263–275.

———. *The Message of the Psalms: A Theological Commentary*. Minneapolis: Fortress, 1985.

———. *The Psalms and the Life of Faith*. Edited by Patrick D. Miller. Minneapolis: Fortress, 1995.

———. "Voice as Counter to Violence." *CTJ* 36 (2001): 22–33.

Budd, Philip J. *Numbers*. WBC 5. Dallas: Word, 1984.

Bullock, C. Hassell. *Encountering the Book of Psalms*. Grand Rapids: Baker, 2001.

Burbank, Ray. "Bhajans and Biblical Theology: An Evaluation of the Indigenous Indian Devotional Song Genre's Educational Potential." *Global Forum on Arts and Christian Faith* 6 (2018): A1–A13.

Butler, Trent C. *Joshua*. WBC 7. Dallas: Word, 1984.

Byassee, Jason. *Praise Seeking Understanding: Reading the Psalms with Augustine*. Radical Traditions. Grand Rapids: Eerdmans, 2007.

Cable, Dana G. "Grief in the American Culture." In *Living with Grief: Who We Are, How We Grieve*, edited by Kenneth J. Doka and Joyce D. Davidson, 61–70. New York: Routledge, 1998.

Campbell, Antony F. "Form Criticism's Future." In *The Changing Face of Form Criticism for the Twenty-First Century*, edited by Marvin A. Sweeney and Ehud Ben Zvi, 15–31. Grand Rapids: Eerdmans, 2003.

Campbell, D. Keith. "New Testament Lament in Current Research and Its Implications for American Evangelicals." *JETS* 57 (2014): 757–772.

Capps, Donald. *Biblical Approaches to Pastoral Counseling*. Philadelphia: Westminster, 1981.

———. *Life Cycle Theory and Pastoral Care*. Theology and Pastoral Care. Philadelphia: Fortress, 1983.

Carson, D. A. *The Gospel According to John*. PNTC. Leicester: Apollos, 1991.

Chilton, Bruce. "Altar." In *NIDB* 1:115–119.

Chisholm, Robert B. Jr. *1 & 2 Samuel*. TTCS. Grand Rapids: Baker, 2013.

Chiu, José Enrique Aguilar. *The Psalms: An Introduction*. Mahwah: Paulist, 2014.

Cogan, Mordechai. *I Kings: A New Translation with Introduction and Commentary*. AYB 10. New Haven: Yale University Press, 2001.

Cogan, Mordechai, and Hayim Tadmor. *II Kings: A New Translation with Introduction and Commentary*. AYB 11. New Haven: Yale University Press, 1988.

Cohen, David J. *Why O Lord? Praying Our Sorrows*. Milton Keynes: Paternoster, 2013.

Cole, Allan Hugh, Jr. *Good Mourning: Getting through Your Grief*. Louisville: Westminster John Knox, 2008.

Cole, R. Dennis. *Numbers: An Exegetical and Theological Exposition of Holy Scripture*. NAC 3b. Nashville: B&H, 2000.

———. "Numbers." In *Zondervan Illustrated Bible Backgrounds Commentary: Old Testament, Vol. 1: Genesis, Exodus, Leviticus, Numbers, Deuteronomy*, edited by John H. Walton, 338–417. Grand Rapids: Zondervan, 2009.

Common, Kate. "What Do People Mean by 'Theopoetics'?" n.p. Online: https://artsreligionculture.org/definitions.

Cook, J. A. "Dad's Double Binds: Rethinking Father's Bereavement from a Men's Studies Perspective." *Journal of Contemporary Ethnography* 17 (1988): 285–308.

Coppes, Leonard J. "הָלַל." In *TWOT* 1:217–218.

Corless, Inge B., et al. "Languages of Grief: A Model for Understanding the Expressions of the Bereaved." *Health Psychology and Behavioral Medicine* 2 (2014): 132–143.

Coward, Harold G, and David J. Goa. *Mantra: Hearing the Divine in India*. New York: Columbia University Press, 1996.

Craigie, Peter C., and Marvin E. Tate. *Psalms 1–50*. 2nd ed. WBC 19. Nashville: Thomas Nelson, 2004.

Creswell, John W. *Qualitative Inquiry and Research Design: Choosing Among Five Approaches*. 3rd ed. Thousand Oaks: SAGE, 2013.

Crisp, Roger "Compassion and Beyond." *Ethical Theology and Practice* 11 (2008): 233–246.

Cross, F. L. ed. "Burial Services." In *The Oxford Dictionary of the Christian Church*, 3rd rev. ed., edited by E. A. Livingstone, 255. New York: Oxford University Press, 2005.

deClaissé-Walford, Nancy L. "The Theology of the Imprecatory Psalms." In *Soundings in the Theology of Psalms: Perspectives and Methods in Contemporary Scholarship*, edited by Rolf A. Jacobson, 77–92. Minneapolis: Fortress, 2008.

deClaissé-Walford, Nancy L., et al. *The Book of Psalms*. NICOT. Grand Rapids: Eerdmans, 2014.

Denzin, Norman K. "The Art and Politics of Interpretation." In *A Handbook of Qualitative Research*, edited by Norman K. Denzin and Yvonna S. Lincoln, 500–515. Thousand Oaks: SAGE, 1994.

Derrett, J. Duncan M. *Law in the New Testament*. Eugene: Wipf & Stock, 2005.

DeVries, Simon J. *1 Kings*. WBC 12. Waco: Word, 2003.

Dickie, June F. "Practising Healthy Theology in the Local Church: Lamenting with Those in Pain and Restoring Hope." *Stellenbosch Theological Journal* 7.1 (2021) n.p. http://dx.doi.org/10.17570/stj.2021.v7n1.a3.

Dickson, John. *Life of Jesus: Who He Is and Why He Matters*. Grand Rapids: Zondervan, 2010.

Dillard, Raymond B. *2 Chronicles*. WBC 15. Dallas: Word, 1987.

Doehring, Carrie. *The Practice of Pastoral Care: A Postmodern Approach*. Rev. and Exp. ed. Louisville: Westminster John Knox, 2015.

Doka, Kenneth J., and Joyce D. Davidson, eds. *Living with Grief: Who We Are, How We Grieve*. New York: Routledge, 1998.

Douglas, Mary. *Natural Symbols: Explorations in Cosmology*. London: Barrie and Rockcliff, 1970.

Drakeford, John W., and E. Ray Clendenen. "Grief and Mourning." In *Holman Illustrated Bible Dictionary*, edited by Chad Brand et al., 690–691. Nashville: Holman, 2003.

Duhm, Bernhard L. *The Book of Isaiah Translated and Explained*. 5th ed. Göttingen: Vandenhoeck & Ruprecht, 1968.

Eklund, Rebekah. *Practicing Lament*. Cascade Companions. Eugene: Cascade, 2021.

Ellington, Scott A. *Risking Truth: Reshaping the World through Prayers of Lament*. PTMS 98. Eugene: Pickwick, 2008.

———. "The Costly Loss of Testimony." *Journal of Pentecostal Theology* 8 (2000): 48–59.

Elwell, Walter A., and Philip W. Comfort, eds. "Burnt Offering." In *Tyndale Bible Dictionary*. Wheaton: Tyndale, 2001.

Evans, Mary J. *1 & 2 Samuel*. UBCS. Grand Rapids: Baker, 2000.

Farnell, Brenda. "Techniques of the Body." In *International Encyclopedia of Anthropology*, edited by Hilary Callan, 1–3. West Sussex: Wiley Blackwell, 2018. DOI: 10.1002/9781118924396.wbiea2263.

Fensham, F. Charles. *The Books of Ezra and Nehemiah*. NICOT. Grand Rapids: Eerdmans, 1982.

Ferrell, Betty R., and Nessa Coyle. *The Nature of Suffering and the Goals of Nursing*. New York: Oxford University Press, 2008.

Ferris, P. W., Jr. "Prayer." In *Dictionary of the Old Testament: Prophets*, edited by Mark J. Boda and J. Gordon McConville 583–587. Downers Grove: InterVarsity, 2005.

Firth, David G. *1 & 2 Samuel*. AOTC. Nottingham: Apollos, 2009.

Fisher, Milton C. "Burial, Burial Customs." In *Baker Encyclopedia of the Bible*, edited by Walter A. Elwell, 1:386–389. Grand Rapids: Baker, 1988.

Fløysvik, Ingvar. *When God Becomes My Enemy: The Theology of the Complaint Psalms*. St. Louis: Concordia Academic Press, 1997.

Ford, S. Dennis. *Sins of Omission: A Primer on Moral Indifference*. Philadelphia: Fortress, 1990.

Fowler, Gene. *The Ministry of Lament: Caring for the Bereaved*. St. Louis: Chalice, 2010.

Fretheim, Terence E. *Creation Untamed: The Bible, God, and Natural Disasters*. Grand Rapids: Baker Academic, 2010.

Fritz, Volkmar. *1 & 2 Kings*. A Continental Commentary. Translated by Anselm Hagedorn. Minneapolis: Fortress, 2003.

Futato, Mark D. *Interpreting the Psalms: An Exegetical Handbook*. Handbooks for Old Testament Exegesis. Grand Rapids: Kregel, 2007.

———. *Joy Comes in the Morning: Psalms for All Seasons*. Phillipsburg: P&R, 2004.

Garrett, Greg. *Stories from the Edge: A Theology of Grief*. Louisville: Westminster John Knox, 2008.

Geertz, Clifford. *After the Fact*. Cambridge: Harvard University Press, 1995.

———. *The Interpretation of Cultures: Selected Essays by Clifford Geertz*. New York: Basic, 1973.

Gerstenberger, Erhard S. *Psalms: Part 1 with an Introduction to Cultic Poetry*. FOTL 14. Grand Rapids: Eerdmans, 1987.

Gibbs, Jason. "Nhac Tien Chien: The Origins of Vietnamese Popular Song." n.p. Online: http://thingsasian.com/story/nhac-tien-chien-origins-vietnamese-popular-song#note22.

Goldingay, John. *Psalms, Vol: 1: Psalms 1–41*. Baker Commentary on the Old Testament Wisdom and Psalms. Grand Rapids: Baker Academic, 2006.

Graham, Elaine L. *Transforming Practice: Pastoral Theology in an Age of Uncertainty*. London: Mowbray, 1996.

Green, Joel B. "Mourning." In *NIDB* 4:161–162.

Greenberg, Moshe. *Biblical Prose Prayer: As a Window to the Popular Religion of Ancient Israel*. Berkeley: University of California Press, 1983. Reprint, Eugene: Wipf & Stock, 2008.

Gregory, T. M. "Mourning." In *ZPEB* 4:302–307.

Grenz, Stanley J. *Prayer: The Cry for the Kingdom*. Rev ed. Grand Rapids: Eerdmans, 2005.

Grollman, Earl A. "What You Always Wanted to Know About Your Jewish Clients' Perspectives Concerning Death and Dying – But were Afraid to Ask." In *Living with Grief: Who We Are, How We Grieve*, edited by Kenneth J. Doka and Joyce D. Davidson, 27–37. New York: Routledge, 1998.

Gunkel, Hermann. *The Psalms: A Form-Critical Introduction*. Translated by Thomas M. Horner. Biblical Series 19. Philadelphia: Fortress, 1967.

Gunkel, Hermann, and Joachim Begrich. *An Introduction to the Psalms: The Genres of the Religious Lyric of Israel*. Mercer Library of Biblical Studies. Macon: Mercer University Press, 1998.

Gutiérrez, Gustavo. *A Theology of Liberation: History, Politics, and Salvation*. Translated by Matthew J. O'Connell. 15th Ann. ed. Maryknoll: Orbis, 1988.

————. *On Job: God-Talk and the Suffering of the Innocent*. Translated by Matthew J. O'Connell. Maryknoll: Orbis, 1987.

Hale, Christopher D. "Reclaiming the Bhajan: Ancient Music Styles of India Transform Modern Worship of Christ." *Mission Frontiers* 23 (2001): 16–17.

Hamilton, Victor P. *The Book of Genesis: Chapters 1–17*. NICOT. Grand Rapids: Eerdmans, 1990.

————. *The Book of Genesis: Chapters 18–50*. NICOT. Grand Rapids: Eerdmans, 1995.

Harasta, Eva, and Brian Brock, eds. *Evoking Lament: A Theological Discussion*. London: T. & T. Clark, 2009.

Harper, G. Geoffrey, and Kit Barker, eds. *Finding Lost Words: The Church's Right to Lament*. ACTM. Eugene: Wipf & Stock, 2017.

Harrichand, James J. S. "Recovering the Language of Lament for the Western Evangelical Church: A Survey of the Psalms of Lament and their Appropriation within Pastoral Theology." *MJTM* 16 (2014–15): 101–130.

Harrington, Hannah K. *The Books of Ezra and Nehemiah*. NICOT. Grand Rapids: Eerdmans, 2022.

Hartley, John E. *Genesis*. UBCS. Grand Rapids: Baker, 2000.

Hauerwas, Stanley. *Naming the Silences: God, Medicine, and the Problem of Suffering*. London: T. & T. Clark, 1993.

Herr, Larry G. "Sackcloth." In *ISBE* 4:256.

Heschel, Abraham J. *The Prophets: An Introduction*. New York: Harper & Row, 1962.

Hess, Richard S. "Joshua." In *Zondervan Illustrated Bible Backgrounds Commentary: Old Testament, Vol. 2: Joshua, Judges, Ruth, 1 & 2 Samuel*, edited by John H. Walton, 2–93. Grand Rapids: Zondervan, 2009.

Hill, Andrew E. *1 & 2 Chronicles*. NIVAC. Grand Rapids: Zondervan, 2003.

Hoang, Dieu-Hien T. "Death Rituals in Vietnamese Society." n.p. Online: http://webs01.hsl.washington.edu/clinical/end-of-life/death-in-viet.

Hobbs, T. R. *2 Kings*. WBC 13. Dallas: Word, 1985.

Holladay, William L. *The Psalms through Three Thousand Years: Prayerbook of a Cloud of Witnesses*. Minneapolis: Augsburg Fortress, 1995.

Hopkins, Denise Dombkowski. *Journey through The Psalms*. Rev. and Exp. ed. St. Louis: Chalice, 2002.

Hopkins, Denise Dombkowski, and Michael S. Koppel. *Grounded in the Living Word: The Old Testament and Pastoral Care Practices*. Grand Rapids: Eerdmans, 2010.

House, Paul R. *1, 2 Kings: An Exegetical and Theological Exposition of Holy Scripture*. NAC 8. Nashville: B&H, 1995.

Hovda, Robert W. *Dry Bones*. Living Worship Guides to Good Liturgy. Washington, DC: Liturgical Conference, 1979.

Howard, David M., Jr. *Joshua: An Exegetical and Theological Exposition of Holy Scripture*. NAC 5. Nashville: B&H, 1998.

Hubbard, Robert L., Jr. *Joshua*. NIVAC. Grand Rapids: Zondervan, 2009.

———. *Ruth*. NICOT. Grand Rapids: Eerdmans, 1988.

Idestrom, Rebecca G. S. "Habakkuk." In *The Book of the Twelve: A Pentecostal Commentary*, edited by John Christopher Thomas, 409–453. Pentecostal Commentary Series. Leiden: Brill, 2020.

Imes, Carmen Joy. *Bearing God's Name: Why Sinai Still Matters*. Downers Grove: IVP Academic, 2019.

Ince-Carvalhal, Lorraine. "The Unfortunate Reality of Grieving." n.p. Online: https://guyanatimesgy.com/the-unfortunate-reality-of-grieving/.

Irish, Donald P. "Multiculturalism and the Majority Population." In *Ethnic Variations in Dying, Death, and Grief: Diversity in Universality*, edited by Donald P. Irish et al., 1–10. Washington: Taylor & Francis, 1993.

Irish, Donald P., et al. *Ethnic Variations in Dying, Death, and Grief: Diversity in Universality*. Washington: Taylor & Francis, 1993.

Jacobson, Rolf A. "Burning Our Lamps with Borrowed Oil: The Liturgical Use of the Psalms and the Life of Faith." In *Psalms and Practice: Worship, Virtue, and Authority*, edited by Stephen Breck Reid, 90–98. Collegeville: Liturgical, 2001.

Jones, Logan C. "The Psalms of Lament and the Transformation of Sorrow." *Journal of Pastoral Care & Counselling* 61 (2007): 47–58. DOI: 10.1177/154230500706100106.

Jonker, Louis C. *1 & 2 Chronicles*. UBCS. Grand Rapids: Baker, 2013.

Jung, K. J. "Rachel's Tomb." In *ISBE* 4:32.

Kaiser, Walter C., Jr. *I Will Lift My Eyes unto the Hills: Learning from the Great Prayers of the Old Testament*. Wooster: Weaver, 2015.

Kazen, Thomas. "Disgust in Body, Mind, and Language: The Case of Impurity in the Hebrew Bible. In *Mixed Feelings and Vexed Passions: Exploring Emotions in Biblical Literature*, edited by F. Scott Spencer, 97–115. Atlanta: SBL, 2017.

Kedar-Kopfstein, Benjamin. "דם." In *TDOT* 3:237–238.

Keefe-Perry, L. B. C. "Theopoetics: Process and Perspective." *Christianity and Literature* 58 (2009): 579–601.

Keller, Timothy. *On Death*. New York: Penguin, 2020.

Khoshaba, Deborah. "About Complicated Bereavement Disorder." n.p. Online: https://www.psychologytoday.com/ca/blog/get-hardy/201309/about-complicated-bereavement-disorder-0.

Kim, Matthew D. *Preaching with Cultural Intelligence: Understanding the People Who Hear Our Sermons*. Grand Rapids: Baker Academic, 2017.

King, Philip J., and Lawrence E. Stager. *Life in Biblical Israel*. Library of Ancient Israel. Louisville: Westminster John Knox, 2001.

Kitchen, K. A. "Burial and Mourning." In *The New Bible Dictionary*, 3rd ed., edited by D. R. W. Wood, 149–150. Downers Grove: InterVarsity, 1996.

Klein, Ralph W. *2 Chronicles: A Commentary*. Hermeneia. Minneapolis: Fortress, 2012.

Kleinman, Arthur. *Social Origins of Distress and Disease: Depression, Neurasthenia, and Pain in Modern China*. New Haven: Yale University Press, 1986.

Konkel, August H. *1 & 2 Kings*. NIVAC. Grand Rapids: Zondervan, 2006.

LaCocque, André. *Ruth*. Translated by K. C. Hanson. A Continental Commentary. Minneapolis: Fortress, 2004.

Laderman, Gary. *Rest in Peace: A Cultural History of Death and the Funeral Home in Twentieth-Century America*. New York: Oxford University Press, 2003.

Lam, Minh Van. *God's Miracles: His Faith, and His Escape from Vietnam by Boat*. Bloomington: WestBow, 2016.

Lamb, David T. *God Behaving Badly: Is the God of the Old Testament Angry, Sexist and Racist?* Exp. ed. Downers Grove: InterVarsity, 2022.

LaMothe, Kimerer. "Dancing in the Face of Death: 'Santuario' and the Pulse Nightclub Shootings. n.p. Online: https://www.psychologytoday.com/us/blog/what-body-knows/201703/dancing-in-the-face-death.

Lane, Patty. *A Beginner's Guide to Crossing Cultures: Making Friends in a Multicultural World*. Downers Grove: InterVarsity, 2002.

LaNeel Tanner, Beth. "How Long, O Lord! Will Your People Suffer in Silence Forever?" In *Psalms and Practice: Worship, Virtue, and Authority*, edited by Stephen Breck Reid, 143–152. Collegeville: Liturgical, 2001.

Lartey, Emmanuel Y. *In Living Color: An Intercultural Approach to Pastoral Care and Counseling*. 2nd ed. London: Jessica Kingsley, 2003.

———. *Pastoral Theology in an Intercultural World*. London: Epworth, 2006. Reprint, Eugene:Wipf & Stock, 2013.

———. *Postcolonializing God: New Perspectives on Pastoral and Practical Theology*. London: SCM, 2013.

———. "Postcolonializing Pastoral Theology: Enhancing the Intercultural Paradigm." In *Pastoral Theology and Care: Critical Trajectories in Theory and Practice*, edited by Nancy J. Ramsay, 79–97. West Sussex: Wiley Blackwell, 2018.

Lemche, N. P. *The Canaanites and Their Land,* JSOTSup 110. Sheffield: Sheffield Academic, 1991.

Lemcio, Eugene E. "The Story's Conclusion: The Revelation to John." In *A Compact Guide to the Whole Bible*, edited by Robert W. Wall and David R. Nienhuis, 137–148. Grand Rapids: Baker Academic, 2015.

Leung Lai, Barbara M. "The Costly Loss of Lament and Protest: Toward a Biblical Theology of Lament and Protest (Psalm 44)." In *Between the Lectern and the Pulpit: Essays in Honour of Victor A. Shepherd*, edited by Rob Clements and Dennis Ngien, 281–291. Vancouver: Regent College Publishing, 2014.

Lewis, C. S. *A Grief Observed*. London: Faber and Faber, 1961.

———. *Mere Christianity*. New York: HarperCollins, 2001.

———. *Reflections on the Psalms*. New York: HarperCollins, 2017.

Li, Jie. "Guilt in Bereavement: Review and Conceptual Framework." *Death Studies* 38 (2014): 165–171.

Littlewood, Jane. *Aspects of Grief: Bereavement in Adult Life*. London: Routledge, 1992.

Lochtefeld, James G. *The Illustrated Encyclopedia of Hinduism, Vol. 1: A–M*. New York: Rosen, 2002.

Long, V. Philips. "2 Samuel." In *Zondervan Illustrated Bible Backgrounds Commentary: Old Testament, Vol. 2: Joshua, Judges, Ruth, 1 & 2 Samuel*, edited by John H. Walton, 412–492. Grand Rapids: Zondervan, 2009.

Longman, Tremper, III. *How to Read the Psalms*. Downers Grove: IVP Academic, 1988.

———. *Psalms: An Introduction and Commentary*. TOTC 15–16. Downers Grove: IVP Academic, 2014.

———. *The Fear of the Lord is Wisdom: A Theological Introduction to Wisdom in Israel*. Grand Rapids: Baker Academic, 2017.

Luthar, Suniya S., and Laurel B. Zelazo. "Research and Resilience: An Integrative Review. In *Resilience and Vulnerability: Adaptation in the Context of Childhood Adversities*, edited by Suniya S. Luthar, 510–550. New York: Cambridge University Press, 2003.

Luther, Martin. "Preface to Georg Rhau's Symphoniae Iucundae." In *Luther's Works, Vol. 53: Liturgy and Hymns*, edited by Ulrich S. Leupold, 321–324. Philadelphia: Fortress, 1965.

Lynch, Peter. "Tested by Practice." In *An Introduction to Catholic Theology*, edited by Richard Lennan, 164–183. Mahwah: Paulist, 1998.

MacIntyre, Alasdair. *After Virtue: A Study in Moral Theory*. 3rd ed. Notre Dame: University of Notre Dame, 2007.

Madigan, Kevin J., and Jon D. Levenson. *Resurrection: The Power of God for Christians and Jews*. New Haven: Yale University Press, 2008.

Mathews, Kenneth A. *Genesis 11:27 – 50:26*. NAC 1B. Nashville: B&H, 2005.

Mauss, Marcel. "Techniques of the Body." In *Sociology and Psychology: Essays by Marcel Mauss*, translated by B. Brewster, 95–135. London: Routledge & Kegan Paul, 1979.

Mayeroff, Milton. *On Caring*. New York: Harper Perennial, 1990.

McBride, J. LeBron. *Spiritual Crisis: Surviving Trauma to the Soul*. New York: Routledge, 2009.

McCann, J. Clinton. "Prayer and Activity: Vengeance, Catharsis, and Compassion." In *A Theological Introduction to the Book of Psalms: The Psalms as Torah*, 112–126. Nashville: Abingdon, 1993.

McCarter, P. Kyle, Jr. *II Samuel: A New Translation with Introduction, Notes, and Commentary*. AYB 9. New Haven: Yale University Press, 1984.

McComiskey, Thomas E. "זָכַר." In *TWOT* 1:241–243.

McCutchan, Stephen P. "Illuminating the Dark: Using the Psalms of Lament." *Christian Ministry* 24 (1993): 14–17.

McGrath, Alister E. *Christian Theology: An Introduction*. 25th Ann. ed. West Sussex: Wiley Blackwell, 2017.

Meninger, William. "Aspects of Prayer." In *Word and Spirit: A Monastic Review*. Number 1, *In Honor of Saint Basil the Great*, 147–149. Still River: St. Bede's, 1979.

Merleau-Ponty, Maurice, J. J. *Phenomenology of Perception*. Translated by Colin Smith. India: Motilal Banarsidass, 1995.

Merrill, Nan C. *Psalms for Praying: An Invitation to Wholeness*. 10th Ann. ed. London: Bloomsbury, 2016.

Milgrom, Jacob. *Leviticus 1–16: A New Translation with Introduction and Commentary*. AYB 3. New Haven: Doubleday, 1991.

———. *Numbers*. The JPS Torah Commentary. Philadelphia: Jewish Publication Society, 1989.

Millar, J. Gary. *Calling on the Name of the Lord: A Biblical Theology of Prayer*. NSBT 38. London: Apollos, 2016.

Miller, Douglas L. "Funeral Customs." In *Baker Encyclopedia of the Bible*, edited by Walter A. Elwell, 1:820–821. Grand Rapids: Baker, 1988.

Miller, Patrick D. "Heaven's Prisoners: The Lament as Christian Prayer." In *Lament: Reclaiming Practices in Pulpit, Pew, and Public Square*, edited by Sally A. Brown and Patrick D. Miller, 15–26. Louisville: Westminster John Knox, 2005.

———. *Interpreting the Psalms*. Philadelphia: Fortress, 1986.

———. *They Cried to the Lord: The Form and Theology of Biblical Prayer*. Minneapolis: Fortress, 1994.

Mortari, Luigina. "The Ethic of Delicacy in Phenomenological Research." *International Journal of Qualitative Studies on Health and Well-Being* 3 (2008): 3–17.

Moltmann, Jürgen. *Experiences of God*. Philadelphia: Fortress, 1980.

———. *The Crucified God: The Cross of Christ as the Foundation and Criticism of Christian Theology*. Translated by R. A. Wilson and John Bowden. Minneapolis: Fortress, 1993.

Morganthaler, Sally. *Worship Evangelism: Inviting Unbelievers into the Presence of God*. Grand Rapids: Zondervan, 1999.

Mowinckel, Sigmund. *The Psalms in Israel's Worship*. Trans. D. R. Ap-Thomas. 3rd ed. Grand Rapids: Eerdmans, 2004.

Muck, Terry. "*Psalm*, Bhajan, *and* Kirtan." In *Psalms and Practice: Worship, Virtue, and Authority*, edited by Stephen Breck Reid, 7–27. Collegeville, MN: Liturgical, 2001.

Muddiman, John. "Fast, Fasting." In *ABD* 2:773–74.

Muraoka, Takamitsu. "1 Sam 1,15 Again." *Biblica* 77 (1996): 98–99.

Murray, Henry A., and Clyde Kluckhohn. *Personality in Nature, Society, and Culture*. New York: Alfred A. Knopf, 1948.

Myers, Jacob M. *Ezra, Nehemiah: Introduction, Translation, and Notes*. AYB 17. New Haven: Yale University Press, 1965.

———. *II Chronicles: Introduction, Translation, and Notes*. AYB 13. New York: Doubleday, 1965.

Nehrbass, Daniel Michael. *Praying Curses: The Therapeutic and Preaching Value of the Imprecatory Psalms*. Eugene: Pickwick, 2013.

Nelsen, Vivian Jenkins. "One Woman's Interracial Journey." In *Ethnic Variations in Dying, Death, and Grief: Diversity in Universality*, edited by Donald P. Irish et al., 21–27. Washington: Taylor & Francis, 1993.

Nelson, Judith Kay. *Seeing Through Tears: Crying and Attachment*. New York: Routledge, 2005.

Newbigin, Lesslie. *The Gospel in a Pluralist Society*. Grand Rapids: Eerdmans, 1989.

New GPC Inc. "Limacol." n.p. Online: http://limacol.com/limacol.php.

Newman, Judith H. "Prayer." In *NIDB* 4:579–89.

———. *Praying by the Book: The Scripturalization of Prayer in Second Temple Judaism*. SBLEJL 14. Atlanta: Scholars, 1999.

Ngien, Dennis. *Fruit for the Soul: Luther on the Lament Psalms*. Minneapolis: Fortress, 2015.

Nichols, Stephen J. *Welcome to the Story: Reading, Loving, and Living God's Word*. Wheaton: Crossway, 2011.

Nouwen, Henri J. M. *A Letter of Consolation*. New York: Harper & Row, 1982.

———. *The Wounded Healer: Ministry in Contemporary Society*. New York: Doubleday, 1972; Reprint, New York: Image, 1979.

Oates, Wayne E. *Grief, Transition, and Loss: A Pastor's Practical Guide*. Creative Pastoral Care and Counseling. Minneapolis: Fortress, 1997.

Olyan, Saul M. *Biblical Mourning: Ritual and Social Dimensions*. New York: Oxford University Press, 2004.

Omanson, Roger L., and John Ellington. *A Handbook on the First and Second Books of Samuel*. New York: United Bible Societies, 2001.

Orloff, Judith. "The Health Benefits of Tears: Learn How Tears Can Benefit You and Improve Your Health." n.p. Online: https://www.psychologytoday.com/us/blog/emotional-freedom/201007/the-health-benefits-tears.

Ortlund, Eric N. *Suffering Wisely and Well: The Grief of Job and the Grace of God*. Wheaton: Crossway, 2022.

Ortner, Sherry, ed. *The Fate of "Culture": Geertz and Beyond*. Berkeley: University of California Press, 1999.

Oswalt, John N. "בָּרַךְ." In *TWOT* 1:132–133.

———. *The Book of Isaiah: Chapters 1–39*. NICOT. Grand Rapids: Eerdmans, 1986.

Parunak, H. D. V. "A Semantic Survey of *NHM*." *Biblica* 56 (1975): 512–532.

Patton, Corrine L. "From Heroic Individual to Nameless Victim: Women in the Social World of the Judges." In *Biblical and Humane: A Festschrift for John F. Priest*, edited by Linda Bennet Elder et al., 33–46. Scholars Press Homage Series 20. Atlanta: Scholars, 1996.

Patton, John H. *From Ministry to Theology: Pastoral Action & Reflection*. Eugene: Wipf & Stock, 2009.

Payne, J. Barton. "Burial." In *ISBE* 1:556–561.

Pemberton, Glen. *After Lament: Psalms for Learning to Trust Again*. Abilene: Abilene Christian University Press, 2014.

———. *Hurting with God: Learning to Lament with the Psalms*. Abilene: Abilene Christian University Press, 2012.

Perrine, Laurence. *Sound and Sense: An Introduction to Poetry*. 4th ed. New York: Harcourt, 1973.

Perry, Hosea L. "Mourning and Funeral Customs of African Americans." In *Ethnic Variations in Dying, Death, and Grief: Diversity in Universality*, edited by Donald P. Irish et al., 51–65. Washington: Taylor & Francis, 1993.

Peterman, Gerald W., and Andrew J. Schmutzer. *Between Pain and Grace: A Biblical Theology of Suffering*. Chicago: Moody, 2016.

Petter, Donna, and Thomas Petter. *Ezra–Nehemiah*. NIVAC. Grand Rapids: Zondervan, 2021.

Pham, Xuan Huong Thi. *Mourning in the Ancient Near East and the Hebrew Bible*. JSOTSup 302. Sheffield: Sheffield Academic Press, 1999.

Provan, Iain W. *1 & 2 Kings*. UBCS. Grand Rapids: Baker, 1995.

Ramshaw, Elaine J. *Ritual and Pastoral Care*. Theology and Pastoral Care. Minneapolis: Fortress, 1987.

———. "Singing at Funerals and Memorial Services." *Currents in Theology and Mission* 35 (2008): 206–215.

———. "The Personalization of Postmodern Post-Mortem Rituals." *Pastoral Psychology* 59 (2010): 171–178.

Ramshaw, Gail. "The Place of Lament within Praise: Theses for Discussion." *Worship* 61 (1987): 317–322.

Rando, Therese A. *Treatment of Complicated Mourning*. Champaign, IL: Research, 1993.

Resner, Andre. "Lament: Faith's Response to Loss." *Restoration Quarterly* 32 (1990): 129–142.

Richards-Greaves, Gillian. "Come to My 'Kwe-Kwe': African Guyanese Ritual Music and the Construction of a Secondary Diaspora in New York City." *The World of Music* 4 (2015): 83–97.

———. "[Re]Constructing 'Home' in the USA through African-Guyanese Ritual." *CeTEAL Newsletter* n.v. (2015): 2–3.

Robinson, Thomas A., and Hillary P. Rodrigues. *World Religions: A Guide to the Essentials*. 2nd ed. Grand Rapids: Baker Academic, 2014.

Ross, Allen P. *A Commentary on the Psalms: Vol. 1 (1–41)*. Kregel Exegetical Library. Grand Rapids: Kregel Academic & Professional, 2011.

Sailhamer, John H. "Genesis." In *The Expositor's Bible Commentary, Vol. 1: Genesis–Leviticus*, edited by Tremper Longman III and David E. Garland, 21–332. Grand Rapids: Zondervan, 2009.

Sanders, J. Oswald. *Facing Loneliness: The Starting Point of a New Journey*. Grand Rapids: Discover House, 1990.

Sarna, Nahum M. *Genesis*. The JPS Torah Commentary. Philadelphia: Jewish Publication Society, 1989.

———. *Exodus*. The JPS Torah Commentary. Philadelphia: Jewish Publication Society, 1991.

Scalise, P. J. "Rachel." In *ISBE* 4:31–32.

Scazzero, Peter. *Emotionally Healthy Spirituality: Unleash A Revolution in Your Life in Christ*. Nashville: Thomas Nelson, 2006.

Schapira, Lidia. "Communication at the End of Life." *Journal of Oncology Practice* 4 (2008) 54, DOI: 10.1200/JOP.08215501.

Schultz, S. J., and G. L. Knapp. "Postures; Attitudes." In *ISBE* 3:911–12.

Seecharan, Clem. "Guyana." n.p. Online: https://www.everyculture.com/Ge-It/Guyana.html.

Sharma, T. R. "Psychological Analysis of Bhakti." In *Love Divine: Studies in Bhakti and Devotional Mysticism*, edited by Karel Werner, 85–95. Durham Indological Series 3. New York: Routledge, 2013.

Sharp, Melinda McGarrah. "Globalization, Colonialism, and Postcolonialism." In *The Wiley Blackwell Companion to Practical Theology*, edited by Bonnie J. Miller-McLemore, 422–431. West Sussex: Wiley Blackwell, 2014.

Sherbino, David. *Re:Connect: Spiritual Exercises to Develop Intimacy with God*. Pickering: Castle Quay, 2013.

Shipp, R. Mark. *Timeless: Ancient Psalms for the Church Today, Vol. 1: In the Day of Distress: Psalms 1–41*. Abilene: Abilene Christian University Press, 2011.

Sire, James W. *The Universe Next Door: A Basic World Catalog*. 6th ed. Downers Grove: IVP Academic, 2020.

Slotki, Judah J. *Daniel, Ezra and Nehemiah*. London: Soncino, 1951.

Smith, Robert S. "Belting Out the Blues as Believers: The Importance of Singing Lament." *Themelios* 42 (2017): 89–111.

Soelle, Dorothee. *Suffering*. Translated by Everett R. Kalin. Philadelphia: Fortress, 1975.

Soll, William M. "The Israelite Lament: Faith Seeking Understanding." *Quarterly Review* 8 (1988): 77–88.

Sparks, Kenton L. "Form Criticism." In *Dictionary of Biblical Criticism and Interpretation*, edited by Stanley E. Porter, 111–113. New York: Routledge, 2009.

Staudacher, Carol. *Men and Grief: A Guide for Men Surviving the Death of a Loved One: A Resource for Caregivers and Mental Health Professionals*. Oakland, CA: New Harbinger, 1991.

Stenhouse, Tara J. "The Psalms of Lament in the Experience of Suffering Christians." In *Stirred by a Noble Theme: The Book of Psalms in the Life of the Church*, edited by Andrew G. Shead, 181–204. Nottingham: Apollos, 2013.

Stott, John R. W. *The Cross of Christ*. Study Guide Edition. Downers Grove: InterVarsity, 2006.

Stroebe, Margaret et al. "Guilt in Bereavement: The Role of Self-blame and Regret in Coping with Loss." *PLoS One* 9 (2014) e96606. DOI: 10.1371/journal. pone.0096606.

Swanson, James A. *A Dictionary of Biblical Languages: Hebrew Old Testament*. 2nd ed. Bellingham: Logos, 2001.

Sweeney, Marvin A. "Form Criticism." In *Dictionary of the Old Testament: Wisdom, Poetry, and Writings*, edited by Tremper Longman III and Peter Enns, 227–241. Downers Grove: InterVarsity, 2008.

Sweeney, Marvin A., and Ehud Ben Zvi, editors. *The Changing Face of Form Criticism for the Twenty-First Century*. Grand Rapids: Eerdmans, 2003.

Swinton, John. *Raging with Compassion: Pastoral Responses to the Problem of Evil*. Grand Rapids: Eerdmans, 2007.

———. "Researching Personal Experience." In *Practical Theology and Qualitative Research*, edited by John Swinton and Harriet Mowat, 101–132. London: SCM, 2006.

———. *Finding Jesus in the Storm: The Spiritual Lives of Christians with Mental Health Challenges*. Grand Rapids: Eerdmans, 2020.

Swinton, John, and Harriet Mowat. *Practical Theology and Qualitative Research*. London: SCM, 2006.

The Editors of the Encyclopaedia Britannica. "Burial: Death Rite." n.p. Online: https://www.britannica.com/topic/burial-death-rite.

Thiselton, Anthony C. *Systematic Theology*. Grand Rapids: Eerdmans, 2015.

Thomas, John C., and Gary R. Habermas. *Enduring Your Season of Suffering*. Lynchburg, VA: Liberty University Press, 2011.

Thompson, J. A. *1, 2 Chronicles: An Exegetical and Theological Exposition of Holy Scripture*. NAC 9. Nashville: B&H, 1994.

Toffelmire, Colin M. "Form Criticism." In *Dictionary of the Old Testament: Prophets*, edited by Mark J. Boda and J. Gordon McConville, 257–271. Downers Grove: InterVarsity, 2012.

Tracy, David. *Blessed Rage of Order: The New Pluralism in Theology*. Chicago: University of Chicago Press, 1996.

Tsumura, David Toshio. *The First Book of Samuel*. NICOT. Grand Rapids: Eerdmans, 2006.

———. *The Second Book of Samuel*. NICOT. Grand Rapids: Eerdmans, 2019.

Tucker, Gene M. *Form Criticism of the Old Testament*. Guides to Biblical Scholarship. Philadelphia: Fortress, 1971.

Anonymous UCA News reporter. "Vietnamese Bishops Issue Guidelines on Ancestor Veneration." n.p. Online: https://www.ucanews.com/news/vietnamese-bishops-issue-guidelines-on-ancestor-veneration/86469.

Vanderkam, James C. "Feasts and Fasts." In *NIDB* 2:443–47.

van Manen, Max. *Researching Lived Experience: Human Science for an Action Sensitive Pedagogy*. 2nd ed. Edmonton: Althouse, 1997.

van Tongeren, Louis. "Individualizing Ritual: The Personal Dimension in Funeral Liturgy." *Worship* 78 (2004): 117–138.

van Wolde, Ellen. "Sentiments as Culturally Constructed Emotions: Anger and Love in the Hebrew Bible." *Biblical Interpretation* 16 (2008): 1–24.

Vieira, Caitlin. "Grieving and Mental Health." n.p. Online: https://guyanachronicle.com/2018/07/21/grieving-and-mental-health/.

Villanueva, Federico G. *It's OK to Be Not OK. Preaching the Lament Psalms*. Carlisle: Langham Preaching Resources, 2017.

———. "Preaching Lament." In *Reclaiming the Old Testament for Christian Preaching*, edited by Grenville J. R. Kent et al., 64–84. Downers Grove: IVP Academic, 2010.

———. *The 'Uncertainty of a Hearing': A Study of the Sudden Change of Mood in the Psalms of Lament*. VTSS 121. Leiden: Brill, 2008.

Vitelli, Romeo. "Can Rituals Help Us Deal with Grief? Using Rituals Can Be More Effective in Controlling Grief Than You Think." n.p. Online: https://www.

psychologytoday.com/ca/blog/media-spotlight/201403/can-rituals-help-us-deal-grief.

Volf, Miroslav. *Exclusion and Embrace: A Theological Exploration of Identity, Otherness, and Reconciliation*. Nashville: Abingdon, 1996.

Walton, John H. "Genesis." In *Zondervan Illustrated Bible Backgrounds Commentary: Old Testament, Vol. 1: Genesis, Exodus, Leviticus, Numbers, Deuteronomy*, edited by John H. Walton, 2–159. Grand Rapids: Zondervan, 2009.

Watts, John D. W. *Isaiah 1–33*. WBC 24. Nashville: Thomas Nelson, 2005.

Webb, Barry G. *The Book of Judges*. NICOT. Grand Rapids: Eerdmans, 2012.

Weems, Ann. *Psalms of Lament*. Louisville: Westminster John Knox, 1995.

Weil, Simone. *Awaiting God*. Abbotsford: Fresh Wind, 2012.

———. *Gravity and Grace*. New York: G. P. Putnam's Sons, 2007.

Wenham, Gordon J. *Genesis 16–50*. WBC 2. Waco: Word, 1994.

———. *Psalms as Torah: Reading Biblical Song Ethically*. Studies in Theological Interpretation. Grand Rapids: Baker Academic, 2012.

———. *The Book of Leviticus*. NICOT. Grand Rapids: Eerdmans, 1979.

———. *The Psalter Reclaimed: Praying and Praising with the Psalms*. Wheaton: Crossway, 2013.

Westerhoff, John. *Spiritual Life: The Foundation for Preaching and Teaching*. Louisville: Westminster John Knox, 1994.

Westermann, Claus. *Genesis 37–50*. Translated by John J. Scullion. A Continental Commentary. Minneapolis: Fortress, 2002.

———. *Praise and Lament in the Psalms*. Translated by Keith R. Crim and Richard N. Soulen. Atlanta: John Knox, 1981.

———. *The Living Psalms*. Translated by J. R. Porter. Grand Rapids: Eerdmans, 1989.

———. *The Psalms: Structure, Content, and Message*. Translated by Ralph D. Gehrke. Minneapolis: Fortress, 1980.

Whitbourne, Susan Krauss. "The Definitive Guide to Guilt: Five Types of Guilt and How You Can Cope with Each." n.p. Online: https://www.psychologytoday.com/ca/blog/fulfillment-any-age/201208/the-definitive-guide-guilt.

Wildberger, Hans. *Isaiah 1–12*. Translated by Thomas H. Trapp. A Continental Commentary. Minneapolis: Fortress, 1991.

Williams, Raymond. *Keywords: A Vocabulary of Culture and Society*. New York: Oxford University Press, 2015.

Williamson, H. G. M. *Ezra, Nehemiah*. WBC 16. Dallas: Word, 1985.

Wimberly, Edward P. *African American Pastoral Care*. Rev. ed. Nashville: Abingdon, 2008.

———. *Recalling Our Own Stories: Spiritual Renewal for Religious Caregivers*. Minneapolis: Fortress, 2019.

Witvliet, John D. "A Time to Weep: Liturgical Lament in Times of Crisis." *Reformed Worship* 44 (1997): 22–26.

Witvliet, John D., et al. *Psalms for All Seasons: A Complete Psalter for Worship.* Grand Rapids: Baker, 2012.

Wolfelt, Alan D. *Creating Meaningful Funeral Ceremonies.* New York: Routledge, 1994.

———. *Creating Meaningful Funeral Experiences: A Guide for Caregivers.* 2nd ed. Fort Collins, CO: Companion, 2011.

Wolterstorff, Nicholas. *Lament for A Son.* Grand Rapids: Eerdmans, 1987.

Woudstra, Marten H. *The Book of Joshua.* NICOT. Grand Rapids: Eerdmans, 1981.

Wray Beal, Lissa M. "Biblically Sanctioned Speech? The Psalms We Avoid." Online: https://cateclesia.com/2020/08/12/biblically-sanctioned-hate-speech-the-psalms-we-avoid/.

———. *1 & 2 Kings.* AOTC. Nottingham: Apollos, 2014.

Wright, Christopher J. H. *Old Testament Ethics for the People of God.* Downers Grove: IVP Academic, 2004.

———. "Preaching and Teaching from the Psalms." In *How to Preach and Teach the Old Testament for All Its Worth,* 246–61. Grand Rapids: Zondervan, 2016.

———. *To the Cross: Proclaiming the Gospel from the Upper Room to Calvary.* Downers Grove: InterVarsity, 2017.

———. *The God I Don't Understand: Reflections on Tough Questions of Faith.* Grand Rapids: Zondervan, 2008.

Wright, N. T. *Christian Origins and The Question of God, Vol. 1: The New Testament and The People of God.* Minneapolis: Fortress, 1992.

———. *Christian Origins and The Question of God, Vol. 3: The Resurrection of the Son of God.* Minneapolis: Fortress, 2003.

Yamauchi, Edwin M. "Ezra-Nehemiah." In *Zondervan Illustrated Bible Background Commentary: Old Testament, Vol. 3: 1 & 2 Kings, 1 & 2 Chronicles, Ezra, Nehemiah, Esther,* edited by John H. Walton, 394–467. Grand Rapids: Zondervan, 2009.

Yancey, Philip. *Prayer: Does It Make Any Difference?* Grand Rapids: Zondervan, 2006.

Youngblood, Ronald F. "1 & 2 Samuel," in *The Expositor's Bible Commentary, Vol. 3: 1 Samuel–2 Kings,* edited by Tremper Longman III and David E. Garland, 21–614. Grand Rapids: Zondervan, 2009.

Zenger, Erich. *A God of Vengeance? Understanding the Psalms of Divine Wrath.* Translated by Linda M. Maloney. Louisville: Westminster John Knox, 1996.

Zylla, Phil C. "Aspects of Men's Sorrow: Reflection on Phenomenological Writings about Grief." *PastPsych* 66 (2017): 837–854. DOI 10.1007/s11089-017-0768-y.

———. "Inhabiting Compassion: A Pastoral Theological Paradigm." *HTS Teologiese Studies/Theological Studies* 73 (2017): 1–9, DOI: 10.4102/hts.v73i4.4644.

———. "Shades of Lament: Phenomenology, Theopoetics, and Pastoral Theology." *PastPsych* 63 (2014): 763–776, DOI: 10.1007/s11089-014-0616-2.

———. *The Roots of Sorrow: A Pastoral Theology of Suffering*. Waco: Baylor University Press, 2012.

———. *Virtue as Consent to Being: A Pastoral-Theological Perspective on Jonathan Edwards's Construct of Virtue*. McMaster Ministry Studies Series 2. Hamilton, ON: McMaster Divinity College Press, 2011.

———. "What Language Can I Borrow? Theopoetic Renewal in Pastoral Theology." *MJTM* 9 (2007–2008): 129–143.

Langham Literature, with its publishing work, is a ministry of Langham Partnership.

Langham Partnership is a global fellowship working in pursuit of the vision God entrusted to its founder John Stott –

to facilitate the growth of the church in maturity and Christ-likeness through raising the standards of biblical preaching and teaching.

Our vision is to see churches in the Majority World equipped for mission and growing to maturity in Christ through the ministry of pastors and leaders who believe, teach and live by the word of God.

Our mission is to strengthen the ministry of the word of God through:
- nurturing national movements for biblical preaching
- fostering the creation and distribution of evangelical literature
- enhancing evangelical theological education

especially in countries where churches are under-resourced.

Our ministry

Langham Preaching partners with national leaders to nurture indigenous biblical preaching movements for pastors and lay preachers all around the world. With the support of a team of trainers from many countries, a multi-level programme of seminars provides practical training, and is followed by a programme for training local facilitators. Local preachers' groups and national and regional networks ensure continuity and ongoing development, seeking to build vigorous movements committed to Bible exposition.

Langham Literature provides Majority World preachers, scholars and seminary libraries with evangelical books and electronic resources through publishing and distribution, grants and discounts. The programme also fosters the creation of indigenous evangelical books in many languages, through writer's grants, strengthening local evangelical publishing houses, and investment in major regional literature projects, such as one volume Bible commentaries like the *Africa Bible Commentary* and the *South Asia Bible Commentary*.

Langham Scholars provides financial support for evangelical doctoral students from the Majority World so that, when they return home, they may train pastors and other Christian leaders with sound, biblical and theological teaching. This programme equips those who equip others. Langham Scholars also works in partnership with Majority World seminaries in strengthening evangelical theological education. A growing number of Langham Scholars study in high quality doctoral programmes in the Majority World itself. As well as teaching the next generation of pastors, graduated Langham Scholars exercise significant influence through their writing and leadership.

To learn more about Langham Partnership and the work we do visit **langham.org**

Milton Keynes UK
Ingram Content Group UK Ltd.
UKHW051016160424
441246UK00015B/441